A WITNESS OF
JESUS CHRIST

A WITNESS OF JESUS CHRIST

The 1989 Sperry Symposium on the Old Testament

Edited by
Richard D. Draper

Deseret Book Company
Salt Lake City, Utah

Library of Congress Cataloging-in-Publication Data

Sperry Symposium on the Old Testament (1989 : Brigham Young University)
    A witness of Jesus Christ : the 1989 Sperry Symposium on the Old Testament / edited by Richard D. Draper.
        p.   cm.
    Proceedings of the symposium held Oct. 28, 1989.
    Includes bibliographical references.
    ISBN 0-87579-362-2
    1. Bible.   O.T. — Criticism, interpretation, etc. — Congresses.
2. Jesus Christ — Mormon interpretations — Congresses.   I. Draper, Richard D.   II. Title.
BS1171.2.S67   1989
221.6'4 — dc20   90-34274
                                                                                                        CIP

Printed in the United States of America
10   9   8   7   6   5   4   3   2   1

Contents

Preface

Many have sought to destroy the Old Testament. In relentless war for more than two millennia, perverse hands have attempted to remove or obscure once-clear teachings and priceless promises and unbelieving minds have sought to expose the God of the book as a myth, a fable, a lie. Time has not been their ally. The testimony of that old, war-torn book has withstood all the machinations of men.

And what is that testimony? No one statement will answer that question. The Old Testament testifies of many things: that there is a living and caring God, that he created the world and mankind, that he calls men and women to assist him in his work, that wickedness never results in happiness, and so on. But focusing on its testimony is oblique to what the Old Testament is really all about. In fact, its title is even a bit misleading.

The English title "Old Testament" derives from word choices used in the Septuagint, the Greek version of the Hebrew Bible that was translated by Jewish scholars around 300 B.C. Those translators chose to render the Hebrew *b'rith,* which means "covenant," by the Greek word *diathaka,* which denotes a "will" or "testament." They did not use the more appropriate Greek word, *sunthaka,* meaning "covenant," out of a misguided reverence for Deity. *Sunthaka* gave the sense of an agreement made between equals having power to negotiate terms, and the Jewish translators seemed to have feared giving the impression that they thought men were equal to God. The idea of a "will" seemed more respectful because a testator dictates all terms of a will. But the result weakened the importance of personal commitment in the covenantal relationship with Deity.

Diathaka, the Greek word the Jewish scholars chose to use to translate the Hebrew, is in turn rendered very well by the English word *testament.* That English word is derived from the Latin *testamentum,* which originally meant a will but particularly a published one. The

Latin *testamentum* originated from *testis*, also Latin, meaning "witness."
This word is akin to the words *tres*, "three," and *stare*, "to stand." It
referred to the witness who functioned as the third party in litigation
or as the verifier of a will.

The Old Testament does function as a witness to the power, might,
majesty, grace, and love of Jehovah. It also witnesses to his involvement
in history, his dealings with people, and his power over nature. Most
of all, it witnesses to his striving to save mankind. But being a witness
is not its primary function.

The Old Testament is primarily a celebration of covenants. The
very idea that God and mortal man could be bound together in a spiritual
relationship thrilled the ancient patriarchs. The promises they derived
from that relationship fired them with hope and continued good works.
In their fear of making man equal to God, the scholars who translated
the Hebrew scriptures into Greek did not know or forgot that man is
the offspring of Deity and that the purpose of covenants, so heralded
in the Bible, was to establish and preserve a relationship of equality
between God and his children by which they became heirs of God and
joint-heirs with Christ in all things.

The importance of covenant making permeates the pages of the
book. It also dramatically underscores the consequences of keeping or
breaking them. And another point should be noted: Jehovah, or Jesus
Christ, initiated all covenants. Covenant making is one of the ways he
interacted and still interacts with his children and binds them to him.
Out of this truth grows the central message of the entire work. President Marion G. Romney stated it in these words: "The message of
the Old Testament is the message of Christ and his coming and his
atonement." (*A Symposium on the Old Testament* [Salt Lake City: The
Church of Jesus Christ of Latter-day Saints, 1979], p. 5.)

To emphasize this message, the eighteenth annual Sidney B.
Sperry Symposium was held Saturday, 28 October 1989, on the Brigham
Young University Campus in Provo, Utah. The symposium, sponsored
jointly by Religious Education of Brigham Young University and the
Church Educational System, is named in honor of Dr. Sperry, whose
faith and scholarship have set examples of excellence for those who
follow in his instructive footsteps.

The theme of the symposium, "The Old Testament: A Witness of
Jesus Christ," was chosen in an attempt to rectify, in part, the effects
that the war against the book has had in obscuring that witness of

Christ and the importance of his covenants. We must remember that the Old Testament is a wounded book. Ignorant, often perverse, and even apostate hands have slashed, and cut, and sliced at its most plain and precious parts. The result has been not only to the remove some parts but to leave much of what remains mutilated to the point that it is barely recognizable. (1 Nephi 13:26.) Jesus said to the Jewish rulers of his day, "Ye have taken away the key of knowledge, the fulness of the scriptures." (JST Luke 11:52.) That key of knowledge is that Jehovah and Jesus are one and the same and that he governs the dispensation of the gospel in any age and renews the covenant as he sees fit.

And yet, not all the plain and precious parts have been removed. The idea of covenants and covenant making still remains strong within the pages of the Old Testament. The witness of the atoning work of the Messiah yet cries from its pages. These points must not be overlooked. The old book has been under God's care, and he has not permitted perversity to have all its own way. Even in its wounded condition, the Old Testament lives and witnesses of that life which sustains all lives. The Apostle Paul bore witness to its vigor when he wrote: "Now to him that is of power to stablish you according to my gospel, and the preaching of Jesus Christ, according to the revelation of the mystery, which was kept secret since the world began, but now is made manifest, and by the scriptures of the prophets." (Romans 16:25–26.)

For Paul and the early Christians, the Old Testament was the scriptural source out of which the mystery of Christ and his gospel were revealed. As it was then, so is it today; if you look for it, you can still find the revelation of Jesus Christ within its pages.

The eighteenth annual Sperry Symposium afforded the opportunity to underscore those places where the mystery of Christ is yet revealed and where the importance of covenants can still be found. This task was made easier through the restoration in modern scripture of truths known to the ancient prophets. The Book of Mormon restores many plain and precious teachings that are missing from the old text. The Doctrine and Covenants contains many insights helpful in understanding covenants, priesthood, commandments, and how God works with his people. Finally, the Pearl of Great Price restores a world of information bearing directly on the witness of the Old Testament. Along with the standard works, prophetic insight is indispensable: Joseph

Smith's translation of the Bible, his many teachings, and those of the other prophets of the Restoration.

The papers in this volume, for the most part, focus on the witness and covenants of Jesus Christ in the Old Testament. With skill and discernment the participants have brought relevant passages together from all the prophetic works to help everyone better understand the testimony of Christ revealed in the Old Testament. Even though they have sought to be in harmony with Church doctrine, their presentations represent their own ideas and are not necessarily those of the Church Educational System, Brigham Young University, or The Church of Jesus Christ of Latter-day Saints.

Sperry Symposium Committee

Richard D. Draper, Editor
Roger R. Keller
John M. Madson
Bruce A. Van Orden

CHAPTER ONE

Isaiah: Disciple and Witness of Christ

L. LaMar Adams

Brigham Young University

Why did Jesus the Christ turn to Isaiah for a witness of the authenticity of His own ministry? Isaiah is heralded as a prophet's prophet, and his writings are unequaled in "splendor of diction, brilliance of imagery, versatility and beauty of style."[1] All this magnificence lies in the greatness of his witness. Among the books of the Old Testament, Isaiah stands as the foremost witness of Christ and His mission.

Why Christ Turned to Isaiah

Jesus turned to Isaiah as His witness because of what Isaiah wrote and who he was. Why is Isaiah's word so great? It is great because of what he wrote and how he wrote it. Compared to all other prophets in the Old Testament, Isaiah's writings have more prophecies about Christ; more diversified details about the First Coming, the Atonement, and the redemptive process; more extensive details about the Second Coming and millennial reign of the Savior; more promises of the covenant and man's access to redemption; more majestic, poetic language, which excels that of all other Hebraic writers; and more melodic beauty, which impels reading and quoting.

One of the great latter-day authorities, Elder Bruce R. McConkie, stated: "Isaiah is a prophet's prophet; his words live in the hearts of those who themselves are authoring holy writ."[2] The following is a Book of Mormon example: "I, Nephi, write more of the words of Isaiah, for my soul delighteth in his words . . . and I will send them forth unto all my children, for he verily saw my Redeemer, even as I have seen him." (2 Ne. 11:2.)

Biblical scholars likewise recognize the greatness of Isaiah's writings. Nagelsback stated: "Isaiah is the great Central-Prophet . . . the one on whom all later prophets lean as their greatest exemplar and

highest prophetic authority . . . of the highest rank, authority, and esteem . . . a master of the Hebrew language . . . unparalleled by any other
prophet . . . all rhetorical forms of art were at Isaiah's command."[3] Note
the beautiful diction and imagery in the following song of the redeemed:

> Behold, God is my salvation;
> I will trust, and not be afraid:
> for the Lord Jehovah is my strength and my song;
> he also is become my salvation.
> Therefore with joy shall ye draw water out of the wells of salvation.
> . . . Cry out and shout, thou inhabitant of Zion:
> for great is the Holy One of Israel in the midst of thee. (Isa. 12:2–6.)

In addition to the reasons given above, Jesus the Christ turned to
Isaiah as a witness of the authenticity of His own ministry because of
the vast extent of Isaiah's revelations, his esoteric prophecies, his
knowledge of the mysteries of God, and the greatness of his life.

The Vast Extent of Isaiah's Revelations

Isaiah was one of the many for whom the heavens were opened.
He saw and prophesied of earth's events from the beginning (Isa. 14)
to the end (66). Likewise, Isaiah's visions and revelations span the
entire rainbow of gospel verities. From the horizon of his perspective,
having beheld premortal councils (14), the creation (40–41), all of history unfolding (11–18), Christ's first and second advent (11), our day
(2), and the Millennium (60–66), he is in an authoritative position to
bear record, warn, and comfort all who read his writings. The Savior
said: "Yea, a commandment I give unto you that ye search these things
diligently; for great are the words of Isaiah. For surely he spake as
touching *all things concerning my people* which are of the house of
Israel." (3 Ne. 23:1–2; italics added.) Thus, Isaiah's writings bear witness of Christ from a perspective held by no other Old Testament
prophet.

Isaiah's Esoteric Prophecies

Esoteric means "to be understood by the specially initiated alone."
Most of Isaiah's prophecies are more deep, detailed, and extensive than
those of any other Old Testament prophet. Like deep water, they can

be fully observed only by those who are equipped to swim deep. They exceed the prophecies of all others who were permitted to reveal God's secrets of heaven and earth—not of plainness, as were those of Ether, who was commanded to seal his up, but of majestic grandeur to camouflage the message otherwise rejected and deleted by the scribes of deceit. Jeremiah chided these scribes: "How say ye, We are wise, and the law of the Lord is with us? Lo, certainly the false pen of the scribes worketh for falsehood." (Jer. 8:8; from the Hebrew.) And to Isaiah, the people say: "Prophesy not unto us right things, speak unto us smooth things, prophesy deceits: . . . cause the Holy One of Israel to cease from before us." (Isa. 30:10–11.)

Because Isaiah's prophecies were esoteric—couched in a language understood only by the specially initiated—the Old Testament scribes and editors, focusing on the beauty of the language, left unscathed, at least in part, the divine message of redemption, which they themselves rejected: "This is a rebellious people, lying children, children that will not hear the law of the Lord: Which say to the seers, See not." (Isa. 30:9–10.) Thus preserved, Isaiah's esoteric prophecies stand as majestic witnesses to Isaiah's specially prepared audience of the authenticity of the redemptive power of Jesus the Christ.

Although some elements of Isaiah's witness can be appreciated by the novice, the more profound portions of Isaiah's witness are enjoyed only by the well informed—in the Savior's words, those who "hunger and thirst after righteousness." (3 Ne. 12:6.) Elder McConkie stated: "No one, absolutely no one . . . can understand the writings of Isaiah until he first learns and believes what God has revealed by the mouths of his Nephite witnesses as these truths are found in that volume of holy writ."[4]

Just as the novice will not understand Isaiah 29 if he is unaware of the circumstances of the coming forth of the Book of Mormon, so also can only the enlightened covenant people understand the power and beauty of Isaiah's messianic witness in Isaiah 22. Those familiar with the temple covenant recognize the glorious meaning of the nail in the sure place as representing Christ and his atonement: "And I will fasten him as a nail in a sure place; and he shall be for a glorious throne to his father's house. And they shall hang upon him all the glory of his father's house, the offspring and the issue, all vessels of small quantity, from the vessels of cups, even to all the vessels of flagons. In that day, saith the Lord of hosts, shall the nail that is fastened in the sure place be removed, and be cut down, and fall; and the burden that was upon it shall be cut off: for the Lord hath spoken it." (Isa. 22:23–25.)

Isaiah himself warns us that only the prepared will be able to understand: "Whom shall he teach knowledge? and whom shall he make to understand doctrine: them that are weaned from the milk." (Isa. 28:9.)

Of those not ready for the meat, the Lord told the Prophet Joseph Smith: "For they cannot bear meat now, but milk they must receive; wherefore, they must not know these things, lest they perish." (D&C 19:22.)

So it is with us today. Only those prepared with enough milk can be nourished by the meat of the living witness of Isaiah.

Because the living message of Isaiah is to teach us to come unto Christ, only those prepared (those of Isaiah's latter-day audience), those who fully understand all that the Savior is, can receive of the full witness of Isaiah's testament. The book of Isaiah is written to a specific remnant in the last days: "Now go, write it before them in a table, and note it in a book, that it may be for the latter days." (Isa. 30:8; from the Hebrew.)

Isaiah's latter-day audience are those who have the restored gospel, temple ordinances, the Book of Mormon, and other modern scripture — all of which are necessary to comprehend Isaiah's grand sea of witness of the Savior. Having the restored gospel is assumed in Isaiah's writings. His purpose is not that of a lecturer, to explain the deep verities of Christ, but that of a testator, to testify and prophesy of Christ to prepare a covenant people to receive Christ as the Second Comforter[5] and for the Second Coming.

Isaiah delineated the milk prerequisites needed to understand the meat witness: "Who among us shall dwell with the devouring fire? who among us shall dwell with everlasting burnings? He that walketh righteously, and speaketh uprightly; he that despiseth the gain of oppressions, that shaketh his hands from holding of bribes, that stoppeth his ears from hearing of blood, and shutteth his eyes from seeing evil." (Isa. 33:14–15.)

Then Isaiah's depiction of the glorious state awaiting those who can be nourished by meat is also a witness of Christ as the King: "He shall dwell on high: his place of defence shall be the munitions of rocks: bread shall be given him; his waters shall be sure. Thine eyes shall see the king in his beauty: they shall behold the land that is very far off." (Isa. 33:16–17.)

What greater witness and knowledge can one have? Isaiah declared that those who fully accept his witness will dwell with Christ the King, joint heirs with him. It is assumed that we know that the "king in his beauty" is Christ in his glory and that the "land very far off" is this earth under Christ's millennial and celestial reign. Isaiah adds: "And I will bring forth a seed out of Jacob, and out of Judah an inheritor of my mountains: and mine elect shall inherit it, and my servants shall dwell there." (Isa. 65:9.)

Isaiah's Knowledge of the Mysteries of God

As the Savior told the Nephites, Isaiah knew of "all things concerning the house of Israel." (3 Ne. 23:2.) Isaiah's knowledge of the mysteries of God and the meat of his knowledge provide more verities of the Atonement and the gospel than do any other witness. Isaiah's writings outweigh those of any other Old Testament prophet, not only in sheer number of chapters (I am assuming that the book of Psalms was written by more than one author), but also in the vast sea of his doctrines and in the richness of his witness of Christ and his atonement.

Because there are far too many to examine here individually, I will give a very small sample of doctrinal topics from the book of Isaiah and give a brief overview of many others.

Some of the beautiful metaphorical passages considered in this exposition could be the result of the heavenly visions of Isaiah. A partial view of Isaiah's sea of doctrinal themes include the following. A sample chapter reference is also given, though usually each theme can be found in several other places. A diligent study of the many recondite concepts in Isaiah's writings can reveal the manner in which each "points to Christ and him crucified." (1 Cor. 2:2.)

Sanctification (13)

Repentance (1)

Broken heart and contrite spirit (57)

The Crucifixion (53)

The Atonement (63)

The Resurrection (26)

How to abide the day (26)

Signs of the Savior's Coming (24)

Spirit prison (49)

Scattering (30)

Gathering (2)

Restoration (2)

The covenant (49)

The Millennium (60)

Glory (28)

Judgment (11)

The holy seed (6)

Greatest sin (11)

Overpopulation (30)

Preparations for the Second Coming (48)

Order of events (11)

Rewards of righteousness (32)

The ensign (18)

The endowment (22)

Latter-day conditions (13)

The Lord's ransomed (35)

Results of sin (33)

The missionary system (18)

The Savior's birth (7)

The Light (9)

His holy mountain (11)

Premortal council (14)

The watchman (21)

Mysteries of God (28)

Foreordination (49)

Latter-day stakes (54)

God's thoughts (55)

The fast (58)

The wicked flood (59)

The gentiles (60)

The new name (62)

Red garments (63)

Purpose (66)

Demonstrations (26)

The righteous remnant (1)

Abiding the indignation (26)

Zion's redemption (1)

The temple (2)

Punishment of disobedience (3)

Abiding the day (33)

Care for the weak (35)

Song of the redeemed (12)

The Book of Mormon (29)

Baptism (8)

Day of visitation (10)

The Judge (11)

Latter-day Arabs (19)

Waiting on the Lord (25)

Care for the needy (10)

Refugees (49)

The water (54)

Peace (26)

The Sabbath (58)

Kingdoms (60)

Children of Abraham (63)

New heavens (65)

New earth (65)

The holy mountain (65)

The Greatness of Isaiah's Life

The greatness of Isaiah's life is a representation and example of Christ in both life and death. A man is great because of what he does. Isaiah was a prophet of prophets for two reasons. First, he had a long life of more than forty years of witnessing Christ to a backsliding nation and her kings, most of whom did not want his witness and hated him for it. Other prophets have been killed for their witness by their own people, but Isaiah first lived out a long, arduous life before sealing his witness with his blood. Only one of the five kings — Uzziah, Jothan, Ahaz, Hezekiah, and Manasseh — reigning during his prophetic leadership is recorded as making Isaiah a friend of the king's court. Second, Isaiah's witness was strong and undaunting to a people who rejected that witness and hated him for it. He stood to prophesy in the face of the storms of angered people who rejected him. Isaiah preached to one of the most difficult people on the earth: "Ah sinful nation, a people laden with iniquity, a seed of evildoers, children that are corrupters:

they have forsaken the Lord, they have provoked the Holy One of Israel unto anger, they are gone away backward. . . . ye will revolt more and more." (Isa. 1:4–5.) Thus, Isaiah's courage was forcefully evident in the warnings and judgments he pronounced with unwearyingness upon those who resented his words. Isaiah's name, life's mission, and death were in similitude of Christ's.

Elder McConkie stated that all prophets testified of Christ — indeed, that very act caused them to be prophets. Elder McConkie added, "Many of them lived in special situations or did particular things that singled them out as types and patterns and shadows of that which was to be in the life of" Jesus Christ.[6] Isaiah said, "Behold, I and the children whom the Lord hath given me are for signs and for wonders in Israel from the Lord of hosts, which dwelleth in Mount Zion." (Isa. 8:18.)

Hebrew Names of Isaiah and His Sons

Not only was Isaiah's life in similitude of Christ's but his name and the names of his two sons served as the most important message to Israel. Isaiah's name has several meanings, but they all have the same message: In Jehovah is salvation, or Jehovah is the Savior. The name of Isaiah's son Mahershalalhashbaz means "make speed the spoil, hasten the prey," or, literally, "Make speed the spoil, hasten the mire." And the name for Sherajashub, Isaiah's second son, means "the remnant shall return." Thus the three names associated with Isaiah are a type of Christ to the house of Israel:

1. True hope and salvation are only in the Lord; Jehovah is the Savior.

2. Those who will not repent will soon be scattered and destroyed.

3. A righteous remnant will be left to return unto the Lord in the last days. (That's us.)

Both individual and national salvation depended upon trust in the Lord. That is the literal meaning of Isaiah's name. And if Isaiah came to deliver a message to you, which son would you want to see with him?

Isaiah's Life and Mission

In addition to the names of Isaiah and his children, the life, mission, and death of Isaiah were in similitude of Christ. While officiating in the temple as a prophet, Isaiah received a visitation from Christ. Isaiah said: "I heard the voice of the Lord, saying, Whom shall I send, and who will go for us? Then said I, Here am I; send me." (Isa. 6:8.)

If we are familiar with latter-day scripture, we can recognize the call to take a special message to Israel as a personification of Jehovah's call in the premortal councils, evidence of the foreordination of Jesus, who also answered, "Here am I, send me." (Abr. 3:27.) Isaiah's message for more than forty years was for all to come unto Christ and accept His redemptive power.

Isaiah's exceptional span of prophetic years outlasted the lives of four of the five kings during whose reign he testified and prophesied. During these long years, he carried the Savior's message to righteous and wicked alike: "Seek ye the Lord while he may be found, call ye upon him while he is near . . . for he will abundantly pardon." (Isa. 55:6–7.)

Isaiah, the Witness for Christ

Isaiah's life was intense in discipleship and witness of Christ. Thus, Isaiah was a type, pattern, and shadow for Christ, which pointed to the future comings of the Messiah. All prophets have testified of Christ, but each has done so with a special mission or cause. Of all the prophets, ancient or modern, Isaiah is known as *the* witness for Christ and was called upon by other prophets for the proof of their messages:

1. Nephi, in proving the reality of Christ and the Atonement (2 Nephi 11:2–4).

2. New and Old Testament writers, and the Savior, who quoted Isaiah more than they quoted any other prophet in proving the fulfillment of messianic prophecies.

3. Book of Mormon prophets, and the Savior, who quoted Isaiah more than they quoted any other prophet.

4. The Doctrine and Covenants, which lists Isaiah as *the* prophet testifying of the Redeemer.

More than a dozen prophets from Adam to Malachi are named in Doctrine and Covenants 138, along with the unique characteristic of each prophet. Here Isaiah is the only one known as the witness of Christ, the Redeemer anointed to free the captives: "Isaiah, who declared by prophecy that the Redeemer was anointed to bind up the broken-hearted, to proclaim liberty to the captives, and the opening of the prison to them that were bound." (D&C 138:42.)

This symbolic depiction is typical of Isaiah's writings. In fact, it is that very symbolism that contributes to the melodic beauty of Isaiah's linquistic style, especially in the Hebrew, but it is marvelously retained in the English of the King James Version: "And they shall be gathered together, as prisoners are gathered in the pit, and shall be shut up in the prison, and after many days shall they be visited." (Isa. 24:22.)

Both these passages symbolize Christ's messianic visit to the spirit world.

Isaiah's Messianic Symbolism

Isaiah's writings were full of messianic symbolism. His witness of the Messiah can be seen throughout his beautiful metaphorical discourses. He foretold of Christ's first coming—birth, mission, crucifixion, and resurrection; his second coming—day of judgment and consummation; and his reign as the millennial King upon the throne of David.

The birth of Christ. Whether Isaiah was chastising a king or delivering a warning of the future, his messianic symbolism is evident. For example, the chastisement and warnings given to wicked King Ahaz were symbolic of the Savior's birth. The Talmud indicates that wicked King Ahaz, king of Judah, despised and feared Isaiah and his messages so much that when Ephraim and Syria waged war against Judah, King Ahaz ran from Isaiah, hiding under a woman's wash tub,[7] "at the end of the conduit of the upper pool in the highway of the fuller's field"—the wash field where the women washed their clothes. (Isa. 7:3.) The Lord told Isaiah where to find the runaway king and to deliver his message to trust in the Savior and ignore the warring kings. Because Ahaz would not trust in the Lord, a sign of Ahaz's own choosing was offered, but Ahaz did not want that, either.

"Therefore the Lord himself shall give you a sign; behold, a virgin shall conceive, and bear a son, and shall call his name Immanuel. Butter and honey shall he eat that he may know to refuse the evil and choose the good." (Isa. 7:14–15.)

How was the virgin birth of Christ a sign to Ahaz when it was so far removed from him and his day? Here we apply the grand key to scriptural symbolism: all things point to Christ. Among other things, it was as if to say, "Ahaz, if you could only have the faith to believe in the virgin birth of Christ who is to come, you could trust in the Lord's message about this war. If you could repent and believe in the miracle of the virgin birth, you could trust in your Savior and ignore the warring kings." But because Ahaz was too wicked to repent and trust in Christ for all his problems, how could he trust Isaiah and the Lord's word in this life-threatening problem?

Some scholars not of Isaiah's latter-day audience and without the language of the fathers[8] in modern scriptures tend to avoid or at least water down the greatness of the messianic witness in the Immanuel passage.[9] The well-known second prophecy of Christ's birth was also given in relation to Israel's destruction. The melodic beauty of this passage draws us to read and reread it. As we do so, we can almost hear the choirs of heaven: "For unto us a child is born, unto us a son is given: and the government shall be upon his shoulder: and his name shall be called Wonderful, Counsellor, The mighty God, The everlasting Father, The Prince of Peace. Of the increase of his government and peace there shall be no end, upon the throne of David, and upon his kingdom, to order it, and to establish it with judgment and with justice from henceforth even for ever." (Isa. 9:6–7.)

The mission of Christ. Isaiah's book is the foremost of Old Testament writings to witness of Christ and his mission. But what does "to witness of Christ" mean? It means at least two things: first, to testify that Jesus is the Christ, and, second, to testify of the mission of Christ. Isaiah testified that Jesus is the Christ by detailed identification of Jesus' life, especially in chapters 7, 9, and 49 through 53. But what does the word *Christ* mean, and what is Christ's mission? The word *Christ* is simply the Greek for the Hebrew equivalent, *Messiah,* meaning "the anointed." So, the question now is, "anointed to what, to what mission?"

The anointed mission foreordained from the foundation of the world, was for God—in this case, Jehovah—to

1. Take upon himself a mortal body (*Immanuel,* meaning "God with us"—Isa. 9:14).

2. Atone for sins (pay the debt required by justice: Redeemer—Isa. 43:1–3; 53:6; etc.) by an infinite suffering (the suffering servant—Isa. 42; 49–53; etc.) and by sacrificing his undefiled life in crucifixion (Isa. 22:23–25; 53:9–12).

3. Overcome death and provide for resurrection: an unconditional Savior (Isa. 25:8, 43, 45).

4. Deliver from spiritual prison (a conditional Savior—Isa. 24:22, 49, etc.) all who believe, through faith, repentance, and knowledge of God (Isa. 1:16–20; 28:9–12; etc.).

5. Return in judgment to reign as the Prince of Peace and the millennial King upon the throne of David (Isa. 9:6–7; 11:3–4; 60:10–22; etc.).

These references confirm two glorious truths. First, they confirm the latter-day scripture that states that Isaiah "declared by prophecy that the Redeemer was anointed to bind up the broken-hearted, to proclaim liberty to the captives, and the opening of the prison to them that were bound." (D&C 138:42.) Second, they confirm that the mission of the Messiah consists of two comings: the First Coming, including his birth, atonement, and resurrection; and the Second Coming in great power and glory, including a day of judgment, destruction of all wickedness, a new heaven and new earth with millennial peace for the righteous.

Jehovah the Redeemer, the Savior, and the Creator. Isaiah is the unique Old Testament prophet who establishes Jehovah as the Redeemer, the Savior, the Creator, the Holy One of Israel, and the God of the Old Testament. Isaiah, in chapters 41, 43 through 45, and 47 through 49, testifies to the identity of the Savior and Redeemer with that of Jehovah. For example, Jehovah said: "And all flesh shall know that I the Lord am thy Saviour and thy Redeemer, the mighty One of Jacob" (Isa. 49:26) and "I, even I, am the Lord; and beside me there is no saviour" (Isa. 43:11). Chapters 40 through 44 testify that Jehovah the Savior and Redeemer is also the Creator: "Thus saith the Lord, thy redeemer, and he that formed thee from the womb, I am the Lord that maketh all things; that stretcheth forth the heavens alone; that spreadeth abroad the earth by myself." (Isa. 44:24.)

Witness of Christ as the God of the Old Testament. Because Isaiah testifies that Jehovah is the Redeemer, the Savior, and the Creator, it naturally follows that he, the Messiah, is the God of the Old Testament. That is also evident in Isaiah's living message: "For thy Maker is thine husband; the Lord of hosts is his name; and thy Redeemer the Holy One of Israel; The God of the whole earth shall he be called." (Isa. 54:5.)

It is evident from chapters 40 through 49 that Jehovah, the Redeemer, Savior, and Creator, is also the Holy One of Israel, King of Israel, Lord of hosts, First and Last, mighty One of Jacob, God of Israel, and the everlasting God. Thus, Jesus the Christ is the Redeemer and Savior of the world; he is Jehovah, the Creator and God of the Old Testament—the God who works with Israel: "Thou also hast wrought

all our works in us." (Isa. 26:12.) From this perspective we can see
how Jehovah is, in one real sense, the only God to Israel. He is God,
symbolically and in all working relationships — there is no other. He is
the First and Last to Israel in more ways than one.

When Isaiah saw "the Lord sitting upon a throne, high and lifted
up, and his train [glory] filled the temple," he declared, "mine eyes
have seen the King, the Lord [Jehovah] of hosts." (Isa. 6:1–5.) Thus
Isaiah saw Jehovah, the Messiah anointed to become the King, the
Christ.

In Isaiah 10 Jehovah is also called Lord, Lord of hosts, light of
Israel, his Holy One, Lord [Jehovah], the Holy One of Israel, and the
mighty God. There are many other names in the book of Isaiah that
the Savior has. Each name refers to some aspect of the mission of the
Messiah or some particular characteristic of his calling.

Characteristic Names for Christ. The book of Isaiah gives more
characteristic names and insight into Christ's mission than any other
Old Testament book, and more than all the others put together. The
following is a partial list. Most names are found many times throughout
the book, so only a few references are given here.

1. Holy One (of Israel, of Jacob), 1:4; 5:24
2. Lord (Jehovah), 1:4, 18
3. Lord, 4:4; 6:1
4. Lord (Jehovah) of hosts, 5:24; 6:3
5. Lord God of hosts, 3:15; 10:23
6. Lord of hosts, 10:16
7. Creator, 40:28; 41:20
8. Savior, 43:11; 49:26
9. Redeemer, 41:14; 43:14
10. Immanuel, 7:14
11. Wonderful, 9:6; 28:29
12. Counsellor, 9:6; 28:29
13. The mighty God 9:6; 49:26
14. Mighty and Strong One, 28:2
15. Everlasting Father, 9:6
16. Everlasting God, 40:28
17. Prince of Peace, 9:6
18. Mighty One (of Jacob, of Israel), 1:24; 60:16
19. Beloved, 42:1
20. He that speaks in righteousness, 63:1; 54:5

21. Deliverer from prison, 24:22
22. The Judge, 11:3–4; 33:22
23. Lawgiver, 33:22
24. First and Last, 41:4; 44:6
25. Shepherd, 40:11
26. Lord of the vineyard, 5:7
27. Lamb of God, 16:1; 53:7
28. The King, 6:5; 33:17
29. A Great Light, 9:1–3
30. Light of Israel, 10:17
31. Light to the Gentiles, 42:6; 49:6
32. Stem of Jesse, 11:1
33. Nail in the sure place, 22:23–24
34. Sure Foundation, 28:16
35. My [His] Servant, 42:1; 50:10
36. Whom man despiseth, 49:7; 53:3
37. Comforter, 40:1–2; 66:13
38. Mighty to save, 63:1
39. Thine Maker, 54:5
40. Thine husband, 54:5
41. God of the whole earth, 54:5

Diligent and prayerful study of these name characteristics, especially in context of the passages in which they were written, can result in a great knowledge of Christ. To know all of Christ's many characteristics is to know Christ, at least in part. This reason may well be one of the reasons the Savior commanded us to diligently study the words of Isaiah. (3 Ne. 23:1.)

A prerequisite to understanding Isaiah's witness of Christ's mission is to distinguish between the two advents of Christ and their interrelationship. Isaiah's witness of the two advents is found throughout his book. From the partial listing that follows, it is evident that both advents are major themes throughout the book of Isaiah.

MESSIANIC SYMBOLISMS AND REFERENCES

	First Coming		Second Coming
7:11–15	A virgin shall conceive	1:24–31	Zion redeemed by purging

9:1–6	A Great Light, a child is born	2:3–4:6	Millennial judgments and peace
11:1–2	As the stem of Jesse	6:13	The holy seed
16:1	Send the Lamb	9:7–21	Millennial reign and judgments prior
22:20–25	The Crucifixion	Ch. 10	Judgments, in glory, a remnant
24:17–22	Spirit prison after Resurrection	11:3–12:6	The Judge, a remnant, Zion's Song
25:8	Christ's death and resurrection	Chs. 13–16	Day of the Lord, of destructions
28:16–29	Christ promised	17:1–19:17	Latter-day preparations
40:1–11	John the Baptist and Christ	17:18–25	Millennial state of Egypt
Chs. 41–49	A Redeemer, Servant, Savior	24:13–23	Signs at Second Coming and millennial state
44:22–24	The redemption wrought	26:19–20	The Resurrection
49:1–8	Christ, a light, despised	Ch. 27	Millennial state
49:9	Sets spirit prisoners free	28:5	Glory of the Lord
Chs. 50–54	Symbolic details of Christ's arrest and crucifixion	30:18–33	The Second Coming and signs
61:1–3	Christ proclaims liberty and second coming	Ch. 32	Messiah as King shall reign
63:2–3	Symbolic of Atonement (see D&C 133:46–48)	33:17–24	Christ as King, Lawgiver, etc.
		Chs. 34–35	Day of vengeance and Millennium
		47:11–14	Wicked burned as stubble
		51:18–20	Two prophets in Jerusalem
		55:12–13	Millennial state
		60:13–22	Millennial gathering and conditions
		61:4–11	Millennial state
		Ch. 63	Christ on Mount of Olives
		65:17–25	New heavens and new earth
		66:12–24	Christ comes with fire, new earth

From the intermixture of the two advents throughout Isaiah's writing, it is easy to see how the children of Israel and modern scholars could confuse the two into one, especially when they are sometimes both represented in the same passage and in reverse chronological order. The following example is from Isaiah 63:1–3, but because the passage is a bit garbled there, I quote from Doctrine and Covenants 133:46–50. Both texts are metaphorically and melodically beautiful. First is the reference to the Second Coming:

"Who is this that cometh down from God in heaven with dyed garments; yea, from the regions which are not known, clothed in his glorious apparel, traveling in the greatness of his strength? And he shall say: I am he who spake in righteousness, mighty to save. And the Lord shall be red in his apparel, and his garments like him that treadeth in the wine-vat. And so great shall be the glory of his presence that the sun shall hide his face in shame, and the moon shall withhold its light, and the stars shall be hurled from their places." (D&C 133:46–49.)

Then it is foretold that the Savior himself will refer to his first coming:

"And his voice shall be heard: I have trodden the wine-press alone, and have brought judgment upon all people; and none were with me." (D&C 133:50.)

Then we have a mixture of first and second advents:

"In all their afflictions he was afflicted. And the angel of his presence saved them; and in his love, and in his pity, he redeemed them, and bore them, and carried them all the days of old." (D&C 133:53; see Isa. 63:8.)

The purpose of the first advent is to prepare us for the second one (Isa. 61:2), to be caught up to meet Christ in his glory (Alma 13:24). Isaiah gives us a grand key by which we can prepare for the Second Coming: "Wisdom and knowledge shall be the stability of thy times, and strength of salvation: the fear of the Lord is his treasure" (Isa. 33:6) and "thou wilt keep him in perfect peace, whose mind is stayed on thee." (Isa. 26:3).

The strength of our salvation is in possessing the knowledge necessary to be caught up at the Second Coming. And if we keep our mind stayed on the Savior, we can obtain that knowledge. The Lord said: "Seek the face of the Lord always, that in patience ye may possess your souls, and ye shall have eternal life" (D&C 101:38) and "come unto me, that ye might feel and see" (3 Ne. 18:25; D&C 6:37). When

we fulfill the covenant-witness of Christ through obtaining this necessary knowledge of God, we too become a witness with Isaiah that
others can "come, . . . feel and see."

Conclusions

In conclusion, it is evident why Jesus the Christ turned to Isaiah
to witness the authenticity of His own ministry. Isaiah's witness stands
as the foremost witness of Christ and his covenant in Old Testament
writings. Isaiah is heralded as the prophet of prophets and a prophet's
prophet. His words are unparalleled in splendor of diction, brilliance of
symbolism, and melodic beauty of style. His witness is unique in identifying the mission, characteristics, and personage of Jehovah as the
Christ, the God of the Old Testament. The greatness of the book of
Isaiah as a prophecy-witness of Christ lies partially in the fact that the
life of Isaiah was in great similitude to the life, mission, and death of
Christ himself.

The vast sea of symbolic witnesses of Christ in the writings of
Isaiah can only be fully appreciated by those who are of Isaiah's latter-
day audience, those of the covenant "whom he shall make to understand
doctrine." (Isa. 28:8.) The Book of Mormon and other modern scriptures restore missing links to the covenant witness of Christ no longer
found in the Bible. Isaiah's witness can be fully understood only with
the new light found in latter-day scriptures. Because the mode of Isaiah's writings is that of a testator, teaching and explaining are left to
the Book of Mormon and other latter-day scripture—which itself is
attested to by Isaiah. Use of these scriptures in diligent study of Isaiah's
words and symbolism can greatly enhance our knowledge and witness
of Christ. Therefore, Jesus and other Book of Mormon authors quoted
extensively from Isaiah to verify and explain the covenant and mission
of Christ. Prayerful study of these texts can help us fulfill the covenant-
witness in our individual lives.

Isaiah's witness is a marvelous type, sign, and wonder of Christ.
It is up to us individually to determine what to do with that witness
and be judged at the Second Coming accordingly. The grand key given
by Isaiah is to keep our minds stayed upon the Savior to avoid hearing
and seeing the evils of our day, that we may seek and obtain the face
of the Lord as the Second Comforter. Isaiah's witness of Christ is
fulfilled in us when we are prepared for the Second Coming. That is
Isaiah's witness and the greatness of his marvelous and beautiful writ-

ings. As Nephi said, "My soul delighteth in Isaiah's words. . . . for he verily saw my Redeemer." (2 Ne. 11:2.) Isaiah is the great disciple and witness of Jesus the Christ.

NOTES

1. Merrill F. Unger, *Introductory Guide to the Old Testament* (Grand Rapids, Mich.: Zondervan Publishing, 1951), p. 311.

2. Bruce R. McConkie, "Ten Keys to Understanding Isaiah," *Ensign*, Oct. 1973, p. 81.

3. Carl Nagelsback, *The Prophet Isaiah* (New York: C. Scribner's Sons, 1878), p. 2.

4. McConkie, "Ten Keys," p. 81.

5. Joseph Smith, *Teachings of the Prophet Joseph Smith*, sel. Joseph Fielding Smith (Salt Lake City: Deseret Book Co., 1938), pp. 149–50.

6. Bruce R. McConkie, *The Promised Messiah* (Salt Lake City: Deseret Book Co., 1978), p. 448.

7. Isadore Epstein, ed. and trans., *The Babylonian Talmud* (London: Soncino Press, 1948), p. 706.

8. L. LaMar Adams, *The Living Message of Isaiah* (Salt Lake City: Deseret Book Co., 1981), pp. 41–45, 52–56.

9. Victor L. Ludlow, *Isaiah: Prophet, Seer, and Poet* (Salt Lake City: Deseret Book Co., 1982), p. 143; and Monte S. Nyman, *Great Are the Words of Isaiah* (Salt Lake City: Bookcraft, 1980), pp. 56–58.

CHAPTER TWO

The Law of Moses
and the Law of Christ

Edward J. Brandt

Correlation Department of The Church of Jesus Christ of Latter-day Saints

When many people hear the words "the law of Moses," they tend to associate that law with something very undesirable — a program or a system that is all outward and temporal and so far removed from what they would hope or expect to be associated with the gospel of Christ that some might wonder if there were any worth in it at all. Such a view of the law of Moses is false.

The law of Moses could not influence a person's life unless that person had some measure and portion of the Spirit of the Lord in his or her life. The lack of that spiritual influence caused great difficulties in ancient Israel. They lost the spirit of the law, which is why the law turned into such a burden, as is illustrated later in the scriptural record. All of the standard works, not just the Old and the New Testament, teach of this law. A proper perspective on this law provides a meaningful dimension to gospel understanding.

The most important text to help us fully appreciate the spirit and purpose of the law of Moses is the Book of Mormon. The Book of Mormon people maintained the spirit of the law of Moses, and it served them well. Their faithful observance finally helped prepare a responsive group to receive the Messiah in their day.

In a great revelation on priesthood, Doctrine and Covenants 84, the Lord established an important foundation for understanding the relationship between the law of Moses and the law of Christ. After reviewing the line of authority in conferring the priesthood in ancient times, we read:

"And the Lord confirmed a priesthood also upon Aaron and his seed, throughout all their generations, which priesthood also continueth and abideth forever with the priesthood which is after the holiest order of God.

18

"And this greater priesthood administereth the gospel and holdeth the key of the mysteries of the kingdom, even the key of the knowledge of God.

"Therefore, in the ordinances thereof, the power of godliness is manifest. [That is to say, in the ordinances of the Melchizedek, or the higher, priesthood is the power of godliness manifest.]

" And without the ordinances thereof [or the ordinances of the higher priesthood], and the authority of the priesthood, the power of godliness is not manifest unto men in the flesh;

" For without this [that is, the temple ordinances] no man can see the face of God, even the Father, and live." (D&C 84:18–22.)

This passage is often used and misused by anti-Mormons against the claims of the First Vision. They are fond of quoting verse 22 out of context, contending that if you have to have priesthood to see the face of God and live, then, they ask, how was it possible for Joseph Smith to see the claimed vision because he had not yet received priesthood. Such an interpretation is a wresting of the context of the passage. The proper context of this revelation is that without the ordinances of the higher priesthood [the temple ordinances], no man can see the face of God and *live in His presence.*[1] These verses provide a true perspective of purpose and power of the priesthood ordinances. Then follows the scriptural explanations of the law of Moses:

"Now this Moses plainly taught to the children of Israel in the wilderness, and sought diligently to sanctify his people that they might behold the face of God;

"But they hardened their hearts and could not endure his presence; therefore the Lord in his wrath, for his anger was kindled against them, swore that they should not enter into his rest while in the wilderness, which rest is the fulness of his glory. [To enter into the rest of the Lord is to enter into his presence – into his glory.]

"Therefore, [as a consequence of this rebellion] he took Moses out of their midst, and the Holy Priesthood also;

"And the lesser priesthood continued [now ask yourselves, what did the lesser priesthood minister?], which priesthood holdeth the key of the ministering of angels and the preparatory gospel;

"Which gospel is the gospel of repentance and of baptism, and the remission of sins, and the law of carnal commandments, which the Lord in his wrath caused to continue with the house of Aaron among the

children of Israel until John, whom God raised up, being filled with the
Holy Ghost from his mother's womb." (D&C 84:23–27.)

The Doctrine and Covenants says that the law of Moses consists
of the preparatory gospel and the law of carnal commandments. The
preparatory gospel includes the elements of faith in Jesus Christ, repentance, and baptism. We are counseled to "come unto Christ," which
ultimately means to become Christlike. The Lord has established a
path to help us achieve that end. There are many significant steps along
the way, all centered in the gospel of Jesus Christ. Some fundamentals
open the door and set one on the path. These fundamentals are called
the first principles of the gospel: faith in Jesus Christ, repentance,
baptism. They are a part of the preparatory gospel, which is part of the
law of Moses. Other scriptures include the law of sacrifice or the burnt
offering as an integral part of the preparatory gospel.[2] Doctrine and
Covenants 84 indicates that the Lord added something to these fundamental things. He described it in verse 27 as the "law of carnal
commandments." The purpose of the law of carnal commandments was
to help the children of Israel focus on the basic fundamentals of the
gospel. These two elements, then—the preparatory gospel and the law
of carnal commandments—are what we commonly call the law of
Moses.[3]

Law of Moses
1. Preparatory Gospel
   a. Burnt offering
   b. Faith in Jesus Christ, repentance,
      and baptism
   c. The Ten Commandments
   d. The law of the covenant
2. Law of Carnal Commandments
   a. Ordinances—Offerings
   b. Performances—including dietary
      and purification laws

To accurately describe the law of Moses, we would have to say
that it contained the basic part of the gospel of Jesus Christ. It was
never intended to be something apart, separated, or even lower than
the gospel of Christ. It was simply to help the people in their focus
and understanding.

An instructive perspective about this law is found in Mosiah 13 in
the Book of Mormon. This is the great discourse given by the prophet

Abinadi as he labored with the wicked priests of King Noah. They had questioned the prophet, asking the meaning of a verse in Isaiah 52: "How beautiful upon the mountains are the feet of him that bringeth good tidings." (Mosiah 12:21; see also Isa. 52:8.) The prophet answered and in the process revealed something of the nature of the law of Moses that the people of Noah were practicing:

"And now I say unto you that it was expedient that there should be a law given to the children of Israel, yea, even a very strict law; for they were a stiffnecked people, quick to do iniquity, and slow to remember the Lord their God;

"Therefore, there was a law given them, yea, a law of performances and of ordinances, a law which they were to observe strictly from day to day, to keep them in remembrance of God and their duty towards him." (Mosiah 13:29–30.)

Verse 30 states that this law, which included the law of carnal commandments, consisted of a law of ordinances and performances. The ordinances and performances were teaching instruments of the law of carnal commandments. A synonym for the word *carnal* is *flesh.* The law of carnal commandments was, therefore, commandments intended to help the children of Israel to control the flesh — to develop self-control and self-discipline in their lives. It was to help them to get a handle on their lives so they could begin to focus on the basic fundamentals that would lead them to Christ. That was its primary purpose and the spirit and the intent of the law of carnal commandments.

Perhaps a brief explanation of the two systems — ordinances and performances — might be helpful. Ordinances had to do with the law of offerings. In ancient Israel a number of offerings were offered by the children of Israel, some of them with special intent: the peace offering, the sin offering, and the trespass offering.[4] The first ten chapters of Leviticus provide the scriptural instruction for these offerings.

The peace offering[5] was intended to help individuals express that they had made peace with God, that they had come to grips with their problems in life. It was offered at one of those moments in life when an individual was at peace, ready to take the next step in personal development and growth. The children of Israel were asked to acknowledge being blessed with that peace in their lives through the peace offering.[6]

The peace offering was also called a vow offering and a thank offering. Done periodically, the vow offering[7] was one of recommitment to the covenants the Israelites had made. It had a similar value for ancient Israel as partaking of the sacrament has in the Church today. The thank offering was to offer thanks[8] to God for the great blessings that had been extended to the Israelites, his grace and his goodness in their lives. In Luke 2 we discover that Joseph and Mary went to the temple to offer an offering. (Luke 2:22–23.) It was a thank offering because they had received a blessing of peace in the gift of this son who had come to their family and, more importantly to Israel, to the whole world.

All these offerings were free-will offerings, not by command or upon demand. These offerings were to help the Israelites to focus on God and their relationship to him, and for them to acknowledge who it was that gave them great blessings in their lives.

The sin offering and the trespass offering were the most important offerings under the law of carnal commandments. A sin offering[9] was given in recognition that a person had come to grips with the sins in his life that were not generally well known by others. There were sins of omission, or sins in one's heart and thoughts, not so much outwardly manifest as inwardly manifest. The trespass offering,[10] on the other hand, was a direct result of outward transgressions. An integral part of the trespass offering was the requirement upon the participant to have repented of the sin and made some sort of restitution. The law was very specific about the kinds of restitutions that were to be offered. For example: if one had stolen five of another man's finest sheep, the law required that he restore to him double, or ten. If people were really sincere in honoring the law, they thought twice about borrowing their neighbor's sheep. In some instances, the law required a recompense or restitution of only 20 percent; but in other instances, it was as much as 100 percent.[11]

Now, what was the purpose of the sin offering and the trespass offering? To teach the people to repent and to obtain the power of repentance in their personal lives, so that they could develop self-control and get their feet on the path that leads to salvation. That was the simple purpose of it. Could a person go through the outward practice of the law and never do it with full intent? Yes. Does that ever happen when an individual partakes of the sacrament thoughtlessly? They also had to struggle with their intent in their religious practice. These offerings were the chief ordinances that were a part of the law of carnal commandments.

There was also the heave offering, or the wave offering,[12] which was a very specialized offering given by the priests only. It was possible, for example, if you chose the right kind of an animal, to offer one offering for all of the offerings. Some have the misconception that the Israelites were running in every day burning up sheep or goats. That was not the purpose of the offering. Usually a family presented an offering once or twice a year during their lives on a special occasion, such as at a feast or conference time, the birth of a child, or other special events, or when they had come to grips with their problems and really wanted a renewal and a refreshment. If they had sufficient resources, they provided the sheep or the goat. If not, the law in some instances permitted lesser substitutions.[13] They took the offering to the tabernacle or, later in their history, to the temple, where the priest would receive them at the gate. The family was not allowed to go past the precincts for the congregation into the area for offerings and sacrifices. The priests took the animal and ceremonially slaughtered it. The priest was allowed to receive or keep the hide as part of the payment for his service.[14] Some of the inner parts were burnt, and some were disposed of in other ways.[15] The animals that were slaughtered were prepared in a special way so as to teach the people of the Atonement. Then the family took the animal of the offerings home, roasted it, and had a special religious meal in commemoration of the things they were trying to accomplish, or it was taken to the priest's family, depending on which type of offering was given.[16]

The priest did not have time to keep flocks as others did, so he was allowed to keep one quarter of an animal as payment for his service. He usually took one of the front quarters of the animal. Again one brought the animal to the priest, and he took it into the precincts. One could watch him as he prepared the animal for the family. He took the hide and probably gave it to one of his sons who attended him there, and then he removed the quarter that was to be payment for his family. He then took that quarter and lifted it up, pointing towards the area where the individual was waiting, and the priest heaved it or waved it above his head, indicating, "This is my payment." Then the individual acknowledged, "Yes, that is your payment." That was the heave or the wave offering — payment for his service.[17]

The priest was required to tithe his portion. He took a small amount of the meat to the altar and acknowledged that this was a gift from God for the service that he had rendered as a priesthood bearer in behalf of one of the children of Israel.[18] Then he could take that roast home for his family and they would be cared for. It was a very practical system, and it all had significance to enable people to have focus in their personal lives and to help them develop self-control.

The performances of the law of carnal commandments are enumerated in numerous places in the Old Testament — such as, do not mix crops in the field.[19] The Israelites were not to sow oats and barley together. They could not have three rows of corn and four rows of peas. They were not to mix the fabric of garments — no wool with linen, for example. The fibers had to be separate. What was the purpose of such performances? To remind them of their covenants. When they sowed a field, they were always reminded that Israel was a part of the covenant people, and they were not to intermingle with nations outside the covenant. That simple reminder was intended to remind them of their covenants. These are only a sample of a multitude of examples, all of which had a practical purpose.

The Book of Mormon teaches of the full spirit of all of these laws that were revealed. In 2 Nephi 11:4 we read: "Behold, my soul delighteth in proving unto my people the truth of the coming of Christ; for, for this end hath the law of Moses been given; and all things which have been given of God from the beginning of the world, unto man, are the typifying of him."

Notice how Nephi reminds them that everything involved in the practices of the law of Moses, as he identified it, was associated with Christ; and it was done with the intent to bring them to Christ.

In 2 Nephi is recorded:

"And, notwithstanding we believe in Christ, we keep the law of Moses, and look forward with steadfastness unto Christ, until the law shall be fulfilled.

"For, for this end was the law given; wherefore the law hath become dead unto us, and we are made alive in Christ because of our faith; yet we keep the law because of the commandments.

"And we talk of Christ, we rejoice in Christ, we preach of Christ, we prophesy of Christ, and we write according to our prophecies, that our children may know to what source they may look for a remission of their sins.

"Wherefore, we speak concerning the law that our children may know the deadness of the law; and they, by knowing the deadness of the law, may look forward unto that life which is in Christ, and know for what end the law was given [that they may look for what end the law was given, all to focus on Christ]. And after the law is fulfilled in Christ, that they need not harden their hearts against him when the law ought to be done away. (2 Ne. 25:24–27.)

The Spirit of the Lord was essential to the full significance of this system of performances and ordinances.

Additional examples of performances can be cited from the great passover feast established in Exodus 11 and 12 in the Old Testament. Many symbols in this feast are associated with the Atonement. Some of them are very obvious, for example, the firstborn animal—the lamb without blemish.[20] Study the book of Leviticus in detail to see how the priests were to slaughter the lamb. They were careful never to break the bones. The throat was to be cut in just a special way, so that the blood would be let out totally. What was the significance of all of that? To teach and remind of the atonement of Christ.[21]

There were other, more subtle types of performances. First, the animal chosen was to be sufficient to feed the group that one was hosting at the home. It was to be, however, just enough to feed all who were present because the law required that it was to be totally consumed.[22] In other words, the sacrifice of the animal had to be complete or total. To use Book of Mormon language, it was to be an infinite sacrifice like unto the "infinite" atonement.[23] There was to be none left. If some was left, it was to be burned. Why did they put the blood on the doorpost? Because only under the covenant of Christ, or under the blood of the lamb, could Israel be saved. That is to say, unless we fall under the effects of the blood of the atonement of Jesus Christ, there is no salvation in Israel.[24]

There are many ramifications in the symbolism and the practices of the feasts in ancient Israel. As Nephi said, "We are made alive in Christ because of our faith." (2 Ne. 25:25.) This statement is indeed true, but only if one has the Spirit of the Lord. The Book of Mormon prophets saw this system of laws with that perspective, and it had great power in their lives. In 2 Nephi 5:10, Nephi reports on this observation and practice: "And we did observe to keep the judgments, and the statutes, and the commandments of the Lord in all things according to the law of Moses."

In Jacob 4:5, the brother of Nephi testified of the effect of the law of Moses through all the ages:

"Behold, they believed in Christ and worshipped the Father in his name, and also we worship the Father in his name. And for this intent we keep the law of Moses, it pointing our souls to him [not just by way of remembrance, you see; even the practices were to help them in their personal lives to start down the road and to find edification from it]; and for this cause it is sanctified unto us for righteousness, even as it was accounted unto Abraham in the wilderness to be obedient unto the commands of God in offering up his son Isaac, which is a similitude of God and his Only Begotten Son."

The prophet Alma likewise taught:

"Yea, and they did keep the law of Moses; for it was expedient that they should keep the law of Moses as yet, for it was not all fulfilled. But notwithstanding the law of Moses, they did look forward to the coming of Christ, considering that the law of Moses was a type of his coming, and believing that they must keep those outward performances until the time that he should be revealed unto them.

"Now they did not suppose that salvation came by the law of Moses; but the law of Moses did serve to strengthen their faith in Christ; and thus they did retain a hope through faith, unto eternal salvation, relying upon the spirit of prophecy, which spake of those things to come." (Alma 25:15–16.)

"Therefore, it is expedient that there should be a great and last sacrifice; and then shall there be, or it is expedient there should be, a stop to the shedding of blood; then shall the law of Moses be fulfilled; yea, it shall be all fulfilled, every jot and tittle, and none shall have passed away.

"And behold, this is the whole meaning of the law, every whit pointing to that great and last sacrifice; and that great and last sacrifice will be the Son of God, yea, infinite and eternal." (Alma 34:13–14.)

What of New Testament times? How understood was the true spirit of the law in the days of the Savior and his apostles? In Luke 24:44 is a significant statement. Jesus reminded the disciples what had happened when he was with them and then said that "all things must be fulfilled, which were written *in* the law of Moses [what is the focus of the law of Moses? Christ is the focus; He is the purpose], and in the prophets [their testimonies were of the Messiah], and in the psalms, concerning me." (Italics added.)

What book of the Old Testament was the most frequently quoted scripture by Jesus and the apostles in the New Testament?[25] The book of Psalms. What was the second most quoted scripture in the New

Testament by Jesus and the apostles? The book of Isaiah, of which about 80 percent is written in poetic form. Why would they choose these two books instead of others? Because the people were best acquainted with these particular books. For the common folk (the Bedouin) in the desert, the Semitic tradition of the Middle East was for the people to sit around the campfires and sing the songs of their religious heritage. The poetic writings (songs) were chiefly the Psalms and Isaiah. They memorized them, or at least parts of them, through the long established tribal system of oral transmission. They learned to sing from the books of Psalms and Isaiah, for these books were the most readily accessible to them. The third most quoted book in the New Testament is the book of Deuteronomy and then other books of the Pentateuch. In comparison to the Psalms and Isaiah, however, they are almost insignificant, because most people had little familiarity with, or at best a limited access to, the rest of the scriptural record. In view of the teachings of the Savior and his reminder of what the scriptural sources taught of him, his testimony was that if one had the spirit of those scriptures, they all pointed to Him.

At a special time when some were permitted to go to the apostle Paul in his place of residence in Rome, he taught them about his great ministry and testimony and witness as an apostle. "And when they had appointed him a day, there came many to him into *his* lodging; to whom he expounded and testified the kingdom of God, *persuading them concerning Jesus, both out of the law of Moses, and out of the prophets."* (Acts 28:23; italics added.)

When the spirit of the law of Moses is really understood, can one teach of Christ? Paul did, and he used it in power while teaching.

In the first chapter of the Gospel of John, the apostle reports of the power of the proper spirit of the law with great power and testimony: "The day following Jesus would go forth into Galilee, and findeth Philip, and saith unto him, Follow me. Now Philip was of Bethsaida, the city of Andrew and Peter. Philip findeth Nathanael, and saith unto him, We have found him, *of whom Moses in the law, and the prophets, did write, Jesus of Nazareth*, the son of Joseph." (John 1:43; italics added.) They had found the Messiah. It is this Messiah, this Christ, of whom the law of Moses taught, as well as other prophets. Those who had the true spirit of the law in New Testament times or in Book of Mormon times recognized the efficacy and power of the law of Moses in helping them to focus on what would bring them to Christ.

What caused many of God's people to detour from the purpose of the law? Again, the Book of Mormon again provides the answer:

"Behold, my brethren, he that prophesieth, let him prophesy to the understanding of men; for the Spirit speaketh the truth and lieth not. Wherefore, it speaketh of things as they really are, and of things as they really will be; wherefore, these things are manifested unto us plainly, for the salvation of our souls. [If you are able to maintain the spirit of the law of Moses, it gives you focus and foundation to lead you to salvation.] But behold, we are not witnesses alone in these things; for God also spake them unto prophets of old.

"But behold, the Jews were a stiffnecked people; and they despised the words of plainness, and killed the prophets, and sought for things that they could not understand. Wherefore, because of their blindness, which blindness came by looking beyond the mark [when they lost the spirit of it, they could not keep the focus; they didn't know the direction they were heading; and problems developed], they must needs fall; for God hath taken away his plainness from them, and delivered unto them many things which they cannot understand, because they desired it. And because they desired it God hath done it, that they may stumble." (Jacob 4:13–14.)

The New Testament record provides an excellent illustration of this problem. Matthew 9:16 and 17 discusses a metaphor that new cloth is not put on or sewn with old cloth and new wine is not put in old bottles.[26] These verses certainly illustrate a principle that seems to be out of context with the law of Moses. In the Joseph Smith Translation, we find the Prophet Joseph Smith added four verses, which suggests that something was lost from the text. This restored text gives a perspective to the problem that had come to the Israelites because of their looking beyond the mark.

"Then said the Pharisees unto him, Why will ye not receive us with our baptism, seeing we keep the whole law?

"But Jesus said unto them, Ye keep not the law. If ye had kept the law, ye would have received me [if you had the spirit of the law, you would have known what I was trying to teach you], for I am he who gave the law.

"I receive not you with your baptism, because it profiteth you nothing.

"For when that which is new is come, the old is ready to be put away." (JST Matt. 9:18–21.)

What had happened? Why did the Jews use the phrase "our baptism," as opposed to "his baptism?" Baptism was a part of the preparatory gospel of the law of Moses.[27] The Apostle Paul, in 1 Corinthians
10, bears testimony that Israel was baptized in the Red Sea with
Moses.[28] Doctrine and Covenants 84 is a confirming testimony that this
principle was inherent in the law that the ancients practiced. The Book
of Mormon bears testimony that baptism was a part of the law of Moses,
which they brought with them, for the practice of it is found in the
record from the very beginning to the end.[29] But the Jews had lost the
spirit and power of it and had confused and eventually combined it with,
or in some cases, substituted it, for something else. Some of the performances given under the law of carnal commandments were a series
of washings and cleansings that were to be performed in different times
in people's lives. There were many washings of purification.[30] Some of
them had very practical purposes, but everything that was done under
the law of carnal commandments was spiritually based. The performances were intended to teach a principle or to give focus and perspective. Therefore, there was no separation, so to speak, of church
and state, of the temporal and the spiritual.

But when Judah (the Jews) fell into apostasy and lost priesthood,
they took the principle of baptism and some of these washings and
mixed them together, forming a new interpretation and initiating the
tradition that is still practiced today. They call it the *Mikveh,* meaning
"gathering of water." It is a ritual bath, an immersion, of cleansing or
washing.[31] Jews of varying religious interpretations use it in a variety
of different ways. Some do it only once or twice in their lifetime,
whereas others do it frequently. In Qumran near the Dead Sea are
numerous of these washing pools. They look like baptismal fonts, but
they are the *mikveh* (bath) of the Jews who lived there.[32] The ancient
fortress of Masada likewise has these pools.[33] The excavations south
of the Temple Mount in Jerusalem also reveal many *mikveh.*[34]

The reintroduction of gospel principles in Jesus' day came with
John, who was to prepare the way. Was there great concern over John
the Baptist's immersing or cleansing people? No. They never raised a
question about that. Why? Because the *mikveh* bath of purification was
a common practice and part of their religious worship. It was not a
strange thing. In fact, Jewish law says that the purest form of washing
in the *mikveh* is with a running stream.[35] When John chose to baptize
in the Jordan River, he chose the purest pool of washing that their

tradition allowed. Why, then, all the contention about John the Baptist? Because of his message! He announced himself as one sent to prepare the way for the Messiah.[36] It was the directness of this theological assertion that threatened the Jewish leaders. He also came with priesthood authority and power to baptize and restored the ordinance of baptism to its proper order. The great lavern basin in the Temple of Solomon was a baptismal font for the living.[37] That knowledge was lost from the Old Testament record as we have it. That is why this restored text in the Matthew account of the Savior's teaching to the Pharisees who had developed another tradition is so important.

The full history of the *mikveh* bath is very difficult to trace. By the time the recorded oral tradition of the Jews was established, which is called the Mishnah, the tradition and practice of the *mikveh* was firmly in place. It obviously had Old Testament roots. The Mishnah is usually dated as early as 200 B.C. The *mikveh* bath is an apostate form of baptism that came down from the Old Testament times with this modified purpose. The full significance of the baptismal ordinance had been lost to them. The Mishnaic tradition specified that the convert to Judaism must fulfill three requirements.[38] First, male converts had to be circumcised. Second, all converts were to wash themselves clean by immersion in a *mikveh* bath.[39] Third, they were to offer sacrifice in the temple. Many Jews were never able to make such a pilgrimage during the time of the temple. How then did they fulfill the requirement of sacrifice? They commissioned another person to offer a proxy sacrifice for them. After the temple was destroyed, how was the requirement of sacrifice satisfied? The traditional rabbinical substitute for the law of sacrifice and offerings was prayer and the study of the Torah.[40]

In Matthew 23 is a great discourse by Jesus that reveals some additional principles that were stumbling blocks to wayward Israel:

"Then spake Jesus to the multitude, and to his disciples, Saying, The scribes and the Pharisees sit in Moses' seat:

"All therefore whatsoever they bid you observe, *that* observe and do; but do not ye after their works: for they say, and do not.

"For they bind heavy burdens and grievous to be borne, and lay *them* on men's shoulders; but they *themselves* will not move them with one of their fingers.

"But all their works they do for to be seen of men: they make broad their phylacteries, and enlarge the borders of their garments." (Matt. 23:1–5; italics added.)

Christ openly condemned some of the religious paraphernalia and tradition that had already long been used among the Jews of his day. He mentioned specifically the phylactery boxes that were used for their prayers and their prayer shawls.[41] He condemned these practices as not being in the spirit of the law. He described them as "heavy burdens to be borne." These and other added practices are often confused with the law of Moses. Also from some of the performances of the law of carnal commandments developed a whole system of traditions that are misinterpretations and distortions of the law of Moses. These traditions deprived the children of Israel of the spirit of the law of Moses and robbed them of the power and direction that that law could give them. The Savior's condemnation continues:

"But woe unto you, scribes and Pharisees, hypocrites! for ye shut up the kingdom of heaven against men; for ye neither go in yourselves, neither suffer ye them that are entering to go in.

"Woe unto you, scribes and Pharisees, hypocrites! for ye devour widows' houses, and for a pretence make long prayer: therefore ye shall receive the greater damnation." (Matt. 23:13–14.)

"Woe unto you, scribes and Pharisees, hypocrites! for ye compass sea and land to make one proselyte, and when he is made, ye make him twofold more the child of hell than he was before like unto yourselves." (JST Matt. 23:12; see also Matt. 23:15.)

Christ is very condemnatory in this setting. Why? Because they surfeited even the proselyte (the convert) with these false traditions. Later in the same chapter He taught another great principle: "Woe unto you, scribes and Pharisees, hypocrites! for ye pay tithe of mint and anise and cumin, and have omitted the weightier matters of the law [you've lost the whole spirit and direction of it, and what it means in a person's life, such as], judgment, mercy, and faith: these ought ye to have done, and not to leave the other undone." (Matt. 23:23.)

Another familiar New Testament scriptural passage, Luke 14:34, seems to have little to do with the law of Moses. "Salt is good: but if the salt have lost his savor, wherewith shall it be seasoned?"

The Joseph Smith Translation provides the proper context for this passage as an example of the Pharisaic traditions:

"Then certain of them came to him, saying, Good Master, we have Moses and the prophets, and whosoever shall live by them, shall he not have life?

"And Jesus answered, saying, Ye know not Moses, neither the

prophets; for if ye had known them, ye would have believed on me; for to this intent they were written. For I am sent that ye might have life. Therefore I will liken it unto salt which is good;

"But if the salt has lost its savor, wherewith shall it be seasoned?" (JST Luke 14:35–37.)

They had corrupted the law — the salt — to the extent that the salt had lost its savor. Their traditions had contaminated the law, and it had lost its purpose and power to bring people to Christ.

The net effect of these traditions on the adherents of the law of Moses in the apostles' day is described in modern revelation: "And it came to pass that the children, being brought up in subjection to the law of Moses, gave heed to the traditions of their fathers and believed not the gospel of Christ, wherein they became unholy." (D&C 74:4.)

Remember what the Apostle Paul said of the law in Galatians 3:17–25:

"And this I say, that the covenant, that was confirmed before of God in Christ, the law, which was four hundred and thirty years after, cannot disannul, that it should make the promise of none effect.

"For if the inheritance be of the law, it is no more of promise: but God gave it to Abraham by promise.

"Wherefore then serveth the law? It was added because of transgressions, till the seed should come to whom the promise was made; and it was ordained by angels in the hand of a mediator.

"Now a mediator is not a mediator of one, but God is one.

"Is the law then against the promises of God? God forbid: for if there had been a law given which could have given life, verily righteousness should have been by the law.

"But the scripture hath concluded all under sin, that the promise by faith of Jesus Christ might be given to them that believe.

"But before faith came, we were kept under the law, shut up unto the faith which should afterwards be revealed.

"Wherefore the law was our schoolmaster to bring us unto Christ, that we might be justified by faith.

"But after that faith is come, we are no longer under a schoolmaster."

Why was the law of carnal commandments given? "It was added because of transgressions." To what was it added? The preparatory gospel. And what was the purpose of the added law of carnal commandments? To teach the children of Israel how to repent, so they could increase the Spirit in their lives to become more focused and come unto Christ. In Galatians 3:24, Paul makes a great statement in which he described the law as a "schoolmaster to bring us unto Christ." The Joseph Smith Translation adds a very significant change: "The law was our schoolmaster until Christ." (JST Gal. 3:24.) The law was not just to bring us to Christ but a schoolmaster till Christ came; and then it was fulfilled.

The fulfillment of the law and its purposes, particularly the law of carnal commandments, was fulfilled at Christ's first advent, both to the Church established in the holy land[42] and also to the peoples of the Americas. Jesus declared that this law was fulfilled in him and that it therefore had an end:

"And it came to pass that when Jesus had said these words he perceived that there were some among them who marveled, and wondered what he would concerning the law of Moses; for they understood not the saying that old things had passed away, and that all things had become new.

"And he said unto them: Marvel not that I said unto you that old things had passed away, and that all things had become new.

"Behold, I say unto you that the law is fulfilled that was given unto Moses.

"Behold, I am he that gave the law, and I am he who covenanted with my people Israel; therefore, the law in me is fulfilled, for I have come to fulfil the law; therefore it hath an end.

"Behold, I do not destroy the prophets, for as many as have not been fulfilled in me, verily I say unto you, shall all be fulfilled.

"And because I said unto you that old things have passed away, I do not destroy that which hath been spoken concerning things which are to come.

"For behold, the covenant which I have made with my people is not all fulfilled; but the law which was given unto Moses hath an end in me.

"Behold, I am the law, and the light. Look unto me, and endure to the end, and ye shall live; for unto him that endureth to the end will I give eternal life." (3 Ne. 15:2–9.)

In 2 Corinthians 3 the apostle Paul wrote to the Saints at Corinth who were, for the most part, converts from Judaism:

"Forasmuch as ye are manifestly declared to be the epistle of Christ ministered by us, written not with ink, but with the Spirit of the living God; not in tables of stone, but in fleshy tables of the heart.

"And such trust have we through Christ to God-ward:

"Not that we are sufficient of ourselves to think any thing as of ourselves; but our sufficiency is of God;

"Who also hath made us able ministers of the new testament [or the new covenant]; not of the letter, but of the spirit: for the letter killeth, but the spirit giveth life." (Vv. 3–6.)

The key that made the law of Moses operative in their lives was the Israelites' ability to obtain and keep the spirit of it. If they followed only the letter of the law, it became dead to them. Many, today, tend to interpret the law of Moses with "the letter" alone. That is an error. The law of Moses viewed in the proper perspective had the Spirit and power and made it possible for individuals to obtain the Spirit in their own lives.

The scripture continues: "But their minds were blinded: for until this day remaineth the same vail untaken away in the reading of the old testament; which vail is done away in Christ." (2 Cor. 3:14.) When Christ is recognized in the Old Testament, then comes understanding and a love of it! But even to this day when Moses (or the Old Testament) is read, "the vail is upon their heart." Paul gave us the key that removes the veil from one's mind: "Nevertheless when it shall turn to the Lord, the vail shall be taken away." (2 Cor. 3:16.) The Joseph Smith Translation adds two words that give a clearer focus: *their heart.* Nevertheless, "when their heart shall turn to the Lord, the vail shall be taken away." (JST 2 Cor. 3:16.) In other words, there must be humility, teachableness, meekness, and obedience. To have the veil removed makes it possible for the individual to repent and come unto Christ. That was the true spirit of the law of Moses.

Do we ever wander in a "wilderness" as a people? Do we have a "law of Moses" added because of transgressions? Are we really ready to build Zion? What then is the true purpose of the law of tithing and the Welfare Services program? Do we have "schoolmasters" to bring us to consecration, to Zion, to prepare for the Millennium? President Joseph F. Smith prophetically declared:

"We expect to see the day, if we live long enough (and if some of us do not live long enough to see it, there are others who will), when every council of the Priesthood in the Church of Jesus Christ of Latter-day Saints will understand its duty; will assume its responsibility, will magnify its calling, and fill its place in the Church. . . . When that day shall come, there will not be so much necessity for work that is now being done by the auxiliary organizations, because it will be done by the regular quorums of the Priesthood. The Lord designed and comprehended it from the beginning, and he has made provision in the Church whereby every need may be met and satisfied through the regular organizations of the Priesthood."[43]

Are not the auxiliaries and various programs "schoolmaster" to us? Are we really so different from ancient Israel?

May the Lord bless us and help us that we might capture the spirit of the law of Moses, for I testify that it was an integral part of the gospel of Jesus Christ and its intent was to lead that people to Christ and help them become Christlike. We should hope that abiding by our "laws and performances" might also have a similar effect in leading us to a more Christlike character.

NOTES

1. Joseph Fielding Smith, *Answers to Gospel Questions,* 5 vols. (Salt Lake City: Deseret Book Co., 1979), 3:115–17; 5:84–86.

2. See Moses 5:5–8.

3. Smith, *Answers to Gospel Questions,* 4:155–60. See also 1:116–18; 3:154–57.

4. Edward J. Brandt, "The Priesthood Ordinances of Sacrifice," *Ensign,* Dec. 1973, pp. 49–53.

5. See Lev. 3; 7:11–38.

6. See Lev. 7:16; 22:18, 21, 23; Num. 15:3; 29:39; Deut. 12:6, 13; 16:10; 23:23.

7. See Lev. 7:16; 22:18, 21, 23; Num. 15:3, 8; 29:39; Deut. 12:6.

8. See Lev. 7:12–13, 15; 22:29.

9. See Lev. 4; 5:1–13; 6:25–30; JST Matt. 26:24.

10. See Lev. 5:15–19; 6:1–7; 7:1–10.

11. See Lev. 5:16; 6:5–17; 27:13, 15, 19, 27, 31; Num. 5:6–10.

12. See Ex. 29:26–27; Lev. 7:14, 32–34; Num. 18.

13. See Lev. 5:7, 11.

14. See Lev. 6:25–30; 7:7–8, 16; 14:13.

15. See Lev. 3:3–5.

16. See Lev. 7:16.

17. See Lev. 7:35–36; Deut. 18:1–8.

18. See Lev. 2:2, 9, 16; 5:12; 6:15; Num. 5:26; 18:26–29

19. See Lev. 19:19; Deut. 22:9–11.

20. See Ex. 12:5; 13:46.

21. See Lev. 16.

22. See Ex. 12:4.

23. See 2 Ne. 9:7; 25:16; Alma 34:10, 12, 14.

24. See Ex. 12:7.

25. See Bible Dictionary, LDS edition of the King James Version of the Bible, s.v. "Quotations."

26. See Matt. 9:16–17; Mark 2:21–22; Luke 5:36–37.

27. D&C 84:27.

28. See 1 Cor. 10:1–4. See also Louis Ginzberg, *The Legends of the Jews* (Philadelphia: Jewish Publication Society of America, 1968), 3:88; 6:34.

29. See 2 Ne. 31:5; Mosiah 18:10; 21:35; Alma 7:14; 3 Ne. 1:27; Moro. 8:25.

30. See notes to Ex. 30:19–21; 40:31; Lev. 11, 15.

31. Philip Birnbaum, *A Book of Jewish Concepts* (New York: Hebrew Publishing Co., 1964), pp. 239, 391.

32. Frank Moore Cross, Jr., *The Ancient Library of Qumran,* rev. ed. (Garden City, N.Y.: Anchor Books, 1961), pp. 67–68; see also William Sanford LaSor, *The Dead Sea Scrolls and the New Testament* (Grand Rapids, Mich.: William B. Eerdmans Publishing Co., 1972), pp. 40, 134, 149–51.

33. Yigael Yadin, *Masada* (London: Sphere Books Ltd., 1973), pp. 164–67. See also Hershel Shanks, *Judaism in Stone* (New York: Harper & Row, 1979), pp. 18–19, 26–30.

34. Nahman Avigad, *Discovering Jerusalem* (Nashville: Thomas Nelson Publishers, 1983), pp. 139–43. See also Benjamin Mazar, *The Mountain of the Lord* (Garden City, N.Y.: Doubleday & Co., 1975), pp. 128–29, 145–47.

35. Herbert Danby, *The Mishnah* (Oxford: Oxford University Press, 1967), pp. 732–33.

36. See John 1:19–28.

37. See 1 Kgs. 7:23–26; 2 Chr. 4:2–5.

38. Ginzberg, *Legends of the Jews,* 3:88.

39. Birnbaum, *Book of Jewish Concepts,* p. 239.

40. Ibid., p. 551.

41. See Deut. 6:8, n. 8b.

42. See Heb. 8:13; see also 2 Cor. 5:17.

43. Joseph F. Smith, *Gospel Doctrine* (Salt Lake City: Deseret Book Co., 1977), p. 159.

CHAPTER THREE

The Waters of Destruction and the Vine of Redemption

Allen J. Christenson

Provo, Utah

As recorded in the Gospel of John, the first public miracle performed by Jesus was the transmutation of water into wine at a marriage feast in Cana. (John 2:1–11.) The Lord did not perform miracles in a capricious manner. The act of producing wine from water must therefore have had some purpose beyond providing for the temporal entertainment of those who attended the marriage feast. According to John, the miracle "manifested forth his glory" and caused his disciples to "believe on him." (John 2:11.)

The significance of this miracle may be better appreciated if the unique symbolism of water and wine in Old Testament theology is recognized. Water appears in ancient scripture as a powerful symbol of universal death, particularly that which results from disobedience to God. The destruction of the earth by a flood of water is an important example of this tradition and figures prominently in the writings of most ancient cultures of the Old World. In contrast, wine represented divine mercy or atonement, a means whereby sin and grief might be forgotten. In light of the significance of water and wine within ancient scripture, the importance of the miracle at Cana as the inaugurating event of the Savior's ministry becomes apparent. The transmutation of water to wine foreshadowed the work of the Lord in overcoming death and providing the means whereby mankind might achieve redemption. This paper will consider the symbolic nature of water and wine in the Old Testament, the Talmud, Dead Sea literature, Pseudepigraphal texts, and early Christian writings as well as modern revelation. Ancient writings outside Judaeo-Christian tradition will also be considered briefly to demonstrate the widespread prevalence of these symbolic elements in the Old World.

Within the tradition of the Old Testament, the most universal pronouncement of divine judgment to have been passed on the world was the Great Flood in the days of Noah. This judgment was decreed by God because "all flesh had corrupted his way upon the earth." (Gen. 6:12.) The destruction was to be total, "both man, and beast, and the creeping thing, and the fowls of the air," so that the earth might be cleansed from all corruption. (Gen. 6:7.)

Early rabbinical scholars stressed that although God gave mankind ample opportunity to repent and save themselves, divine justice was meted out to the full measure when the floodwaters finally came. Noah is traditionally believed to have waited until the waves reached his ankles before entering the ark, hoping for God to show mercy on the world, but there was to be none.[1]

In Old Testament prophecy waters frequently symbolize death. Salvation was therefore described as being drawn "out of many waters." (Ps. 18:16.) Modern revelation continues to stress the potential destructive nature of water for those who are not faithful. In a revelation given to Joseph Smith, the Lord declared: "Behold, there are many dangers upon the waters, and more especially hereafter; for I, the Lord, have decreed in mine anger many destructions upon the waters. . . . Nevertheless, all flesh is in mine hand, and he that is faithful among you shall not perish by the waters." (D&C 61:4–6.)

When the waters of the Flood abated and all flesh had been destroyed, a bow was set in the heavens as a token that God would never again destroy mankind by flood. Immediately following the appearance of this sign, Noah planted a vineyard. From the fruit of this vine, Noah made wine and fell into a drunken stupor from its effects. (Gen. 9:20–21.)

The Genesis account of the drunkenness of Noah has greatly tarnished the reputation of the great prophet. Most modern rabbinical scholars are at a loss to explain why Noah would have conducted himself in such a manner: "Noah made himself profane, degraded himself. He should have planted anything but the vine, which is the source of so much sin and crime among the children of men."[2] Some scholars have argued that since Noah was traditionally the first man to cultivate the vine, he could not have known of its intoxicating effects and could therefore not be blamed for his drunkenness.[3] Certainly the incident as described in the extant version of the Old Testament does not seem to be in keeping with Noah's noble character. Elsewhere in Genesis, Noah is described as "a just man and perfect in his generations" who "walked with God." (Gen. 6:9.) Peter described him as a "preacher of righteousness." (2 Peter 2:5.) Through modern revelation, we know that he was baptized in the name of Jesus Christ,[4] taught the same everlasting gospel that the Savior taught,[5] and received the Melchizedek Priesthood at the unusually young age of ten under the hand of Methuselah. (D&C 107:52.) It is this same Noah who appears in the scriptures as the angel Gabriel, standing in authority second only to Michael in the priesthood hierarchy of heaven.[6]

Why would a prophet of Noah's stature plant the grapevine and prepare wine after the destruction of the Flood? It is because wine represented a symbol of redemption, a token of reconciliation with God. According to ancient Jewish tradition, the wine produced by Noah was first used to consecrate a burnt offering to the Lord so that he "might thereby seek atonement for himself and for his sons."[7] By divine commandment, wine was also offered by Aaron and his sons as atonement for the sins of the Israelites. Under the law of Moses this ritual continued to be carried out periodically. (Ex. 29:40; Lev. 23:13; Num. 15:5, 7, 10; 28:7, 14.)

The symbolic effect of wine is to restore goodwill between God and man. In ancient prophecy, the Lord often promised the bestowal of wine as a token of reconciliation and forgiveness. The prophet Joel prophesied: "So shall ye know that I am the Lord your God dwelling in Zion, my holy mountain: then shall Jerusalem be holy, and there shall no strangers pass through her any more. And it shall come to pass in that day, that the mountains shall drop down new wine. . . . For I will cleanse their blood that I have not cleansed: for the Lord dwelleth in Zion." (Joel 3:17–18, 21; see also Joel 2:19,24; Micah 2:11; Zech. 8:12; 9:17.) Isaiah equated the mercy of God with wine, which is given "without price." (Isa. 55:1.) Solomon wrote that for those whose works are accepted by God, wine is to be drunk with a merry heart. (Eccl. 9:7.) Wine indeed was created by God to gladden man's heart. (Ps. 104:15.) Josephus wrote that "God bestows the fruit of the vine upon men for good; which wine is poured out to him, and is the pledge of fidelity and mutual confidence among men; and puts an end to their quarrels, takes away passion and grief out of the minds of them that use it, and makes them cheerful."[8] Jotham's parable of the trees in Judges 9 stresses that wine gives joy to God as well as to man. (Judges 9:11–13.)

Anciently, those undergoing the process of repentance or mourning were forbidden to drink wine lest they forget their sin or affliction before it was resolved. In the Testament of Reuben, the firstborn son of Jacob relates that he abstained from wine during his time of penance: "With determination of soul, for seven years I repented before the Lord: I did not drink wine or liquor.... Rather, I was mourning over my sin, since it was so great."[9]

By tradition, all of Joseph's brethren abstained from wine after selling him into slavery out of regret for the evil they had done. Their abstention from wine was ended twenty-two years later when they were reunited with Joseph in Egypt. Joseph had also abstained from wine during this time out of grief for his father.[10]

Nazarites took a solemn vow to abstain from wine, grapes, and every product of the vine, so as to be in constant remembrance of the vow taken.[11] Upon completion of the vow, the Nazarite was brought to the door of the tabernacle to offer a burnt sacrifice, a sin offering and a peace offering, symbolic of his reconciliation with God.[12] Following this, he was then freed of his vow and could again partake of the fruit of the vine.

Writers of the early Christian period familiar with ancient Jewish tradition recognized Noah's vine as symbolic of redemption. In the Greek Apocalypse of Baruch, the fruit of the vine planted by Noah was equated with the atoning blood of the Savior, whereby man could be forgiven of sin and prepare to return to God:

"When God caused the Flood over the earth and destroyed all flesh ..., the water entered Paradise and killed every flower, but it removed the sprig of the vine completely and brought it outside. And when the earth appeared from the water and Noah left the ark, he started to plant [some] of the discovered plants. He also found the sprig, and taking it, he considered in his mind what it was. ...

"And God sent the angel Sarasael, and he said to him, 'Rise, Noah, plant the sprig, for the Lord says this: "Its bitterness will be changed into sweetness, and its curse will become a blessing, and its fruit will become the blood of God, and just as the race of men have been condemned through it, so through Jesus Christ Emmanuel in it [they] will receive a calling and entrance into Paradise." ' "[13]

Augustine also compared the vine of Noah with the atonement of Jesus Christ, which brought forgiveness to mankind.[14] Wine therefore symbolized the atoning blood of God, given to take away the reproach of the wicked and to cause the repentant to rejoice.

In the days of Noah, the corruption of mankind had in effect broken the covenant with God and all flesh was therefore under condemnation. After the earth was violently cleansed by water, the covenant was renewed through Noah with the bow given as a sign of God's favor. (Gen. 9:11–17.) Noah planted the grapevine as a token of his reconciliation with God, to symbolize that the corruption of the earth had been forgotten and that the time for mourning was ended. That this wine was drunk in excess may reflect the terrible sadness the aged prophet felt for those who had been destroyed.

Because of the universal nature of the Great Flood it is no surprise that a number of ancient cultures recorded their recollections of the event, however distorted. Flood epics throughout the ancient world include references to wine as a symbol of reconciliation with heaven following the flood. In Egypt, the association between wine and the floodwaters of destruction was remarkably explicit. The fullest extant account of the Great Flood in Egyptian texts is found in "The Book of the Divine Cow," portions of which were common in New Kingdom funerary literature, including the tombs of Tutankhamen, Seti I, and Ramses II. As in Israelite tradition, this text relates that in ancient times mankind transgressed the laws of heaven. The sun god, Re, therefore ordained that all flesh be destroyed by a universal flood. He commissioned his daughter Hathor to take the sacred Eye of heaven and with it go down to the earth and cover it again with the primal waters that had inundated it before creation. The presence of the gods withdrew from men, the skies darkened, and the weeping Eye of Re destroyed mankind with a terrible flood. The thunder and lightning of the darkened skies combined with the waters of the flood to destroy everything. The vengeful goddess trod the bodies of the wicked until their blood mixed with the waters covering the earth, making them red. Seeing that the destruction of mankind was nearly complete, Re desired to save a remnant. He therefore ordered that red wine be prepared from the bloody waters of the flood and be given to the goddess to assuage her thirst for destruction. Seven thousand vessels of red intoxicant were thus prepared: "When the goddess came in the morning she found them flooded, and her gaze was pleased by it. She drank and it pleased her heart. She returned drunk without having perceived mankind."[15]

The annual rising of the Nile in Egypt was believed to recapitulate the Great Flood at the dawn of time. The feast commemorating the

Nile inundation was called the Feast of Intoxication in honor of the miraculous changing of the floodwaters to wine. All Egyptians drank heavily during the feast, believing that the sweetness of the wine and their own drunkenness would ritually cause the gods to forget men's faults and limit the floodwaters from destroying them again.

It is significant that the first plague sent upon Egypt in the days of Moses was to turn the waters of the Nile to blood. (Ex. 7:16– 25.) This was a terrifying sign to the Egyptians, as it immediately called to mind their traditions of the destruction of the earth, implying that they were again under condemnation by the gods. Water served as the means whereby the arrogance of the Egyptians was ultimately punished, because God destroyed the forces of Pharoah in the depths of the Red Sea as they pursued the children of Israel. (Ex. 14:26–28.)

The apostle Paul wrote to the Corinthians that their Israelite ancestors "all passed through the sea; and were all baptized unto Moses in the cloud and in the sea." (1 Cor. 10:1–2.) Paul recognized that the passage of the Israelites through the Red Sea was a form of baptism, washing away that which was unclean, just as the Egyptians were drowned in its depths. In descending beneath the floodwaters, the Israelites trusted in the mercy of God to save them from what would otherwise have brought them certain death.

Having survived the floodwaters of the Red Sea, the Israelites were promised a fruitful land where they were to dwell as the people of God. The fruit of the vine again figures prominently in the account of their arrival in the promised land. When spies were first sent into Canaan they brought back a single cluster of grapes that was so great in size that it required two men to carry it. (Num. 13:20– 24.) The grapes were a token of God's favor and the promise of redemption after their many trials in the Sinai wilderness.

It is significant in this regard that as part of the Passover meal, several cups of wine are drunk to symbolize the spiritual triumph of the Israelites that followed their suffering in Egypt. As the wine is blessed, Psalms 113 through 118 are read as hymns of thanksgiving for their delivery from death. Psalm 116 in particular stresses this redemption:

"The sorrows of death compassed me, and the pains of hell gat hold upon me: I found trouble and sorrow. Then called I upon the name of the Lord; O Lord, I beseech thee, deliver my soul. . . . Return unto thy rest, O my soul; for the Lord hath dwelt bountifully with thee. For thou hast delivered my soul from death, mine eyes from tears, and my feet from falling." (Ps. 116:3–4, 7–8.)

Modern Jewish families in celebrating the Passover unitedly lift a cup of wine and recite the words: "We shall then sing a new song of praise to You for our redemption and for the liberation of our souls. Blessed are You, Hashem [Lord], Who has redeemed Israel. Blessed are You, Hashem [Lord] Our God, King of the universe, Who creates the fruit of the vine."[16]

Jewish legend relates that floodwaters were also the means of punishment for the wicked among Israel. The Zohar relates that when the Israelites worshipped a golden calf in the wilderness, the oceans threatened to rise and flood the earth again. The waters were finally assuaged when Moses cast those who had committed idolatry, along with the dust of the destroyed calf, into the depths of the sea. He then poured out a great draught of water over the place of idolatry as if to drown it. Those who subsequently drank from that water brought a curse upon themselves.[17] In contrast, God provided a miraculous well to sustain the Israelites in the wilderness, a well that produced water that tasted like sweet wine.[18]

Another example of the use of wine as a symbol of reconciliation is the prophecy of the feast of wine to be held following the destruction of the wicked. This great banquet of the Lord was a common motif in messianic literature, symbolizing the ultimate triumph of God over the forces of death and evil. In Joel 3, the fury of God in the last days was seen to leave the nations of Egypt and Edom desolate, while the redeemed lands of Judah would become fruitful once more. Verse 18 declares that the mountains shall drop down new wine "when the Lord comes again to dwell in Zion." Amos also declared that in that day "the mountains shall drop sweet wine." (Amos 9:13.)

Isaiah prophesied that after the destruction of the wicked, a vintage feast will be given by the Lord as a token of his victory over death: "And in this mountain shall the Lord of hosts make unto all people a feast of fat things, a feast of wines on the lees, of fat things full of marrow, of wines on the lees well refined." (Isa. 25:6.)

The Scroll of the Rule, one of the Dead Sea texts from the Qumran community, describes a messianic banquet in which the elect will drink wine as a community with the Messiah and his high priest.[19]

Later tradition greatly embellished the account of this banquet. The Syriac Apocalypse of Baruch relates that when the Messiah is revealed, grapes will grow to a miraculous degree: "The earth will also yield fruits ten thousandfold. And on one vine will be a thousand branches, and one branch will produce a thousand clusters, and one cluster will produce a thousand grapes, and one grape will produce a cor of wine. And those who are hungry will enjoy themselves and they will, moreover, see marvels every day."[20]

The Pirqe Mashiah prophesies that when the Messiah comes, rivers of wine will flow from the Holy of Holies within the House of the Lord, barring the angel of death from crossing it to afflict the people of God.[21]

Prior to his death, Jesus referred to this great messianic banquet when he declared that he would not drink of the fruit of the vine until he could do so with his elect in the kingdom of God. (Matt. 26:29; Mark 14:25; Luke 22:16–18.)

Doctrine and Covenants 27 also describes this banquet, given to Joseph Smith as he was procuring wine for the sacrament in August 1830: "The hour cometh that I will drink of the fruit of the vine with you on the earth, and with Moroni, . . . and also with Elias, to whom I have committed the keys of bringing to pass the restoration of all things spoken by the mouth of all the holy prophets since the world began, concerning the last days." (D&C 27:5–6.) The passage continues with a list of the major prophets of past dispensations who would meet together to partake of the banquet of the Lord.

The close association of destructive waters and the wine of reconciliation is also found in ancient Mesopotamia. According to the Epic of Gilgamesh, the man chosen to escape the Great Flood was Utnapishtim, who built a special boat and loaded it with animals to save them from destruction. Upon landing on solid ground, Utnapishtim immediately offered a sacrifice and poured out a libation of wine to appease the gods and stanch their anger.[22]

The Babylonian New Year's festival commemorated the end of the Flood and the renewal of life. As part of the festival, a crescent-shaped boat, patterned after that which escaped the Great Flood, was built and filled with sacrificial animals. On the fifth day of the festival, a sheep was sacrificed and thrown into the river so that the waters would bear away the impurities of the people. This ritual recapitulated the cleansing of the earth by the Flood. At the culmination of the festival, a sacred marriage feast was held with the king playing the role of the bridegroom.[23] This was primarily a feast of wine,[24] and many libations of new wine were poured out to the gods to overpower the forces of death and to encourage the fertility of the crops.

The ancient Greeks called the survivor of the Great Flood Deucalion. According to Pindar, the festival of Deucalion was celebrated with large amounts of wine while the people sang songs of the destruction of the world by great storms which covered the earth with black waters.[25] The name Deucalion itself comes from the roots *deucos* and *halieus*, meaning "new wine sailor."[26]

The Greek god of wine was Dionysus. In Dionysian tradition water was also a symbol of death, whereas wine was the instrument of new life. Soon after birth, the infant Dionysus was hacked to pieces and submerged in boiling water. He miraculously achieved rebirth to immortality by means of a sacred grape vine.[27] Through the wine of Dionysus man can achieve reconciliation with the gods: "He [Dionysus] invented the liquid draught of the grape and introduced it to mortals. When they get their fill of the flowing grape, it stops their grief. It gives them sleep and forgetfulness of daily sorrows. There is no other medicine for trouble. The libations we pour are the god himself making our peace with gods, so that through him mankind may obtain blessings."[28]

Water as a symbol of destruction and wine as a symbol of redemption have been seen to be common motifs in Old Testament writings as well as the traditions of the major ancient cultures outside Israelite tradition. Recognition of the symbolic significance of water and wine in the ancient world sets the stage for a proper understanding of these elements in Jewish culture at the time of Christ. The ordinances of baptism and sacramental wine reflect this ancient tradition and are known to have been practiced by the Jewish inhabitants of Qumran just before the advent of the Savior.[29] The theme finds its ultimate expression in the ministry of Jesus Christ. The institution of Christian baptism by immersion in water followed by a sacrament of wine served as tokens of the purging of sin and the promise of redemption.

The apostle Peter likened baptism to the Flood and compared the escape of Noah and his family from death to the resurrection of all flesh through Jesus Christ:

"He [Jesus Christ] went and preached unto the spirits in prison; which sometime were disobedient, when once the long-suffering of God waited in the days of Noah, while the ark was a preparing, wherein few, that is, eight souls were saved by water. The like figure whereunto even baptism doth also now save us (not the putting away of the filth of the flesh, but the answer of a good conscience toward God,) by the resurrection of Jesus Christ." (1 Peter 3:19–21.)

Baptism by water was therefore equated with death, specifically the destruction of mankind in the days of Noah. It is only through symbolic death in a watery flood that sin can be washed away, making possible man's redemption to a new life in Christ. This was a favorite theme in the writings of Paul:

"Know ye not, that so many of us as were baptized into Jesus Christ were baptized into his death? Therefore we are buried with him by baptism into death: that like as Christ was raised up from the dead by the glory of the Father, even so we also should walk in newness of life. For if we have been planted together in the likeness of his death, we shall be also in the likeness of his resurrection." (Rom. 6:3–5; see also Col. 2:12.)

Modern revelation also stresses the connection between the waters of baptism and death:

"The ordinance of baptism by water, to be immersed therein in order to answer to the likeness of the dead, that one principle might accord with the other; to be immersed in the water and come forth out of the water is in the likeness of the resurrection of the dead in coming forth out of their graves. . . . Consequently, the baptismal font was instituted as a similitude of the grave, and was commanded to be in a place underneath where the living are wont to assemble." (D&C 128:12–13; see also 76:51.)

In remembrance of the covenants made at baptism and as a symbol of the Lord's promise always to be with them, those who were baptized partook of a sacrament of wine, blessed as a token of the atoning blood of the Savior. Among ancient Christians, the sacramental bread and cup of wine were offered immediately after baptism to symbolize the initiate's reconciliation with God.[30] At least as early as the second century, Easter was set aside for baptism and the administration of the sacrament, so as to emphasize the initiate's spiritual death and resurrection in imitation of Jesus Christ.[31] According to Cyril, who was bishop of Jerusalem in the fourth century, baptisms were conducted in a special building with a font of water.[32] This ceremony took place at night to symbolize its association with death. Having been baptized, the initiate was led into another building, called the "Church of the Resurrection," where the individual was offered the sacrament.[33]

Most early Christian writers referred to the sacrament by the Greek word *eucharistia*, "thanksgiving."[34] This word exemplifies the attitude of the early Saints toward the sacrament as an expression of gratitude to God for their redemption from spiritual death. Ignatius thus refers to the sacrament as "the medicine of immortality, and the sovereign remedy by which we escape death and live in Jesus Christ for evermore."[35]

The symbolism of wine as a token of divine mercy and forgiveness was used by Jesus throughout his earthly ministry. The apostle John in particular emphasized this association, as is evident from the fifteenth chapter of his Gospel:

"I am the true vine, and my Father is the husbandman. Now ye are clean through the word which I have spoken unto you. . . . I am the vine, ye are the branches: He that abideth in me, and I in him, the same bringeth forth much fruit: for without me ye can do nothing." (John 15:1–3, 5.)

The powerful symbol of God as a vine, offering salvation to those who partake of it, is very ancient. In explaining the vision of the tree of life, the prophet Nephi equated Jehovah with a vine: "And then at that day will they not rejoice and give praise unto their everlasting God, their rock and their salvation? Yea, at that day, will they not receive the strength and nourishment from the true vine? Yea, will they not come unto the true fold of God?" (1 Nephi 15:15.)

In the Septuagint version of Psalms 80:14–16, the suffering of the promised Messiah was compared to the destruction of a grapevine, planted by God: "Take care of this vine and [protect] what your right hand has planted, the son of man whom you yourself made strong; for they have burned it with fire and cut it down."[36]

Early Christians interpreted the famous messianic prophecy of Isaiah concerning the "stem of Jesse" or the "Branch" (Isa. 11:1) to represent Jesus Christ as the true vine. In the Didache, the early apostles declared: "We give thanks to thee, our Father, for the holy Vine of thy servant David, which thou hast made known to us through thy servant Jesus."[37]

Wine was designated by Jesus at the Last Supper as the symbol of his atoning blood, shed for the sins of the world: "And he took the cup, and when he had given thanks, he gave it to them: and they all drank of it. And he said unto them, This is my blood of the new testament, which is shed for many." (Mark 14:23–24.)

Having instituted the sacrament, Jesus declared that he would not partake of wine again until the great sacrifice was complete and reconciliation with God was possible for mankind: "Verily I say unto you, I will drink no more of the fruit of the vine, until that day that I drink it new in the kingdom of God." (Mark 14:25; see also Matt. 26:29; Luke 22:16–18.) In keeping with this promise, Jesus refused wine mixed with myrrh that was offered to him to ease his suffering on the cross. (Mark 15:23.) To have accepted wine on the cross would have represented the premature reconciliation of God to man before the atoning sacrifice was completed.

The use of wine as a sacrament in remembrance of the Atonement was also instituted by Christ among the ancient inhabitants of the New World. Jesus specifically commanded that this ordinance follow baptism as a symbol of God's presence with his elect. (3 Nephi 18:1–11.)

Modern revelation to the prophet Joseph Smith preserved the use of wine in the sacrament. (D&C 20:75–78; 27:3–4.) The Word of Wisdom allows the drinking of wine only in connection with this sacred ordinance (D&C 89:6), although an earlier revelation had made it clear that the substance used in the sacrament is not as important as proper remembrance of the Atonement. (D&C 27:2.)

The miracle at Cana was, of course, performed at a marriage feast. Jesus frequently referred to his appearance in glory in the last days as a bridegroom coming to claim the church of the faithful as his bride. (Matt. 9:15; 22:2–9; 25:1–10; Mark 2:19; Luke 5:34; John 2:9; 3:29; Rev. 19:7–9; 21:2,9; 22:17.) In referring to himself as the bridegroom, Jesus recalled the prophecy of Isaiah that in the last days God would rejoice over the just "as the bridegroom rejoiceth over the bride." (Isa. 62:5; see also Jer. 3:14.) Jewish legend declares that in that day the great banquet of the Messiah will be convened for the pious in the Garden of Eden as a bridegroom greets his guests at a wedding feast. There they are to be given "wine preserved in its grapes since the six days of creation."[38] This image is also a frequent motif in the Doctrine and Covenants, particularly in those sections dealing with the preparations of the Saints to greet the Savior in the last days. (D&C 33:17; 65:3; 88:92; 133:10, 19.)

The ceremonies of baptism and the sacrament were often equated in early Christian literature with the marriage of Christ with the soul of the initiate. The marriage was consummated by partaking of the sacramental meal. Cyril of Jerusalem wrote: "[Jesus] once in Cana of Galilee, turned the water into wine, akin to blood, and is it incredible that He should have turned wine into blood? When called to a bodily marriage, He miraculously wrought that wonderful work; and on the children of the bridechamber, shall He not much rather be acknowledged to have bestowed the fruition of His Body and Blood?"[39]

In early Christian congregations, light for the ritual of the sacrament was provided by a series of lamps, which recalled the lights held by virgins going forth to meet the bridegroom in the parable of the wedding feast. Gregory Nazianzen recorded the instructions given to the new members prior to this ceremony: "The Station in which you shall presently stand after your Baptism before the Great Sanctuary is a foretype of the future glory. . . . The lamps which you will kindle are a Sacrament of the illumination there with which we shall meet the Bridegroom, shining and virgin souls, with the lamps of our faith shining."[40] As marriage feasts, the sacrament and the great messianic banquet spiritually unite the redeemed people of God with the Savior.

Paul wrote that the laws and prophecies of the Old Testament served as schoolmasters to bring us to a knowledge of Jesus Christ. (Gal. 3:24.) The ancient prophet Jacob, although he lived many centuries before the birth of the Savior, wrote:

"For this intent have we written these things, that they may know that we knew of Christ, and we had hope of his glory many hundred years before his coming; and not only we ourselves had a hope of his glory, but also all the holy prophets which were before us. Behold, they believed in Christ and worshiped the Father in his name." (Jacob 4:4–5.)

It is important to remember that the prophets of the Old Testament knew of Jesus Christ and looked forward in hope to his day. The great prophet Noah taught, "Believe and repent of your sins and be baptized in the name of Jesus Christ, the Son of God, even as our fathers did, and ye shall receive the Holy Ghost, that ye may have all things made manifest."[41] The apostle Paul wrote that it was by faith that Noah carried out the will of the Lord. (Heb. 11:7.) Despite the terrible judgment meted out upon his generation, Noah did not lose that hope of redemption, which comes through faith in Jesus Christ. In token of this hope he planted a vineyard, so that the bitterness of the floodwaters could be forgotten in the sweetness of new vine.

In the context of these ancient traditions, understood at the time of Jesus Christ, the significance of the miracle performed at the marriage feast at Cana becomes apparent. The conversion of water to wine by the power of the Messiah dramatically symbolized the Savior's mission in providing for mankind's reconciliation with God. As such, the miracle served to foreshadow the ministry of the Lord in overcoming death, offering himself as an atoning sacrifice, and in providing the means by which man might spiritually unite himself with God forever.

NOTES

1. Moshe Weissman, *The Midrash Says: The Book of Beraishis* (Brooklyn: Yakov Publications, 1980), p. 93.

2. Rashi, in *Pentateuch and Haftorahs – Hebrew Text, English Translation and Commentary*, ed. J. H. Hertz (London: Soncino Press, 1960), p. 34.

3. Ibid.

4. JST Gen. 8:11.

5. Joseph Smith, *Teachings of the Prophet Joseph Smith*, sel. Joseph Fielding Smith (Salt Lake City: Deseret Book Co., 1976), p. 264; see also JST Gen. 8:4, 7.

6. Smith, *Teachings*, p. 157.

7. Jubilees 7.3–5, in *The Old Testament Pseudepigrapha*, ed. James H. Charlesworth, 2 vols. (Garden City, N.Y.: Doubleday and Co., 1983), 2:69.

8. Josephus, *Antiquities of the Jews* 2.5.2, in *The Life and Works of Josephus*, trans. William Whiston (Philadelphia: John C. Winston Co., 1936), p. 65.

9. Testament of Reuben 1.9–10, in Charlesworth, *Old Testament Pseudepigrapha*, 1:782.

10. Testament of Joseph 3.5, in Charlesworth, *Old Testament Pseudepigrapha*, 1:820.

11. Numbers 6:3–4; Luke 1:15; 7:33; Nazir 1.2; 2.4, in *The Mishnah*, trans. Herbert Danby (Oxford: Oxford University Press, 1933), pp. 281–82.

12. Numbers 6:13–21; Nazir 6.9, in Danby, *Mishnah*, p. 289.

13. Greek Apocalypse of Baruch (3 Baruch) 4.10–15, in Charlesworth, *Old Testament Pseudepigrapha*, 1:667, 669.

14. Augustine, *City of God*, trans. Henry Bettenson (London: Penguin Books, 1972), 16.1–2, pp. 649–51.

15. The Book of the Divine Cow 6.13–21, in *Ancient Egyptian Literature*, trans. Miriam Lichtheim (Berkeley and Los Angeles: University of California Press, 1976), 2:199.

16. Nosson Scherman, *The Family Haggadah* (Brooklyn: Mesorah Publications, Ltd., 1981), p. 49.

17. *Zohar* 2.113b, trans. Harry Sperling, Maurice Simon, and Paul P. Levertoff (London: Soncino Press, 1984), 3:338–39.

18. Louis Ginzberg, *The Legends of the Jews* (Philadelphia: Jewish Publication Society of America, 1939, 1981), 3:65.

19. The Scroll of the Rule 11–22, trans. G. Vermes, in *The Essene Writings from Qumran*, ed. A. Dupont-Sommer (Cleveland: World Publishing Co., 1962), pp. 108–9.

20. Syriac Apocalypse of Baruch (2 Baruch) 29.5–6, in Charlesworth, *Old Testament Pseudepigrapha*, 1:630.

21. Pirqe Mashiah, BhM 3.74, in *The Messiah Texts*, ed. Raphael Patai (New York: Avon Books, 1979), p. 233.

22. The Epic of Gilgamesh, Old Babylonian Version, Tablet 11.155–61, trans. N. K. Sandars, in *Ancient Near Eastern Texts*, ed. James B. Pritchard (Princeton: Princeton University Press, 1958, 1973), 1:70.

23. Theodore H. Gaster, *Thespis* (New York: W.W. Norton and Co., 1977), pp. 62–64.

24. The Epic of Gilgamesh, Tablet 11.72–4, in Pritchard, *Ancient Near Eastern Texts*, 1:69.

25. Pindar, *Olympian Ode* 9.41–57, in *The Odes of Pindar*, trans. Richard Lattimore (Chicago: University of Chicago Press, 1976), pp. 30–31.

26. Robert Graves, *The Greek Myths* (Middlesex, England: Penguin Books, 1972), 1:141.

27. Euripides, *Bacchants* 519, in *Euripides: Ten Plays*, trans. Moses Hadas and John McLean (New York: Bantam Books, 1960), p. 292; see also Jane Harrison, *Prolegomena to the Study of Greek Religion* (Cleveland: Meridian Books, 1966), pp. 436–37.

28. Euripides, *Bacchants* 275–85, in Hadas and McLean, *Euripedes: Ten Plays*, p. 287.

29. Community Rule 3, 5; Messianic Rule 2, trans. G. Vermes, in *The Dead Sea Scrolls in English* (Harmondswirth, Middlesex, England: Penguin Books, 1975), pp. 45–47.

30. Justin Martyr, *Apology* 1.65, in *Marcus Aurelius and His Times*, ed. Walter J. Black (Roslyn, N.Y.: Walter J. Black, 1945), p. 289.

31. Tertullian, *On Baptism* 19, in *Early Christians Speak*, ed. Everett Ferguson (Austin, Tex.: Sweet Publishing Co., 1971), p. 39; see also Gregory Nazianzen, *Oration on Baptism*, 40.29, in *Nicene and Post-Nicene Fathers of the Christian Church*, ed. Philip Schaff and Henry Wace (Grand Rapids, Mich.: Eerdmans Publishing Co., 1978), 7:368.

32. Cyril of Jerusalem, *Lecture on the Mysteries*, 20.4, in Schaff and Wace, *Nicene and Post-Nicene Fathers*, 7:147.

33. Cyril of Jerusalem, *Lecture* 14.14, in Schaff and Wace, *Nicene and Post-Nicene Fathers*, p. 97; Cyril of Jerusalem, *Lecture* 23 (On the Mysteries 5), in Schaff and Wace, *Nicene and Post-Nicene Fathers*, pp. 153–57.

34. Ignatius, *Philadelphians* 4, in *Early Christian Writings*, trans. Maxwell Staniforth (New York: Penguin Books, 1968), p. 112; Ignatius, *Smyrnaeans* 8, ibid., pp. 121–22; Justin Martyr, *Apology* 1.65–66, in Black, pp. 289–90.

35. Ignatius, *Ephesians* 20, in Staniforth, *Early Christian Writings*, p. 82.

36. Septuagint Psalms 80:14–16, in *The Anchor Bible: Gospel According to John 13–21*, trans. Raymond E. Brown (Garden City, N.Y.: Doubleday and Co., 1970), p. 670.

37. Didache 9.2, in Staniforth, *Early Christian Writings*, p. 231.

38. Numbers Rabbah 13:2, in Patai, p. 238.

39. Cyril of Jerusalem, *Lecture on the Mysteries* 22.2, in Schaff and Wace, *Nicene and Post-Nicene Fathers,* 7:151.

40. Gregory Nazianzen, *Oration on Holy Baptism* 40.46, in Schaff and Wace, *Nicene and Post-Nicene Fathers,* 7:337.

41. JST Gen. 8:11.

CHAPTER FOUR

The Abrahamic Test

Larry E. Dahl
Brigham Young University

Everyone who achieves exaltation must successfully pass through an Abrahamic test. Let me repeat. Everyone who achieves exaltation must successfully pass through an Abrahamic test. Joseph Smith, in speaking to the Twelve Apostles in Nauvoo said: "You will have all kinds of trials to pass through. And it is quite as necessary for you to be tried as it was for Abraham and other men of God. . . . God will feel after you, and he will take hold of you and wrench your very heart strings, and if you cannot stand it you will not be fit for an inheritance in the Celestial Kingdom of God."[1] That is not a particularly comforting thought, but it is one that cannot be ignored if the scriptures are taken seriously. Why must there be an Abrahamic test? And how can we all be tested like Abraham was tested? Why use Abraham as the standard? What is there about the test Abraham experienced that is universally applicable? When our test comes, will we recognize it? How can we prepare?

Mortal Testing Intended and Purposeful

It is interesting to review the Lord's own statements about his intent to test and try his people. In the very beginning, in the planning stages of this earth, the Lord said, "We will take of these materials, and we will make an earth whereon these may dwell; and we will prove them herewith, to see if they will do all things whatsoever the Lord their God shall command them." (Abr. 3:24–25.) *All* things, not just *some* things! The angel taught King Benjamin this same truth: "For the natural man is an enemy to God, and has been from the fall of Adam, and will be forever and ever, unless he yields to the enticings of the Holy Spirit, and putteth off the natural man and becometh a saint through the atonement of Christ the Lord, and becometh as a child, submissive, meek, humble, patient, full of love, *willing to submit to all things which the Lord seeth fit to inflict upon him, even as a child doth submit to his father.*" (Mosiah 3:19; italics added.) To the beleaguered Saints being driven out of Jackson County, Missouri, the Lord affirmed that he would "give unto the faithful line upon line, precept upon precept; and I will try you and prove you herewith. And whoso layeth down his life in my cause, for my name's sake, shall find it again, even life eternal. Therefore, be not afraid of your enemies, for I have decreed in my heart, saith the Lord, that I will prove you in all things, whether you will abide in my covenant, even unto death, that you may be found worthy. For if ye will not abide in my covenant ye are not worthy of me." (D&C 98:12–15.)

Five months later the Lord declared, "Therefore, they must needs be chastened and tried, even as Abraham, who was commanded to offer up his only son. For all those who will not endure chastening, but deny me, cannot be sanctified." (D&C 101:4–5.) Notice the two words *chastened* and *tried.* Is there a difference in meaning between the two? A careful examination of the scriptural use of these two words shows that *chasten* is generally employed when people are being corrected or punished because of disobedience. *Tried,* on the other hand, is used to describe what happens to the righteous. In Doctrine and Covenants 98:12 the Lord specifies that the *faithful* were to be tried, even unto death. Both chastening and trying are needed in the process of becoming sanctified. Indeed, one of the meanings of *chasten* is "to make chaste or pure; purify; refine,"[2] and one of the meanings of *try* is "to make pure by melting or boiling."[3] The Saints needed to be chastened "in consequence of their transgressions." (D&C 101:2.) In addition, they needed to be tried, even as Abraham, in consequence of their righteousness. In a revelation to President Brigham Young, the Lord explained, "My people must be tried in all things, that they might be prepared to receive the glory that I have for them, even the glory of Zion; and he that will not bear chastisement is not worthy of my kingdom." (D&C 136:31.)

The Lord's intent is clear—those worthy of his kingdom will be tried and proven, even as Abraham.

Abraham's Test

Even as Abraham! Concerning Abraham's test, the biblical record says simply: "God did tempt [the JST says 'try' instead of 'tempt'] Abraham, and said unto him, Abraham: and he said, Behold, here I am.

And he said, Take now thy son, thine only son Isaac, whom thou lovest, and get thee into the land of Moriah; and offer him there for a burnt offering upon one of the mountains which I will tell thee of." (Gen. 22:1–2.) What is not discussed at that point in the record is the seeming incongruities, even contradictions, that Abraham must have faced when he received that command.

First, consider the matter of human sacrifice. Abraham, as a young man, had been saved by the Lord from being offered as a sacrifice himself at the hands of an apostate priesthood who worshiped false gods. These idol worshipers offered to their gods "men, women, and children," specifically those who "would not bow down to worship gods of wood or of stone." (Abr. 1:8–11.) The Lord had told Abraham to leave the area because of those evil practices (Abr. 1:14) and go to a strange land that would eventually belong to his descendants (Abr. 1:16–18; 2:6). Now he was being asked to offer a human sacrifice – a hard thing to reconcile. Further, God had made it clear to Abraham on several occasions that it was through Isaac the blessings of the covenant were to come to Abraham and to the whole world. Those blessings are the heart and soul of bringing salvation to the children of men, for the promise was that the seed of Abraham, through Isaac, would be scattered among and bless "all the families of the earth." (See Abr. 2:8–11.) How could that promise be fulfilled if Isaac were killed?

Besides, Abraham loved Isaac dearly. After all, he had waited anxiously for Isaac to be born for at least twenty-five years from the time the Lord first promised him an heir.[4] That wait alone would be an Abrahamic test for many. And this long wait troubled Abraham. Several years after the promise of a son at Haran, after Abraham had traveled from Haran, through Canaan, to Egypt, and back to Canaan, and still no child, Abraham asked the Lord for an explanation. He even proposed that perhaps a child born "in my house," meaning a child of one of his servants, could become his heir. Without any details about how or when, the Lord simply reaffirmed the original promise of literal seed:

"Fear not, Abram: I am thy shield, and thy exceeding great reward. And Abram said, Lord God, what wilt thou give me, seeing I go childless, and the steward of my house is this Eliezer of Damascus? And Abram said, Behold, to me thou hast given no seed: and, lo, one born in my house is mine heir. And, behold, the word of the Lord came unto him, saying, This shall not be thine heir; but he that shall come forth out of thine own bowels shall be thine heir. And he brought him forth

abroad, and said, Look now toward heaven, and tell the stars, if thou
be able to number them: and he said unto him, So shall thy seed be."
(Gen. 15:1–5.)

To Abraham's credit, "he believed in the Lord; and he counted it
to him for righteousness." (Gen. 15:6.) More time passed. Sarai gave
Hagar to Abraham, and Ishmael was born. Thirteen more years passed.
Abraham was now ninety-nine years old, and Sarai was eighty-nine.

"And God said unto Abraham, As for Sarai thy wife, thou shalt not
call her name Sarai, but Sarah shall her name be. And I will bless her,
and give thee a son also of her: yea, I will bless her, and she shall be
a mother of nations; kings of people shall be of her. Then Abraham fell
upon his face, and laughed [the JST says "rejoiced"], and said in his
heart, Shall a child be born unto him that is an hundred years old? and
shall Sarah, that is ninety years old bear? And Abraham said unto God,
O that Ishmael might live before thee! And God said, Sarah thy wife
shall bear thee a son indeed; and thou shalt call his name Isaac: and I
will establish my covenant with him for an everlasting covenant, and
with his seed after him." (Gen. 17:15–19.)

When Sarah heard the news, she "laughed within herself," realizing
that both she and Abraham were "old and well stricken in age; and it
ceased to be with [her] after the manner of women." (Gen. 18:11.) I
suspect most of us can empathize with Sarah's reaction. But the Lord's
response was sobering—"Is anything too hard for the Lord? At the
time appointed I will return unto thee, according to the time of life,
and Sarah shall have a son." (Gen. 18:12–14.) "At the set time of which
God had spoken" Isaac was born. (Gen. 21:2.)

Can you imagine the joy that Abraham and Sarah must have felt—
joy accompanied by deep gratitude and an undeniable realization of the
power of God and the surety of his promises. They had waited for such
a long time, yearning and praying and living righteously. The blessing
had finally come. Surely now all would go smoothly. In their old age
they could quietly witness the continued fulfillment of God's promises
through Isaac. Or could they? First came family problems: Ishmael
mocked Isaac and concern grew over who would be Abraham's heir.
Hagar and Ishmael were sent away to be cared for by the Lord. Shortly
thereafter came the unthinkable requirement: offer Isaac as a sacrifice!

Now, keeping in mind the historical events we have reviewed, try
to put yourself in Abraham's place for a moment. How might you have
reacted? I can feel myself wanting to say "No. It can't be. Human

sacrifice is an abomination. All the blessings of the covenant are to come through Isaac. This doesn't make any sense to me. I have been obedient. I have been patient. And besides all that, I love him with all my heart. I don't want him to die. This is too painful. Why does it have to be this way?" For some reason it did have to be that way, with all its seeming incongruities and inconsistencies. And it was painful for Abraham. Joseph Smith taught that "if God had known any other way whereby he could have touched Abraham's feelings more acutely and more keenly he would have done so."[5]

In spite of the hurt, Abraham passed his test. The Genesis account does not describe Abraham's thoughts or feelings or questions. It mat-ter-of-factly says: "And Abraham rose up early in the morning . . . and went unto the place of which God had told him." (Gen. 22:3.) But the apostle Paul bears witness of Abraham's profound faith in God: "By faith Abraham, when he was tried, offered up Isaac: and he that had received the promises offered up his only begotten son, Of whom it was said, That in Isaac shall thy seed be called: accounting that God was able to raise him up, even from the dead; from whence also he received him in a figure." (Heb. 11:17–19.)

In spite of the mind-boggling contradictions of the situation, Abra-ham had faith to proceed. He had full confidence that *somehow* God could and would fulfill all his promises, even though the one through whom the promises were to come was bound on an altar and Abraham's knife was raised to slay him. It was not until the last, precarious moment that the Lord stopped Abraham, saying, "Abraham, Abraham: . . . Lay not thine hand upon the lad, neither do thou anything unto him; for I know that thou fearest God, seeing thou hast not withheld thy son, thine only son from me." (Gen. 22:11–12.)

What faith! What discipline! What a sterling example! No wonder Abraham is held up as the model.

Our Tests

What about us? How are we to be tested "even as Abraham?" Being asked to offer a child as a sacrifice just does not relate to our time and circumstance. But wrenching heart strings does relate — to all times and circumstances. And there are many ways to wrench the heart in any age: being asked to choose God over other things we dearly love, even when those things are good and have been promised, and when we have worked for them, yearned for them, prayed for them, and have been obedient and patient; or being asked to persevere in righteousness and service (perhaps even Church service) in the face of terrible difficulty, uncertainty, inequities, ironies, and even contradictions; or watching helplessly as the innocent suffer from the brutal misuse of God-given agency in the hands of evil men.

We should remember that not all the difficulties that try the souls of men are specially designed Abrahamic tests from God. Most, in fact, are the inevitable consequences of living in a mortal, fallen world, where natural law and agency, for the most part, are allowed full sway. It is true that such conditions come from God in the sense that he created the earth and that the conditions here are allowed by him, even designed by him to be a universal, probationary testing ground for his children. Everyone experiences bumps in the road of life, which expose weaknesses and strengths, giving opportunity for self-understanding, growth, and refinement. We are not wise enough to sort out all the factors that contribute to our challenges in this life.

The critical issue is not the source of the challenges, anyway. The critical issue is how we respond to them. We can lose our focus and our progress if we constantly examine every bump in the road to determine whose fault it is.

The same principle applies to anticipating tests. It is self-defeating to spoil the present by worrying incessantly about the "big test" that will someday come. And it just may be that the "big test" will be very different from what we expect. It is enough to know that God will try us — in his own time, and in his own way, and that the very best way to prepare for that eventuality is by faithfully dealing with present tasks.

It appears that in addition to the general trials of life that all people face, those who claim to be the people of the Lord are faced with special challenges both collectively and individually.

Collective, or Generational, Tests

The Prophet Joseph Smith, writing from Liberty Jail in March 1839 about the Saints being driven out of the state of Missouri, addressed the idea of different but equal generational Abrahamic trials:

"And now, beloved brethren, we say unto you that inasmuch as God hath said that He would have a tried people, that He would purge them as gold, now we think that this time He has chosen His own crucible, wherein we have been tried; and we think if we get through with any degree of safety, and shall have kept the faith, that it will be a sign to this generation, altogether sufficient to leave them without excuse; and we think also, it will be a trial of our faith equal to that of Abraham, and that the ancients will not have whereof to boast over us in the day of judgment, as being called to pass through heavier afflictions; that we may hold an even weight in the balance with them; but now, after having suffered so great sacrifice and having passed through so great a season of sorrow, we trust that a ram may be caught in the thicket speedily, to relieve the sons and daughters of Abraham from their great anxiety, and to light up the lamp of salvation upon their countenances, that they may hold on now, after having gone so far unto everlasting life."[6]

The Saints in 1839 were being persecuted, hounded by mobs, and driven from their homes, which the Prophet said was a test equal to that of Abraham and "the ancients." What "ancients" might be included? Could the early Christians of nearly two thousand years ago qualify? Their generational trial involved a number of horrifying possibilities — being tortured, eaten by lions, dipped in oil and set afire, or being run through with a sword. Others of the ancients were stoned to death, scourged, forced to languish in vile prisons, burned at the stake.

Knowing what the ancients suffered and what the early Saints of this dispensation went through leads naturally to the question of our own generation. What is our collective, generational trial? Consider the teachings of President Ezra Taft Benson, as he spoke to regional representatives of the Church in 1977, while he was president of the Council of the Twelve Apostles:

"Every generation has its tests and its chance to stand and prove itself. Would you like to know of one of our toughest tests? Hear the warning words of President Brigham Young, 'The worst fear I have about this people is that they will get rich in this country, forget God and His people, wax fat, and kick themselves out of the Church and go to hell. This people will stand mobbing, robbing, poverty and all manner of persecution and be true. But my greatest fear is that they cannot stand wealth.'

"Ours then seems to the toughest test of all for the evils are more subtle, more clever. It all seems less menacing and it is harder to detect. While every test of righteousness represents a struggle, this particular test seems like no test at all, no struggle and so could be the most deceiving of all tests.

"Do you know what peace and prosperity can do to a people—It can put them to sleep. The Book of Mormon warned us of how the devil, in the last days, would lead us away carefully down to hell.

"The Lord has on the earth some potential spiritual giants whom He saved for some six thousand years to help bear off the Kingdom triumphantly, and the devil is trying to put them to sleep. The devil knows that he probably won't be too successful in getting them to commit many great and malignant sins of commission. So he puts them into a deep sleep, like Gulliver, while he strands them with little sins of omission. And what good is a sleepy, neutralized, lukewarm giant as a leader?

"We have too many potential spiritual giants who should be more vigorously lifting their homes, the kingdom, and the country. We have many who feel they are good men, but they need to be good for something—stronger patriarchs, courageous missionaries, valiant genealogists and temple workers, dedicated patriots, devoted quorum members. In short, we must be shaken and awakened from a spiritual snooze."[7]

President Harold B. Lee adds his testimony about our current collective test:

"We are tested and we are tried, we are going through some of the severest tests today and we don't realize perhaps the severity of the tests that we're going through. In those days, there were murderings, there were mobbings, there were drivings. They were driven out into the desert, they were starving and they were unclad, they were cold. They came here to this favored land. We are the inheritors of what they gave to us. But what are we doing with it? Today we are basking in the lap of luxury, the like of which we've never seen before in the history of the world. It would seem that probably this is the most severe test of any test that we've ever had in the history of this Church."[8]

That is a rather astonishing notion: ease and affluence can be an Abrahamic test equal, in the sense of proving one's faith, to the sufferings and deprivations of earlier generations. But that is the testimony of the prophets, and the testimony of history. Given a choice (and maybe we were given such a choice long before we came to earth), who wouldn't choose ease and affluence rather than pain and suffering? It sounds so attractive, so generous of the Lord. And all we have to do is keep the commandments, using our affluence to build the kingdom of God and serve others. Why is that so difficult? Because ease and affluence tend toward self-indulgence and self-importance. We can become spiritually flabby and casual in our prayers because we seem to need nothing, indifferent to the needs of others because we do not know how it feels to go without. Not liking to be reminded that others have needs, we remove ourselves from the inner city of life to the "quiet hedonism of suburbia," both temporally and spiritually.[9] We can gorge ourselves with temporal things to the point of spiritual death. Mormon's editorial comment about a deteriorating Nephite society adds another witness:

"And thus we can behold how false, and also the unsteadiness of the hearts of the children of men. . . . Yea, and we may see at the very time when he doth prosper his people . . . then is the time that they do harden their hearts, and do forget the Lord their God, and do trample under their feet the Holy One—yea, and this because of their ease, and their exceedingly great prosperity." (Hel. 12:1–2.)

The test of ease and affluence is real for much of the Church today. And it will become more a factor as the Church expands into third-world countries where there is poverty instead of abundance. It will take the best within us to meet the challenge.

One more brief note about an additional collective trial we face today. It involves affluence but of a different kind. It is the affluence of knowledge. Elder Harold B. Lee called it sophistication. He said, "We are now going through another test—a period of what we might call sophistication. This is a time when there are many clever people who are not willing to listen to the humble prophets of the Lord. And we have suffered from that. It is rather a severe test."[10]

The prophet Jacob warned of that very challenge and told us how to successfully meet it: "O the vainness, and the frailties, and the foolishness of men! When they are learned they think they are wise, and they hearken not unto the counsel of God, for they set it aside, supposing they know of themselves, wherefore, their wisdom is foolishness and it profiteth them not. And they shall perish. But to be learned is good if they hearken unto the counsels of God." (2 Ne. 9:28–29).

It behooves us to take stock of ourselves and come to grips with our generational Abrahamic tests—tests of luxury and sophistication.

Individual Tests

There are individual tests in addition to collective ones. Each person faces unique circumstances. Each person has a particular aggregation of strengths and weaknesses. What is a challenge for one may be simple for another, and vice versa. Elder Boyd K. Packer explained:

"The crucial test of life, I repeat, does not center in the choice between fame and obscurity, nor between wealth and poverty. The greatest decision of life is between good and evil.

"We may foolishly bring unhappiness and trouble, even suffering upon ourselves. These are not always to be regarded as penalties imposed by a displeased Creator. They are part of the lessons of life, part of the test.

"Some are tested by poor health, some by a body that is deformed or homely. Others are tested by handsome and healthy bodies; some by the passion of youth; others by the erosions of age.

"Some suffer disappointment in marriage, family problems; others live in poverty and obscurity. Some (perhaps this is the hardest test) find ease and luxury.

"All are part of the test, and there is more equality in this testing than sometimes we suspect."[11]

Our minds are almost paralyzed by the thought that these very different tests can be considered equal. Some of them seem so much more attractive than others. Would you rather be handsome, healthy, bright, and rich, or the opposite of those characteristics? And yet we are assured that all are being adequately tested with their particular circumstances and their unique combination of characteristics. Accepting and understanding that principle may be an Abrahamic test for some, maybe even for many. In our immaturity, we "see through a glass darkly." (1 Cor. 13:12.) We "cannot behold with [our] natural eyes, for the present time, the design of [our] God concerning those things which shall come hereafter, and the glory which shall follow after much tribulation." (D&C 58:3.)

"In time," Neal A. Maxwell observed, "each person will receive a 'customized challenge' to determine his dedication to God."[12] The Prophet Joseph Smith taught that before one can have his calling and election made sure he must be "thoroughly proved"; God must find "that the man is determined to serve Him at all hazards."[13] "All hazards" may at times mean there will be no ram in the thicket, no angel to stop the knife, as there were with Abraham. Paul faced that reality. He said, "And lest I should be exalted above measure through the abundance of the revelations, there was given to me a thorn in the flesh, the messenger of Satan to buffet me. . . . For this thing I besought the Lord thrice, that it might depart from me. And he said unto me, My grace is sufficient for thee: for my strength is made perfect in weakness." (2 Cor. 12:7–9.)

Paul's particular "thorn in the flesh" is reminiscent of the more general principle spoken by the Lord to Moroni: "I give unto men weakness that they may be humble; and my grace is sufficient for all men that humble themselves before me; for if they humble themselves before me, and have faith in me, then will I make weak things become strong unto them." (Ether 12:27.) Not only Paul but many of us may suffer from a thorn in the flesh or a weakness that is painful but purposeful, and which God may see fit not to remove. All of us know people, faithful people, who are afflicted with some debilitating illness that lasts and lasts, maybe for a lifetime. Neither prayers nor tears nor blessings nor medicine relieves the condition. All that is left is to endure patiently. Truly, that wrenches the heartstrings. Why is it necessary? What is gained?

The Purposes of Being Tested

There just have to be exalted purposes in all this testing. The scriptures help to identify some. Lehi explained that without opposition, neither righteousness nor happiness could be brought about. (2 Ne. 2:11.) In a revelation to Joseph Smith the Lord said, "If they never should have the bitter they could not know the sweet." (D&C 29:39; see also Moses 6:55). To Brigham Young came the word that "my people must be tried in all things, that they may be prepared to receive the glory that I have for them, even the glory of Zion," though just how it prepares them is not said. (D&C 136:31.) The Lord indicates that being chastened and tried is a prerequisite to being sanctified. (D&C 101:4–5.) James taught that the "trying of your faith worketh patience." (James 1:3.) We learn from 2 Chronicles 32:31 that being tried exposes the heart: "God left him, to try him, that he might know all that was in his heart." Note what Christ's suffering did for him, in addition to all that it did for us. Alma taught, "And he will take upon him their infirmities, that his bowels may be filled with mercy, according to the flesh, that he may know according to the flesh how to succor his people according to their infirmities." (Alma 7:12.) Paul wrote, "For in that he himself hath suffered being tempted, he is able to succour them that are tempted." (Heb. 2:18.) In Abraham's case, his trial, being "a similitude of God and his Only Begotten Son" (Jacob 4:5), brought to him a piercing understanding of Another's feelings.[14] The same is true for all of us — experiencing trials can bring deep empathy.

Perhaps all these purposes just mentioned are encompassed in the following explanation given in the *Lectures on Faith:*

"An actual knowledge to any person, that the course of life which he pursues is according to the will of God, is essentially necessary to enable him to have that confidence in God without which no person can obtain eternal life. . . .

"Such was, as always will be, the situation of the saints of God, that unless they have an actual knowledge that the course they are pursuing is according to the will of God they will grow weary in their minds, and faint. . . .

"Let us here observe, that a religion that does not require the sacrifice of all things never has power sufficient to produce the faith necessary unto life and salvation; for from the first existence of man, the faith necessary unto the enjoyment of life and salvation never could be obtained without the sacrifice of all earthly things. It was through this sacrifice, and this only, that God has ordained that men should enjoy eternal life; and it is through the medium of the sacrifice of all earthly things that men do actually know that they are doing the things that are well pleasing in the sight of God."[15]

Simply put, choosing to do the will of God at all hazards brings a righteous and necessary self-awareness and self-confidence, a perfect faith in God and in our ability to do his will. We then know something about ourselves that God has known all along. President Hugh B. Brown, in answer to the question of why Abraham was asked to "offer as a sacrifice his only hope for the promised posterity," said: "Abraham needed to learn something about Abraham."[16] Knowledge about ourselves thus gained puts our relationship to God on a higher plane. We truly become heir to "all that my Father hath" (D&C 84:38), and our "confidence" will "wax strong in the presence of God." (D&C 121:45.) That confidence is not arrogance or self-righteousness; it is not a feeling we have simply received that which we have earned. It is, rather, being at ease or comfortable in the presence of Goodness, having complete faith and trust in One who has been gracious — who has *given* us that which we could never, on our own, achieve, once we have proven what the deepest yearnings of our heart and soul really are. Note the confidence with which Job, as he successfully dealt with his own Abrahamic trials, withstood those who accused him of unrighteousness:

"Hold your peace, let me alone, that I may speak, and let come on me what will. . . . Though he slay me, yet will I trust in him. . . He also shall be my salvation: for an hypocrite shall not come before him. Hear diligently my speech, and my declaration with your ears. Behold now, I have ordered my cause; I know that I shall be justified." (Job 13:13–18.)

"But he knoweth the way that I take; when he hath tried me, I shall come forth as gold." (Job 23:10.)

"For I know that my redeemer liveth, and that he shall stand at the latter day upon the earth: and though after my skin worms destroy this body, yet in my flesh shall I see God: whom I shall see for myself, and mine eyes shall behold, and not another; though my reins be consumed within me." (Job 19:25–27.)

There is a profound difference between submitting to God by choosing to serve him at all hazards, and submitting to God by simply giving up, crumbling as it were under the load of suffering. The first brings power and confidence; the other results in impotence and despair. President John Taylor described the spirit of that difference:

"I was not born a slave! I cannot, will not be a slave. I would not be a slave to God! I'd be His servant, friend, His son. I'd go at His behest; but would not be His slave. I'd rather be extinct than a slave. His friend I feel I am, and He is mine. A slave! The manacles would pierce my very bones—the clanking chains would grate against my soul—a poor, lost, servile, crawling wretch, to lick the dust and fawn and smile upon the thing who gave the lash! . . . But stop! I am God's free man; I will not, cannot be a slave!"[17]

The object of Abrahamic tests is to make us God's free men and women, not slaves. There is no eternal life in slavery. Eternal life comes with freely choosing to become an heir, at all hazards.

About Perspective

The stark reality is that understanding the need for Abrahamic tests and the and nature of such tests does not take away the pain that comes with them. It helps, however, to realize that we are not alone. Others have traveled similarly and endured it well. And so can we. It is at the same time both comforting and somewhat disquieting to read the exchange between the Lord and Joseph Smith as the Prophet cried out in frustration from his cell in Liberty Jail:

"O God, where art thou? And where is the pavilion that covereth thy hiding place?

"How long shall thy hand be stayed? . . . (D&C 121:1–2.)

"My son, peace be unto thy soul; thine adversity and thine afflictions shall be but a small moment;

"And then, if thou endure it well, God shall exalt thee on high; thou shalt triumph over all thy foes. . . .

"Thou art not yet as Job." (D&C 121:1–2, 7–8, 10.)

"Know thou, my son, that all these things shall give thee experience, and shall be for thy good.

"The Son of Man hath descended below them all. Art thou greater than he?

"Therefore, hold on thy way. . . . Thy days are known, and thy years shall not be numbered less; . . . God shall be with you forever and ever." (D&C 122:7–9.)

That promise applies to us. Few of us are as Job, and none of us suffers as did the Son of Man. To be sure, God will try us—to see if we are determined to serve him at all hazards. Just as surely, he will be with us and sustain us in our faithful strivings to meet those trials successfully.

NOTES

1. As reported by President John Taylor in *Journal of Discourses*, 26 vols. (Liverpool: F. D. Richards & Sons, 1851–86), 24:197.

2. *World Book Dictionary* (Chicago: Doubleday & Co., 1986), s.v. "chasten."

3. Ibid., s.v. "try."

4. The promise of a great nation coming from Abraham came while he resided in Haran. (Gen. 12:1–3; Abr. 2:1–11.) According to Genesis 12:4, Abraham was seventy-five years old when he left Haran. Isaac was born when Abraham was one hundred years old. (Gen. 21:5.) Hence the twenty-five-year wait. If, however, Abraham 2:14 gives Abraham's correct age at leaving Haran (sixty-two years old), then the wait was thirty-eight years.

5. Taylor, in *Journal of Discourses*, 24:264.

6. Joseph Smith, *Teachings of the Prophet Joseph Smith*, sel. Joseph Fielding Smith (Salt Lake City: Deseret Book Co., 1938), pp. 135–36.

7. Ezra Taft Benson, "Our Obligation and Challenge," Regional Representatives Seminar, 30 Sept. 1977, pp. 2–3. Unpublished typescript in author's possession.

8. Harold B. Lee, address to Church employees, Salt Lake City, 13 Dec. 1973. Unpublished typescript in author's possession.

9. Neal A. Maxwell, "The Gospel Gives Answers to Life's Problems" (address to seminary and institute personnel), Provo, Utah, Brigham Young University, Summer 1970, p. 2.

10. Harold B. Lee, "Sweet Are the Uses of Adversity," *Instructor*, June 1965, p. 217.

11. Boyd K. Packer, in Conference Report, Oct. 1980, p. 29.

12. Neal A. Maxwell, as quoted in *Daily Universe*, Brigham Young University, Provo, Utah, 7 Oct. 1983.

13. Smith, *Teachings*, p. 150.

14. Rabbinic traditions and apocryphal writings contain the notion that Isaac was a grown man and fully subscribed to his being offered as a sacrifice. Such an idea, though not affirmed in the scriptures, makes the comparison with the atonement of Christ more poignant and meaningful. (See Louis Ginzberg, *The Legends of the Jews* (Philadelphia: Jewish Publication Society of America, 1968), pp. 271–283; and *The Book of Jasher* (Salt Lake City: J. H. Parry & Co., 1887), pp. 59–63.

15. Joseph Smith, "Lecture Sixth," *Lectures on Faith* (Salt Lake City: Deseret Book Co., 1985), pars. 2, 4, 7.

16. As reported by Truman G. Madsen in *Joseph Smith the Prophet* (Salt Lake City: Bookcraft, 1989), p. 93.

17. *Oil for Their Lamps*, comp. M. Lynn Bennion (Salt Lake City: LDS Department of Education, 1943), p. 73; see also Elder Boyd K. Packer in "Follow the Brethren" (address to Brigham Young University students), Provo, Utah, 23 Mar. 1965.

CHAPTER FIVE

A Major Change in Israel: Effects of the Babylonian Captivity

Dean Garrett

Brigham Young University

One of the great struggles in the Old Testament was the struggle within the hearts of the people of Judah as they vacillated between worshiping the God of Israel and worshiping the idol gods of the Canaanites. As Moses prepared the people of Israel to enter the promised land, the Lord warned:

"Take heed to thyself, lest thou make a covenant with the inhabitants of the land whither thou goest, lest it be for a snare in the midst of thee: but ye shall destroy their altars, break their images, and cut down their groves: for thou shalt worship no other god . . . lest thou make a covenant with the inhabitants of the land, and they go a whoring after their gods, and do sacrifice unto their gods, and one call thee, and thou eat of his sacrifice; and thou take of their daughters unto thy sons, and their daughters go a whoring after their gods, and make thy sons go a whoring after their gods." (Ex. 34:12–16.)

The battle raged within the hearts of the people of both Israel and Judah until the God of Israel took second place to the carnal gods of the pagan nations. When this happened, disaster struck both Israel and Judah. Israel was taken captive by the Assyrians and was lost from the pages of history. Judah fought the battle longer, struggling through cycles of idolatry, returning to the God of Israel, turning back to idolatry, and then returning to the God of Israel. Often the reigning king was an important factor in this cycle.

Eventually Judah also felt the sting of captivity. The Babylonian captivity had a profound effect on the relationship of the people of Judah and the God of Israel. Not until Judah came out of captivity did the people have a resolve to worship the God of Israel. No longer would they struggle with idolatrous worship. That transformation is the subject of this paper.

Judah before the Captivity

Before the captivity, Judah's struggle with idolatry was mixed with wars and treaties with neighboring countries and with frequent turmoil within its own borders. Twenty kings had ruled over this kingdom, only a few of them righteous. These righteous kings, however, enabled Judah to survive nearly one hundred and fifty years longer than the northern kingdom of Israel.

After the Assyrians conquered northern Israel in 721 B.C. and took many of the people into captivity, King Hezekiah governed the people of the southern kingdom (Judah) and did, as the scriptures plainly state, "that which was right in the sight of the Lord." (2 Kgs. 18:3.) Hezekiah was keenly aware that northern Israel was taken captive by the Assyrians because of Israel's disobedience to God's laws. Consequently, he instituted a series of reforms to help his people renew their covenants with God. He immediately reopened the temple and called the Levites to repair and cleanse it. Sacrifices were again offered in the temple.[1] Hezekiah removed the high places of prostitution and the images of false gods from among the people of Judah, "for he clave to the Lord, and departed not from following him, but kept his commandments, which the Lord commanded Moses. And the Lord was with him; and he prospered whithersoever he went forth." (2 Kgs. 18:6-7.)

During this entire time, Hezekiah felt great military and political pressure from Assyria. After Sennacherib ascended to the Assyrian throne in 705 B.C., the pressure intensified. Hezekiah became "sick unto death" (2 Kgs. 20:1), but the Lord granted him fifteen years of life, although the Lord warned through Isaiah that Judah would be captured by Babylon. After two Assyrian invasions, Judah, with the direct intervention of Jehovah, was able to defeat the Assyrians under King Sennacherib in 689 B.C. (See 2 Kgs. 19:35-37.)

At the death of this good and righteous king, the foundation for the prophesied Babylonian captivity was laid by Hezekiah's twelve-year-old son, Manasseh, who ascended the throne. He built up the high places again, made a grove, and set up a graven image in it. He made his sons pass through the fire, meaning he "burnt his children in the fire, after the abominations of the heathen" (2 Chr. 28:3), used enchantments, and dealt with familiar spirits and wizards. The people followed him, and "they hearkened not: and Manasseh seduced them to do more evil than did the nations whom the Lord destroyed before the children of Israel." (2 Kgs. 21:9.)

Manasseh's son Josiah, the last righteous king of Judah, succeeded him. Josiah tried to bring the people back to the God of Israel. A young king, he led a religious reformation that extended even to the remnants of the northern kingdom. He restored the temple to its proper use, worked hard to destroy the idolatrous images and the high places from the land, replaced idolatrous priests, and reinstituted the celebration of the Passover. (2 Kgs. 23.)

During Josiah's reign, a Book of the Law was found in the temple and read to the people. This practice so impressed the people that it led to the centralization of all sacrificial worship at Jerusalem, thus controlling all sacrificing and impeding idolatrous worship. Unfortunately, Josiah became politically involved in the conflict between Assyria and Egypt and was killed at the battle of Meggido attempting to keep the king of Egypt out of Judah. (2 Chr. 35.)

After the death of Josiah, Judah's history was marked with a vacillation of faith, which led the Lord to declare, "I will remove Judah also out of my sight, as I have removed Israel, and will cast off this city Jerusalem which I have chosen, and the house of which I said, My name shall be there." (2 Kgs. 23:27.)

Jehoahaz replaced Josiah as king, but after reigning only three months he was taken captive by Nechoh, the pharaoh of Egypt, and was replaced by Jehoiakim. (2 Kgs. 23:31–36.) Jehoiakim led Judah through two important transitions that had great effects on Judah's future. The first was that the king returned to pagan worship. The evils in Judah intensified under King Jehoiakim, for he "headed the movement to restore paganism: altars were erected on every hill to heathen deities, so that there were more gods in Judah than there were towns. Even the sacred animals of Egypt were worshipped in the dark chambers beneath the temple. In the most sacred places of the temple itself idolatrous priests worshipped the rising sun, and the obscene rites of Phoenicians idolatry were performed in private houses."[2] C. Geikie described that period: "The strong Egyptian faction in Jerusalem . . . had introduced the animal worship of the Nile Valley, and had even turned a large room in the temple into a chapel for its services . . . the sun worship of the East had also found a footing in its courts . . . In the very holiest spot of the sanctuary, about twenty-five men, presumably representatives of the high priest . . . stood with their backs to the temple—the open sign of apostasy—and worshipped the rising sun, their faces turned to the east."[3] They even offered their children to the god Molech. (Jer. 32:35.)

The second transition was the political changes that took place in the area. Assyria was defeated by a Babylonian-Median army in 612 B.C.[4] Thus, the power brokers of the region became Babylon and Egypt. During the first three years of Jehoiakim's reign, Judah was a vassal of Egypt. In 609 B.C. Babylon defeated Egypt at Carchemish. (2 Kgs. 24:7.) Jeremiah warned the people of Judah that the king of Babylon would destroy the land (Jer. 20:4), and Judah became a vassal of Babylon soon thereafter in 604 B.C. Three years later Jehoiakim rebelled against Babylon by withholding tribute to Babylonia. This rebellion was an open invitation to strike. Unable to attend to Judea immediately, Nebuchadnezzar, king of Babylon, incited raiders from neighboring lands to devastate the land. These disturbances led to turmoil within Judah, during which Jehoiakim died, leaving the kingdom to his eighteen-year-old son, Jehoiachin. In 598 B.C. Nebuchadnezzar led the Babylonian army against Jerusalem. The new king, Jehoiachin, surrendered to Babylon in 597 B.C. He was exiled to Babylon, along with his mother, many leading figures, and a prophet named Ezekiel.[5]

Nebuchadnezzar appointed a new king, Zedekiah, to rule over his vassal state. For the first four years of his reign, he remained obedient to Babylonian rule. In the fourth year, however, he was visited by emissaries of neighboring nations who encouraged him to assist them in shaking off the yoke of Babylon. The prophet Jeremiah warned forcefully that all nations were to serve Babylon and the nation that would not serve Babylon would be punished by God. (Jer. 27:1–11.) He also warned Zedekiah that Jerusalem would be smitten and Zedekiah taken captive by Nebuchadnezzar. (Jer. 21:1–8.) Nevertheless, Zedekiah paid more heed to the noblemen of his court who cited the Davidic covenant, which stated that the throne would never fall. Therefore, in 589 B.C., Zedekiah went out in open revolt against Babylon. Nebuchadnezzar laid siege to Jerusalem for two and one-half years. No help came from the neighboring nations. Finally in 587 B.C., Zedekiah fled from the city with his family and some members of his court. He was captured by the Babylonians at Jericho. His sons were killed before his eyes. Then the king's eyes were put out by the hot irons of the Babylonians, and he, along with the remaining members of his family and court, was marched to Babylon. After destroying the temple and the city, the Babylonians took many of the people into Babylonian exile.[6]

The Babylonian Captivity

Life for the Jews in their Babylonian captivity consisted not of horror and slavery but rather of social freedom and economic opportunity. Jews proved enterprising in their business and economic affairs. The Babylonian Jews were allowed to move about freely, to live in their communities within or near the great cities, and to carry on their way of life.[7] Indeed, so secure was their life in Babylon, that when Cyrus allowed the captive Jews to return to Judah to build their temple, many of them refused to leave.

The greatest danger faced by the Jewish people in Babylon was that in time the Jewish religion, torn from its historic foundation and physical grounding in the Holy Land, would sink into the sands of the Babylonian culture. The pressure of the Babylonian culture sifted the captive Jews. Some capitulated to the pressures, but most did not "descend to the level of pagan religion. Despite the high degree of cultural assimilation, the religious contrast set up an impassable barrier between the exiles and their environment."[8] This time of exile was a time for solidification of faith and commitment for many of the captives. Jeremiah wrote to the captives in Babylon these words of the Lord: "For I know the thoughts that I think toward you . . . thoughts of peace, and not of evil, to give you an expected end. Then shall ye call upon me, and ye shall go and pray unto me, and I will hearken unto you. And ye shall seek me, and find me, when ye shall search for me with all your heart." (Jer. 29:11–13.)

The captivity seemed to impress upon the minds of the Jewish people that the God of Israel was, indeed, a jealous God. The prophets were right in their warnings of doom and destruction if the people did not repent and follow him and him only. In captivity the nation as a whole accepted the verdict that God's wrath had been poured out upon them for their sins of idolatry. They became totally committed to worship only the God of Israel. Thereafter, Israel became a very zealous nation for its God.

During the captivity some of the Jews tried "with varying degrees of success, to integrate themselves into the tissues of Babylonian life . . . [but] the exiled community as a whole had opted for their continued Jewishness. The priests might have no temple, but they could yet lead the people in hymns and prayers to the God of Israel and, on occasion, devise new forms of devotion and petition."[9] Sacrifice was not practiced, but the Sabbath was elevated in importance as a day of spiritual renewal and became the focal point of the Jewish religious celebration.[10]

Return from Captivity

The spiritual seasoning and conditioning of the Jewish people enabled them to return to the land of their inheritance. Their return was facilitated by the death of the Babylonian king, Nebuchadnezzar, in 562 B.C. His kingdom survived only a short time after his death. Civil strife and political upheaval with threats from foreign nations increased in the years following his death. Nebuchadnezzar's son Evil-merodach, who succeeded him, released Jehoiachin from prison and placed him in the king's court. Soon, however, Evil-merodach was assassinated in a palace revolt. The resulting political instability led to the rise of the Medes and Persians as the real powers; and in 539 B.C. their combined forces under the Persian king, Cyrus, led to the total defeat of the Babylonian empire.[11]

This was the same Cyrus that Isaiah had prophesied God would raise up to free the captive people of Judah. The Lord said of Cyrus: "He is my shepherd, and shall perform all my pleasure: even saying to Jerusalem, Thou shalt be built; and to the temple, Thy foundation shall be laid." (Isa. 44:28.) Cyrus' policies toward those conquered differed greatly from those of other rulers. The Assyrians, for example, imposed the worship of their gods upon captives and sought to eradicate the worship of the gods of the subjected lands. Cyrus, on the other hand, "had no intention of offending his subjects' religious susceptibilities by such policy; on the contrary, he would conciliate those susceptibilities by playing the part of a worshipper of their various gods. 'The Great King' . . . had no objection to bowing in the house of Rimmon if there was anything to be picked up on the floor."[12]

Cyrus' policy toward the subjugated nations was not to deport them but rather to work with them to make them loyal subjects. This philosophy led Cyrus to issue at least two decrees in behalf of the Jewish people concerning the house of God. The first decree was:

"Let the house be builded, the place where they offered sacrifices, and let the foundations thereof be strongly laid; the height thereof threescore cubits, and the breadth thereof threescore cubits; with three rows of great stones, and a row of new timber: and let the expenses be given out of the king's house: and also let the golden and silver vessels of the house of God, which Nebuchadnezzar took forth out of the temple which is at Jerusalem, and brought unto Babylon, be restored, and brought again unto the temple which is at Jerusalem, everyone to his place, and place them in the house of God." (Ezra 6:3–5.)

The charge to build the temple was given to "Sheshbazzar, the prince of Judah" who was given all the vessels and gold and silver to take to Jerusalem. (See Ezra 1:7–11.)

The second decree authorized the people to return to Jerusalem to build the temple: "Who is there among you of all his people? his God be with him, and let him go up to Jerusalem, which is in Judah, and build the house of the Lord God of Israel, (he is the God,) which is in Jerusalem. And whosoever remaineth in any place where he sojourneth, let the men of his place help him with silver, and with gold, and with goods, and with beasts, beside the freewill offering for the house of God that is in Jerusalem." (Ezra 1:3–4.)

Zerubbabbel, the grandson of Jehoiachin, was appointed governor of Judah. He led the returning exiles to Jerusalem, where they set about rebuilding the city and the temple. Building the temple was another significant step in focusing the attention of the Jewish people on the God of Israel. It was the constant reminder of their relationship with their God and the allegiance they owed him.

The task of building the temple was not an easy one. A dispute developed with the citizens of Samaria, who were of the house of Israel and who wanted to participate in the project. (Neh. 2:10–20.) Because they were viewed by the returning exiles as impure in their worship, however, the exiles declined the invitation. "The northerners did not take their rebuff patiently. The Samaritans regarded the tiny area of Judaea as part of their territory, and they made it their business to put so many obstacles in the way of the returned exiles that the work of rebuilding the temple was soon checked, and for fifteen years or so nothing more was done about it."[13] The exiles settled into building houses and cultivating their lands.

In the meantime, Cyrus was killed in battle in 520 B.C., and his son, Cambyses, succeeded him. Cambyses died about eight years later and was succeeded by Darius. In the early part of Darius' reign, renewed interest was given to the building of the temple. Two prophets, Haggai and Zechariah, both taught that the difficulties in Judah and the political upheaval in Persia indicated that God was about to act and that building the temple was necessary for the nation of Judah to receive the blessings of God. They both spoke encouraging words to Zerubbabel, telling him that the Lord would make him "as a signet: for I have chosen thee, saith the Lord of Hosts" (Hag. 2:23) and "the hands of Zerubbabel have laid the foundation of this house; his hands shall also finish it; and thou shalt know that the Lord of hosts hath sent me unto you" (Zech. 4:9). Zerubbabel, along with Jeshua, the priest, resumed the task of building the temple; however, the renewed efforts by the Jews led to renewed efforts by the Samaritans to stop the work. The complaints of the Samaritans finally forced the Persians to search in the records for the terms of the original legislation; but when they found the decrees of Cyrus, the work of rebuilding went forward without hindrance from Persia. Finally, four years after construction had resumed, the temple was completed and dedicated.

Upon the death of Darius in 404 B.C., the next king of Persia, Artaxerxes, faced a different problem with the returned exiles. The people of Jerusalem had commenced rebuilding the walls of Jerusalem. That was beyond what had been specified in the decrees of Cyrus and was, therefore, without legal authorization. Therefore, the people of Samaria sent a letter to the king's court to draw attention to the problem. The king ordered the building of the wall stopped until such time as he could personally issue a decree. Consequently, the Samaritans took upon themselves the role of enforcers and tore down part of the rebuilt walls. Nehemiah, the king's chief cupbearer, was saddened when he heard of the problems in Jerusalem. The king, noticing his sadness, asked Nehemiah, "What would you like me to do for you?" Nehemiah responded by asking that the king send him "to Judah to the city of my father's sepulchers, that I may rebuild it." (Neh. 2:1–6.)

Nehemiah was sent to Judea with specific instructions to rebuild the walls of Jerusalem. What he saw when he arrived disturbed him. Some problems of the past had reappeared. "Money lending and the consequent reduction of insolvent debtors to the status of serfs, had appeared again. The small-holders had not only to maintain themselves by the produce of their land; they had to pay the temple tax and an imperial tax as well, and many of them were driven to mortgage their fields, vineyards and houses to their wealthier neighbors to raise the money. When they were unable to repay the loans, they were forced to sell their children into serfdom."[14]

Nehemiah persuaded the people to discontinue this unrighteous practice, but there were other situations that he as the civil governor could not solve. These involved the regulation of Jewish religious life.

Another official by the name of Ezra was sent from the Persian court to Judea to assist in governing the people. It appears that he came as an official representative of the court as "secretary of state for Jewish affairs."[15] He brought with him from Babylonia nearly two thousand Jews, including a considerable number of priests, Levites, and temple attendants.

The solidification of the religious life that began in Babylon continued under Ezra and Nehemiah. They were supported by Haggai, the prophet who "preached with the fire of nationalism" and reminded the people that economic conditions in the land were precarious because they had left Yahweh's house lying in ruins while they lived in fine, paneled houses.[16] They were also assisted by Zechariah, who expressed a hope for a restored state of Israel with a God-chosen prince and high priest. Zechariah had visions and prophesied about the future of Israel.

The renewed expansion of nationalism was married to recodification of the religious law. Along with two thousand people, Ezra took with him to Judea a copy of the law book. Ezra's focus on the law book had a tremendous effect on the Jewish community: "Jewish and Christian traditions give Ezra an important place in the formation of the Old Testament Canon, but the most important feature that emerges from these traditions, is that Ezra stands at the end of the history of the Pentateuchal Law of the Old Testament as Moses stands at the beginning of it. Not that Ezra was in any sense an author or creative figure such as Moses was; he was not even a legislator, but more probably an editor and codifier. . . .

"Ezra's mission had far-reaching results for the life of the Jews. The law-book which he carried became the officially recognized constitution of the community in Judaea and Jerusalem. From the imperial point of view Judaea was formally constituted a hierocracy or temple state, that is to say, a community the center of whose life was the temple, and whose constitution was founded on the constitution of the temple."[17]

At an important public meeting, the people accepted the law book as their constitution (Neh. 8:1–18) and agreed by covenant to keep the law, to refuse intermarriage with Gentiles, to abstain from trade on the Sabbath and to keep it holy, and to observe the jubilee year by leaving their lands untilled and releasing all of their Jewish debtors, and to pay tithes as well as contributions to the maintenance of the temple. (See Neh. 9.)

Ezra, therefore, took the allegiance to the God of Israel beyond the temple and the Sabbath worship. During this period, two other criteria determined membership in the Jewish community. The first was birth; the second was loyalty to the Book of the Law (the Torah) and support of the temple. After the walls were built, Nehemiah said, "My God put into mine heart to gather together the nobles, and the rulers, and the people, that they might be reckoned by genealogy." (Neh. 7:5.) Those not found in the genealogy list, being polluted, were put from the priesthood. (Neh. 7:63–64.) According to one writer, "In the context of the rest of Nehemiah's work, this can mean only one thing: It was important to be born into the right family and to be able to trace one's ancestry to a Jewish father, grandfather, and so on."[18]

Ezra took this new principle of exclusion one step further and demanded that the Jewish men give up their "strange wives." It appears that Ezra met with the "chief father" of each family and reviewed each family's genealogy. "And they made an end with [removed] all the men that had taken strange wives." (Ezra 10:17.) Thus the religious purity of the people of Judah would be ensured.

Conclusion

With the Torah being fully developed and accepted, the temple in operation again, and a strict definition of loyalty and worthiness invoked, the people of Judah were now ready to face the challenges of political foes. Future powers were able to control them politically but not culturally, and especially not religiously. Even future scattering and subsequent dispersion did not destroy their religion. Ezra had given great impetus to strict conformity with the law — which came to be one major characteristic of postexilic Judaism.[19] They had become so entrenched in their law that when their Messiah came to redeem them, they even rejected him!

Upon their return from Babylon, the Jews were determined that they would not lose their identity nor would they go whoring after the gods of other nations. Never again would they allow themselves the luxury of mingling with and accepting the customs of Gentile nations. Never again would they form alliances with foreign nations. Their strict religious and national identity was developed and maintained by a strict code of religious conduct. The scribes who came into existence after the return from Babylon had the responsibility of interpreting and defending the Torah in relation to the social and religious behavior of the Jewish people. This attitude of isolation developed the Jews into a very strong-willed and peculiar people.

The fall and captivity of Judah had a great effect on the mindset of the people of Judah. Their reaction to these events became so energetic and their feelings toward the law and its application became so strong that the religious practices the Savior met were far different from the ones that Isaiah and Jeremiah dealt with. As one writer so ably put it:

"The Fall [of Judah] is the great watershed of Israel's religious life. From earliest times the sin of 'idolatry' had existed in Israel, and the zealots of every age had combated it. After the fall, however, 'the evil genius of idolatry died.' During the period of the second temple, and forever after, idolatry cease, to exist."[20]

NOTES

1. Geoffery W. Bromley, ed., *The International Standard Bible Encyclopedia*, (Grand Rapids, Mich.: William B. Eerdmans Publishing Co., 1980), 2:705.

2. John Lord, *Beacon Lights of History*, 1:384, as quoted by Leon M. Strong, *Three Timely Treasures* (Independence, Mo.: Zion's Printing & Publishing Co., 1949), p. 46.

3. Cunningham Geikie, *Hours with the Bible (Ezekiel to Malachi)*, p. 384, as quoted by Strong, *Three Timely Treasures*, p. 47.

4. James D. Newsome, Jr., *By the Waters of Babylon* (Atlanta: John Knox Press, 1979), p. 17.

5. *Encyclopedia Judaica* (Jerusalem: Keter, n.d.), 9:1322.

6. *Encyclopedia Judaica*, 16:962–63.

7. Bernhard W. Anderson, *Understanding the Old Testament* (Englewood Cliffs, N. J.: Prentice-Hall, 1966), p. 376.

8. Leo W. Schwarz, ed., *Great Ages and Ideas of the Jewish People* (New York: Random House, 1956), pp. 77–78.

9. Newsome, *By the Waters of Babylon*, pp. 79–81.

10. *Encyclopedia Judaica*, 14:558–62.

11. Newsome, *By the Waters of Babylon*, pp. 109–14.

12. F. F. Bruce, *Israel and the Nations* (Grand Rapids, Mich.: William B. Eerdmans Publishing Co., 1969), p. 100.

13. Ibid., p. 101.

14. Ibid., p. 107.

15. Ibid., p. 108. See also *Encylopedia Judaica*, 6:1103–06.

16. Anderson, *Understanding the Old Testament*, p. 438.
17. Bruce, *Israel and the Nations*, pp. 108–9.
18. Anderson, *Understanding the Old Testament*, p. 450.
19. Ibid., p. 496.
20. Schwarz, *Jewish People*, pp. 78–79.

CHAPTER SIX

The "Hidden" Messiah

Richard Neitzel Holzapfel

Director of Irvine, California, Institute of Religion

When Rabbi Jacob Isaac, one of the founders of the Hasidic movement in Poland, died in 1815, his son traded to an innkeeper a clock that he had inherited from his father. Some time later Issachar Baer, rabbi of Radoshitz and a disciple of Rabbi Isaac, stopped at the inn. The innkeeper gave him the very room in which the clock was hanging:

"All night the Rabbi of Radoshitz did not sleep, but paced back and forth in the room, joyously, with dancing steps. In the morning the [innkeeper] asked him why he did not sleep all night. . . . [Rabbi Baer] said], "When I heard the chimes of the clock I instantly recognized that this was the clock of our Holy Master of Lublin [Rabbi Isaac]. For from every clock one hears a note which tells its owner that he is one hour nearer his death. And although he needs this knowledge, still the note is one of sadness and sorrow. But the clock of the Rabbi of Lublin issued notes of joy and jubilation that an hour has passed until the coming of our true Messiah. This is why I could not sleep, and for sheer joy I danced."[1]

One fundamental tenet of Judaism is the belief in the Messiah.[2] It is well known that Jews have long expected and hoped for the coming of the "true Messiah." Many orthodox Jews still await his coming. "I believe with complete faith," states one of the Thirteen Principles of Faith, "in the coming of the Messiah, and even though he should tarry, nevertheless I shall wait for his coming every day."[3] What is less well known is what the Jews mean and have meant by "Messiah."

The present Old Testament text uses the Hebrew word *Mashiyach* in several different ways. *Mashiyach* means "anointed."[4] The English equivalent, *Messiah,* derives from the verb māshāh meaning "to anoint."[5] Objects consecrated to God in ancient Israel were anointed by olive oil being poured over them. (Ex. 30:26–30; 40:9–11.) Individuals consecrated to the service of God were also anointed with oil. In this context *messiah* refers to at least three important offices in ancient Israel:

1. The high priest, "the anointed of God" (Lev. 4:3, 5, 16).

2. The king, "the anointed of the Lord" (1 Sam. 2:10, 35; 9:16; 16:3; 24:6; 2 Sam. 12:7; 1 Kgs. 1:34). The title included not only the kings of Israel and of Judah but also Cyrus of Persia (Isa. 45:1).

3. The prophet of the Lord. Elijah, for example, anointed Elisha in his own place (1 Kgs. 19:16).[6]

The person thus anointed became sacrosanct; to harm him or even curse him was a capital offense. (2 Sam. 19:22.) Even the anointed David, whom King Saul wanted to kill, refused on two occasions to slay the anointed-but-now-rejected Saul. Finding Saul asleep in a cave, David said to his men, "The Lord forbid that I should do this thing unto my master, the Lord's anointed, to stretch forth mine hand against him, seeing he is the anointed of the Lord." (1 Sam. 24:6.) On another occasion, David and Abishai found Saul asleep within a trench, at which point Abishai said to David, "God hath delivered thine enemy into thine hand this day: now therefore let me smite him. . . . And David said to Abishai, Destroy him not: for who can stretch forth his hand against the Lord's anointed, and be guiltless?" (1 Sam. 26:8–9.)

Although the nature and purpose of these anointed servants are clear, confusion over the mission and identity of a Savior Messiah existed during the six centuries preceding the birth of Jesus. This confusion was caused partly by the convergence from many varied traditions of ideas and beliefs about other specially anointed servants. The Jews did not have a single, clear idea about the relationship between the various anointed figures who were expected to appear before the "day of the Lord." At various times the Jews expected as many as three special messiahs—the Messiah ben Joseph (Ephraim), the Messiah ben Levi (Aaron), and the Messiah ben Israel (David)—all figures who were believed to play various important roles in establishing the kingdom of God on the earth.[7] The relationship of these anointed figures with God was not in itself "essentially different from that of other people, called and appointed by God in the past, but the circumstances in which they appear are radically different."[8]

During the century preceding the birth of Jesus, the Essenes at Qumran near the Dead Sea believed in at least two special messiahs: Messiah ben Israel and Messiah ben Aaron.[9] The Damascus Rule, a text from the Qumran community, contains the belief that the final leadership of the kingdom of God would rest in the hands of a Messiah ben Aaron and a Messiah ben Israel. "The King-Messiah," according to Geza Vermes, "was to be the Prince of the Congregation, and the Priestly Anointed, the Messiah of Aaron and Israel, was to be the Interpreter of the Law." Vermes argues further that "the Davidic Prince was to lead the people to triumph, to defeat the Gentiles, and bring into being the Kingdom of God. In matters of doctrine he was to obey the Priests; the first Commentary on Isaiah states expressly that 'as they teach him, so shall he judge.' At the [Messianic] Banquet, also, he was to follow after the Priest. The Messiah of Aaron, on the other hand, is represented as the High Priest of the Kingdom. He was to conduct the liturgy during the battle against the ultimate foe, and as the final Interpreter of the Law he was to reveal the significance of the Scriptures and their relevance to events of the Messianic age and to the endless time of eternal bliss."[10]

The messianic descendant of Aaron is clearly considered superior to the messiah of Israel. The messianic expectation is further complicated in these sources because the Essenes awaited a third prophetic messiah as well. Somewhat disputed among scholars are the role and identity of this prophetic figure.[11] Sources from the period between the Old Testament and New Testament suggest that "during the century before the birth of Christ the [messianic] hope was steadily reviving."[12] F. F. Bruce, a noted New Testament scholar, argues that no single "form of messianic expectation was cherished by Jesus' contemporaries, but the hope of a military Messiah predominated."[13]

The mission and role of a Savior Messiah were hidden from many Jews in the words of their sacred writings. The Jewish canon, what we now know as the *Tenach* (the Hebrew scriptures, or Old Testament), was both incomplete and unclear in presenting and announcing a Savior Messiah. The New Testament reflects the confusion and diverse beliefs about a Savior Messiah and other "anointed" figures during this period. For example, passages in the Gospel of John show that the Jews, shortly before and during the ministry of Jesus, entertained an expectation of at least two separate Messiahs: "When the Jews sent priests and Levites from Jerusalem to ask [John the Baptist], Who art thou? And he confessed, and denied not; but confessed, I am not the Christ [Savior Messiah]. And they asked him, what then? Art thou Elias [Elijah]? And he saith, I am not. Art thou that prophet [Messiah ben Ephraim]? And he answered, No." (John 1:19–21.)

In the New Testament the Greek word *Christos* is used to translate the Hebrew word *Mashiyach,* both of which mean "anointed," except that the Greek word may not have carried the strong political connotation that the Hebrew word did.[14] The Grecized Aramaic form *Messias* is found a few times in the text. (John 1:41; 4:25.) The Septuagint, the Greek Old Testament, uses *Christos* forty times to translate the Hebrew *Mashiyach.*[15] Only after the passion, death, and resurrection of Jesus did the disciples themselves begin to understand the full meaning of the Old Testament passages on the nature and purpose of the call of a Savior Messiah. (Mark 16:14; Luke 24:44–47; Acts 1:11.)

The New Testament text reveals the Savior Messiah of the Old Testament to the Jews in a clearer manner than earlier records did.[16] One very difficult and misunderstood teaching about the Savior Messiah was his relationship to God, his divine sonship. Many Jews anticipated a Davidic Messiah, but for them his relationship with the Father was hidden. In ancient Israel the idea of being God's son had diverse meanings and connotations. It was used metaphorically in several ways, sometimes representing any of the children of Israel, or a holy or a charismatic Israelite, or the king of Israel. A royal or kingly Messiah was also thought of as a son of God. In a different sense, angelic or heavenly beings were known as the sons of God.[17] This language was understood as metaphorical.

Surprisingly, only three passages in the present Old Testament text allude to the Savior Messiah as being the son of God. Neither do such references exist in any scriptural exegeses, such as the Targum, Mishnah, and Talmud, which began to emerge after the biblical text ended.[18] The first biblical allusion is found in Psalms: "I will declare the decree: the Lord hath said unto me, Thou art my Son; this day have I begotten thee." (Ps. 2:7.) The second and third passages are found in Isaiah: "Therefore the Lord himself shall give you a sign; Behold, a virgin shall conceive, and bear a son, and shall call his name Immanuel" (Isa. 7:14) and "For unto us a child is born, unto us a son is given: and the government shall be upon his shoulder: and his name shall be called Wonderful, Counsellor, The mighty God, The everlasting Father, The Prince of Peace" (Isa. 9:6).

The problematic nature of these passages is evident in the various ways they have been transmitted, translated, interpreted, and understood. The Psalm 2:7 passage is often seen in context of a promise to David that after David's death, Solomon would sit on his throne: "I will be his father," says the Lord, "and he shall be my son. If he commit iniquity, I will chasten him with the rod of men, . . . but my mercy shall not depart away from him." (2 Sam. 7:14–15.) A contemporary Jewish commentary based on the Targum, Talmud, Midrash, and other classical Jewish commentaries explains that the phrase "This day have I begotten thee" should be understood in a figurative sense only. "On the day of his enthronement," A. Cohen argues, "the king was *begotten* of God as His servant to guide the destinies of His people."[19]

Some scholars believe that this so-called royal psalm was recited on the occasion of the enthronement ceremony. This verse was recited by the king as he was invested with royal powers. Anointed as king, he becomes begotten of God. "This has nothing to do with physical descent, however, or with divine kingship as in Egypt," H. Neil Richardson argues. "What we find in the Hebrew Bible is adoption language, qualifying the king for the patrimony Yahweh wishes to bestow upon him."[20] The conclusion is that in ancient Israel and Judah, kings were viewed as having a special father-son relationship with God.

The passage from Isaiah 7:14 has linguistic difficulties that center on the English word *virgin*. A modern Jewish translation renders this passage, "Assuredly, my Lord will give you a sign of His own accord! Look, the young woman is with child and about to give birth to a son. Let her name him Immanuel."[21] The choice of the phrase "young woman" instead of "virgin" is based on the oldest known Hebrew text, sometimes described as "Proto-Masoretic."[22] The King James Version is based on the Masoretic text, or the traditional reading, though at this point the translators deviate from the Hebrew text and reflect the use of the Greek Old Testament word *parthenos*, meaning "virgin."[23] Matthew's use of this passage was probably based on the Septuagint, the primary Christian Bible version during the first century. (Matt. 1:23.)[24] The Hebrew *almah* means "an adolescent woman," one of marriageable age, whereas the Hebrew *bethulah* means "virgin."[25] A translation in Aramaic, the language of Jesus, uses the phrase "young woman."[26]

The passage from Isaiah 9:6–7 is rendered in a recent Jewish version somewhat differently. "For a child is born unto us, . . . And his name is called Pele-joez-el-gibbor-Abi-ad-sar-shalom."[27] I.W. Slotki translates this name as "Wonderful in counsel is God the Mighty, the Everlasting Father, the Ruler of Peace" and adds, "the child will bear

these significant names in order to recall to the people the message
which they embodied."[28]

There is no biblical or extrabiblical evidence that these verses were
understood by Jews in any way other than adoption, before the interpretation provided in the New Testament.[29] Caiaphas, the high priest,
specifically questioned Jesus during his trial about His claim to be the
Savior Messiah. Jesus' affirmation gave Caiaphas and the other Jewish
leaders the needed pretext to bring a charge of treason to Pilate, because in one sense Jesus claimed to be the King of the Jews, which
they understood narrowly as a political ruler. Such a claim was then
dealt with by the Roman law and power, just as the Jewish leaders
expected it to be. (Mark 14:61–62.)

But not only did Jesus give evidence to convict him under Roman
law, he also gave the Jews evidence for convicting him of blasphemy,
a capital crime under the law of Moses, as the claim of being a Messiah
was not. (Matt. 26:64; Mark 16:62; Luke 22:69.) Joel Marcus argues
that there must have been something different about Jesus' claim other
than simply the claim of being the Messiah: "Why should Jesus' claim
to be 'the Messiah, the Son of God' be considered blasphemous if 'Son
of God' is merely a synonym for 'Messiah'? What is blasphemous about
claiming to be the Messiah? One searches Jewish literature in vain for
evidence that a simple claim to be the Messiah would incur such a
charge."[30]

The evidence Jesus gave his interrogators, therefore, was his claim
to sit on the right hand of God. This claim implied divine sonship and
equality with God. F. F. Bruce writes: "One who claimed to be the
Messiah might therefore, as a corollary, speak of sitting at God's right
hand; but to speak thus explicitly [as Jesus did] would be regarded as
going to the very limit of daring, and the same attitude would be taken
to one who, claiming to be the Messiah, accepted the corollary that
because the Messiah is addressed by God as his Son in Psalm 2:7, he
himself therefore was the Son of God."[31]

Jesus' claim of being God's literal son was more controversial to
the Jews than his claim of being the Davidic messiah. Marcus believes
that this claim was "understood in a quite realistic, almost biological
sense" by the New Testament writers.[32] But this biological understanding of Jesus' origin was beyond the comprehension of the Jewish
leaders; the claim, therefore, was simply blasphemous to them. That
the "hidden" Messiah was the Son of God, the Holy One of Israel, was

a belief they could not accept, because it was not part of the tradition handed down to them.

There are several other reasons why the Savior Messiah was hidden from Israel. One is the use of prophetic language and the ability of the individual to understand it, especially the words of Isaiah. For many, only when the prophetic word was fulfilled would they understand the scriptures. Nephi said, "In the days that the prophecies of Isaiah shall be fulfilled men shall know of a surety, at the times when they shall come to pass." (2 Ne. 25:7.) In this case, the messianic passages in Psalm 2 and Isaiah could generally only be understood after their fulfillment in Jesus of Nazareth.

A related problem is the double fulfillment of prophetic language. The resurrected Jesus said that Isaiah's words "have been" and "shall be" fulfilled. (3 Ne. 23:3.) The passage in Isaiah 7:14 may, therefore, have been fulfilled by the wife of Isaiah, the wife of Ahaz, or another woman of the royal family during Isaiah's own time, and then fulfilled a second time in a dramatic way seven hundred years later in the life of Mary, Jesus' mother.[33]

A second problem contributes to the difficulty of preserving a consistent and coherent messianic view: the tendency of Israel to look beyond the mark. Jacob said that Israel "despised the words of plainness . . . and sought for things that they could not understand. Wherefore, because of their blindness, which blindness came by looking beyond the mark, they must needs fall . . . [meaning] they cannot understand [the prophecies]." (Jacob 4:14.) One example was the sacrifice of the lamb required by the law of Moses. (Ex. 12:5, 21; 29:39; Lev 14:10.) For many Jews the sacrifice of a lamb was a symbol, not of what God would do through his anointed Son for mankind, but of what man was now doing through animal sacrifice to restore his relationship with God. By looking beyond the mark, they believed that the lesser animal could be sacrificed for man without seeing that the sacrifice was symbolic of a greater sacrifice in which the greater (that is, God) must atone for the lesser (that is, sinful man).[34] The meaning of the sacrifice was lost in the misunderstanding of the symbols surrounding it.[35]

The scriptural text contributes to the confusion about the Savior Messiah. The transmission and translation of the biblical texts are one of the great miracles of history; nevertheless, there are problems in understanding the meaning of the text. "How do ye say," Jeremiah asked, "we are wise, and the law of the Lord is with us? Lo, certainly in vain he made it; the pen of the scribes is in vain." (Jer. 8:8.) Note an alternative translation of this passage: "How can you say, 'We are wise, since we have Yahweh's Law?' Look how it has been falsified by the lying pen of the scribes!"[36] Though this reading is disputed, Jeremiah may have been hinting at a corruption of the text by his time.[37] Six hundred years later, Jesus said, "Woe unto you, lawyers! for ye have taken away the key of knowledge: ye entered not in yourselves, and them that were entering in ye hindered." (Luke 11:52.) The Joseph Smith Translation amplifies Jesus' meaning of the "key of knowledge" by describing it as nothing less than "the fulness of the scriptures."[38]

Jeremiah and Jesus imply that problems with the text, or at least with the proper interpretations of the text, were present very early. The textual problems seem to fit under several categories, including transmission problems, translation problems (from Hebrew into Greek, for example), and more important, problems in original composition.[39]

While the New Testament begins to reveal the "Hidden" Messiah, the Book of Mormon stands not only as a second witness of the Christ but as a revealer of the "hidden" Messiah in a deeply profound way that was often only hinted at by the New Testament writers. The difficulties of many Old Testament passages are made "plain" by the Nephite record. One purpose of the Book of Mormon is to "prov[e] to the world that the holy scriptures are true." (D&C 20:11.) Or, as Nephi said, the coming forth of the Book of Mormon by "the power of the Lamb, from the Gentiles [is to] convinc[e] . . . the Gentiles and the remnant of the seed of my brethren, and also the Jews . . . that the records of the prophets [the Old Testament] and of the twelve apostles of the Lamb [New Testament] are true." (1 Ne. 13:39.)

Not only does the Book of Mormon confirm the doctrine of the Savior Messiah, which is clearly spelled out in the Old Testament, but it confirms prophetic intention, gives inspired commentary, and restores important messianic texts and context. Joseph Smith said, "From sundry revelations which had been received, it was apparent that many important points touching the salvation of men, had been taken from the Bible, or lost before it was compiled."[40] I feel that crucial teachings concerning the Savior Messiah were lost to Israel and would be unavailable to us without the Book of Mormon. The "restoration" of the fulness of the gospel enables us to regain some of the intentions of the prophetic teachings in the Old Testament; in this sense, the "Hidden" Messiah is rerevealed.

The knowledge of the Savior Messiah was lost very early through a series of apostasies, only to be restored when a prophet was called again. This cycle of apostasy/restoration, apostasy/restoration, continued until the coming of Jesus Christ.[41] A restoration of the deeper meaning of the sacrificial system of the Jews and also of specific messianic passages and the restoration of other lost knowledge can be seen in the life of Lehi and Nephi, who lived at Jerusalem about 600 B.C. A clear understanding of a Savior Messiah who would offer for sinful Israel a sacrifice does not appear to have been found among Jews during that period.

Lehi's visions, as described by Nephi, show surprise at the new understanding of the mission of the Savior Messiah. Much of Lehi's new understanding comes from reading an unknown book shown to him by an angel. It does not seem to have been found in the understanding of contemporaries of Lehi and may not have been clearly taught in the text in use at the time. Only after reading this book was Lehi able to testify about the Savior Messiah, because the book "manifested plainly of the coming of a Messiah." (1 Ne. 1:19.) In recounting his father's experience, Nephi explained that Lehi taught his family that "a prophet would the Lord God raise up among the Jews—even a Messiah, or, in other words, a Savior of the world." (1 Ne. 10:4.) The context of the passage seems to indicate that this teaching was something new for Lehi's family, something not commonly known. The first use of the title "Lamb of God" is found in verse 10, and it is possible that Lehi discovered in his visions and revelations the connection between the sacrifice of the lamb and the death of the Messiah. In verse 11, Lehi mentioned that the Messiah will be slain.

Nephi was moved by his father's revelations on the birth and death of the Savior Messiah to know more about the things his father had taught. Exactly what did he want to know? That is not specifically indicated, but in the following chapter Nephi learned, seemingly for the first time, that the Lamb, already identified by Lehi as the Savior Messiah, is also the literal Son of God. (1 Ne. 11:21.) That is a genuinely profound revelation concerning the condescension of God.

The literal sonship of the Savior Messiah was rejected when it was revealed. The biblical text does not explicitly address this problem, but a case example of this rejection is found in the Book of Mormon among those who claimed to follow the traditions of Moses. It appears that two separate traditions about the Savior Messiah's origin came to the New World. Possibly Laman and Lemuel, who sided with the Jews at Jerusalem against their father and brother, brought a separate tradition concerning the Messiah with them. Abinadi presents a message very similar to the prophetic messages found in the Old Testament. It is God's call to return to his law and a reaffirmation of the commandments given to Moses at Sinai. Although this call for repentance challenges the king and his court, it is the doctrine of the Savior Messiah's divine sonship for which Abinadi finally brings upon himself the death penalty from Noah's priests. The Nephite record states: "[Noah] said unto him: Abinadi, we have found an accusation against thee, and thou art worthy of death. For thou has said that God himself should come down among the children of men; and now, for this cause thou shalt be put to death unless thou wilt recall all the words." (Mosiah 17:7–8.)

What Abinadi said to the court of Noah was that "God himself shall come down among the children of men, and shall redeem his people. And because he dwelleth in flesh he shall be called the Son of God." (Mosiah 15:1–2.) Abinadi quoted Isaiah 53 and connected the Savior Messiah with being God's son. Thus, for Abinadi, the Savior Messiah was not only the Lord's special, anointed servant foreseen by Isaiah, but God's own son and the Holy One of Israel, Israel's God. Abinadi was executed shortly after this pronouncement.

Did the Jews seek Lehi's life for a similar reason when he taught them "plainly" concerning the Savior Messiah and the redemption of the world? (1 Ne. 1: 19–20.) Perhaps the messianic passages that deal with the Savior Messiah's divine sonship have not survived transmission in the Old Testament because they were ultimately rejected and the prophets who "plainly" taught this doctrine were put to death. The New Testament disciple, Stephen, may have had that in mind when he said: "Which of the prophets have not your fathers persecuted? and they have slain them which shewed before of the coming of the Just One." (Acts 7:52.) Was the difficulty Jesus encountered among his disciples related to their failing to understand the relationship of the Savior Messiah and God, namely, that he would be God's son?

That this relationship between the Savior Messiah and God was known before the mortal ministry of Jesus is clearly detailed in texts restored through Joseph Smith.[42] The restoration of pre-New Testament teachings found in the Book of Mormon, Pearl of Great Price, and the Joseph Smith Translation reveal the great knowledge that biblical prophets had once made available. Only vestiges of this knowledge can be found in our current Old Testament text. Several years ago, a young Jew, Larry Gassin, joined the Church in southern California. He was raised in a Conservative Jewish congregation in the San Fernando Valley. After meeting with the missionaries for the first time and during their subsequent visits, Larry often read his Hebrew scriptures. The divine sonship of the crucified Jesus, a stumbling block to the Jews (1 Cor. 1:23), was hard to grasp. Larry had difficulty making correlations with the prophetic writings he read, especially Isaiah, to the message of the Savior Messiah. Eventually, having gained a testimony of the Book of Mormon, he and his family were baptized. Over the next two years, Larry attended several extended family gatherings—a bar-mitzvah for a nephew, a funeral for his grandmother, and family Hanukkah and Passover celebrations. Each time, an opportunity allowed him to share his newfound faith in Jesus the Savior Messiah. Often scriptural passages were read, but for Larry these passages had new meaning. At first he could not understand why his family and the rabbi could not "see" Jesus in the text. After reflection, Larry realized that he now "saw" Jesus in the Hebrew scriptures because he had received a witness of the truth of his new Old Testament commentary, the Book of Mormon. For Larry Gassin, the Savior Messiah was no longer hidden, but revealed as the divine Son of God Almighty.

The calling, mission, suffering, death, and resurrection of the Savior Messiah were announced by the prophet Isaiah, though the servant mentioned is identified as Israel by Jewish commentators. (Isa. 42:1–4; 49:1–6; 50:4–9; 52:13–53:12.)[43] The Book of Mormon testifies to the identity of the "suffering servant" as Jesus of Nazareth, the Christ or Messiah. (Mosiah 13:33–15:31.)

By substituting the word *messiah* for all the pronouns, we can see the "hidden" Messiah in Isaiah 53:

"Who hath believed our report? and to whom is the arm of the Lord revealed?

"For he [the Messiah] shall grow up before him [God] as a tender plant, and as a root out of a dry ground: he [the Messiah] hath no form nor comeliness; and when we shall see him [the Messiah], there is no beauty that we should desire him [the Messiah].

"He [The Messiah] is despised and rejected of men; a man of sorrows, and acquainted with grief: and we hid as it were our faces from him [the Messiah]; he [the Messiah] was despised, and we esteemed him [the Messiah] not.

"Surely he [the Messiah] hath borne our griefs, and carried our sorrows: yet we did esteem him [the Messiah] stricken, smitten of God, and afflicted.

"But he [the Messiah] was wounded for our transgressions, he [the Messiah] was bruised for our iniquities: the chastisement of our peace was upon him [the Messiah]; and with his [the Messiah's] stripes we are healed.

"All we like sheep have gone astray; we have turned every one to his own way; and the Lord has laid on him [the Messiah] the iniquity of us all.

"He [the Messiah] was oppressed, and he [the Messiah] was afflicted, yet he opened not his mouth: he [the Messiah] is brought as a lamb to the slaughter, and as a sheep before her shearers is dumb, so he [the Messiah] openeth not his mouth.

"He [the Messiah] was taken from prison and from judgment: and who shall declare his [the Messiah's] generation? for he [the Messiah] was cut off out of the land of the living: for the transgression of my [God's] people was he [the Messiah] stricken.

"And he [the Messiah] made his grave with the wicked, and with the rich in his [the Messiah's] death; because he [the Messiah] had done no violence, neither was any deceit in his [the Messiah's] mouth.

"Yet it pleased the Lord to bruise him [the Messiah]; he hath put him [the Messiah] to grief: when thou shalt make his [the Messiah's] soul an offering for sin, he [the Messiah] shall see his seed, he [God] shall prolong his [the Messiah's] days, and the pleasure of the Lord shall prosper in his [the Messiah's] hand.

"He [God] shall see of the travail of his [the Messiah's] soul, and shall be satisfied: by his [God's] knowledge shall my righteous servant [the Messiah] justify many; for he [the Messiah] shall bear their iniquities.

"Therefore will I [God] divide him [the Messiah] a portion with the great, and he [God] shall divide the spoil with the strong; because he [the Messiah] hath poured out his [the Messiah's] soul unto death: and he [the Messiah] was numbered with the transgressors; and he [the Messiah] bare the sin of many, and made intercession for the transgressors."[44]

With the scriptural interpretations of the disciples of Jesus, the restoration of ancient scripture, and the Holy Spirit as a guide, one is now in a position to have the Savior Messiah of the Hebrew Scriptures revealed, so that he is no longer hidden from view.

NOTES

1. Quoted in Raphael Patai, *The Messiah Texts* (New York: Avon Books, 1979), pp. 50–51.

2. While many Reconstructionist, Reform, and Conservative Jews no longer anticipate the appearance of a Savior Messiah, Orthodox and Hasidic Jews still pray, "Let the Shoot of David Thy servant sprout up" as part of the Eighteen Benedictions edited by Rabbi Gamaliel II in A.D. 70.

3. Quoted in Patai, *Messiah Texts*, p. 47.

4. Francis Brown, S. R. Driver, and C. A. Briggs, *A Hebrew and English Lexicon of the Old Testament* (Oxford: Oxford University Press, 1977), p. 603.

5. Ibid., pp. 602–3.

6. See also Isaiah 61:1; Psalm 105:15 for the parallelism "mine anointed" with "my prophets."

7. See Joseph Klausner, *The Messianic Idea in Israel: From Its Beginning to the Completion of the Mishnah* (New York: Macmillan, 1955); Gershom Scholem, *The Messianic Idea in Judaism and Other Essays on Jewish Spirituality* (New York: Schocken Books, 1971); Joachim Becker, *Messianic Expectation in the Old Testament* (Philadelphia: Fortress Press, 1980); and Jacob Neusner, *Messiah in Context: Israel's History and Destiny in Formative Judaism* (Philadelphia: Fortress Press, 1984). The parallels between the Ephraimite Messiah and Joseph Smith are examined in Joseph Fielding McConkie, *His Name Shall Be Joseph: Ancient Prophecies of the Latter-day Seer* (Salt Lake City: Hawkes Publishing, 1980), pp. 153–84.

8. M. de Jonge, "The Use of the Word 'Anointed' in the Time of Jesus," *Novum Testamentum* 8 (1966): 147.

9. See also the Testament of Judah in R. H. Charles, *The Apocrypha and Pseudepigrapha of the Old Testament* (Oxford: The Clarendon Press, 1977), p. 322. In the Testament of the Twelve Patriarchs the same scheme of dual messiahship is present, and in which Judah declares, "For to me the Lord gave the kingdom, and to him [Levi] the priesthood, and He set the kingdom beneath the priesthood. To me He gave the things upon the earth; to him the things in heavens. As the heaven is higher than the earth, so is the priesthood of God higher than the earthly kingdom, unless it falls away through sin form the Lord and is dominated by earthly kingdom. For the angel of the Lord said unto me: The Lord chose him rather than thee, to draw near to Him, and to eat of His table and to offer Him the first-fruits of the choice things of the sons of Israel; but thou shalt be king of Jacob." (Testament of Judah 21:2–5.) On the relationship between the messianism of the Tes-

taments and that of Qumran, see K. G. Kuln, "Two Messiahs," *The Scrolls and the New Testament*, K. Stendahl, ed. (New York: Harper and Row, 1957), pp. 57–58.

10. Geza Vermes, *The Dead Sea Scrolls in English* (Baltimore, Md.: Penguin Books, 1968), p. 49.

11. See Robert Eisenman, *Maccabees, Zadokites, Christians and Qumran* (Leiden, Netherlands: E. J. Brill, 1983), pp. xi-xvii, 1–3.

12. See Bible Dictionary, LDS edition of the King James Version of the Bible, s.v. "Messiah." A collection of this literature is found in George W. E. Nickelsburg, *Jewish Literature between the Bible and the Mishnah* (Philadelphia: Fortress Press, 1981).

13. F. F. Bruce, *New Testament History* (Garden City, N.Y.: Doubleday, 1980), p. 133.

14. William F. Arndt and F. Wilbur Gingrich, *A Greek-English Lexicon of the New Testament and Other Early Christian Literature* (Chicago: University of Chicago Press, 1957), p. 895.

15. George Morrish, comp., *A Concordance of the Septuagint* (Grand Rapids, Mich.: Zondervan Publishing House, 1976), p. 261.

16. The New Testament identifies the Savior Messiah as not only an eschatological King but as a preexistent heavenly being and a participant in the creative enterprise. (John 1:1–4.)

17. George Arthur Buttrick, ed., *The Interpreter's Dictionary of the Bible*, 5 vols. (Nashville: Abingdon Press, 1962), 4:408–9.

18. Though not necessarily considered a scriptural exegesis in the traditional sense, the Isaiah Targum, an Aramaic translation of the Hebrew book of Isaiah, reflects a contemporary understanding of a passage, since no translation is objective or neutral. Bruce Chilton argues, "The translator always — and necessarily — conveys his own understanding of what he translates." Bruce D. Chilton, *The Isaiah Targum: Introduction, Translation, Apparatus and Notes* (Wilmington, Del.: Michael Glazier, 1987), ix.

19. A. Cohen, ed., *The Psalms: Hebrew Text & English Translation with an Introduction and Commentary* (New York: Soncino Press, 1985), p. 4.

20. H. Neil Richardson, "The Old Testament Background of Jesus as Begotten of God," *Bible Review*, vol. 2, Nov. 11 (Fall 1986): 24.

21. *Tanach: A New Translation of the Holy Scriptures according to the Traditional Hebrew Text* (Philadelphia: Jewish Publication Society, 1985), p. 631.

22. Frank Moore Cross, David Noel Freedman, and James A. Sanders, eds., *Scrolls from Qumran Cave I: The Great Isaiah Scroll, The Order of the Community, The Pesher to Habakkuk* (Jerusalem: The Albright Institute of Archaeological Research and The Shrine of the Book, 1974), p. 13.

23. See LDS Bible Dictionary, s.v. "Masoretic."; *The Septuagint with Apocrypha: Greek and English* (Grand Rapids, Mich.: Zondervan Publishing House, 1980), p. 842.

24. See also Robert G. Bratcher, *Old Testament Quotations in the New Testament* (New York: United Bible Societies, 1984), p. 1. For additional information on the Septuagint see Ernst Wurthwein, *The Text of The Old Testament: An Introduction to the Biblia Hebraic* (Grand Rapids, Mich.: William B. Eerdmans Pub-

lishing Co., 1979), pp. 49–74, especially, pp. 51–53. For a Jewish polemical view of this issue see Gerald Sigal's *The Jew and the Christian Missionary: A Jewish Response to Missionary Christianity* (New York: KTAV Publishing House, 1981), pp. 20–28.

25. The Hebrew *almah* is translated, "a young woman, ripe sexually, maid or newly married" in Brown, Driver, and Briggs *Hebrew and English Lexicon*, p. 761. For a complete discussion of the use of *virgin* in the Old Testament see G. J. Botterweck and Helmer Ringgren, *Theological Dictionary of the Old Testament*, John T. Willis, trans., 5 vols. (Grand Rapids, Mich.: William B. Eerdmans Publishing Co., 1975), 2:338–343.

26. The antiquity of this document is based on some scholars' belief that the Targum reflects similarities with documents from the first and second centuries A.D. For the use of *young woman,* see Bruce D. Chilton, *The Isaiah Targum*, p. 17.

27. I. W. Slotki, ed., *Isaiah: Hebrew Text & English Translation with an Introduction and Commentary* (New York: Soncino Press, 1980), p. 44.

28. Ibid., pp. 44–45.

29. See Gerald Cooke, "The Israelite King as Son of God," *Zeitschrift Fur Die Alttestamentliche Wissenschaft* 72 (1961): 202–25.

30. See Joel Marcus, "Mark 14:61: 'Are You the Messiah Son-of-God?'" *Novum Testamentum* 31 (April 1989): 127.

31. Bruce, *New Testament History*, p. 198.

32. Marcus, "Mark 14:61," p. 140.

33. See Avraham Gileadi, *The Book of Isaiah: A New Translation with Interpretive Keys from the Book of Mormon* (Salt Lake City: Deseret Book Co., 1988), especially pp. 66–69.

34. "For it is expedient," according to Amulek, "that there should be a great and last sacrifice; yea, not a sacrifice of man, neither of beast, neither of any manner of fowl; for it shall not be a human sacrifice; but it must be an infinite and eternal sacrifice." (Alma 34:10.)

35. An additional doctrine lost to Israel was the Messiah's ultimate rejection and crucifixion. A crucified Messiah was a contradiction in terms for Jews of the Pharisaic-Rabbinic tradition. See Galatians 3:13 for Paul's original reason for rejecting a "crucified" Jesus whom he thought was obviously accursed of God. See also Roy A. Rosenberg, "The Slain Messiah in the Old Testament," *Zeitschrift fur die Alttestamentliche Wissenschaft* 99 (1987): 259–61.

36. *The New Jerusalem Bible* (Garden City, N.Y.: Doubleday, 1985), p. 1311.

37. For an alternative reading of this text see Michael A. Fishbane, *Biblical Interpretation in Ancient Israel* (Oxford: Clarendon Press, 1985), pp. 33–36.

38. LDS Bible Luke 11:52 (n. 52c).

39. For a complete discussion see Robert J. Matthews, *A Plainer Translation, Joseph Smith's Translation of the Bible: A History and Commentary* (Provo, Utah: Brigham Young University Press, 1975), especially pp. 4–8.

40. Joseph Smith, *Teachings of the Prophet Joseph Smith*, sel. Joseph Fielding Smith (Salt Lake City: Deseret Book Co., 1977), pp. 9–11.

41. Information about the Savior Messiah was lost following the apostasy of

the New Testament Dispensation. For example, the relationship of Jesus to his Father's other sons and daughters, including Lucifer, is no longer understood among the Christian community.

42. See the Triple Combination index headings of "Jesus Christ — Messiah," "Only Begotten Son," "Son of God," and "Son of Man."

43. Unlike other Jewish sources, the Isaiah Targum does identify the Messiah with the servant in Isaiah 53, but it is the New Testament and restoration scriptures that give us a more profound view of the suffering servant's person. See Bruce D. Chilton, *The Isaiah Targum*, pp. 103–5.

44. This idea was introduced to me by Keith Meservy of the BYU Ancient Scripture Department. See also Irving H. Cohen, "A Jew Finds the True Messiah," in *No More Strangers*, comp. Hartman and Connie Rector (Salt Lake City: Bookcraft, 1971), pp. 56–66.

CHAPTER SEVEN

Job's Relevancy in the Twenty-First Century

Clark V. Johnson

Brigham Young University

Because Job struggled to know God, he did not understand why he lost everything: prosperity, children, health, even his good name. He continued in faith, however; even his friends' betrayal caused him only to turn more desperately to God.

Some scholars feel that Job is a book of fiction that views life philosophically. Others feel the book relates the experiences of a historical figure. Both views agree that the book of Job is "the greatest work of genius in the Old Testament" as it considers the question of man's destiny in mortality, a question that historians and philosophers have debated throughout the world's history.[1] Those who argue that Job was a real person note that the prophet Ezekiel referred to Job in the Old Testament, the apostle James cited him in the New Testament, and the Lord mentioned him in the Doctrine and Covenants. I personally feel these references indicate that Job was a historical figure and that these same references are three keys that unlock the book of Job.

Though the book of Job is placed among tenth-century works, it is most likely that Job lived much earlier, during the time of the patriarchs Abraham, Isaac, and Jacob.[2] Yet Job's struggle to understand life and to come to grips with his suffering makes his book relevant today. Continued suffering through heart failure, cancer, AIDS, alcoholism, respiratory failure, and a myriad of other diseases that afflict people in the twentieth century make the message in the book of Job timeless.

My own study of Job has grown out of my continuing struggle with cancer. Had I an understanding of Job's life before finding myself afflicted with cancer, it might have alleviated some of the frustration I felt. In a letter to a friend, I wrote: "The pain one endures through cancer and its variety of prescribed treatments is exotic. My experience has been that having cancer is like being on a roller coaster — one day you're up and feel reasonably good, and the next day you're down. The pain and mental anguish are so great that they become unbearable."[3]

Job, a Righteous Man

When I began to study Job, I found that nowhere in the book of Job is he ever referred to as a prophet. Job is a good man who struggled to support a family, build the kingdom of God, and to understand his relationship with God.

Job's prominence is revealed in the Old Testament by Ezekiel, who wrote, "Though these three men, Noah, Daniel, and Job, were in it, they should deliver but their own souls by their righteousness, saith the Lord God." (Ezek. 14:14.) In other words, Ezekiel referred to Noah and Daniel as well as Job as righteous men.

The opening verses of the book of Job refer to Job as "perfect and upright, and one that feared God, and eschewed evil." (Job 1:1.)

In the New Testament the Savior taught, "Be ye therefore perfect, even as your Father which is in heaven is perfect." (Matt. 5:48.) During the 1830s when Joseph Smith retranslated the Bible, he changed this verse to read, "Ye are therefore commanded to be perfect, even as your Father which is in heaven is perfect." (JST Matt. 5:50.) The word *perfect* is used to translate the Hebrew word *shalam*, meaning "whole or complete or full." The Lord confirmed this definition when he told the Prophet Joseph Smith, "Ye are not able to abide the presence of God now, neither the ministering of angels; wherefore, continue in patience until ye are perfected." (D&C 67:13.) The scriptures teach that perfection is growing toward heavenly blessings through discipline, not a stagnant confirmation of something divine.

In the gospel sense, to be perfect, whole, or complete is to exercise our agency to receive all that God wants us to receive. Speaking of the priesthood, the Savior revealed: "And this greater priesthood administereth the gospel and holdeth the key of the mysteries of the kingdom, even the key of the knowledge of God. Therefore, in the ordinances thereof, the power of godliness is manifest. And without the ordinances thereof, and the authority of the priesthood, the power of godliness is not manifest unto men in the flesh." (D&C 84:19–21.) To be perfect, a person must receive the priesthood and have the mysteries of godliness revealed through the ordinances of the priesthood. When a man receives the higher priesthood and a man and woman go to the temple to make covenants and to receive their washings and anointings, endowments and sealings, they become whole. They are complete; they have received all that God will give them in mortality. Perfection is achieved when people keep the covenants they make with God. In this sense, Ezekiel's description of Job becomes clearer.

Job had received all the blessings of the priesthood; he kept his covenants; thus, he was whole, or complete. It is then necessary to fear God and to eschew evil, as Job did. Those who fear God keep his commandments; they love, respect, and revere him. In addition, those who fear God "eschew" or shun evil.

Job, a Family Man

The opening verses of the book of Job depict him as a family man. He had three daughters and seven sons. (Job 1:2.) He supported his large family in various enterprises. He had "seven thousand sheep, and three thousand camels, and five hundred yoke of oxen, and five hundred she asses, and a very great household; so that this man was the greatest of all the men of the east." (Job 1:3.) Job had servants and employees to help oversee his holdings; he was, in short, a wealthy man.

But Job was more concerned about his children than about his possessions. After his sons and daughters had feasted, Job "sanctified them, and rose up early in the morning, and offered burnt offerings according to the number of them all" as was required by patriarchal law. Job reasoned, "It may be that my sons have sinned, and cursed God in their hearts. Thus did Job continually." (Job 1:3–5.)

Many parents can identify with Job's concern for his children. During my years of teaching I have encountered several students who complained bitterly against God about the death of one of their parents. That has always been a matter of great concern for me. Years ago, when it looked as though I was going to die soon of cancer, I did not want my children to be bitter and blame their Father in Heaven. At Christmastime we returned home to Preston, Idaho, where we spent the Christmas season with our parents. During that week I took my four oldest children to four different places that were special to me while I was growing up and taught them concerning Heavenly Father's love for them. I told them that it looked as though I would have to return to be with him, so I would not have the opportunity of being with them as they grew up. I promised them that if they would live the gospel and go to the temple to be sealed, it did not matter if I lived or died—I would be with them when they went to the temple. After carefully teaching them many things, I gave each one a father's blessing.

When I finished with my youngest daughter, who turned four years old that Christmas, I thought my heart would melt. I found myself exclaiming, "Oh, God, how much can she possibly understand?" As though she divined my thoughts, she reached towards me. With her tiny arms extended upwards, and opening and closing her hands as a child does when it wants to be held, she said, "Daddy, Daddy, I love you." As I took her into my arms, I knew that somehow she had understood. I knew that my children would not be bitter but would love their Father in Heaven.

While in the Missionary Training Center, our eldest son wrote to us about one of the elders in his district who bore testimony concerning his father's death from cancer. The elder described the bitterness that he had felt, and he told of the years of pain the death of his father had caused him. Then Paul wrote:

"Dad, I remember the time you took me to my great-grandfather's old farm. We talked about the Indian battle that had been fought there. We spoke of other things, and you explained that you were dying of cancer and that it looked as though you would not be here to help me as I grew up. You told me that if I would keep the commandments and get married in the temple, you would be there to see me married. You said that it didn't matter whether you were here on earth or with Heavenly Father. Then I knelt in the snow and you blessed me. I love you, Dad, for preparing a way so that I would not be bitter."

Occasionally we have family problems that might not seem to be so serious. One son called me late at night and said, "Dad?" I answered, "Yes?" He responded, "Something's wrong with the car." I said, "Oh, what?" The answer, "Well, the roads are slick, and I hit a curb. I think you'd better come, Dad." I asked, "Are you hurt?" "No," he replied. I asked, "Was there another car involved?" He answered, "No." "I'll be right there, Son." He had hit a curb, bending the left front wheel forty-five degrees, and "thought something was wrong" with the car. As I pondered my reaction to this minor crisis, it struck me that the gospel teaches us that children are more important than things.

Parents today do not offer animal sacrifices in behalf of their children as Job did, but they sanctify their children through prayer and fasting according to the law of the gospel.

Job, a Teacher

The Old Testament notes that Job's concern extended beyond his immediate family to others. Eliphaz said to Job, "Thou hast instructed many, and thou hast strengthened the weak hands." Job probably served as the Old Testament equivalents of Aaronic Priesthood advisor, scoutmaster, and even Gospel Doctrine teacher. A second witness of Job's greatness as a teacher was given by Eliphaz, who pointed out to Job that his "words have upholden him that was falling, and thou hast strengthened the feeble knees." (Job 4:3–4.) When Job lost his family, his businesses, and all his wealth, he reminisced about his life when it was good. He reminded his friends that he "delivered the poor that cried, and the fatherless, and him that had none to help him. The blessing of him that was ready to perish came upon me: and I caused the widow's heart to sing for joy. . . . I was eyes to the blind, and feet was I to the lame. I was a father to the poor. . . . And I brake the jaws of the wicked, and plucked the spoil out of his teeth." (Job 29:12–17.)

Job would have been a good home teacher.

Contemporaries of Job admired him and sought counsel with him. Job's success as a businessman, rancher, and farmer made him prominent in the eyes of his neighbors and friends. His genuine concern for the welfare of others was also well known. It was at the time of spiritual and physical prosperity that Job's trials began.

Satan's Influence

It is difficult for some people to accept Satan's influence in the presence of God as presented in the book of Job. One teacher proposed that Job's trials were not satanic but priesthood trials. She read to her class: "And the days of the children of men were prolonged, according to the will of God, that they might repent while in the flesh; wherefore, their state became a state of probation, and their time was lengthened, according to the commandments which the Lord God gave unto the children of men." (2 Nephi 2:21.) This verse points out that mortality is a state of probation in which men and women are tried and tested. Other scriptures also substantiate what this teacher taught about man's mortality. Mormon, while abridging the plates which later became the Book of Mormon, wrote about the "greater things" revealed by Christ to the Nephites: "I was about to write them [the greater things], all which were engraven upon the plates of Nephi, but the Lord forbade it, saying: I will try the faith of my people." (3 Nephi 26:11.)

Mormon's son, Moroni, wrote that man will be tried as he seeks God in faith. He wrote, "Dispute not because ye see not, for ye receive no witness until after the trial of your faith." (Ether 12:6.) Those who seek to know God through faith and obedience will be tried before they will receive a witness. While Brigham Young was preparing the Saints at Winter Quarters, Nebraska, to cross the plains in 1847, the Lord revealed to him, "My people must be tried in all things, that they may be prepared to receive the glory that I have for them, even the glory of Zion; and he that will not bear chastisement is not worthy of my kingdom." (D&C 136:31.) These four scriptures show that man is on earth to be proven. We prove ourselves through physical, mental, emotional, and spiritual trials.

Satan is portrayed in scripture in two different ways. First, he is a usurper. In our premortal life when our Father in Heaven presented his plan for the salvation and exaltation of his children, Lucifer responded, "Behold, here am I, send me, I will be thy son, and I will redeem all mankind, that one soul shall not be lost, and surely I will do it; wherefore give me thine honor." (Moses 4:1.) Satan wanted to deprive men and women of their agency, and he sought to take God's place by demanding his honor. The scriptures teach that Lucifer rebelled against God and was banished from the presence of God. He became Satan, "the devil, the father of all lies, to deceive and to blind men, and to lead them captive at his will, even as many as would not hearken unto my voice." (Moses 4:4.)

Second, Satan is a deceiver. In his encounter with Eve in the Garden of Eden, he said, "Yea, hath God said—Ye shall not eat of every tree of the garden? . . . And the woman said . . . We may eat of the fruit of the trees of the garden; But of the fruit of the tree which thou beholdest in the midst of the garden, God hath said—Ye shall not eat of it, neither shall ye touch it, lest ye die." Satan said to her, "Ye shall not surely die; for God doth know that in the day ye eat thereof, then your eyes shall be opened, and ye shall be as gods, knowing good and evil." (Moses 4:7–12.) Thus Satan tries to destroy man through manipulation and deception, for he wants that "all men might be miserable like unto himself." (2 Nephi 2:25–27.)

Each time Satan appears in holy writ he deceives those with whom he has contact. Job's trials were not confrontations with Satan but were natural or man-made. There is no evidence in the book of Job that he was enticed or deceived by Satan. Rather, Job's actions demonstrate a complete trust in God, even though his personal world collapsed. Rowley said that Job's "innocent suffering" enriched his life because in his suffering he had "fellowship with God."[4]

Trial 1: Job Lost All His Possessions

At the height of his prosperity, Job received news of economic and family setbacks that shocked him. Four servants reported to him that the Sabeans had stolen the asses, fire from heaven had consumed the sheep, the Chaldeans had taken the camels, and a "wind from the wilderness" had caused his eldest son's home to collapse where his children were feasting. All of the children were killed, along with many servants and employees. (Job 1:14–19.)

These natural and manmade disasters caused his economic and personal world to collapse. Job's reaction to these calamities reveals his character. "Job arose, and rent his mantle, and shaved his head, and fell down upon the ground, and worshipped, And said, Naked came I out of my mother's womb, and naked shall I return thither: the Lord gave, and the Lord hath taken away; blessed be the name of the Lord. In all this Job sinned not, nor charged God foolishly." (Job 1:20–22.)

Job's loss of material wealth did not cause him to lose his perspective. Even the tragic deaths of his ten children did not cause him to turn from God.

Trial 2: Physical Affliction

Job's ordeals did not diminish with the loss of his property and family. Disease racked his body, and he was smitten with boils from the "sole of his foot unto the crown" of his head. (Job 2:7.) Job was so miserable that he took a potsherd (a broken piece of pottery or glass) and sat down among the ashes. (Job 2:8.) He became an outcast. Society no longer accepted him, and he took refuge with the lepers and other diseased persons on the refuse heaps outside the town.[5] Job described his physical condition: "My flesh is clothed with worms and clods of dust; my skin is broken, and become loathsome." (Job 7:5.) His physical pain caused him mental anguish. He often could not sleep, and when he did, nightmares plagued him. (Job 7:4, 13–15.) Some feel that Job had elephantiasis, because boils are one of the symptoms.[6]

Job's wife told him to "curse God and die." (Job 2:9.) But Job refused to blame God for his suffering. (Job 2:10.)

Trial 3: Job's Friends

One key to interpreting Job's relationship with his three friends — Eliphaz the Temanite, Bildad the Shuhite, and Zophar the Naamathite — is in the Doctrine and Covenants. During the winter of 1838–39, the Prophet Joseph Smith spent about six months in Liberty Jail in Missouri. After being confined for almost four and one-half months, the Prophet received three revelations, which were later published as sections 121, 122, and 123 of the Doctrine and Covenants. The Lord referred to Joseph's situation and compared him to Job: "Thou art not yet as Job; thy friends do not contend against thee, neither charge thee with transgression, as they did Job." (D&C 121:10.) In the Old Testament account, Job's three friends met and decided to visit him. According to the text, their purpose was "to mourn with him, and to comfort him." (Job 2:11.) But the Doctrine and Covenants suggests that they came to contend against him.

When they first saw Job he was suffering so much and was so disfigured that they "knew him not, they lifted up their voice, and wept; and they rent every one his mantle, and sprinkled dust upon their heads toward heaven." (Job 2:12.) They sat by his side and mourned with him for "seven days and seven nights, and none spake a word unto him: for they saw that his grief was very great." (Job 2:13.) They were troubled by his affliction, and they didn't know what to say.

After a while, however, they found their tongues and had much to say to Job. Most of the chapters in Job relate to these conversations. A cycle occurs between chapters 4 and 32 in which each of Job's friends takes a turn speaking to him. After each one finishes, Job answers him. Eliphaz and Bildad each address Job three times; Zophar argues with him twice. That number leads some scholars to believe that part of the book of Job is missing, namely, Zophar's last speech. A youth, Elihu, who is silent during the first thirty-one chapters, criticizes his elders from chapters 32 through 37. Elihu neither adds to nor takes away from our understanding of Job. I will examine the so-called "comforting words" of each of the three friends and then discuss Job's response to them.

Eliphaz, the Temanite. Eliphaz began his remarks with a philosophical approach about mortality: "Man is born unto trouble, as the

sparks fly upward. . . . happy is the man whom God correcteth: therefore despise not thou the chastening of the Almighty. . . . Man that is
born of a woman is of few days, and full of trouble." (Job 5:7, 17; 14:1.)
He reminded Job that man is born on the earth to be tried and tested
by God; therefore, Job ought to be content because his trials show that
God is mindful of him.

Comforting words became harsh accusations during his second
speech, however. Eliphaz said to Job, "Thou castest off fear, and re-
strainest prayer before God." (Job 15:4.) Here Eliphaz accused him of
failing to worship God and of neglecting to keep the commandments.
Later he told Job that "the wicked man travaileth with pain all his days,
and the number of years is hidden to the oppressor." (Job 15:20.) In
his third speech Eliphaz explained to Job why Job was a wicked man.
He reasoned: "Trouble and anguish shall make him afraid . . . For he
[a wicked man] stretcheth out his hand against God, and strengtheneth
himself against the Almighty. . . . He dwelleth in desolate cities, and in
houses which no man inhabiteth, which are ready to become heaps.
He shall not be rich." (Job 15:24–25, 28–29.) Eliphaz logically explained
that wicked men do not prosper. Job had lost all his possessions and
business; therefore, Job was a wicked man.

Bildad, the Shuhite. Bildad began his "comforting words" by
directly accusing Job of sin: "If thou wert pure and upright; surely now
he would awake for thee, and make the habitation of thy righteousness
prosperous." (Job 8:6.) Bildad continued his accusations with, "Behold,
God will not cast away a perfect man, neither will he help the evil
doers." (Job 8:20.) When Job refused to admit to any sin, Bildad resorted
to the definition that indisputably proved Job a sinner. According to
Bildad, a wicked man's "roots shall be dried up beneath, and above
shall his branch be cut off. His remembrance shall perish from the
earth, and he shall have no name in the street. He shall be driven from
light into darkness, and chased out of the world. He shall neither have
son nor nephew among his people, nor any remaining in his dwellings. . . . Surely such are the dwellings of the wicked, and this is the
place of him that knoweth not God." (Job 18:16–19, 21.) According to
the Old Testament the greatest curse that could come upon a man
anciently was to have no descendants to carry on the family name.
Bildad reasoned that Job was a sinner because he had lost all his
children.

Zophar, the Naamathite. From his opening remarks Zophar attacked Job: "Should thy lies make men hold their peace? and when thou mockest, shall no man make thee ashamed? . . . Know therefore that God exacteth of thee less than thine iniquity deserveth." (Job 11:3, 6.) Zophar accused Job of lying to them when Job insisted that he had not sinned. (Job 20:11.)

Zophar returned to the theme introduced by Eliphaz: Wicked men do not prosper. (Job 20:27–29.) "His bones are full of the sin of his youth, which shall lie down with him in the dust." (Job 20:11.) Finally, in exasperation Zophar told Job, "The triumphing of the wicked is short, and the joy of the hypocrite but for a moment." (Job 20:5.) Zophar reasoned that Job was a liar and a hypocrite. His former wealth was little more than fool's gold and not a testimony of his once being righteous.

Each of Job's friends turned on him. Outright malice may not have been their intent, but it was the result.

Job's Reaction to His Friends

Job insisted that he had done nothing wrong and that he was not guilty of sin. "Return, I pray you," he said, "let it not be iniquity; yea, return again, my righteousness." (Job 6:29.) "Thou knowest that I am not wicked." (Job 10:7.) Countering the attack of Zophar and Eliphaz, Job insisted that wicked men do prosper. "The wicked live," he argued, "become old, yea, are mighty in power. Their seed is established in their sight with them, and their offspring before their eyes. Their houses are safe from fear, neither is the rod of God upon them. Their bull gendereth, and faileth not; their cow calveth, and casteth not her calf. They send forth their little ones like a flock, and their children dance. They take the timbrel and harp, and rejoice at the sound of the organ. They spend their days in wealth, and in a moment go down to the grave. Therefore they say unto God, Depart from us; for we desire not the knowledge of thy ways." (Job 21:7–14.)

Stressing his righteousness, Job reasoned: "I have understanding as well as you; I am not inferior to you. . . . I am as one mocked of his neighbor." (Job 12:3–4.) He emphasized his trust in God and said to his friends, "I will maintain mine own ways before him." (Job 13:15.) If the situation were reversed, he said, "I also could speak as ye do: if your soul were in my soul's stead, I could heap up words against you, and shake mine head at you. But I would strengthen you with my mouth, and the moving of my lips should assuage your grief." (Job

16:4–5.) Finally he said to them, "I have heard many such things: *miserable comforters are ye all.*" (Job 16:2; italics added.)

Three Modern Friends

In 1971 the doctors diagnosed my cancer. They explained that it had spread to my left lung and that I must go to Stanford University Medical Center where they would begin treating the tumor with chemotherapy. For eight days I vomited continually. During this time my body broke out in open sores, my tongue swelled, and my mouth broke out in ulcers. For several weeks I could barely talk or chew my food.

During this time my wife and I discussed my situation. One evening I said to her, "If we're trying to prolong my life and our Father in Heaven wants me in the spirit world, then we might be doing the wrong thing." She agreed and asked what I proposed. I explained that we ought to have a family fast. I explained to her we should not request that I get well but rather to know our Father in Heaven's will.

Arrangements were made, and our home teacher and bishop came to give me a special blessing. At one point in the blessing the bishop said, "I bless you with peace. It is so strong that I can feel it filling your whole being. At this moment I have peace too. I bless you that your body will have power to mend itself." Later my wife and I pondered the truly marvelous and significant blessing I had received.

This blessing had an interesting effect upon my close friends, who asked me about it. I told them that I remembered the bishop saying, "Your body will have power to mend itself."

One person said to me, "Of course you'll stay on the drugs?" I answered, "Well, I am not sure if that is what the blessing meant." He responded, "What are you going to do when you get to the spirit world and the Lord looks at you and says, 'What are you doing here? You're forty years too early'?"

Another good friend said, "That's great. Your body will resurrect your spirit, and you'll be exalted in the celestial kingdom." He had forgotten Alma's teachings that the spirit resurrects the body. (See Alma 39, 41.)

The third person questioned, "Are you really a man of faith, or are you afraid of the chemotherapy because it makes you sick?" Even though these people meant well, their counsel undermined the purity of the blessing I had received, until I became confused and lost the spirit of peace that had been with me. I did not know what to do. My friends meant well. They would have done nothing to harm me, but their lack of understanding brought confusion instead of peace.

The Victory of Faith

Like many people who are afflicted with disease or who lose their business or members of their family, Job strove to understand the reasons behind his calamities: "I will not refrain my mouth; I will speak in the anguish of my spirit; I will complain in the bitterness of my soul." (Job 7:11.) He wanted to know the purpose of his suffering and his purpose in living when he said, "I am full of confusion; therefore see thou mine affliction." (Job 10:15.) His suffering became so acute that he said, "My soul is weary of my life." (Job 10:1.)

Reaching this point of despair, he turned to God, whom he addressed, "Though he slay me, yet will I trust in him." On another occasion he addressed his maker exclaiming, "I have sinned; what shall I do unto thee, O thou preserver of men? Why hast thou set me as a mark against thee, so that I am a burden to myself? And why dost thou not pardon my transgression, and take away mine iniquity? for now shall I sleep in the dust; and thou shalt seek me in the morning, but I shall not be." (Job 7:20–21.)

Job pleaded with God continually: "I will say unto God, Do not condemn me; shew me wherefore thou contendest with me. . . . Oh that I knew where I might find him! that I might come even to his seat! . . . Will he plead against me with his great power? No; but he would put strength in me. . . . But he knoweth the way that I take: when he hath tried me, I shall come forth as gold." (Job 10:1–2; 23:3, 6, 10.)

Job wanted the Lord to answer him, so he continued to pray: "My desire is, that the Almighty would answer me, and that mine adversary had written a book. Surely I would take it upon my shoulder, and bind it as a crown to me. I would declare unto him the number of my steps; as a prince would I go near unto him." (Job 31:35–37.) Perhaps one of the greatest evidences of the conviction Job had of his own righteousness was his lack of fear to account to his Father in Heaven.

Job Accounted to His Maker

James gave the key to Job's future when he wrote, "Behold, we count them happy which endure. Ye have heard of the patience of Job, and have seen the end of the Lord; that the Lord is very pitiful, and of tender mercy." (James 5:11.)

Job received his wish:

"The Lord answered Job out of the whirlwind, and said,

"Who is this that darkeneth counsel by words without knowledge?

"Gird up now thy loins like a man; for I will demand of thee, and answer thou me.

"Where wast thou when I laid the foundations of the earth? declare, if thou hast understanding.

"Who hath laid the measures thereof, if thou knowest? or who hath stretched the line upon it?

"Whereupon are the foundations thereof fastened? or who laid the corner stone thereof;

"When the morning stars sang together, and all the sons of God shouted for joy? . . .

"Hast thou commanded the morning since thy days; and caused the dayspring to know his place . . . ?" (Job 38:1–7, 12.)

"Hast thou entered into the springs of the sea? or hast thou walked in the search of the depth?

"Have the gates of death been opened unto thee? or hast thou seen the doors of the shadow of death?

"Hast thou perceived the breadth of the earth? declare if thou knowest it all.

"Where is the way where light dwelleth? . . .

"Hast thou entered into the treasures of the snow? or hast thou seen the treasures of the hail . . . ?" (Job 38:16–19, 22.)

"By what way is the light parted, which scattereth the east wind upon the earth?

"Who hath divided a watercourse for the overflowing of waters, or a way for the lightning of thunder;

"To cause it to rain on the earth, where no man is; on the wilderness, wherein there is no man;

"To satisfy the desolate and waste ground; and to cause the bud of the tender herb to spring forth?" (Job 38:24–27.)

"Knowest thou the ordinances of heaven? canst thou set the dominion thereof in the earth?

"Canst thou lift up thy voice to the clouds, that abundance of waters may cover thee? (Job 38:33–34.)

Job insisted that he was not wise enough to answer these questions.

He said to the Lord: "I am vile; what shall I answer thee? I will lay mine hand upon my mouth. Once have I spoken; but I will not answer: yea, twice; but I will proceed no further." (Job 40:4–5.)

Later, however, as his understanding and confidence in God grew, Job declared: "I know that thou canst do everything, and that no thought can be withholden from thee. . . . therefore have I uttered that I understood not; things too wonderful for me, which I knew not. Hear, I beseech thee, and I will speak. . . . I have heard of thee by the hearing of the ear: but *now mine eye seeth thee*. Wherefore I abhor myself, and repent in dust and ashes. (Job 42:2–6; italics added.)

Job found himself in the presence of God. His victory was complete.

Job's experience with God was like that of the brother of Jared in the Book of Mormon. The brother of Jared, after building the ships the Lord had commanded him to build, approached God with a request for light to light the vessels. God said to the brother of Jared, "What will ye that I should do that ye may have light in your vessels? For behold, ye cannot have windows, for they will be dashed in pieces; neither shall ye take fire with you, for ye shall not go by the light of fire." (Ether 2:24.)

The brother of Jared went to Mount Shelem and "did molten out of a rock sixteen small stones; and they were white and clear, even as transparent glass." (Ether 3:1.)

Again he approached the Lord in prayer, saying:

"O Lord, and do not be angry with thy servant because of his weakness before thee; for we know that thou art holy and dwellest in the heavens, and that we are unworthy before thee; because of the fall our natures have become evil continually; nevertheless, O Lord, thou hast given us a commandment that we must call upon thee, that from thee we may receive according to our desires. . . .

"O Lord, . . . suffer not that they shall go forth across this raging deep in darkness; but behold these things which I have molten out of the rock.

"And I know, O Lord, that thou hast all power, and can do whatsoever thou wilt for the benefit of man; therefore touch these stones, O Lord, with thy finger, and prepare them that they may shine forth in darkness; and they shall shine forth unto us in the vessels which we have prepared, that we may have light while we shall cross the sea." (Ether 3:2–4.)

The Lord yielded to the brother of Jared's request and touched the stones. "And the veil was taken from off the eyes of the brother of Jared, and he saw the finger of the Lord; and it was as the finger of a man, like unto flesh and blood; and the brother of Jared fell down before the Lord, for he was struck with fear."

When the Lord saw that the brother of Jared had fallen he asked him, "Why hast thou fallen?"

The brother of Jared replied, "I saw the finger of the Lord, and I feared lest he should smite me; for I knew not that the Lord had flesh and blood."

God asked, "Sawest thou more than this?" The brother of Jared answered, "Nay; Lord, show thyself unto me."

The Lord responded with one final question, "Believest thou the words which I shall speak?"

The brother of Jared answered, "Yea, Lord, I know that thou speakest the truth, for thou art a God of truth, and canst not lie." Once he had said these words, the veil was withdrawn and the brother of Jared found himself in the presence of the great Jehovah, who said to him, "Because thou knowest these things ye are redeemed from the fall; therefore ye are brought back into my presence; therefore I show myself unto you." (Ether 3:6–13.)

Job's experience, like that of the brother of Jared's, redeemed him from the fall, and he found himself in the presence of Jesus Christ.

Conclusion

Job was a righteous man. He suffered economic, physical, social, cultural, emotional, and spiritual trials. But through all his afflictions, he came to know God. Moreover, he came to know himself, and he became secure in his relationship with his peers.

Like Job, during my years of pain I have learned things about myself that are too special to live without. Do not misunderstand—my own sufferings are in no way comparable to Job's, but I believe that Job is the friend of everyone who knows pain. I believe that by studying the life of Job, a person can receive courage. I find in Job an overwhelming desire to understand God and to know God. Through Job's life I have learned that a person can know peace. His central message is that the road to perfection takes patience and implicit trust in God, no matter what the temporal circumstances. Reliance on God brings strength to an individual in times of trial, which is an important part of this life.

My life, like Job's life, has been one miracle after another. And yet, while I have written of miracles, I also realize that for some there has been no miracle. During the years I have lived with cancer I have met children who have lost a parent, wives who have lost a husband, husbands who have lost a wife, and parents who have lost a child. They always ask, "Where is my miracle?"

Part of the answer to their question lies in scripture. The Savior instructed priesthood holders to bless the sick and to "pray for and lay their hands upon them in my name; and *if they die they shall die unto me*, and *if they live they shall live unto me. . . .* And again, it shall come to pass that he that hath faith in me to be healed, and is *not appointed unto death, shall be healed.*" (D&C 42:44, 48; italics added.) We must never forget that each of us has a divine mission. President Kimball wrote: "God controls our lives, guides and blesses us, but gives us our agency. We may live our lives in accordance with his plan for us, or we may foolishly shorten or terminate them. I am positive in my mind that the Lord has planned our destiny."[7]

NOTES

1. H. H. Rowley, *The Growth of the Old Testament* (London: Hutchinson University Library, 1966), p. 138.

2. "The Age of the Patriarchs, 1967–1606 B.C.," *The Chronological Bible*, ed. Ed Reese (Np.: 1977), pp. i, 19–54.

3. Letter to Stewart Miller, Dec. 7, 1981.

4. Rowley, *Growth of the Old Testament*, pp. 141–42.

5. Keith H. Meservy, "Job: Yet Will I Trust in Him," *1978 Sperry Symposium on the Old Testament* (Provo, Utah: Brigham Young University Religious Studies Center, 1978), p. 5; see also *The Westminster Study Edition of the Holy Bible* (Philadelphia: Westminster Press), p. 641 n.

6. Meservy, "Job," p. 5; see also *Westminster Study Edition of the Holy Bible*, p. 641.

7. Spencer W. Kimball, "Tragedy or Destiny," *Improvement Era*, Mar. 1966, p. 216.

CHAPTER EIGHT

The Old Testament, a Witness for Jesus Christ

Daniel H. Ludlow

Brigham Young University

Before I begin my remarks on the subject of this symposium, perhaps it would be appropriate to say just a few words about the fine teacher and close friend after whom the symposium is named. It was more than one-third of a century ago, 1955 to be exact, that I first joined the faculty of Brigham Young University and met Dr. Sperry. I had just completed my master's and doctoral studies at Indiana University and Columbia University when I decided to accept the invitation of President Ernest L. Wilkinson to become a member of this faculty rather than to return to my position at Utah State University, where I had served on the faculty for five years and where I had been a student for four years before. My only earlier visits to the BYU campus had been to participate in high school and college debate tournaments.

The one name that was really familiar to me at that time among the faculty of the Division of Religion, as it was then called, was the name Sidney B. Sperry. Although I had never personally met Dr. Sperry, I still remember my feelings of inadequacy and concern when I entered a room in the Joseph Smith Building for my first faculty meeting. Several of the faculty were in the room when I entered, and one of them immediately left the cluster of teachers and came to me, shook my hand, and said, "You must be Brother Ludlow. I am Sidney Sperry. I have heard a great deal about you and am anxious to become better acquainted with you." That cordial welcome has always meant a great deal to me, and I remember it with deep feeling and fondness.

Subsequently I had many visits with Dr. Sperry in his office, and during his illness near the end of his life, I visited in his home on several occasions and became acquainted with the warm and friendly spirit of Sister Sperry. Their descendants have every reason to be proud of their noble heritage.

Now to my assigned subject.

Although the Old Testament as a witness for Jesus Christ will certainly be the main thrust of this paper, the Old Testament is also a witness for other things in other areas. For example, the Old Testament is also a witness for the gospel plan of progression and salvation and a witness for the other scriptures, especially for the Book of Mormon. In other words, the Old Testament is a key part of God's system of witnesses.

In Deuteronomy 19:15 we read, "At the mouth of two witnesses, or at the mouth of three witnesses" shall matters "be established." Matthew 18:16 states, "In the mouth of two or three witnesses every word may be established." And in 2 Corinthians 13:1 we read, "In the mouth of two or three witnesses shall every word be established." As we hope to establish in this discussion, the Old Testament is a very important witness in establishing the *words* and the *truths* of our Heavenly Father.

You should know at the very beginning of our discussion that I am firmly convinced the Old Testament is one of the greatest books on the face of the earth today. It is indeed the book of books.

The Old Testament is the basic scripture for the Jewish people, and — together with the New Testament — is the basic scripture for all Christians. So far as Latter-day Saints are concerned, the Old Testament ranks with the New Testament, the Book of Mormon, the Doctrine and Covenants, and the Pearl of Great Price as important scripture that our Heavenly Father has given us for our blessing and for which we each will be held accountable at our day of judgment.

As you know, the Old Testament is the focus of study for adults every fourth year in the Sunday School Gospel Doctrine classes, the Relief Society Spiritual Living lessons, and the Melchizedek Priesthood personal study guides of the Church. Of course, the fact that the Old Testament is emphasized every fourth year in the adult curriculum programs does not mean that we should study the Old Testament *only* during those years. The First Presidency has told us that we should be reading in the Bible daily.

Reasons to Read the Old Testament

We should read the Old Testament consistently and thoroughly for many reasons, including the following:

1. It is a commandment of God. The Lord and his prophets have

instructed us to read, study, and ponder all of the scriptures available to us. That should be sufficient for us to read the Old Testament. When Adam was questioned about why he did a particular thing, he replied simply, "I know not, save the Lord commanded me." (Moses 5:6.)

2. The Old Testament contains many principles of salvation and provides many examples of righteousness. Stories of faith, devotion, diligence, perseverance, and bravery are in the Old Testament. These, in turn, have inspired and illuminated much of the best literature in the world. The heroic attributes and characteristics of many of these role models—Abraham, Jacob, Joseph, Moses, Elijah, Job, and Daniel, to name a few—are sorely needed in today's world. President Spencer W. Kimball stated: "To know the patriarchs and prophets of ages past and their faithfulness under stress and temptation and persecution strengthens [us and our] resolves."[1]

Learning and living the principles of righteousness contained in the Old Testament would help us solve many problems we face today. In the scriptures the Lord teaches us correct principles, and then he expects us to use our free agency in living the truths of these principles so we can receive the blessings associated with such obedience. In the Old Testament, the Lord promised his covenant people that if they lived the principles of righteousness contained in the scriptures, he would bless them with "the rain of your land in his due season," "send grass in thy fields for thy cattle," and "prolong your days in the land." (Deut. 11:14, 15, 9.) Similar blessings await us today.

3. The Old Testament is a strong witness of the divinity of Jesus Christ. Indeed, the Old Testament was essentially the scripture that was available to the Jewish people at the time Jesus Christ was upon the earth and admonished them: "Search the scriptures . . . they are they which testify of me." (John 5:39.)

Statements of Leaders

Several leaders, both political and religious, have spoken of the worth of the Bible, of which the Old Testament is a vital part.

Abraham Lincoln called the Bible "the best gift God has ever given to man."[2]

When President Ronald Reagan proclaimed 1983 to be the Year of the Bible, he encouraged "all citizens, each in his or her own way, to reexamine and rediscover its priceless and timeless message."[3]

The following message was prepared by the First Presidency of the Church: "We commend to all people everywhere the daily reading, pondering and heeding of the divine truths of the Holy Bible. . . . When it is read reverently and prayerfully, the Holy Bible becomes a priceless volume, converting the soul to righteousness. . . . As we read the scripture, we avail ourselves of the better part of this world's literature."[4]

Brigham Young stated: "The doctrines contained in the Bible will lift to a superior condition all who observe them; they will impart to them knowledge, wisdom, charity, fill them with compassion and cause them to feel after the wants of those who are in distress, or in painful or degraded circumstances. They who observe the precepts contained in the Scriptures will be just and true and virtuous and peaceable at home and abroad. Follow out the doctrines of the Bible, and men will make splendid husbands, women excellent wives, and children will be obedient; they will make families happy and the nations wealthy and happy and lifted up above the things of this life."[5]

As Latter-day Saints, we are all well acquainted with the statement of the Prophet Joseph Smith that helps explain the eighth article of faith: "We believe the Bible to be the word of God as far as it is translated correctly. The Prophet said: "I believe the Bible as it read when it came from the pen of the original writers. Ignorant translators, careless transcribers, or designing and corrupt priests have committed many errors."[6]

This qualifying statement by the Prophet Joseph Smith should not be interpreted to mean that we do not accept the Bible as inspired scripture from the Lord. Brigham Young stated: "The Bible is true. It may not all have been translated aright, and many precious things may have been rejected in the compilation and translation of the Bible; but we understand . . . that if all the sayings and doings of the Savior had been written, the world could not contain them. I will say that the world could not understand them. . . . the Bible, when it is understood, is one of the simplest books in the world, for, as far as it is translated correctly, it is nothing but truth, and in truth there is no mystery save to the ignorant. The revelations of the Lord to his creatures are adapted to the lowest capacity, and they bring life and salvation to all who are willing to receive them."[7]

Another statement by Brigham Young on the value of the Bible in learning the truths of the gospel has had a great influence on me: "In all my teachings, I have taught the gospel from the Old and New Testaments. I found therein every doctrine, and the proof of every

doctrine, the Latter-day Saints believe in, as far as I know, therefore
I do not refer to the Book of Mormon as often as I otherwise should.
There may be some doctrines about which little is said in the Bible,
but they are all couched therein, and I believe the doctrines because
they are true, and I have taught them because they are calculated to
save the children of men."[8]

Let me repeat a key sentence from this statement by Brigham
Young: *"I found therein [in the Bible] every doctrine and the proof of every
doctrine the Latter-day Saints believe in, as far as I know."*

I love the Book of Mormon, and I love to teach the doctrines of
the gospel from the Book of Mormon. But after reading this statement
from Brigham Young, I decided to put the statement to a test. I reread
the Book of Mormon, noting and recording every basic, essential doctrine of the gospel that was mentioned in that glorious scripture. Then
I reread the Bible, and placed appropriate references from the Bible
next to the doctrines I had listed from the Book of Mormon. There
was at least one biblical reference for each doctrine from the Book of
Mormon, *without exception.* I challenge you to try that same exercise
with the Book of Mormon and the Bible. Not only would it help you
in reading these two books again, but you will obtain a greater knowledge of the gospel and a greater appreciation of the Bible.

The Old Testament Is Not Read

Despite these and other similar statements on the importance of
the Bible, a modern evangelist has called it the "great unread book."
Also, a popular book about the Bible written by Bruce Barton was given
the apt title: *The Book Nobody Knows.*

Certainly the Old Testament is not being given much attention
among Christian churches today, with but few exceptions. Many of the
Jewish people have also deserted the Old Testament, either through
neglect or by a preference for other books containing their oral or
written traditions. Even among Latter-day Saints, the Old Testament
is perhaps the least read and the least understood and appreciated of
all our standard works.

Some of you may have heard me mention a study made for the
Church several years ago by a professional polling institution of Shen-
andoah, Iowa, called Central Surveys, Incorporated. One purpose of the
study was to determine the extent to which members of the Church
had read the various scriptures. The Church members surveyed were

asked the following questions concerning each of the five standard works of the Church:

"To what extent have you read _____" and the name of a particular book of scripture was listed. For example, the participants were asked, "To what extent have you read the Old Testament?" The participants responded with the most accurate of five possible responses:

"I have read this scripture completely through at least once."

"I have probably read half of this scripture but have not read all of it."

"I have read some of this scripture but probably have not read half of it."

"I have not read any of this scripture."

"I choose not to answer this question."

Most of the members of the Church who were interviewed answered the questions concerning the Old Testament with one of the first three responses, indicating they had read at least part of this scripture. But relatively few of them were able to respond that they had read the Old Testament *completely through* at least once.

Reasons for Not Reading the Old Testament

Why is it that many, if not most, of us have never bothered to read the Old Testament completely through?

One excuse I have heard is that the Old Testament is "simply or primarily a history book about a people who lived a long time ago, with strange customs, in a land that is far away." It is true the Old Testament contains history; but it is not *simply* or *primarily* a history book. It is much, much, much more than that. In fact, not one of the seventeen topics dealt with in this symposium is simply or primarily history.

Another excuse is that it is "too hard to understand." When questioned further, the person might make such observations as "it is too long," or "the language is too difficult," or "it doesn't seem very relevant today." Although the first two of these excuses might be based on some facts, they are still *excuses*, and we should recognize them as such. The last excuse isn't at all true if you concentrate on the basic doctrines and gospel teachings in the book. There is such a thing as basic, fundamental truth, and truth is eternal. Thus the truths contained in the Old Testament apply just as much today as they applied at the time they were given thousands of years ago.

How to Understand the Old Testament

Actually the Old Testament is not an extremely hard or difficult book to understand. It is a relatively simple book if you understand how and why the book is put together the way it is. Remember the words from Brigham Young: "The Bible, *when it is understood*, is one of the simplest books in the world, for, as far as it is translated correctly, it is nothing but truth, and in truth there is no mystery *save to the ignorant*."⁹ This statement gives us a clue to understanding the Old Testament: We must remove our *ignorance* concerning it. In other words, we must study and ponder the book, become acquainted with its makeup and format, and learn its doctrines and teachings.

A statement in the Book of Mormon also gives us a hint about how we should study the scriptures. In Alma 17:2 we read that the sons of Mosiah "had waxed strong in the knowledge of the truth; for they were men of a sound understanding and they had *searched* the scriptures *diligently*, that they might know the word of God." (Alma 17:2; italics added.)

Note again the principle: The scriptures must be *searched diligently*.

The reason why the scriptures should be searched diligently is in the statement by the Savior in John 5:39, "They are they which testify of me."

The Scriptures Testify of Jesus Christ

The requirement is clear: We should search the scriptures diligently so we might have a stronger testimony of Jesus Christ.

Now let's see how the Old Testament is a key scripture to learn of the mission of Jesus Christ. It includes many statements and prophecies of Jesus Christ as the great Jehovah of the Old Testament, prophecies concerning the life, mission, and atonement of Jesus Christ on the earth as recorded in the New Testament, prophecies relating to events on the earth immediately preceding his second coming, and still other prophecies relating to his millennial reign as King of Kings and Lord of Lords. The strength of multiple witnesses in the Old Testament of the total mission of Jesus Christ can prove to be a weakness, however, if the reader does not recognize which prophecies were fulfilled during Old Testament times, which were fulfilled during the New Testament period, which are being fulfilled at the present time, and which are still to be fulfilled in the future.

For example, one reason the Jewish people as a nation did not accept Jesus Christ as the Messiah at his first coming was that they felt some of the prophecies pertaining to his second coming should have been fulfilled at that time. Some felt he should have led the Israelites to victory over the Romans and established at his first advent his great millennial reign of peace and righteousness. No wonder Peter warned us: "Knowing this first, that no prophecy of the scripture is of any private interpretation. For the prophecy came not in old time by the will of man: but holy men of God spake as they were moved by the Holy Ghost." (2 Peter 1:20–21.)

Thus, one reason we should search the Old Testament diligently is so we can truly understand it. Then, and only then, will it become "one of the simplest books in the world," as Brigham Young told us.

The Old Testament Testifies of Jesus Christ

The Old Testament contains the essential things the world needs to know to gain a testimony of Jesus Christ and of his gospel. A serious, diligent study of the Old Testament will reveal the many essential doctrines the prophets of ancient Judah knew about the birth, life, and atonement of the Messiah, the Anointed One, whom we know by the name-title Jesus Christ. I will mention very briefly a few of these essential doctrines, together with at least one key scriptural reference pertaining to each. I also suggest some titles from the Topical Guide and the Bible Dictionary that you might review for additional information and insight.

1. The Messiah would be born of a virgin.

Isaiah 7:14; see also "Jesus Christ, Birth of" in the Topical Guide and "Christ, Names of" in the Bible Dictionary.

2. The Messiah would be born in Bethlehem of Judea.

Micah 5:2; see also "Jesus Christ, Messiah" and "Jesus Christ, Prophecies about" in the Topical Guide and "Bethlehem" and "Messiah" in the Bible Dictionary.

3. The Messiah would be reared in the tribal lands assigned to Zebulun and Naphtali, which includes Nazareth and the Galilee.

Isaiah 9:1–2; see also "Jesus Christ, Messiah" and "Jesus Christ, Prophecies about" in the Topical Guide and "Galilee," "Messiah," "Naphtali," "Nazareth," and "Zebulun" in the Bible Dictionary.

4. The Messiah would have power over the physical elements of

the earth, including the physical body. Thus He could heal the sick, cause the blind to see, and so forth.

Isaiah 42:5–7; see also "Jesus Christ, Mission of" and "Jesus Christ, Power of" in the Topical Guide and "Messiah" in the Bible Dictionary.

5. The Messiah would bear the sin of the world and the iniquities and transgressions of many.

Isaiah 50:6; 53:4–6; see also "Iniquity," "Jesus Christ, Atonement through," "Jesus Christ, Savior," "Sin," and "Transgress, Transgression" in the Topical Guide and "Christ, Names of" and "Messiah" in the Bible Dictionary.

6. The Messiah would be "be lifted up on a tree" (crucified) and have his hands and feet pierced."

Psalm 22:16; Zechariah 12:10; 13:6; see also "Jesus Christ, Crucifixion of" and "Jesus Christ, Death of" in the Topical Guide and entitled "Crucifixion" in the Bible Dictionary.

7. The Messiah would be resurrected from the dead and provide resurrection for all mankind.

Job 19:25; Isaiah 25:8; 26:19; 53:12; Ezekiel 37:12; Hosea 13:14; see "Jesus Christ, Resurrection" and "Resurrection" in the Topical Guide and "Death," "Messiah," and "Resurrection" in the Bible Dictionary.

The Old Testament teachings on the resurrection of the Messiah are particularly important as the resurrection of Jesus Christ is the proof of his divinity.

In addition to these essential teachings associated directly with the atonement of Jesus Christ, the Old Testament includes many other interesting and confirming prophecies about his life on earth. Again, I shall mention briefly only a few, with a related scripture or two:

1. The Messiah would be of the loins of David; indeed, the title "Son of David" would be one of his sacred titles.

2 Samuel 7:13; Psalms 89:4; 132:17; Isaiah 9:7; 11:1; Jeremiah 23:5; 33:15.

2. The Messiah would come forth out of Egypt.
Hosea 11:1.

3. The Messiah would ride into Jerusalem on the foal of an ass.
Zechariah 9:9.

4. The Messiah would be betrayed for thirty pieces of silver.
Zechariah 11:12–13.

5. The Messiah would be with the wicked in his death. Isaiah 53:9.
6. The Messiah would be with the rich in his grave. Isaiah 53:9.
7. The Messiah would be called by many titles, including the sacred title "Son of Man," meaning "Son of Man of Holiness" or "Son of God."

If the readers of the Old Testament realized the multitudinous titles in that scripture that refer to Jesus Christ, I feel confident they would have a greater understanding and appreciation of the teachings of the Old Testament on the life, mission, and atonement of Jesus Christ. Many of these titles are listed in the Bible Dictionary under "Christ, Names of." In just this brief passage from Isaiah 54:5, "for thy Maker is thine husband; the Lord of hosts is his name; and thy Redeemer the Holy One of Israel; The God of the whole earth shall he be called," Isaiah included at least five titles referring to Jesus Christ. Notice other titles for Jesus Christ in just a few samples of the writings of Isaiah:

"Behold, a virgin shall conceive, and bear a son, and shall call His name *Immanuel*" meaning "God with us. " (Isa. 7:14; italics added.)

"For unto us a *child* is born, unto us a *son* is given: and the government shall be upon his shoulder: and his name shall be called Wonderful, Counsellor, The mighty God, The everlasting Father, The Prince of Peace." (Isa. 9:6; italics added.)

"Behold, God is my salvation . . . the Lord Jehovah is my strength and my song." (Isa. 12:2; italics added.)

"Thus saith the Lord, your redeemer, the Holy One of Israel . . . I am the Lord, your Holy One, the creator of Israel, your King." (Isa. 43:14–15.)

"Thus saith the Lord the King of Israel, and his redeemer the Lord of hosts: I am the first, and I am the last; and beside me there is no God." (Isa. 44:6.)

"All flesh shall know that I the Lord am thy Saviour and thy Redeemer, the mighty One of Jacob." (Isa. 49:26.)

The Topical Guide has more headings beginning with the words "Jesus Christ" than with any other words. These headings are all followed by scores of separate references pertaining to that particular topic. Many of these headings include a word or a term that might also be used as a title for Jesus Christ:

Jesus Christ, Advocate; . . . Creator; . . . Davidic Descent of; . . .

Exemplar; . . . Firstborn; . . . Good Shepherd; . . . Head of the Church;
. . . Jehovah; . . . Judge; . . . King; . . . Lamb of God; . . . Light of the
World; . . . Lord; . . . Mediator; . . . Messenger of the Covenant; . . .
Messiah; . . . Only Begotten Son; . . . Redeemer; . . . Rock; . . . Savior;
and . . . Son of Man.

I hope with these examples I have convinced you that the Old
Testament contains many teachings related to the important doctrine
that Jesus Christ is the Messiah, the Anointed One. Every time we
read one of the titles which refer to him we should think of him. Truly,
these scriptures are they which testify of him.

Suggestions on Studying the Old Testament

Now let me share with you a few observations concerning the
organization and format of the Old Testament.

I'm sure that you already know that the essential meaning of the
word *Bible* is "books," and as the Old Testament is part of the Bible,
it is really made up of a series of *books*. Some of the books are not
closely related to the books that precede them or follow them. Thus
the Old Testament does not always have the consistent flow of story
or chronology that might be found in some of the other scriptures.

One major purpose of the Old Testament is to lead people to Jesus
Christ and to the gospel of Jesus Christ; however, the prophecies about
Christ and the doctrines of the gospel are so frequently intertwined
with the history and daily affairs of the people that the reader might
easily become too involved with the history and miss the really essential
teachings. Again, please don't let this happen to you.

The Old Testament Contains the
Religious History of Selected Families

The Old Testament is essentially a brief synopsis of the religious
history of a series of families. To understand this history, you need to
know something about the background of the practices, traditions, beliefs, and customs of those families. Many of these "manners and customs of the Hebrews"—a term riveted in our minds through the title
of a book and a course by Dr. Sperry—will be covered in some of the
specialized discussions today. An understanding of these customs will
help you to picture these people as real people, with real challenges.

In other words, an understanding of these customs will help the Old Testament to come alive for you.

Also, you need to realize that the peoples of the Old Testament were in a relative state of apostasy during most of their history as recorded in this scripture. Thus, do not expect to find in the Old Testament the preciseness and clarity of teachings about these doctrines that you will find in the Book of Mormon. The prophet Nephi correctly noted that the teachings of the Old Testament were not always as "plain and precious" as corresponding doctrinal teachings that had been recorded on the brass plates of Laban.

Why Is It So Important to Use the Latter-day Saint Edition of the King James Version of the Bible?

Let's turn our attention to another area of study of the Old Testament: Why is it so important to use the Latter-day Saint edition of the King James Version of the Bible? I am absolutely convinced the Latter-day Saint edition of the Bible is the very best edition that has been published in modern times. Let's examine the major elements and contributions of this edition, and I believe you will soon see its great value.

Title Page. You will note from the title page and the two pages of explanatory introduction that the text of the LDS edition of the Bible is the authorized King James text, word for word and comma for comma. The LDS edition was first printed in 1979, and any printing since then should be acceptable.

Contents Page. The Contents page lists all of the thirty-nine books of the Old Testament and the twenty-seven books of the New Testament in the order the books appear in the scriptures. The Appendix includes the sections headed "Topical Guide," "Bible Dictionary," "Joseph Smith Translation," "Gazetteer," and "Maps." Each of these sections will be discussed in detail later.

Explanation Concerning Footnotes. Turn to the page headed "Explanation Concerning Footnotes." Make certain that you understand each of the major points made on this page. Note, for example, the explanations of the abbreviations used in the footnotes:

GR: An alternate translation from the Greek.

HEB: An alternate translation from the Hebrew.

IE: An explanation of idioms and difficult constructions.

JST: Joseph Smith Translation.

TG: Topical Guide.

OR: Signifies that alternate words follow to clarify the meaning of archaic English expressions.

The footnotes identified by these abbreviations are extremely important to a more complete understanding of the Old Testament. In fact, these footnotes are so important that each of them should be marked with a distinctive color, both the superscript letter in the text that leads to the footnote and the abbreviation in the footnote itself. The only exception to this marking might be the TG (Topical Guide) footnotes, because there are so many.

Let me explain this marking system further.

You will note in Genesis 1:1 that the word *created* is preceded by the small superscript letter *c*. In the footnotes on this page, Genesis 1:1 note *c* gives the abbreviation HEB with the explanation that in this instance the word *created* could also have been translated as *shaped* or *fashioned*. The content of this footnote is so important to understanding the first verse of Genesis that I mark in the same color both the superscript letter *c* in the text as well as the abbreviation HEB in the footnote. Then, when I read the text again, the marking on the superscript letter automatically leads me to the appropriate significant footnote.

All of the footnotes headed by the abbreviations GR, HEB, IE, JST, and OR are so important that *each of them* should be marked with a different color.

Cross-references in the Footnotes

The voluminous cross-references in the footnotes will lead you to related scriptures in all the standard works, not only to other references in the Old Testament and the New Testament but also to appropriate references in the Book of Mormon, the Doctrine and Covenants, and the Pearl of Great Price. If you will consistently use the cross-references, you will increase your understanding and appreciation of the great gospel plan of salvation and exaltation, and of the life, mission, and atonement of Jesus Christ, because these are the common messages of all the standard works.

The footnotes are at the very heart and core of anyone's diligent study of the Old Testament.

Chapter Headings

As you know, the chapter headings were especially prepared for the LDS edition of the Bible by General Authorities who were serving as prophets, seers, and revelators. The headings were then carefully reviewed by members of the Scriptures Publication Committee, headed by three members of the Quorum of the Twelve Apostles and by the members of the Correlation Executive Committee of the Church. In a sense, these chapter headings might be considered the closest thing to scripture in the Church outside of the text of the scriptures themselves. I urge you to read each of these chapter headings, without exception. In fact, I recommend that at least one time in your life you read all the chapter headings consecutively, one after the other, without taking time to read the text itself. Reading the chapter headings will show you the grand sweep of the organization of the Old Testament in a manner that might not be possible when you become involved with the details of the accounts in the text.

In preparing for this discussion, I decided to do two things in relation to the chapter headings in the Old Testament. First, I wanted to see if I could read all of the chapter headings without reading the text of the scriptures. Second, I wanted to identify every chapter heading that contained information related to the gospel—the "good news"—of Jesus Christ: his life, mission, or atonement.

In regard to the first goal, in one hour and fifteen minutes I had read and marked all of the chapter headings from Genesis through Esther. Later, in less than one hour, I completed reading the chapter headings from Job through Malachi. It was a very worthwhile and enlightening experience. I highly recommend that you do the same.

In regard to the second goal, I listed all the chapters in all the books of the Old Testament where the chapter heading pertained to the life, mission, or atonement of Jesus Christ. I was amazed and delighted at the number of chapters I listed. Granted, it was sometimes a judgment call about whether or not a particular chapter should be listed, but usually the chapter heading was so detailed there was no question. An asterisk following the chapter number indicates that the chapter heading includes a key word or phrase that clearly pertains to Jesus Christ. These key words or phrases include: "Christ," "Messiah," "Son of God," "speaking Messianically," "Second Coming," "Millennium," or "in the last days." I did not include an asterisk if the chapter heading used "Jehovah" or "I AM," even though we as Latter-day Saints know these terms also apply to Jesus Christ.

Here is a list of the chapters, arranged by book:

Genesis 1–2, 3*, 4, 6–9, 12–14, 16–17, 21–22, 24–28, 32–33, 35, 48, 49*, (JST 50). (Summary: 26 of 50; 2 asterisks.)

Exodus 3, 4, 6, 12–13, 18–20, 24, 27–35, 39–40. (Summary: 20 of 40.)

Leviticus 1, 4–11, 16–17, 19–23, 25–27. (Summary: 19 of 27.)

Numbers 3, 6–11, 14–15, 18, 21, 24*, 27–29. (Summary: 15 of 36; 1 asterisk.)

Deuteronomy 4–11, 13–17, 18*, 26–30, 32–33. (Summary: 21 of 34; 1 asterisk.)

Joshua 1, 5, 24. (Summary: 3 of 24.)

Judges 2, 10. (Summary: 2 of 21.)

Ruth 4. (Summary: 1 of 4.)

1 Samuel 3, 8–10, 16. (Summary: 5 of 31.)

2 Samuel 7*, 22–24. (Summary 4 of 24; 1 asterisk.)

1 Kings 3, 6–8, 17–19. (Summary 7 of 22.)

2 Kings 2, 4, 13, 18, 23. (Summary: 5 of 25.)

1 Chronicles 13, 17, 28. (Summary: 3 of 29.)

2 Chronicles 4–8, 15, 29–30, 34–35. (Summary: 10 of 36.)

Ezra 2, 6, 9. (Summary: 3 of 10.)

Nehemiah 7–8, 10, 13. (Summary: 4 of 13.)

Esther 0. (Summary: 0 of 10.)

Job 1–2, 4, 12–14, 19*, 38, 42. (Summary: 9 of 42; 1 asterisk.)

Psalms 1, 2*, 3–7, 8*, 9*, 11, 13–15, 16*, 17–20, 21*, 22*, 23–25, 27–30, 31*, 33, 34*, 36–37, 40*, 44, 45*, 46–49, 50*, 53, 59, 62, 67*, 68*, 69*, 72*, 73, 76, 78–87, 89*, 90, 91*, 92–94, 97*, 102–7, 108*, 110*, 111–13, 115–17, 118*, 119, 121, 123–30, 132*, 134–36, 138–39, 144–50. (Summary: 104 of 150; 22 asterisks.)

Proverbs 1–4, 8–9, 14, 29. (Summary: 8 of 31.)

Ecclesiastes 2, 3, 7–9, 11–12. (Summary: 7 of 12.)

Song of Solomon 0. (Summary: 0 of 8.)

Isaiah 1, 2*, 3, 4*, 5, 6*, 7*, 8*, 9*, 10*, 11*, 12*, 13*, 14*, 16*, 17–18, 22*, 24*, 25–27, 28*, 29–31, 32*, 33*, 34*, 35, 40*, 41, 42*, 43–44, 45*, 46, 48, 49*, 50*, 51*, 52*, 53*, 54*, 55–58, 59*, 60*, 61*, 62*, 63*, 64*, 65*, 66*. (Summary: 56 of 66; 35 asterisks.)

Jeremiah 1–2, 3*, 4–11, 13–18, 22, 23*, 25*, 30*, 31*, 32, 33*, 50. (Summary: 25 of 52; 6 asterisks.)

Lamentations 3–4. (Summary: 2 of 5.)

Ezekiel 1–4, 8–10, 11*, 12–14, 16*, 17*, 18, 20*, 28, 33, 34*, 36*, 37*, 38*, 39–48. (Summary: 31 of 48; 8 asterisks.)

Daniel 2, 3*, 4–6, 7*, 8*, 9*, 10*, 11*, 12*. (Summary: 11 of 12; 7 asterisks.)

Hoshea 2*, 3*, 12–13, 14*. (Summary: 5 of 14; 3 asterisks.)

Joel 2*, 3*. (Summary: 2 of 3; 2 asterisks.)

Amos 3–8, 9*. (Summary: 7 of 9, 1 asterisk.)

Obadiah 1. (Summary: 1 of 1.)

Jonah 1, 4. (Summary: 2 of 4.)

Micah 2–3, 4*, 5*, 6, 7*. (Summary: 6 of 7; 3 asterisks.)

Nahum 1*, 2*. (Summary: 2 of 3; 2 asterisks.)

Habakkuk 2. (Summary: 1 of 3.)

Zephaniah 1*, 2, 3*. (Summary: 3 of 3; 2 asterisks.)

Haggai 1, 2*. (Summary: 2 of 2; 1 asterisk.)

Zechariah 1, 2*, 3*, 5, 6*, 7, 8*, 9*, 10, 11*, 12*, 13*, 14*. (Summary: 13 of 14; 9 asterisks.)

Malachi 1–2, 3*, 4*. (Summary: 4 of 4; 2 asterisks.)

Summary of all the chapters in the 39 books of the Old Testament: Total number of chapters: 929

Number of chapters referring to the life, mission, or atonement of Jesus Christ: 449 (or 48%)

Number of chapters identified by an asterisk (indicating that the chapter heading contains a key word or phrase pertaining specifically to Jesus Christ: 108 (12% of total, or 24% of those pertaining to Jesus Christ)

Now have I convinced you that the Old Testament is something more than history? It is indeed a strong witness for Jesus Christ.

As impressive as these figures are, however, the fact that a chapter does not include a reference to the life, mission, or atonement of Jesus Christ does not mean we should not read, study, and ponder that chapter. Hundreds of important principles and teachings are contained in many of the other chapters. For example, chapters 1, 5, 6, 7, and 17 of 2 Kings are not in the list. Yet powerful messages are contained in all of those chapters.

To get an idea of the significance and detail of the chapter headings, let's read those for the first three chapters of Genesis:

"Chapter 1: God creates this earth and its heaven and all forms of life in six days; Creative acts of each day set forth — God creates man, both male and female, in his own image—Man given dominion over all things, and commanded to multiply and fill the earth."

"Chapter 2: Creation completed—God rests on the seventh day—Prior spirit creation explained—Adam and Eve placed in Garden of Eden—They are forbidden to eat of the tree of knowledge of good and evil—Adam names every living creature—Adam and Eve are married by the Lord."

"Chapter 3: The Serpent (Lucifer) deceives Eve—She and then Adam partake of the forbidden fruit—Her seed (Christ) shall bruise the Serpent's head—Role of woman, and of man—Adam and Eve cast out of Garden of Eden—Adam presides—Eve becomes the mother of all living."

I hope these samples whet your appetite to read all the chapter headings.

Appendix

Now let's look at the Appendix of the LDS edition of the Bible.

Topical Guide. Thousands of topics are listed in the 598 pages of the Topical Guide. Tens of thousands of references are listed under these topics, with references under each topic arranged in the order of the books and sections of the Old Testament, the New Testament, the Book of Mormon, the Doctrine and Covenants, and the Pearl of Great Price. As you can imagine, the efforts of hundreds of people who contributed tens of thousands of hours, with the aid of computers, were required to prepare the Topical Guide. Elder Bruce R. McConkie said that without the help of the computer, the Topical Guide in the LDS edition of the scriptures could not have been prepared in its thoroughness and accuracy *in this century.*

And all that effort is available to help us in our diligent study of the scriptures.

Bible Dictionary. I believe that the Bible Dictionary in the LDS edition of the Bible is the best Bible Dictionary that has ever been published. Some of the scriptural scholars in the Church received permission to use the best of what had been printed in other Bible dictionaries; then they improved upon these materials through their understanding of latter-day scripture and their acquaintance with the teachings of the prophets of this dispensation. Unfortunately, many members of the Church, even those who already have a copy of the

LDS edition of the Bible, have not learned how to use this magnificent instructional aid. It is the "sealed portion" of the Bible!

The best, and perhaps the only, way to become acquainted with the contents of the Bible Dictionary is to read all the entries in the dictionary, item by item and word for word, from "Aaron" through "Zipporah." Perhaps too many of us wait to use the Bible Dictionary until we feel a definite need for its use; only then do we look up the appropriate topic. Of course, it is better to use the dictionary in this fashion than not to use it at all. But how much better it would be for us if we first acquainted ourselves with what is in the dictionary. For example, average teachers in the Church might never check the Bible Dictionary under the topic "Fall of Adam" because they think they already know all they need to know about the fall of Adam. Nevertheless, I am confident virtually every member of the Church would have his or her understanding of the Fall expanded by reading what has been provided under that topic in the Bible Dictionary. I earnestly invite you to do so. In fact, I invite you — indeed, challenge you — to read all the entries in the Bible Dictionary. Let me share with you three of those entries that will prove of great value to you.

1. On pages 622 to 625 of the Appendix is a series of articles on the subject of the Bible under such subtitles as "Structure of the Bible," "Preservation of the Text of the Old Testament," "Preservation of the Text of the New Testament," and "Bible, English." This information should prove invaluable to you as you diligently study the Old Testament. Additional information on this same general subject is found under the entry "Canon" on page 630.

2. On pages 635 through 645 are chronological tables that should also prove indispensable to you. Note the wealth of information: a list of dates and of the kings and the prophets of both the kingdom of Judah and the kingdom of Israel. Note also the information in the charts under such headings as "Internal History," "External History," "Synchronisms," "Jewish History," "Profane History," "Egypt," "Syria," and "Contemporary Events." Again, the results of the efforts of many students and scholars of the scriptures, requiring thousands of hours, are available to you in a format that can be easily understood and used. You might want to specially mark or tag these tables, as well as the tremendous Harmony of the Gospels charts on pages 684 through 696.

3. On pages 756 to 759 of the Appendix is an extremely interesting article under the heading "Quotations from the Old Testament Found

in the New Testament." This is one of the many worthwhile articles
I mentioned earlier that might never be discovered by even the serious
student of the Bible unless he or she reads the Bible Dictionary from
beginning to end. Yet this valuable list tells you all the Old Testament
passages that have clearly influenced New Testament writers, in the
order of the books of the Old Testament. Thus, you can readily determine that this list includes 64 references from Psalms, 55 from
Isaiah, 26 from both Deuteronomy and Exodus, and 18 from Genesis.
If you want to spend some extremely interesting and informative gospel
study time, read the passages listed from the Old Testament and then
read the corresponding passages from the New Testament. That experience alone will convince you the Old Testament is a valuable witness for Jesus Christ.

Joseph Smith Translation. The next major section of the Appendix is titled "Joseph Smith Translation: Excerpts Too Lengthy for
Inclusion in Footnotes."

Many excerpts from the Joseph Smith Translation are included as
footnotes on the pages of the text of the Bible. It was decided, however,
that if the footnote from the Joseph Smith Translation would take over
nine lines on one of those pages, then it should appear in this special
section.

The first reference in this section is Genesis 9:4–6. That does not
mean that the Joseph Smith Translation does not make many significant
contributions to a correct understanding of the first eight chapters of
Genesis. If you carefully review those early chapters of Genesis, however, you will note the numerous cross-references to the books of
Moses and Abraham in the Pearl of Great Price. These references to
modern scripture provide the student of the Old Testament with invaluable insights into the early chapters of Genesis.

Even then, note the many lengthy contributions of the Joseph Smith
Translation to such chapters as Genesis 9, 14, 15, 17, 19, 21, 48, and
50.

Gazetteer. The items in the Gazetteer should enable the serious
student of the Bible to locate any major place name in the twenty-two
maps that follow. Learn to use the Gazetteer properly so you can quickly
find the location of any places mentioned.

Maps. The twenty-two maps in the LDS edition of the Bible are
among the best biblical maps available. Map number 1, the physical
map of Palestine, can be used to find both Old Testament and New

Testament locations; however, maps 2 through 12 are primarily concerned with Old Testament locations and maps 13 through 22 pertain primarily to the New Testament. As you study the Old Testament, you will want to examine carefully all of the maps of the time period that is most appropriate for each area.

Now that we have completed our summary of the major sections in the Appendix, I hope you agree that the LDS edition of the Bible is indeed a remarkable publication. Use it. It will prove to be one of the most helpful and interesting teachers you have ever had.

The Old Testament as a Witness for Other Scriptures

In addition to serving as a witness for Jesus Christ and for some of the basic doctrines and principles of the gospel of Jesus Christ, the Old Testament also serves as a witness for the other scriptures. The statement by Amos that "surely the Lord God will do nothing, but he revealeth his secret unto his servants the prophets" (Amos 3:7) and the statement by God himself that he is an unchangeable God, the same yesterday, today, and tomorrow, both suggest the possibility of other scriptures.

The Old Testament supports the basic claims of the New Testament, as indicated by the many Old Testament statements quoted by New Testament writers. In addition, the Old Testament serves as a witness of the Book of Mormon, as indicated in Ezekiel 37, and of both the Book of Mormon and the Doctrine and Covenants, as indicated in Psalm 85: "Truth shall spring out of the earth; and righteousness shall look down from heaven." (Ps. 85:11.) President Ezra Taft Benson's inspired interpretation of this expression, which is essentially the same as Moses 7:62, is that it refers to the Book of Mormon ("Truth shall spring out of the earth") and to the revelations of the last days, including those that have "been preserved for us in the Doctrine and Covenants."[10]

Two of the major engravers of the sets of plates from which we get the Book of Mormon—Nephi on the Small Plates, and Mormon on the Plates of Mormon—have also testified of the role of the Old Testament as a scriptural witness.

In the last chapter Nephi engraved, he warned: "And you that will not partake of the goodness of God, and respect the words of the Jews [the Old Testament], and also my words [the Book of Mormon], and the words which shall proceed forth out of the mouth of the Lamb of

God [including the New Testament], behold, I bid you an everlasting farewell, for these words shall condemn you at the last days. For what I seal on earth, shall be brought against you at the judgment bar; for thus hath the Lord commanded me, and I must obey. Amen." (2 Ne. 33:14–15.)

The last chapter engraved by Mormon on his plates includes these words: "Therefore repent, and be baptized in the name of Jesus, and lay hold upon the gospel of Christ, which shall be set before you, not only in this record [the Book of Mormon] but also in the record which shall come unto the Gentiles from the Jews, which record shall come from the Gentiles unto you [the Bible]. For behold, this [the Book of Mormon] is written for the intent that ye may believe that [the Bible]; and if ye believe that [the Bible] ye will believe this [the Book of Mormon] also." (Morm. 7:8–9.)

Although Moroni's famous challenge in the last chapter he engraved on the plates of Mormon is usually interpreted to pertain primarily to the Book of Mormon, a careful reading of his words indicates the Bible is also involved. Let's review first his words in Moroni 10:3: "Behold, I would exhort you that when ye shall read these things [from the plates of Mormon], if it be wisdom in God that ye should read them, that ye would remember how merciful the Lord hath been unto the children of men, from the creation of Adam even down until the time that ye shall receive these things, and ponder it in your hearts."

Let's ponder those words for a moment to make certain we understand what Moroni is asking us to do. It is obvious that he is asking us to read the Book of Mormon, but isn't it equally obvious that he is asking us to read the Bible? Notice again his counsel that we "should remember how merciful the Lord hath been unto the children of men, *from the creation of Adam even down until the time that ye shall receive these things.*" (Emphasis added.) Where do we read about the Creation and about events from the time of the Creation? They are found in the Bible; they are not found in the Book of Mormon. In fact, this same Moroni, when he started his abridgment of the plates of Ether, recorded: "And as I suppose that the first part of this record, which speaks concerning the creation of the world, and also of Adam, and an account from that time . . . is had among the Jews—Therefore I do not write those things which transpired from the days of Adam." (Ether 1:3–4.)

Now let's continue with Moroni 10:4. "And when ye shall receive these things [the Bible, the Book of Mormon, and the way God deals with man], I would exhort you that ye would ask God, the Eternal Father, in the name of Christ, if *these things* are not true; and if ye shall ask with a sincere heart, with real intent, having faith in Christ, he will manifest the truth of it [the Book of Mormon] unto you, by the power of the Holy Ghost." (Italics added.)

And then the tremendous fifth verse: "And by the power of the Holy Ghost ye may know the truth of all things."

No wonder Brigham Young testified of these two powerful scriptural witnesses: "No man can say that this book (laying his hand on the Bible) is true . . . and at the same time say that the Book of Mormon is untrue. There is not that person on the face of the earth who has had the privilege of learning the Gospel of Jesus Christ from these two books, that can say that one is true, and the other is false. . . . If one be true, both are."[11]

And that is my testimony. Both the Bible and the Book of Mormon are true because they teach the same things, and they both teach that Jesus Christ is the Divine Son of God, the Savior and Redeemer of the world. I testify further that the Old Testament is an important part of the biblical testimony of the Messiah, the Anointed One. The Old Testament is a witness for Jesus Christ. Of these things I bear witness in the name of Jesus Christ.

NOTES

1. "What I Hope You Will Teach My Grandchildren" (address to seminary and institute personnel), Provo, Utah, July 11, 1966, p. 6.

2. Abraham Lincoln, as cited in *Church News*, Mar. 20, 1983, p. 3.

3. Ronald Reagan, as cited in *Church News*, Mar. 20, 1983, p. 3.

4. The First Presidency, as cited in *Church News*, Mar. 20, 1983, p. 3.

5. Brigham Young, *Discourses of Brigham Young*, sel. John A. Widtsoe (Salt Lake City: Deseret Book Co., 1941), p. 125.

6. Joseph Smith, *History of The Church of Jesus Christ of Latter-day Saints*, ed. B. H. Roberts, 7 vols., 2d ed. rev. (Salt Lake City: Deseret Book Co., 1932–51), 6:57.

7. Young, *Discourses of Brigham Young*, p. 124.

8. Brigham Young, in *Journal of Discourses*, 26 vols. (London: Latter-day Saints' Book Depot, 1854–86), 16:73–74.

9. Young, *Discourses of Brigham Young*, p. 124; italics added.

10. Ezra Taft Benson, in Conference Report, Oct. 1986, p. 102.

11. Young, in *Journal of Discourses*, 1:38.

CHAPTER NINE

Beyond the Biblical Account: Adam, Enoch, Noah, Melchizedek, Abraham, and Moses in Latter-day Revelation

Robert J. Matthews
Brigham Young University

I am pleased to be part of this symposium named in honor of Dr. Sidney B. Sperry, who for so many years was a major influence in religious education on this campus. Many of the present religion faculty and faculty in other disciplines at Brigham Young University were instructed by him and worked with him. The theme of the Sperry symposium each year focuses on the subject of the coming year in the Church. This is the eighteenth annual symposium, and the subject is the Old Testament as a witness of Jesus Christ. I alone am responsible for the contents of this paper. I am not speaking for the university or the Church; however, I believe that what I say here is correct and in harmony with the Brethren and with what the Lord has revealed.

My topic is the contribution of latter-day revelation in enabling us to correctly understand what the early patriarchs were like and what they taught. The Bible, of course, gives us a great amount of historical information about these things, but it is often vague in doctrinal content. It is a cardinal principle in this Church that many plain and precious things have been deliberately removed from the text of the Bible since the time it was written. The most serious kinds of things that were removed were the doctrinal things. The angel in 1 Nephi 13 said that "many plain and precious things" were "taken away" "out of the book," and also "many covenants were taken away." Most of the extractions occurred in the first century after Christ; thus the Jewish and the Christian world since that time has not had a completely adequate Bible. The Bible is wonderful, even so, and is a force for good and for righteousness in the earth, but think how marvelous it must have been when it was complete and doctrinally much richer than it now is.

Consequences to the Bible When Certain Portions Were Removed

Two problems arise when information is taken out of a record. First, of course, there is the loss of what is gone. But second, the loss of one piece of information often renders some of the remaining information unintelligible or even misleading. Many of the missing parts were vital to a correct understanding of the historical, intellectual, and doctrinal milieu in which the ancient prophets and patriarchs lived. Without those missing parts the picture is fragmented and vague, if not distorted. My purpose is to discuss a number of things that are found only in latter-day revelation, yet that pertain to the biblical story. These are things that we would not know if we had only the Bible.

Let me read some examples from two Bible Dictionaries. First, from the *Cambridge Bible Dictionary* on the fall of Adam. This is the dictionary that was published for many years in the missionary edition of the Bible we used for the Church before the new edition was published.

"**Fall.** This word denotes the first entrance of sin into the world, as described in Gen. 3. The story which is there told should probably be regarded as allegory rather than as literal history. The Bible does not teach that man was originally created perfect, i.e. with all his moral faculties perfectly developed, but that at a certain point in the history of the race the development took a wrong turn, which was not in accordance with God's original purpose. Man consciously set himself to act in opposition to the will of his Creator. This deliberate act of self-assertion produced in the race a natural inclination towards what is wrong, a taint which is handed on from one generation to another, and which is generally called 'original sin'; we are all 'by nature born in sin.' "[1]

And from *Harper's Bible Dictionary:*

"**Fall, the.** The lapse from innocence and goodness, the first apostasy: the loss of Adam's position of integrity, virtue, and innocence, after his sin, as related in the Genesis accounts of the Eden tragedy. . . .

"There is no O.T. [Old Testament] doctrine of the Fall. But the Fall and the atoning grace of Christ are the core of the N.T. [New Testament] theology of Paul."[2]

And now, on the subject of offering sacrifice, as stated in the *Cambridge Bible Dictionary:*

"**Sacrifice.** No Divine command can be quoted for the institution of sacrifice; the desire to offer some thank-offering was instinctive in man. . . . The earliest sacrifices, [were] those of Cain, Abel and Noah. . . . The idea of propitiation became prominent later on, after the Mosaic Law had brought in a fuller knowledge of sin, and had produced a deeper sense of guilt."[3]

In contrast to the foregoing statement about the origin and purpose of sacrifice, the Lord has revealed that God commanded Adam to offer sacrifice and to use the firstlings of his flock for that purpose. An angel later explained to Adam the similitude of this sacrifice of an animal to the forthcoming sacrifice of Jesus Christ. (JST Gen. 4:5–8; Moses 5:4–10.) Furthermore, the Fall is spoken of in latter-day revelation as an actual event, not as an allegory, and is regarded by us as necessary and as part of the eternal plan. Those who prepared these two dictionaries were no doubt good and God-fearing Christian scholars, but they simply did not have the benefit of a complete Bible or of latter-day revelation.

It is true, as *Harper's Bible Dictionary* stated, that the Old Testament now has no doctrine of the Fall, but that is because almost all traces of doctrinal discussions of the Fall have been removed. Latter-day scripture attests that at one time the Old Testament, especially Genesis, had a very clear doctrine of the Fall, beginning with God's revelation to Adam on the subject. We know from latter-day scriptures that the ancient biblical prophets taught the concept of the fall of Adam and the atonement of Christ. That is especially evident in the Book of Mormon and in the Joseph Smith Translation.

Although it is true that nearly all of the doctrines of the gospel are mentioned in the Bible, they are not organized with proximity to one another and are scattered throughout the Bible such that they are not easily recognized nor properly associated. After people have learned the gospel and become acquainted with the plan of salvation from latter-day revelation, they can then see traces of the plan and discover references to it in the Bible, but they cannot initially construct the plan and fit it together from the Bible alone.

Twenty-five years ago another teacher and I were standing along a roadway in Washington state to photograph Mt. Rainier in the distance. Considerable mist in the air made the view hazy and obscure.

My friend told me he could put a filter on his camera, remove much of the haze, and thus the photo would be clearer. That was a new idea to me, but I liked it. In a similar way, we can look through the lens of latter-day revelation today and see the ancient patriarchs with much of the mist and obscurity removed. I believe we can filter out some of the accumulated fog and smog and distant haze. I mean the fog of mistranslation, the smog of neglect or unbelief, and the haze of fragmentary records.

Sources of Information

The chief sources are the standard works of the Church and the teachings of the Prophet Joseph Smith.

1. The Bible is an old book and has been available to mankind through the years. The prophets who wrote it made it plain and doctrinally strong. They made it clear that they knew of and worshiped Jesus Christ as their Redeemer. The prophets are dead, the original manuscripts are gone, and all the copies have suffered many changes and losses at the hand of man. Some losses were unintentional, but some were intentional. The intentional losses are the most serious because they systematically removed basic doctrinal passages.

2. The Book of Mormon is an old book, as old as the Bible, but the manuscript plates were kept hidden in the ground, out of the reach of man, all through the centuries; therefore it did not suffer the changes and alterations that occurred to the Bible. It demonstrates that the same doctrines that were known to the biblical record were known to the Book of Mormon also. In fact, the Book of Mormon says that God speaks the "same words unto one nation like unto another." (2 Ne. 29:8.) Likewise, many of the same persons are spoken of in both records. The Book of Mormon has come as a second witness for Jesus Christ, a companion to the Bible, and it also makes known many of the things that have been taken away from the Bible. (1 Ne. 13:39–40.)

3. The Doctrine and Covenants is a new book, containing revelations from the same Lord who gave revelations to the prophets who wrote the Bible and the Book of Mormon. The Doctrine and Covenants contains many of the same doctrines that those two old books contain, and it speaks often of the ancient biblical prophets.

4. The Pearl of Great Price contains two Old Testament excerpts of ancient material translated by Joseph Smith. The first is an excerpt from his translation of Genesis, now called the book of Moses. The

second is an excerpt from his translation of records containing the
writings of Abraham in Egypt. It is called the book of Abraham.

5. The Joseph Smith Translation of the Bible is a document containing thousands of additions and clarifications to the King James
Version. This work was begun and carried forth by Joseph Smith in
his calling as a prophet and seer and under the express direction of
the Lord commanding him to make such a translation. Many of the
doctrinal revelations now in the Doctrine and Covenants were received
as a consequence of the Prophet Joseph Smith's making this Bible
translation.

6. Joseph Smith's writings and teachings are also used because
Joseph Smith was the great prophet and restorer who received so much
direct revelation from God. He was visited by many of the ancient
biblical prophets, and he understood the work of the Lord that has
taken place on this earth from the beginning. The Lord said of Joseph
Smith: "I have given unto him the keys of the mystery of those things
which have been sealed, even things which were from the foundation
of the world." (D&C 35:18.) Joseph Smith's views about the work of
God and the history of the prophets back to Adam are very important
to us if we want to know about things as they really were.

An interesting phenomenon about gospel study is that the more
you know, the more you want to know. You recall that Abraham said
he wanted to be a greater follower of righteousness and to possess a
greater knowledge. (Abr. 1:2.) Likewise, Moses yearned for another
chance to commune with God, for, said he, "I have other things to
inquire of him." (Moses 1:18.) When a person is once awakened to the
knowledge and inklings of the doctrine and laws of God, the soul thirsts
for gospel knowledge even more vigorously than the body craves food.

A second factor about studying the gospel is that the more one
learns the more he or she is able to learn. Just so, the latter-day
revelation contained in our standard works and in the teachings of
Joseph Smith opens up vistas of understanding and spiritual joy like
nothing else can do.

Unity and Continuity in the Work of God on the Earth

Before examining some of the specific contributions of latter-day
revelation to our understanding of the ancient prophets—things that
are important but are entirely lacking or are clouded and obscured in

the biblical account — I will make some general summary observations about these latter-day revelations.

One item of importance is the continuity or the unity of purpose that latter-day revelation unfolds to us about the ancient order of things. We learn that beginning with Adam, all of the prophets and patriarchs had the gospel of Jesus Christ, and it was the same gospel then as it is now. Adam had the same gospel, the same ordinances, the same endowment, the same celestial marriage, and the same covenants that you and I have received by being members of by The Church of Jesus Christ of Latter-day Saints. Furthermore, these prophets knew of each other. The earlier ones met together, and the later ones knew they were engaged in the same gospel as the earlier ones were engaged in and for the same purposes. These things become more evident as we read the latter-day scriptures and the words of Joseph Smith.

In searching out these facts and comparing the scriptures, we will actually be fulfilling some ancient prophecies. For example, in 2 Nephi 3:12 we read that the writings of the loins of Judah (the Bible) and the writings of the loins of Joseph (the Book of Mormon) shall come together in the last days. That is a parallel passage to Ezekiel 37:14–17, in which it is said that the stick of Ephraim and the stick of Judah shall become one in our hands. But notice the special wording of 2 Nephi 3:12. These writings shall "grow together, unto the confounding of false doctrines." Growing together is more than just being placed together under one cover or in a plastic, zippered carrying case. To "grow," there must be action. It is dynamic. If it grows, it gets better, because understanding and learning increase as study progresses. That is what happens when we use latter-day revelation to understand the Bible.

I have come to the firm conclusion that the Lord wants us to know the doctrine and to know it well. One purpose of the coming forth of the Book of Mormon is so that we can learn — mark what it says — "the very points of his doctrine." (1 Ne. 15:14.) And in Doctrine and Covenants 10:62, the Lord says he wants "the true points of my doctrine" to be brought forth so as to lessen contention. The Lord also says that those who have only the Bible in its imperfect altered condition are in "that awful state of blindness," because they lack the greater knowledge they ought to have about the gospel. (1 Ne. 13:32).

I hope that what is presented in this paper is in harmony with the spirit, the intention, and the proper use of these sacred statements. I will now treat Adam and Eve, then Enoch, Noah, Melchizedek, Abraham, and Moses, in that order. Then I will make a few brief conclusions.

Adam and Eve

It is proper to begin with Adam and Eve, even though we cannot enter into an extensive biography. Rather, I will deal with a few specific points of historical and doctrinal importance.

The idea of a Garden of Eden is taught in each of the standard works and is a frequent topic in Joseph Smith's teachings. There is no indication in the Bible where the Garden was located, and the popular conclusion is that such a place, if it existed at all, was somewhere in the Near East or Asia. Latter-day scripture does not categorically, in ten words or less, pinpoint the Garden in a precise locality. It does, however, place Adam in the western hemisphere, stating that he dwelt at Adam-ondi-Ahman, and speaks particularly of Spring Hill in Davies County, Missouri, as the place where Adam shall come to a future council meeting. Drawing on the information in Doctrine and Covenants 78:15; 116:1; and 117:8–11, Latter-day Saints early concluded that the area now called the state of Missouri is the place where Adam and Eve dwelt after their expulsion from the Garden.

I do not know of an existing document containing the specific and precise declaration in the words of Joseph Smith in which he located the Garden of Eden in an exact spot, but we have several secondary sources saying that he did so. President Brigham Young, President George Q. Cannon, President Heber C. Kimball, and President Joseph Fielding Smith have said that Joseph Smith taught that the Garden of Eden was located in Jackson County, Missouri, where the city of Independence now is. Here are their words:

President Brigham Young declared: "Joseph, the Prophet, told me that the Garden of Eden was in Jackson County, Missouri. When Adam was driven out he went to the place we now call Adam-ondi-Ahman, Daviess County, Missouri."[4]

President George Q. Cannon asked an audience in the Salt Lake Tabernacle in 1867 why the Latter-day Saints talk and pray so much about returning to Zion (Missouri). He then answered his question himself by saying that we are grateful for our home in the west, but "we look forward to that land [Zion] with indescribable feelings, because it is the place where God has said His City shall be built. It is the land where Adam, the Ancient of Days, will gather his posterity again, and where the blessings of God will descend upon them. It is the land for which the wise and learned have travelled and sought in vain. Asia has been ransacked in endeavoring to locate the Garden of Eden. Men have supposed that because the Ark rested on Ararat that the flood commenced there, or rather that it was from thence the Ark started to sail. But God in His revelations has informed us that it was on this choice land of Joseph where Adam was placed and the Garden of Eden was laid out. The spot has been designated, and we look forward with peculiar feelings to repossessing that land."[5]

President Heber C. Kimball, speaking in Provo, Utah, in 1863, discussed several things about Adam and the redemption of the earth: "The spot chosen for the garden of Eden was Jackson County, in the state of Missouri, where Independence now stands; it was occupied in the morn of creation by Adam and his associates who came with him for the express purpose of peopling this earth." He further commented that "the Prophet Joseph frequently spoke of these things in the revelations which he gave, but the people generally did not understand them."[6]

There is an interesting scriptural statement, or formula, that says the "first shall be last and the last shall be first." That, of course, has a lot of meanings and can be applied to a number of things. When applied to the city of New Jerusalem, however, the idea could be quite instructive. The Lord revealed in Doctrine and Covenants 57:1–3 and 84:1–3 that the New Jerusalem and temple should be where Independence now is. On the basis of the first being last and the last being first, we can reason that the Lord's city in the last dispensation should be at the same place where it all began, in the Garden of Eden.

President Joseph Fielding Smith taught that the Garden of Eden and the New Jerusalem were in the same place: "In accord with the revelations given to the Prophet Joseph Smith, we teach that the Garden of Eden was on the American continent located where the City Zion, or the New Jerusalem, will be built. When Adam and Eve were driven out of the Garden, they eventually dwelt at a place called Adam-ondi-Ahman, situated in what is now Daviess County, Missouri."[7]

As to the family of Adam, Genesis gives the names of Cain, Abel, and Seth, as though these were the earliest children of Adam and Eve. It does not say they are first; it simply does not mention any before them, which leads the reader to assume they were the first. Later, in Genesis 4:17, mention is made of Cain's wife, with no explanation about who she is. That has been a problem to some students because no daughters of Adam and Eve had been mentioned. In the Joseph Smith Translation, Genesis 4:1–3 (Moses 5:1–3), we read that Adam and Eve had many sons and daughters, and these sons and daughters had sons and daughters (making Adam and Eve grandparents) before either Cain or Abel were born. Whom did Cain marry? In the Joseph Smith Translation, Genesis 5:27 identifies her as a daughter of one of his brothers. (See Moses 5:28.)

No mention is made in Genesis about how Adam and Eve felt about the Fall and having been cast out of the Garden of Eden. But in the Joseph Smith Translation, Genesis 4:9–12 (Moses 5:10–11), we find both of them rejoicing because of the great new life and spiritual opportunities available to them as a result of the Fall. We don't know how they felt about it immediately, but after they were taught the gospel, they rejoiced because of the Fall.

It is only from latter-day revelation that we learn that Adam and Eve would have had no children without the Fall. The Bible does not define this and therefore many have looked upon the transgression of Adam as a bad thing, believing that if Adam had not transgressed, the earth would have kept its paradisiacal status and the entire human family could have lived in paradise without sin, death, and so forth. Little do these theorists know or realize that none of the human family would have been born if Adam and Eve had not fallen. The references for this very significant and essential doctrine are 2 Nephi 2:23; Moses 5:11; and Moses 6:48.

Furthermore, we learn from latter-day scripture that Adam could read and write, having a perfect and pure language, and that a record was kept which was called the Book of Remembrance. Adam and his immediate posterity kept this record, and they taught their children to read and write in a language which was pure and undefiled. (JST Gen. 6:5–6; Moses 6:5–6.)

Enoch, seven generations and nearly a thousand years later, makes reference to this book (JST Gen. 6:49–50; Moses 6:45–46), as does Abraham another thousand years after that. (Abr. 1:28–31.) Abraham said he had in his possession detailed and informative written records kept by his ancestors back to Adam and the creation. Those records contained information not known to mankind today. (See Fac. 2, items 8–21.)

Nothing in the Bible suggests such a set of records or such a highly developed, literate society among Adam and his immediate family. Yet in latter-day revelation this subject is not simply alluded to or hinted at; it is a major thrust of the revelation about Adam.

Latter-day Saints have opportunity to view Adam in much clearer light than do those who depend on the Bible alone. We read in the Joseph Smith Translation, Genesis 4 and 5 (Moses 5 and 6), that Adam offered animal sacrifice with faith toward the coming Messiah and that he was visited by angels, was taught the doctrine of the Fall and the Atonement, was baptized with water, and held the priesthood. We learn from the teachings of the Prophet Joseph Smith that Adam was visited by Christ and possessed the keys of every dispensation as the father and patriarch of the human race. None of this doctrinal information is discernible from the present Bible record.

The Prophet Joseph Smith said that Adam "is the father of the human family, and presides over the spirits of all men. . . . He is the head, and was told to multiply. The keys [of the priesthood] were first given to him, and by him to others. He will have to give an account of his stewardship [to God] and they [those who have held keys] to him. . . . Christ is the Great High Priest; Adam next."[8]

The Prophet Joseph Smith also said of Adam: "I saw Adam in the valley of Adam-ondi-Ahman. He called together his children and blessed them with a patriarchal blessing. The Lord appeared in their midst, and he (Adam) blessed them all, and foretold what should befall them to the latest generation."[9]

He further said: "[Adam] is Michael, because he was the first and father of all, not only by progeny, but the first to hold the spiritual blessings, to whom was made known the plan of ordinances for the salvation of his posterity unto the end, and to whom Christ was first revealed, and through whom Christ has been revealed from heaven, and will continue to be revealed from henceforth. Adam holds the keys of the dispensation of the fullness of times; i.e., the dispensation of all the times have been and will be revealed through him from the beginning . . . to the end of the dispensations that are to be revealed.

"[The Lord] set the ordinances to be the same forever and ever, and set Adam to watch over them, to reveal them from heaven to man, or to send angels to reveal them. . . . These angels are under the direction of Michael or Adam, who acts under the direction of the Lord."[10]

And further: "This, then, is the nature of the Priesthood; every man holding the Presidency of his dispensation, and one man holding the Presidency of them all, even Adam."[11]

None of the foregoing teachings from the Prophet Joseph Smith could be discerned from the biblical record alone, yet it is basic, indispensable information about Adam, and necessary for us to know if we are to understand much about Adam and the plan of God for this earth.

Adam's son Seth is spoken of as a "perfect man," in the express likeness of Adam's person, and is said to be so much like Adam, he could be distinguished from him only by his age. (D&C 107:43.) This certainty attests to the physical perfection and beauty of Adam and Seth. There is more, however, that we can learn about this. In January 1843 the Prophet Joseph spoke of his own brother Alvin, whom he regarded very highly, and the Prophet said that Alvin, who had died some years before, "was a very handsome man, surpassed by none but Adam and Seth."[12] I do not know Alvin's exact physical dimensions, but the Smiths were a tall family. Joseph Smith, Sr., was 6' 3"; Hyrum and Joseph were 6 feet; their brother William is said to have been 6' 4". We have every reason to believe that Alvin was therefore also tall and long limbed. Beauty and handsomeness are in the eye of the beholder and are relative terms; yet by nineteenth-century standards Joseph Smith believed Alvin to be a handsome man, and by those same standards he judged Adam and Seth, whom the Lord said were perfect men, to be even more handsome than Alvin. It follows, then, in my thinking, that if by modern standards Adam and Seth were very handsome, and this is speaking of their whole appearance, they were not caveman physiques, only one step removed from the apes. Joseph would never have thought a Neanderthal type was more handsome than his beloved brother Alvin. I think we are safe in concluding that Adam and Seth were upright, straight, tall, and well-proportioned by our standards today.

Joseph Smith was not guessing at Adam's appearance, for he had said in 1839: "I saw Adam in the valley of Adam-ondi-Ahman."[13] The Prophet was quoted by Oliver B. Huntington as saying that Adam was "such a perfect man, great and stout, that he never stumbled or fell a joint to the ground."[14] President John Taylor knew about Joseph Smith's acquaintance with Adam and referred to it as follows: "If you were to ask Joseph what sort of a looking man Adam was, he would tell you at once; he would tell you his size and appearance and all about him. You might have asked him what sort of men Peter, James and John were, and he could have told you. Why? Because he had seen them."[15]

Enoch

Enoch is a patriarch frequently spoken of in the Church, yet very little is given about him in the Bible. Today we speak of Enoch and his City of Zion which was translated and taken from the earth nearly five thousand years ago. We also read in the scripture that Enoch's city will return to the earth in the last days to be joined with the New Jerusalem, which will be built upon the earth in Jackson County, Missouri. We speak of Enoch's city having the ideal social and economic system whereby there were no poor among them. None of this information is given in the Bible; all of it is dependent upon latter-day revelation. The Bible tells us that Enoch was translated, but says nothing about a city of Enoch, and nothing of Enoch's ministry as a preacher of the gospel of Jesus Christ.

From Joseph Smith we learn not only all of that about Enoch, but also that after his translation he became a ministering angel to people on other planets of a terrestrial order.[16] The Prophet also told us that Enoch came as a ministering angel and instructed Paul.[17]

Although the Bible gives us to understand that Enoch was a righteous man and a man of faith, it does not categorically tell us what Enoch did. From the Joseph Smith Translation we learn that Enoch was a missionary and a successful expounder of the gospel of Jesus Christ, including the fall of Adam, and he had great visions of eternity, the spirit world, the Judgment, and like things.

One of the greatest statements concerning the fall of Adam and the atonement of Jesus Christ and the effect of the Atonement in freeing little children from so-called original sin is given by Enoch in Moses 6:49–54. We read from Enoch that Adam had been taught that for a remission of any sins he committed after he became mortal, he would have to repent, exercise faith in Jesus Christ, and be baptized in water. But for the transgression in the Garden of Eden, he was forgiven without baptism, etc. Here are Enoch's words:

"But God hath made known unto our fathers, that all men must repent.

"And he called upon our father Adam, by his own voice, saying, I am God; I made the world, and men before they were in the flesh.

"And he also said unto him, If thou wilt, turn unto me and hearken unto my voice, and believe, and repent of all thy transgressions, and be baptized, even in water, in the name of mine Only Begotten Son, who is full of grace and truth, which is Jesus Christ, the only name which shall be given under heaven, whereby salvation shall come unto the children of men; and ye shall receive the gift of the Holy Ghost, asking all things in his name, and whatsoever ye shall ask it shall be given you.

"And our father Adam spake unto the Lord, and said, Why is it that men must repent, and be baptized in water?

"And the Lord said unto Adam, Behold, I have forgiven thee thy transgression in the garden of Eden.

"Hence came the saying abroad among the people, that the Son of God hath atoned for original guilt, wherein the sins of the parents cannot be answered upon the heads of the children, for they are whole from the foundation of the world." (JST Gen. 6:51–56; Moses 6:50–54.)

Nothing surpasses this for clarity in any other passage or reference. Because these are the words of the Lord to Adam, cited by Enoch, and contained in the writings of Moses, it shows that all three of these prophets were acquainted with the doctrine of Christ relative to the Fall and the status of little children.

Enoch was present at a great conference at Adam-ondi-Ahman held three years before the death of Adam. The proceedings of the meeting and the prophecies of Adam uttered at that conference were all written at the time in the book of Enoch and are yet to be revealed to us. (D&C 107:57.)

Enoch had a vision of things from the premortal spirit world through mortality up to and including the Millennium and beyond. He saw Noah and the Flood and Jesus being crucified. He saw the Resurrection and the restoration of the gospel in the last days. That is all recorded in Moses 6 and 7.

Enoch was the great-grandfather of Noah, and he saw in vision Noah and his family. He saw that Noah built the ark, and he saw the coming of the Flood. Enoch received a promise that his seed, or posterity, would never be completely destroyed but would continue on the earth as long as the earth should stand. "And the Lord showed Enoch all things, even to the end of the world." (Moses 7:67.) None of that is in our present Bible.

There is an interesting and highly spiritual event recorded in Moses

7:28–41, in which Enoch witnessed the God of heaven weeping. He expressed his astonishment that the Lord, who had so many creations and so much power, should weep. The Lord explained that he wept because of the wickedness of his children, that they were without natural affection, they hated one another, and would not receive him to be their Father and God, and that because of their wickedness they would have to suffer. Then Enoch also wept with the Lord. That is a most spiritual and touching scene, and we are indebted to the Prophet Joseph Smith's translation of Genesis (also recorded in the book of Moses), which contains this remarkable record.

There is yet another point to be made from this particular episode. When Enoch saw the Lord weep, he said: "How is it that the heavens weep, and shed forth their tears as the rain upon the mountains?" (Moses 7:28.) Remember this was hundreds of years before Noah was born. Many have noted that the Bible does not mention rain until the flood at Noah's time and so have wondered if perchance there was no rain that fell upon the earth until the Flood. The verse in which Enoch compares the heavens weeping to the falling rain strongly suggests that Enoch was well acquainted with rain long before Noah.

Although Enoch was translated some three thousand years before Christ, which means his life in the flesh was extended in such a way that he did not die, we learn from Doctrine and Covenants 133:54–55 that Enoch had undergone a change equal to death and was resurrected at the time of Jesus' resurrection. Such a change could occur in the twinkling of an eye, but it happened, and Enoch—as is the case with all those translated before the time of Christ—is now a resurrected being.

It was with Enoch as with all of the patriarchs and prophets: he was baptized and confirmed, ordained and endowed, in the regular order of the gospel and its ordinances.

Noah

We have already spoken somewhat of Noah, but there are a few other things to be noted. The Genesis story of the Flood is well known to Bible readers. It is mentioned in the Old Testament, the New Testament, and also the Book of Mormon, the Doctrine and Covenants, and the Pearl of Great Price. Strange as it may seem upon inspection, our present book of Genesis does not give a single word of what Noah preached to the people for the 120 years he warned of the coming deluge. Not one word! Genesis 6 through 8 tells the story, but nothing is said about what Noah preached. In these chapters the Lord talks a lot to Noah, but no record is there of what Noah said to the people.

We learn from the Joseph Smith Translation (Moses 8:23–24), however, that Noah preached repentance, and faith in Jesus Christ, and baptism, and the reception of the Holy Ghost. He also warned the people that if they did not accept the gospel of Christ the floods would come upon them. That is important. It was not for rejecting a weather report that the people were destroyed but for rejecting the first principles of the gospel of Jesus Christ. Noah was not a weather prophet but a prophet of the Lord Jesus Christ.

Perhaps you hadn't noticed this great gap and deficiency in Genesis, but it is there. In the New Testament Peter does a little better and says that Noah was "a preacher of righteousness," but no direct word is said about Noah's preaching the gospel of Christ. (2 Peter 2:5.) Because of latter-day revelation we know that Noah, like all the other prophets, was baptized, confirmed, ordained, and endowed, with the same gospel and the same ordinances that are preached among us in the Church today. We don't know who baptized Noah, but we learn from Doctrine and Covenants 107:52 that Noah was ordained at the age of ten years by his grandfather, Methuselah.

We learn from the Prophet Joseph Smith that Noah is Gabriel, and that he stands next to Adam in the hierarchy of the priesthood. Noah was like a second Adam in saving things through the Flood and re-populating the earth.[18]

Because Noah is Gabriel, we realize it was really Noah who came to Zacharias and to Mary and announced the forthcoming birth of John the Baptist and of Jesus (Luke 1). We further learn from Doctrine and Covenants 27:6–7 that this same person, who is called Gabriel and also Elias, has the assignment to bring to pass "the restoration of all things" in the last days. No doubt he, being Noah, holds this position as second to Adam. Adam, you recall, presides over all dispensations. Noah seems to have a special responsibility under Adam to bring about the Restoration. Thus both Adam and Noah have a special relationship to The Church of Jesus Christ of Latter-day Saints.

Many other interesting things about Noah are taught only in latter-day revelation, but time will not permit a more detailed report.

Melchizedek

Like Enoch, Melchizedek has been almost lost to the Bible, yet he is and was one of the greatest of prophets and patriarchs. Alma says of him: "There were many before him, and also there were many afterwards, but none were greater." (Alma 13:19.)

Little is said in Genesis of the ministry of Melchizedek, but from the Joseph Smith Translation we learn that he was valiant even as a youth and wrought great miracles by faith.

We know also that in the ancient Church the priesthood of the Son of God was named the Melchizedek Priesthood because of Melchizedek's great faith and righteousness, so as to avoid the too-frequent use of the name of Deity. (D&C 107:1–2.) Latter-day revelation makes it clear that Melchizedek was a believer in Jesus Christ and was a preacher of the gospel of Christ. For example, Alma says that Melchizedek was a high priest after the order of the holy priesthood. Alma also explains that such a high priest is ordained "after the order of the Son, the Only Begotten of the Father." (Alma 13:9; see also Alma 13:7–8; D&C 107:2–3.) The same declaration is made of Melchizedek in the Joseph Smith Translation, Genesis 14:25–40. Because of latter-day revelation we know that Melchizedek had faith in Christ and was baptized, received the gift of the Holy Ghost, was ordained, and was endowed with the same ordinances in the same gospel we know in the Church today.

In the old sixth-century church of Saint Appollonaire in Ravenna, Italy, is a mosaic showing Melchizedek at an altar with bread and wine – a reflection of Genesis 14:18. The mosaic goes beyond this passage of scripture, however, for on one side of the altar is Abel offering a lamb. On the other side is Abraham with his son Isaac. Above the whole scene is the rainbow, reminiscent of Noah. And through the clouds, reaching down from heaven is the hand of God. This very unusual piece of art brings together many notable prophets, each with a redemptive motif, in association with Christ. The fact that this mosaic exists shows that somebody in Ravenna had ideas about Melchizedek in the sixth century after Christ. It speaks of a unity of purpose in the ministries of Abel, Noah, Abraham, and Melchizedek. Christianity and Judaism have all but lost sight of Melchizedek today, probably because the Bible now contains so very little about him. Later Christian art does not emphasize Melchizedek; therefore, we have to go back to the earliest centuries to find evidence of a tradition about him.

The Prophet Joseph explained that it was Melchizedek who taught Abraham the gospel of Jesus Christ and who also ordained Abraham to the priesthood.[19] (D&C 84:14.)

Genesis 14:17 reports that Melchizedek brought forth bread and wine for himself and Abraham. The Joseph Smith Translation, however, rewords this verse to say: "Melchizedek . . . brake bread and blest it; and he blest the wine, he being the priest of the most high God." This wording suggests that there were two blessings, one for the bread and one for the wine. That would be unusual procedure for a regular meal. If it is not a description of the sacramental emblems of the forthcoming atonement of Jesus Christ, then it surely comes close to being so.

There can be no mistaking the evidence from latter-day scripture and from Joseph Smith's teachings that Melchizedek was a prophet of Jesus Christ.

Abraham

Much has already been said of Abraham, so I will add only a single instance from his writings. I have repeatedly said in this paper that Adam, Enoch, Noah, and Melchizedek each had the gospel of Christ, with the same baptism, the same priesthood, and the same endowment that are found in the Church today. There are several ways to establish this point, but one of the most important is the Prophet Joseph Smith's explanation of Facsimile 2, item 3, in the book of Abraham. It is here stated that the "grand Key-words of the Holy Priesthood" were "revealed to Adam in the Garden of Eden, as also to Seth, Noah, Melchizedek, Abraham, and all to whom the Priesthood was revealed." This language seems to be very direct and easy to be understood. It says, in effect, that the endowment, which is the ceremony by which one receives the grand key words, was given to all the prophets, beginning with Adam.

Moses

There is no question from the New Testament, especially from John 5 through 7 and Luke 24:25–27, that Moses knew of the coming of Jesus Christ and wrote of him. These are New Testament explanations, however, and the Old Testament references are not that clear. Even so, in our present Bible there is more evidence for Moses knowing of Christ than there is for the earlier prophets. That concept is strengthened in latter-day revelation with the glorious vision of Moses recorded in Moses 1. Moses there learned much about the work of Jesus Christ as creator and learned that he is the Savior and the Only Begotten of the Father. (Moses 1:6–21, 32–33.) Just as Genesis is a preface to the Old Testament, so Moses 1 is a preface to Genesis.

In a revelation to the Prophet Joseph Smith we learn that Moses was ordained to the Melchizedek Priesthood by his father-in-law, Jethro, and a priesthood lineage is given from Adam to Moses. (D&C 84:6–15.)

The Continuity of the Lord's Work

Among the many things that latter-day revelation contributes to an understanding of the Old Testament, none is more forceful than the evidence of continuity in the work of the prophets from Adam on down through the centuries. This unity and continuation of purpose is no longer evident in the Bible. I have no doubt it was there in the beginning, but it has become obscured.

The patriarchs from Adam to Methuselah were all on the earth together and knew one another and were all in the meeting at Adam-ondi-Ahman. There was an unbroken line of ordination from Adam to Methuselah and from him on down to Noah, and from Noah to Moses. When the Lord called Noah and taught him of his ministry and commanded him to build an ark, He also told him that he had the same priesthood and covenant that was given to Enoch. (JST Gen. 8:23, enlarging KJV Gen. 6:18; JST Gen. 9:15, 17, enlarging KJV Gen. 9:9, 11; see also JST Gen. 9:21–25, enlarging KJV Gen. 9:16.) Later, when the priesthood and covenant were given to Melchizedek, he was told that it was the same that Enoch possessed. (JST Gen. 14:25–40.) Still later, when Abraham was called and ordained, the Lord compared his calling to that of Enoch and told him to remember Enoch's covenant. (JST Gen. 13:13, enlarging KJV Gen. 13:14.)

These Joseph Smith Translation passages, plus the priesthood genealogy lists of Doctrine and Covenants 84:6–17 and 107:40–52, certify the credentials of the ancient patriarchs, showing that they were called of God and ordained under the hand of a living priesthood bearer. These passages certify that the patriarchs each had the same covenant and sacred work and that each was engaged in the same purposes of God. They certify that the work of God is standardized and unified. There was unity, and there was organization. Unity and organization cannot be discovered in our present book of Genesis, which tends to treat each patriarch and prophet independently as well as scantily.

Every Dispensation Was Governed by the Gospel Law

Everything is governed by a law that was formulated and existed in the premortal existence before the world was created. The gospel and plan of salvation existed then, and the same plan is still operating. Nothing has been added; nothing has been taken away. We read in Doctrine and Covenants 130:20–21: "There is a law, irrevocably decreed in heaven before the foundation of this world, upon which all blessings are predicated—

"And when we obtain any blessing from God, it is by obedience to that law upon which it is predicated."

And in Doctrine and Covenants 132:5, 8–12, we read:

"For all who will have a blessing at my hands shall abide the law which was appointed for that blessing, and the conditions thereof, as were instituted from before the foundation of the world.

"Behold, mine house is a house of order, saith the Lord God, and not a house of confusion.

"Will I accept of an offering, saith the Lord, that is not made in my name?

"Or will I receive at your hands that which I have not appointed?

"And will I appoint unto you, saith the Lord, except it be by law, even as I and my Father ordained unto you, before the world was?

"I am the Lord thy God; and I give unto you this commandment— that no man shall come unto the Father but by me or by my word, which is my law, saith the Lord."

Not every point needs to be repeated in the scripture about each prophet's calling, once we know the laws of the gospel. For example, the Prophet Joseph understood it this way:

"The gospel has always been the same; the ordinances to fulfill its requirements, the same, and the officers to officiate, the same; and the signs and fruits resulting from the promises, the same; therefore, as Noah was a preacher of righteousness he must have been baptized and ordained to the priesthood by the laying on of the hands, etc."[20]

"He [God] set the ordinances to be the same forever and ever."[21]

"It was the design of the councils of heaven before the world was, that the principles and laws of the priesthood should be predicated upon the gathering of the people in every age of the world. . . . Ordinances instituted in the heavens before the foundation of the world, in the priesthood, for the salvation of men, are not to be altered or changed. All must be saved on the same principles."[22]

The concepts taught here by the Prophet Joseph Smith must be understood if one wishes to get a clear perspective of the work of God on the earth. This perspective and cohesiveness is no longer found in the biblical record. We are grateful for latter-day scripture that puts it together for us in a comprehensive package.

Conclusions

What are some contributions of latter-day revelation in understanding the Old Testament?

1. The ancient prophets were real people. Although they lived and died, they are angels now, and many visited the Prophet Joseph Smith.

2. All of the ancient prophets had the gospel of Jesus Christ; therefore, they had the same priesthood, the same covenants, the same ordinances, and the same endowment and celestial marriage that are in the Church today.

3. The plan of salvation—the work of God on the earth in every age—is standardized and unified.

4. The ancient patriarchs were intelligent, effective gospel preachers, and record keepers. They had a highly literate society with a written and spoken language that exceeds any on earth today, and their records contained factual information not known among mankind today.

I am grateful for the Bible and for the latter-day revelation that adds to and clarifies it.

NOTES

1. *Cambridge Bible Dictionary,* s.v. "Fall."

2. *Harper's Bible Dictionary* (New York: Harper and Row, 1961), p. 185.

3. *Cambridge Bible Dictionary,* s.v. "Sacrifice."

4. Cited in Matthias F. Cowley, *Wilford Woodruff: History of His Life and Labors* (Salt Lake City: Bookcraft, 1964), p. 481.

5. George Q. Cannon, in *Journal of Discourses,* 26 vols. (London: Latter-day Saints' Book Depot, 1956), 11:337.

6. Ibid., 10:235.

7. Joseph Fielding Smith, *Doctrines of Salvation,* 3 vols. (Salt Lake City: Bookcraft, 1956), 3:74.

8. Joseph Smith, *Teachings of the Prophet Joseph Smith,* sel. Joseph Fielding Smith (Salt Lake City: Deseret Book Co., 1967), pp. 157, 158.

9. Ibid., p. 158.

10. Ibid., pp. 167–168.

11. Ibid., p. 169.

12. Joseph Smith, *History of The Church of Jesus Christ of Latter-day Saints,* ed. B. H. Roberts, 7 vols., 2d ed. rev. (Salt Lake City: Deseret Book Co., 1964), 5:247.

13. Smith, *Teachings*, p. 158.

14. *Diary of Oliver B. Huntington,* as cited in Hyrum Andrus, *Joseph Smith, the Man and the Seer* (Salt Lake City: Deseret Book Co., 1960), p. 92.

15. John Taylor, in *Journal of Discourses,* 18:326.

16. Smith, *Teachings,* pp. 170–71.

17. Ibid., p. 170.

18. Ibid., p. 157.

19. Ibid., pp. 323, 324.

20. Ibid., p. 264.

21. Ibid., p. 168.

22. Ibid., p. 308.

CHAPTER TEN

Isaiah 53: The Richest Prophecy on Christ's Atonement in the Old Testament

Keith H. Meservy

Brigham Young University

Franz Delitzsch, Jewish convert to Christianity, was greatly impressed with how much Isaiah knew about Christ. He considered Isaiah 53 to be the "most central, the deepest, and the loftiest thing that the Old Testament prophecy, outstripping itself, has ever achieved."[1] His appreciation is not overdone. Many others have drawn on its inspiration. Elder Bruce R. McConkie noted how often New Testament writers quoted it[2] and concluded that we can scarcely imagine how many sermons have been preached, lessons taught, and testimonies borne, based on its message.[3] The apparent reason Isaiah 53 evokes such strong interest and feelings does not seem hard to find: it provides the clearest perception of Christ's atonement—the centerpiece of God's plan of salvation—to be found anywhere in the Old Testament.

Not all Christian scholars, however, agree that it is a prophecy about Christ or that it has anything to do with him. They disagree with the traditional interpretation because they do not believe that God knows the distant future, and because he does not, neither could any of his prophets. Therefore, they believe that no ancient prophet could have known of the coming of Christ. More specifically, in their thinking, Isaiah, who lived seven hundred years before Christ, could not have known a single detail of his life or death. Consequently, they look for someone other than Christ to be the subject of this prophecy.[4] This is not the forum to discuss that issue, but knowing prophetic capabilities determines how we interpret this chapter. And the contents of Isaiah 53 are part of our data about what prophets could and could not do.

Traditionally within the Christian church Isaiah 53 has been interpreted as a prophecy about Christ.[5] But since that traditional interpretation is now disputed, we should ask ourselves, Is the mission of the so-called "suffering Servant," as described in Isaiah 53, doctrinally and historically consistent with what dead prophets in the Old Testament and Book of Mormon have said about Jesus' life and mission? how Jesus carried out his atoning mission? how he and his apostles interpreted his mission? how living prophets today interpret his mission?

If our answer is yes, we might reason with A. Cressy Morrison. In his book, *Man Does Not Stand Alone,* he cited the evidence of statistical improbability as being reason enough for a scientist to believe in God. We might apply his reasoning to the question of whether or not Isaiah knew about Christ. He says that if one were to number ten coins from one to ten and place them in his or her pocket and attempt to draw them out in the numbered sequence, the chance of pulling out number one would be one in ten. The chance of replacing that coin and of pulling out number two next would be one in a hundred. The chance of pulling out all ten coins in their proper sequence would be one in ten billion times of trying! Morrison observes: "The object in dealing with so simple a problem is to show how enormously figures multiply against chance."[6]

When we look at Isaiah's prophecy, let us see how many details of his prophecy are directly related to Jesus' life and ministry, especially his unique atoning ministry. Then we must ask ourselves: how many specific details in Isaiah's prophecy have to be consistent with Jesus' life before we conclude that it is statistically impossible for Isaiah to have known such details without having had any foreknowledge of Christ?

Question of Pronominal Usage

Before getting directly into the text, we raise another question: why did Isaiah use pronouns in his prophecy without supplying their antecedents? Perhaps he was showing that no prophecy stands alone, that each shows part of God's truth about the way things are, were, or will be. (D&C 93:4.) Therefore, whatever he prophesied must fit into the overall plan of God as it was formulated before the creation of the world.[7]

We know that before this earth was founded, God knew that Adam would fall and die. So he formulated a plan to circumvent the detrimental effects of these events — his deified Son would go to earth and live, and die, and live again, so he could break the bands of death and enable those who had been disabled by death to live again.

God's solution to the fall of Adam and Eve and their posterity seems
to be the necessary background against which every prophecy should
be studied. Thus, whoever hears any prophet discuss part of the plan
would understand how the part he or she hears fits into the whole, as
known to God.

Interpretation

Because Isaiah 52:13–15 is usually regarded as being the beginning
of Isaiah 53, many interpreters start their analysis of Isaiah 53 with
these verses. The Book of Mormon, however, applies these verses to
Joseph Smith. (3 Nephi 20:43–45; 21:7–11.) Therefore, I shall follow
the traditional chapter division of the Bible and begin my analysis of
Isaiah 53 with Isaiah 53:1.

Isaiah 53:1. *"Who hath believed our report? and to whom is the arm
of the Lord revealed?"* When God would send his Son to begin his
greatest work on earth, who would hear his report? Who would see
God's hand revealed? These questions raised by Isaiah were also raised
by Jesus with the Jews—were they hearing God's word when Jesus
spoke and seeing God's hand when Jesus worked? Nicodemus did (John
3:2), but many did not. Some said his words were blasphemous and
his deeds were empowered by the devil. (John 10:5–7; see also 10:20–
21; Matt. 12:24.)

But words and works were the means God used to reveal his
Messiah to the world. Jesus cited words and works as evidence that
he was the One who would come. When John's disciples questioned
whether he was or was not the One to come, he asked them simply
to follow him around. And then he said: "Tell John what things ye have
seen and heard." (Luke 7:23.) On another occasion, he said: "I told
you [that is, gave you the report] and ye believed not: the works that
I do in my Father's name, they bear witness of me [that is, reveal the
Father]. But ye believe not." (John 10:25–26; see also 10:5–7; Matt.
12:24.) "Why do ye not understand my speech? even because ye cannot
hear my word." (John 8:43.) When they refused to see God revealed
by his words and works, Jesus called them blind and deaf. Thus John
could say: "Though he had done so many miracles before them, yet
they believed not on him: That the saying of Esaias [Isaiah] the prophet
might be fulfilled, which he spake, Lord, who hath believed our report?
and to whom hath the arm of the Lord been revealed?" (John 12:37–
38.)

Isaiah 53:2. *"For he shall grow up before him as a tender plant, and as a root out of a dry ground..."* We can understand the parts of this prophecy only when we understand the whole. Let's anticipate our fuller discussion of this prophecy by concluding that *he* in this verse applies to Jesus. Therefore, any reference to *his* growing up would relate metaphorically to Jesus' growing up. During that time, according to Isaiah, he was a root or tender suckling seeking moisture and nurture in the surrounding soil–that is, within his normal environment–but finding it dry and sterile, sought for nurture elsewhere instead.

Now, because we know historically that as he grew, Jesus was "strong in spirit, filled with wisdom: and the grace of God was upon him" (Luke 2:40), we might conclude that "growing up before him" might refer to Jesus' growing up under divine grace before his Father. Thus, somewhat like all prophets, he was taught from on high — by visits from his Heavenly Father and His angels and by visions and revelations of the Holy Ghost. Thus, when Jesus reached the age of twelve, "all that heard him were astonished at his understanding and answers." (Luke 2:37.) Eventually people would ask: "How knoweth this man letters, having never learned?" (John 7:15.) That is, "how did this man grow up?"

Scriptures teach us that Jesus grew by divine grace, going from one grace to another. (D&C 93:11–17; Luke 2:40, 46–52.) Thus, "he spake not as other men, neither could he be taught: for he needed not that any man should teach him." (JST Matt. 3:25.)

Jesus typically acknowledged his dependency upon his Father for what he said and did: "I do nothing of myself; but as my Father hath taught me, I speak these things." (John 8:28.) "My doctrine is not mine, but his that sent me." (John 7:16.) "The Father which sent me, he gave me a commandment, what I should say, and what I should speak." (John 12:49.) "The Son can do nothing of himself but what he seeth the Father do: for what things soever he doeth, these also doeth the Son likewise. For the Father loveth the Son, and sheweth him all things that himself doeth." (John 5:19–20.) "For he whom God hath sent speaketh the words of God: for God giveth not the Spirit by measure unto him. The Father loveth the Son, and hath given all things into his hand." (John 3:34–35.) Thus, as he matured in divine wisdom, he spoke and acted by divine revelation rather than from rabbinic precedent.

"... he hath no form nor comeliness; and when we shall see him,

there is no beauty that we should desire him." We know nothing of Jesus' physical appearance to explain what the comparisons in this verse mean.

Isaiah 53:3. *"He is despised and rejected of men . . ."* The idea that Jesus was despised seems incompatible with our perception of him as being one who attracted multitudes from Judea, Idumaea, Perea, Galilee, Tyre, and Sidon. They all came to him for healing, for light, or out of curiosity. When their initial needs were satisfied and they thought they perceived what he was doing, they decided they could no longer walk with him. (John 6:60–66.) Some said he was possessed of a devil. (John 8:48; 10:20; Mosiah 2:9.) Others claimed that he was a Samaritan. (John 8:48.) He was hated, and he warned his disciples not to expect better treatment of a world that hated him first. (John 7: 7; 15:18, 20, 23.) Attempts were repeatedly made on his life, even by hometown neighbors in Nazareth. (John 7:19; 8:37, etc.) Rejected, he was a light shining in an otherwise uncomprehending darkness. Isaiah's words were stronger: he was despised and rejected. (John 1:4–5, 11.)

". . . a man of sorrows, and acquainted with grief . . ." We tend to think that Jesus rose above every sorrow, breasted every storm, and faced every grief this world knows without personally hurting. But if sharing things of great value—especially the gospel—brings great joy, we must conclude that the opposite also is true—that being unable to share things of eternal value, especially the gospel with its atonement so personally, painfully, and lovingly wrought by him must have brought him enormous grief. Paying such a cost to bring the gospel to them and then having them receive it so poorly must have been agonizing indeed for him to bear. So, as he rode over the Mount of Olives in his so-called "triumphal entry" and envisioned the desolation awaiting the inhabitants of this great city when they became thoroughly sick of soul, his tears flowed freely. Perhaps, better than anything else, they summarize his sorrow over Jewish failure to accept him as their Lord when he had come into their midst. The tears at the end of his ministry show how deep the sorrow within his soul really was. (Luke 19:41–44; Matt. 23:37–38.) And perhaps they suggest why, as Elder James E. Talmage believed, his death might have come from a broken heart.[8]

". . . and we hid as it were our faces from him . . ." Individual reaction to Jesus varied, but that poetic parallel shows how the world simply did not countenance him.

". . . he was despised, and we esteemed him not." This parallel again emphasizes worldly rejection of Jesus. That generation was preoccupied

by wickedness and adultery and despised him for testifying that what
they were doing was evil. They resented his intrusion into their self-
complacent, greedy, lustful way of living. Despising him and his values,
they made him into a thing of naught — a critic unworthy of credibility,
whom they thought they could ignore. This attitude astonished Nephi.
For him it was incredible that the world could judge their God "to
be a thing of naught" and trample him under their feet. (1 Nephi
19:7–10.)

Isaiah 53:4. *"Surely he hath borne our griefs and carried our sorrows . . ."* Ironically, while the world despised him, he carried its griefs
and knew its sorrows. At this point Isaiah introduces us to the cardinal
aspect of Christ's unique ministry — his vicarious suffering, death, and
resurrection whereby he would atone for the sins of the world. Of this
atonement and its universal application, Jacob could say: "He suffereth
the pains of all men, yea, the pains of every living creature, both men,
women, and children, who belong to the family of Adam." (2 Nephi
9:21.) That explains why Isaiah refers to *our* griefs and *our* sorrows.
He was referring to the totality of griefs and sorrows suffered by all
mankind, who go astray.

". . . yet we did esteem him stricken, smitten of God, and afflicted."
Because transgression brings punishment and suffering, many infer
that suffering is evidence enough of transgression. "Who ever perished
being innocent?" Don't those who "plow iniquity, and sow wickedness,
reap the same?" Are not the wages of sin death? Do not those who
perish, perish "by the blast of God"? (Job 4:7–9.) Those who observed
Jesus' suffering seem to have concluded that he suffered for his personal
sins. Isaiah, however, had known better.

*". . . But he was wounded for our transgressions, he was bruised for
our iniquities . . ."* By poetic parallel, Isaiah shows the depth of his
understanding of the vicarious nature of Christ's suffering. Only God
can overcome our sickness of soul. Therefore, we might understand
how Isaiah emphasized eleven different times in this single chapter
the vicarious aspect of Christ's atonement. His repetitions drum home
the painful and yet gladdening message in such a way that no one need
misunderstand its basic truth: Christ would suffer and die for all our
sins and do for us what we could not do for ourselves.

Wounded and *bruised* are words that make us cringe, especially
when we know that Jesus was wounded and bruised in our behalf. Who
can tolerate the thought that this holy, compassionate, loving Being,

who never transgressed the will of his Father, was willing to be wounded and bruised for us who would transgress, so that we would not have to be wounded and bruised ourselves? Free-spirited Alma the Younger could not. Before he encountered the reality and horror of personal sin, he thought he could ignore and forget God and eliminate him from his life. When he finally confronted the evil in his life, he experienced the pains of a damned soul. At that point, he discovered how much he preferred annihilation — physically and spiritually — to entering the presence of God knowing that he had broken his commandments. In his state of gall, he felt "encircled about by the everlasting chains of death." But in the depths of his misery, he remembered having heard that "Jesus Christ, a Son of God, [would] atone for the sins of the world." (Alma 36:17.) When he realized what Isaiah had taught and what his own father had been teaching — that the iniquity of us all had, before the foundation of the world, been laid upon Jesus (Isa. 53: 8), he discovered how Jesus could take over his wounding and heal his pain. When this profound truth "seized hold" of Alma's mind, he pleaded to Jesus for release from his horrendous pain, and discovered, while he pleaded, that release did come, but at Jesus' expense. Alma transferred his burdens to Jesus' account for future reckoning when Alma's pains, long since forgotten, would come alive in all their terrible fury within Jesus.

When the time of reckoning had come for Jesus, then he, like Alma, also pleaded for sweet release: "Father, all things are possible unto thee; take away this cup from me." Nevertheless, keeping faith with Alma, Jesus said: "Not what I will, but what thou wilt." (Mark 14:36–37; see also D&C 19:18.)

Presumably, his pain became as intense as Alma's joy had been. (Alma 36:17–20.) But, thus qualified to promise, he assured everyone that *all* manner of sins (excepting blasphemy) could be forgiven. (Isa. 1:18; Ezek. 18:21–23; Matt. 12:31.) Thus, nonvirgins might become virgins again; thieves, honorable again; and abusers, faultless again. All because he could heal broken hearts and comfort mourners, every one.

Knowledge of this truth provides substance to our faith and reason for our hope. It leads repentant sinners to sing in glorious relief: "Oh, it is wonderful that he should care for me / Enough to die for me." (*Hymns of The Church of Jesus Christ of Latter-day Saints*, 1985, no. 195.) It adds grateful souls to Jacob's choir as he sings of the greatness of the mercy of him who "delivereth his saints from that awful monster the devil, and death, and hell, and that lake of fire and brimstone, which is endless torment." (2 Nephi 9:19.)

This truth lies at the heart of every prophetic witness from the time of Adam to the present, as affirmed by John when he said that "the testimony of Jesus is the spirit of prophecy." (Rev. 19:10.) It could not be otherwise. Whoever receives remission of sins and gains reconciliation with God has to know that "no flesh . . . can dwell in the presence of God, save it be through the merits, and mercy, and grace of the Holy Messiah. . . . " (2 Nephi 2:8.) Thus, there is only one name given under heaven whereby we might be saved.

"... the chastisement of our peace was upon him ..." Because the chastisement, or discipline, referred to here brings *our* peace, it must be chastisement due us, because of guilt, before we can attain reconciliation and peace with him. Note again that Christ suffers vicariously for us.

Shalom, meaning "peace," derives from the verb *shillem,* " to reconcile." Atonement brings reconciliation to those who become alienated from God for transgressing his laws. Therefore, his shalom, or peace, is not the shalom, or friendly greeting, given by the world. (John 14:27.) His peace, a gift of the Spirit, is a fruit of his atonement. Thus, his peace passeth all understanding. (1 John 3:24; Philip. 4:7.) This ultimate shalom comes through wholeness of being, wellness of soul, and oneness with God.

"... and with his stripes we are healed." Again, because our healing comes from his stripes (punishment), the stripes he suffers are deserved by us. Again, his vicarious suffering brings healing to us. Elsewhere in his writings, Isaiah attributes a healing role to the Anointed One, precisely because he was anointed to bind up broken hearts, liberate captives, free those imprisoned by sin, comfort mourning hearts, replace ashes with beauty, anoint mourners with joy, and replace heaviness with praise. (Isa. 61:1–3.) Any soul, wounded unto death by living in this world, becomes a candidate for healing by this compassionate Physician.

Isaiah 53:6. *"All we like sheep have gone astray; we have turned every one to his own way."* Isaiah finally explains why this righteous Servant suffers vicariously. As accountable people, we all, including Isaiah, at some point in our lives reject divine counsel and disobey divine commands. In our pride we conclude that we, better than he, know how to find true happiness and therefore demand of him that he not fence us in. Consequently, out of hard experience, we learn that we have "sinned, and come short of the glory of God" (Rom. 3:23) and that none of us is "righteous, no, not one." (Rom. 3:10.)

Those who are wise enough to recognize this truth and honest enough to admit it to themselves and to God are prepared to receive God's solution. ". . . *the Lord hath laid on him the iniquity of us all.*"[9] Thus "when we were yet without strength, in due time Christ died for the ungodly. . . . While we were yet sinners, Christ died for us." (Rom. 5:6–8.) As Peter testified, Jesus bore "our sins in his own body on the tree, that we, being dead to sins, should live unto righteousness; by whose stripes ye were healed. For ye were as sheep going astray; but are now returned unto the Shepherd and Bishop of your souls." (1 Peter 2:24–25.)

Isaiah 53:7. *"He was oppressed, and he was afflicted, yet he opened not his mouth . . ."* Finally, when he had borne the weight of Gethsemane, Jesus was taken by temple guards to Caiaphas' palace for the next phase of his atoning work. At that point he suffered oppression and affliction at the hands of judicial officials. Thus, worldly men sat in judgment upon their Maker in their courts and "judge[d] him to be a thing of naught. Wherefore they scourge[d] him, . . . [smote] him, . . . and spit upon him, and he suffereth it, because of his loving kindness and his long-suffering towards the children of men." (1 Ne. 19:9.) How condescending, because of love, the Lord God Omnipotent had become!

And, just as Isaiah teaches, Jesus remained silent throughout the proceedings of all their courts: twice before Caiaphas, twice before Pilate, and once before Herod. Caiaphas, shocked at Jesus' silence after the many charges had been placed against him, asked: "Answerest thou nothing? What is it which these witness against thee?" But Jesus "held his peace." (Matt. 26:62–63.) Then, in Pilate's court, despite being "accused of the chief priests and elders, he answered nothing." Pilate asked him whether he understood the seriousness of the charges being made against him or not. Again, Jesus "answered him to never a word," causing Pilate to marvel greatly. (Matt. 27:12–14.) Herod "questioned with him in many words; but he answered him nothing," despite the fact that many "chief priests and scribes stood and vehemently accused him." (Luke 23:9–10.) Back in Pilate's court, Pilate asked: "Whence art thou?" Because Pilate was not asking about his hometown but rather about where he was coming from, Jesus "gave him no answer." (John 19:9–11.)

During these proceedings, Jesus did not really defend himself against the injustice of the charges, despite his being set at naught, mocked, taunted, spit upon, falsely accused, scourged, crowned, and ridiculed by Jewish and Roman officials. We also marvel that he bore up under the official affliction and oppression without opening his mouth. But Jesus, by personal example, challenges all Christians, who also suffer unjustly, to follow his example. Said Peter: "This is thankworthy, if a man for conscience toward God endure grief, suffering wrongfully. . . . [or] if, when ye do well, and suffer for it, ye take it patiently, this is acceptable with God. . . . because Christ also suffered for us, leaving us an example. . . . Who, when he was reviled, reviled not again; when he suffered, he threatened not; but committed himself to him that judgeth righteously." (1 Peter 2:19–23.)

Jesus' willingness to be judged a thing of naught by worldly standards without any remonstrance shows how willing he was to descend below all things.

"*. . . he is brought as a lamb to the slaughter . . .*" The metaphor of a lamb about to be slaughtered might have been a popular figure wherewith to portray the suffering Messiah, but it reflects also the attitude of Caiaphas when he ordered that Jesus be arrested. Caiaphas had convinced his Sanhedrin that if Jesus were allowed to continue his work, the Jewish nation and the Sanhedrin would be at risk. Therefore, said Caiaphas, "It is expedient for us, that one man should die for the people and that the whole nation perish not." (John 11:50.) So Jesus was brought by Caiaphas to their slaughter.

"*. . . and as a sheep before her shearers is dumb, so he openeth not his mouth.*" Once again Jesus' silence during the proceedings is highlighted by poetic parallel. This metaphor only partly applies to Jesus because he knew that he was about to be slaughtered, not sheared. But the dumbness of the sheep in both instances applies metaphorically to Jesus' persistent silence.

Isaiah 53:8. "*He was taken from prison and from judgment . . .*" No gospel account speaks of Jesus' being imprisoned, but, having been condemned to death late at night, he must have spent the remainder of that night in the high priest's prison. (One wonders if he got any sleep during that night.) Next morning he was taken from judgments in Jewish and in Roman courts to Calvary for execution of the sentence.

". . . and who shall declare his generation? for he was cut off out of the land of the living." This verse, as well as verses 9 and 12, show how well Isaiah knew that Jesus had to taste "death for every man. . . . that through death he might destroy him that had the power of death, that is, the devil; and deliver them who through fear of death were all their lifetime subject to bondage." (Heb. 2:9, 14–15.)[10]

Because the death of the righteous servant—that is, Jesus—was foreseen by Isaiah, one wonders at what point in his growing up years Jesus learned that *he* would be the Messiah? At what point did he learn what being Messiah meant? Is it possible that while he was studying Isaiah 53, he came to know for the first time on earth what being God's special Son meant? And, is it possible on that occasion that the Father himself came to visit his Son to explain to him how he, the Messiah, would have to be cut off out of the land of the living? We cannot know, but it seems quite possible.

Since he would die, who could talk about his generation—his offspring? Abinidi responds to this question by saying that when his soul would become "an offering for sin he shall see his seed." Atonement brings back life to those spiritually and physically dead. They are born again as new creatures and he is their Begetter, so they become his sons and daughters. Thus, those dead in sin who look to him for "a remission of their sins, . . . [gain new life and become] his seed. . . . these are they whose sins he has borne; these are they for whom he has died, to redeem them from their transgressions. And now, are they not his seed?" (Mosiah 15:10–12; see also Isaiah 53:10.)

". . . for the transgression of my people was he stricken." Once more, like a throbbing drum, Isaiah underlines the vicarious nature of Jesus' suffering.

Isaiah 53:9. *"And he made his grave with the wicked."*

In this parallel context, "being stricken" means "being stricken to death." Thus, dying with transgressors must mean making his grave with the wicked.

". . . and with the rich in his death." Though dying among or with the wicked, he would be buried in the tomb of the rich man, Joseph of Arimathea.

". . . because he had done no violence, neither was any deceit in his mouth." That is, in his death a great injustice would be done. A just man would die. Would there be deceit in his mouth? Why, he was the God of truth, who could not lie. (Ether 3:12.) He had come into the

world to "bear witness unto the truth." (John 18:37.) He was "full of grace and truth." (John 1:14, 17.) He was Truth personified. (John 14:6.)

Violence in him? Rather than commit violence or even have violence carried out in his name, he taught disciples to suffer abuse rather than give it, turn the other cheek, pray for enemies, be peacemakers, be forgiving, be reconciled to other people before trying to be reconciled to God, do to others what one would have them do to oneself, etc. Thus, neither in word nor deed did he commit deception or violence, as confirmed by Pilate to those who charged him with being a malefactor: Pilate found no fault in him. Peter, who best knew him on earth, echoed this judgment when he said that Jesus "did no sin, neither was guile found in his mouth." (1 Peter 2:22.) Being sinless, the Just One died to bring us, the unjust, to God.

Isaiah 53:10. *"Yet it pleased the Lord to bruise him; he hath put him to grief..."* Here *Lord* signifies the Father, and the Father obviously got no pleasure out of bruising his Son. Nevertheless, the Father must have been delighted that his Firstborn volunteered to be his earthly Son and submit himself to be bruised so that justice might be satisfied. (Moses 4:1–2; Abr. 3:27.)

"... when thou shalt make his soul an offering for sin, he shall see his seed..." Isaiah addresses here the One Who would offer His Son.[11] In doing so, Isaiah answers the question posed in verse 8 about his generation — that is, his seed. Having life in himself, he could generate life and give power to those who believe in him "to become the sons [and daughters] of God." (John 1:12–13; D&C 93:22; Mosiah 5:7; Romans 8; John 3:3–5; D&C 93:22.)

By calling his sacrifice an "offering for sin," Isaiah recognized the sacrificial nature of his death. It was the sacrifice that God who loved the world enough was willing to make. It was the necessary sacrifice that had been offered before the world was. (Rev. 13:8.) It was the sacrifice announced by his forerunner when he introduced him as "the Lamb of God, which taketh away the sin of the world." (John 1:29.)

To commemorate the preeminence of this sacrifice, God, from the time of Adam, had required his children to offer the "firstlings of their flocks." These sacrifices became similitudes "of the sacrifice of the Only Begotten of the Father." (Moses 5:5–7, 10–12, 58–59; 6:48–63.) And, being similitudes, their blood, or life, had to be given. For blood is "the life of the flesh." That is, life, or blood, was required to make "an atonement for the soul." (Lev. 17:11.) "Without the shedding of blood" there is no atonement or remission of sins. (Heb. 9:22.) Thus, the very first man who lived on this earth learned that he would be cleansed by "the blood of [God's] Only Begotten." (Moses 6:59.) Likewise, Peter testified that all mankind could be redeemed by "the precious blood of Christ, as of a lamb without blemish and without spot, who verily was foreordained before the foundation of the world." (1 Peter 1:19–20.) And so, having required Christ to become an "offering for sin," God required his children to simulate his offering of Christ. (Alma 34:13–14; 3 Nephi 9:20.)

"*. . . he shall prolong his days, and the pleasure of the Lord shall prosper in his hand.*" Prolonging days is what immortality is all about, and prolonging days through resurrection makes "the pleasure of the Lord" prosper. (See Moses 1:39.) Thus, *in* or *by means of* his hand or *by his power*, he broke the bands of death. Thus, "when we were yet without strength, in due time Christ died for the ungodly." (Rom. 5:6.) Thus, we could become "dead indeed unto sin, but alive unto God through Jesus Christ our Lord." (Rom. 6:11.) And that makes the Lord's pleasure prosper.

Isaiah 53:11. *"He shall see of the travail of his soul, and shall be satisfied . . ."* In this passage *He* is the Father, who required that his Son Jesus suffer travail of soul, and *His* soul was the soul of Jesus. *Travail* poignantly describes what Jesus experienced in working out the Atonement. Alma, in describing his own pain for sin, used phrases reminiscent of the torture chamber—"racked with pain," "filled with horror."

The record is sparse concerning Jesus' anguish: he became very heavy, he was amazed, he trembled, he shrank, he bled at every pore, he suffered both body and spirit, he suffered more than man can suffer, he sweat great drops of blood. (Luke 22:44; D&C 19:16–18; Mosiah 3:7.) These writers grapple as they try to comprehend the unfathomable pain he bore as he carried the burden of this world's sins. Isaiah encompassed this in his phrase "travail of soul," of the kind known only to the Messiah, but of the kind that God found to be sufficient.

Isaiah asserts that God "shall be satisfied" but Alma qualifies that assertion when he says that justice had to be satisfied in order for God's merciful plan to operate. Thus, "God himself atoneth for the sins of the world . . . to appease the demands of justice." Appeasing justice would make him "a perfect, just God, and a merciful God also." (Alma

42:15.) When justice is satisfied, mercy can encircle repentant souls in the "arms of safety" and protect them from the insistent demands of justice. (Alma 34:15–16.) Thus, justice is satisfied when the Messiah bears our griefs, carries our sorrows, is wounded for our transgressions, bruised for our iniquities, bears our chastisement, has our iniquities laid on him, is oppressed and taken from prison and judgment, fathoms our travail of soul, and bears our iniquities. Suffering for us, he satisfies justice, which makes the pleasure of the Lord prosper.

"... *by his knowledge shall my righteous servant justify many; for he shall bear their iniquities.*" Here *his* knowledge must refer to the Father's knowledge that "It is finished." Thus, through his unique service, the righteous Servant will "justify many, for he shall bear their iniquities." Once again Isaiah speaks of Christ's vicarious work in bearing our iniquities. His phrase "justify many" describes the precise effects of his atonement. While the atonement is infinite in power, universal in application, and available to all, it applies nevertheless only to those who freely accept it. God cannot forgive active transgressors nor save those who refuse to believe in and accept the means he provides for their salvation. He never forces his love or his mercy upon anyone. To receive his justification, one must accept his freely-given gift. Thus, he "suffered these things for all, that they might not suffer if they would repent," but if they would not repent they "must suffer even as [he]." (D&C 19:16–17.) Thus, the many to whom Isaiah refers who are justified, are those who "believe on his name"; whereas those who show neither faith nor repentance are "exposed to the whole law of the demands of justice; [and] therefore only unto him that has faith unto repentance is brought about the great and eternal plan of redemption." (Alma 34:16.) "Salvation cometh to none else ... [and] the wicked remain as though there had been no redemption made, except it be the loosing of the bands of death." (Alma 11:40–41.)

Righteous Servant

Isaiah identifies the subject of this prophecy as a "righteous servant." But *servant* is a title that applies to various subjects, so its use here is not definitive.[12] As already noted, however, the kind of unique service that this servant does leads us to conclude that Jesus is the One to whom Isaiah referred.

Other students, of course, for reasons given at the beginning of this chapter, look for alternative identifications. Two other types of candidates appear: Israel personified and a variety of historical persons.

First, as the seed of Abraham, Israel was called to bless, that is, to serve, the nations of the earth. Israel would perform this service by virtue of holding God's priesthood (ministry) and receiving his revelation, that is, by extending God's work throughout the world. (Gen. 12; Abraham 2:11.) Within the book of Isaiah, the Lord sees Israel in this light: "Thou art my servant, O Israel, in whom I will be glorified." (Isa. 49:3; 48:20; 43:10.) Many Christian interpreters accept this use as the proper identification of the servant in Isaiah 53; however, Aston has definitively refuted the idea.[13]

Second, various individuals (messiah, king, prophet) are servants. Some Jews who reject Jesus as the subject of the prophecy in Isaiah 53 nevertheless believe that this is an unfulfilled prophecy about the Messiah who is yet to come.[14] Some identify one or another ancient Israelite leader as the righteous servant: Moses, Hezekiah, Jeremiah, the so-called "Second Isaiah" himself, and so on.[15] But there is no consensus on these identifications.

By making the Atonement for all the people in the world, Jesus rendered the greatest service anyone could render—doing for others what they could not do for themselves. Thus, Jesus was a servant par excellence. His whole life was spent in service. (Mosiah 2:17.) He defined the meaning of his life by service. He came to minister and not to be ministered to, "to give his life a ransom for many." (Matt. 20:27–28; 23:10–12; Mark 10:45.) Service, he taught by word and deed, is the greatest use to which a life can be put. (Luke 22:24–27.) Thus he could promise: "He that is greatest among you shall be your servant." (Matt. 23:11; 20:26.) Thus service earns one the highest commendation in the hereafter. (Matt. 25:31–46.) So, when he washed their feet, he seems to have summarized for them the meaning of his life and teachings. (John 13:12–16; Matt. 20:25–28.) There is no example of anyone rendering greater service to more people than he. How appropriate of Isaiah to epitomize the subject of this marvelous prophecy about his vicarious service by calling him a righteous Servant.

Isaiah 53:12. *"Therefore will I divide him a portion with the great..."* Since *I* identifies the One who provides the reward, it also identifies the One who required the sacrifice, who had to be pleased when it was made, who could reward the One who performed it—that is, Jesus' Father. When Isaiah uses *I* here, he is doing it by divine investiture of authority.

Elsewhere we learn how great Jesus' reward will be when he is glorified, appointed heir of all things, and sits "on the right hand of majesty on high." (Heb. 1:3.) "Angels and authorities and powers [will all become] subject unto him." Until then he sits at God's right hand until his enemies become his footstool. (1 Peter 3:22; Ps. 110:2.) Of him it will be said, Never did the Father say to the angels as he saith unto the Son: "Thy throne, O God, is for ever and ever: a sceptre of righteousness is the sceptre of thy kingdom. Thou hast loved righteousness, and hated iniquity; therefore God, even thy God, hath anointed thee with the oil of gladness above thy fellows." (Heb. 1:8–9.)

"*. . . and he shall divide the spoil with the strong . . .*" Any victor, of course, shares spoils with whomever he pleases. Jesus divides his spoils with the Twelve. Said he: "I appoint unto you a kingdom, as my Father hath appointed unto me; that ye may eat and drink at my table in my kingdom." (Luke 22:29–30; Matt. 19:8.) He identifies the *strong* elsewhere as being those who overcome all things and endure to the end. With these, He again divides the spoil, as he promised: "To him that overcometh will I grant to sit with me in my throne, even as I also overcame, and am set down with my Father in his throne." (Rev. 3:21; D&C 76:53–60.)

"*. . . because he hath poured out his soul unto death . . .*" Again Isaiah repeats the awesome price Christ would pay for his victory and, by his precise words, shows that Jesus participated as an active agent in making the sacrifice by pouring out his own soul. This action had been foreshadowed by the visit of Elijah and Moses on the Mount of Transfiguration when they prepared him for his "decease which he should *accomplish* at Jerusalem." (Luke 9:31; italics added.) Jesus explained how he would accomplish his decease when he said: "I lay down my life. . . . no man taketh it from me, but I lay it down of myself. I have power to lay it down." (John 10:17–18.)

Thus, when his time had fully come, he set his face to go to Jerusalem, refused to call down legions of angels to defend himself, repeated his willingness to drink the cup which the Father had poured for him, and, when he had finished all that he had to do, he announced: "Father, into thy hands I commend my spirit." (Luke 23:46.) Then "he bowed his head, and *gave up* the ghost," and died. (John 19:30; italics added.)

By saying that *he poured out his soul* unto death, Isaiah may be suggesting why it was important for him to die on the cross — for this manner of death allowed him time to do the pouring out. If he had been beheaded, hanged, run through with a sword, or stoned, he would have died instantaneously without having had any time to use his volition in giving up his life. When they put him on the cross to see that he died, all they needed to satisfy their desires was time. Given time, he would die. But by giving him time, they gave him control over the giving. He could decide at what point to lay down his life. Thus, as a priest sacrificing a lamb, he performed the sacrifice. And as a Lamb, he became his own victim. (Heb. 8:1–2; 9:11–16, esp. v. 14.) This crucial detail was known to Isaiah when he said that the righteous servant would pour out his own soul unto death.

"*... and he was numbered with the transgressors ...*" In making the Atonement, Jesus was crucified between "two thieves; the one on his right hand, and the other on his left. And the scripture was fulfilled, which saith, And he was numbered with the transgressors." (Mark 15:27–28; Luke 22:37; see also Isaiah 53:9.)

"*... and he bare the sin of many, and made intercession for the transgressors.*"

Like a death knell, we are reminded once more of the vicarious nature of his suffering. And by saying that he would bear the sin of *many*, Isaiah reminds us by his precise language that Christ bore the sins of those who "come unto God by him, seeing he ever liveth to make intercession for them." (Heb. 7:25; 9:24; see also Isaiah 53:11.)

Conclusion

How clearly Isaiah shows that the work of this unnamed Sufferer is vicarious in nature and that it provides healing for those bruised and wounded by living. How clearly he shows that his costs would be anguish, bruising, humiliation, and ultimately his life, but that he would willingly undertake all this to satisfy the pleasure of the Father and to provide reconciliation for all. How consistently the picture Isaiah gives is the picture of what Christ does, as declared by prophets, of what we know of how Jesus lived his life, of how he worked out his atonement, and how his apostles and all prophets have interpreted his mission.

This being so, what statistical chance is there that a prophecy could be made that would have so many specific historical and doctrinal points in common with Jesus' life without Isaiah knowing of Jesus beforehand?

Don't these technical similarities all rule out the possibility of there being only a chance relationship between the life of Jesus and Isaiah's prophecy? Don't they rule out any idea that these similarities exist because Jesus simply imitated the prophecy? Rather, do they not show that Isaiah knew with precision of the coming of Jesus and of his atoning mission? Especially since scholars cannot agree on any other serious candidate as a substitute? And since the technical similarities show that Isaiah clearly knew of Christ, there is no reason to believe that other prophets might not have known of him also, and this, of course, is what Jesus insisted.

It is amazing that Moffatt, who believed that no prophet anciently knew of Christ, explained away the numerous similarities between Isaiah's prophecy and Jesus' life by saying that the suffering Servant conception was organic to the consciousness of Jesus, and that he often regarded His vocation in the light of this extremely suggestive prophecy.[16] That is, Moffatt says, the similarities exist because Jesus imitated what Isaiah said rather than because Isaiah knew beforehand what Jesus would do. Moffatt, of course, does not explain why Jesus would want to imitate the role of someone who suffers for someone else, or why he would have to die, nor does it explain why the Gospel writers explain that our atonement for sin depends upon Jesus' suffering and death.

We are also amazed at how casually scholars attempt to explain away Jesus' application of these prophecies to himself. (Luke 24:6–27.) In one book, Jesus' and his apostles' testimony that the prophets knew of him is explained away in one footnote. We are told that Jesus simply did what other Jewish interpreters (rabbis and Dead Sea sectarians) of his day did when they likened or applied the scriptures to themselves![17]

But the clarity of Isaiah's vision shows in part why Elder Bruce R. McConkie says of him that he "knew and taught more about redemption and atonement than any of Israel's seers."[18] Martin Luther, who believed in prophetic ability to foretell the distant future, said, "Isaiah 53 is a witness of Christ that stands so bright that even in the New Testament, apart from Paul, there is hardly a passage to equal it."[19]

One reason it was so important for prophets and people to know of the coming of Christ is explained by Alma: "Is not a soul at this time as precious unto God as a soul will be at the time of his coming? Is it not as necessary that the plan of redemption should be made known unto this people as well as unto their children? Is it not as easy at this time for the Lord to send his angel to declare these glad tidings unto us as unto our children, or as after the time of his coming?" (Alma 39:17–19.)

All prophetic witnesses, living and dead, guided by revelation, agree. Those bound by a rational definition of God disagree. How important it is for us to have a second witness to what we are taught in the Bible so we do not misunderstand such a fundamentally important subject as this. The Book of Mormon is thus not only a second witness of Jesus' resurrection and ministry but also of the truth that prophets anciently knew of the distant coming of Christ.

I conclude with Franz Delitzsch's testimony:

"How many are there whose eyes have been opened when reading this 'golden passional of the Old Testament evangelist' as Polycarp the Lysian calls it! In how many an Israelite has it melted the crust of his heart! It looks as if it had been written beneath the cross upon Golgotha, and was illuminated by the heavenly brightness of the full *shev limini* ["sit thou on my right hand" (Ps. 110:1.)] It is the unravelling of Ps. xxii. and Ps. cx. It . . . is the most central, the deepest, and the loftiest thing that the Old Testament prophecy, outstripping itself, has ever achieved."[20]

This I believe.

NOTES

1. C. F. Keil and F. Delitzsch, *Biblical Commentary on the Prophecies of Isaiah,* 2 vols., trans. James Martin (Grand Rapids, Mich.: William B. Eerdmans Publishing Co., 1877; reprint 1965), 2:303.

2. He cites Matt. 8:17; Acts 8:27–35; Rom. 4:25; 1 Pet. 2:24–25.

3. Bruce R. McConkie, *The Promised Messiah* (Salt Lake City: Deseret Book Co., 1978), p. 235.

4. Book of Mormon readers recognize the logic and underlying assumption of this "modern" argument as being the same as that made by Korihor before Christ came to earth. Korihor, like them, assumed that "no man can know anything which is to come," and concluded that no one could "know that there shall be a Christ." (Alma 30:13, 15.) Whoever makes Korihor's assumption must logically draw his conclusion.

Korihor did not enjoy the luxury of waiting to see if prophecies about Christ came to pass. (Deut. 18:21–22.) We might excuse him for not believing that Christ would come. But Christian scholars have better resources. They have the testimony of Jesus and his apostles, affirming that prophets knew he would come. In this light, they know that Jesus called two of his disciples "fools and slow of heart" for

not believing "all that the prophets" had spoken concerning him and that, while
he expounded to them all of the scriptures concerning himself the Spirit testified
to them that what he was teaching was true. (Luke 24:25–32.)

Latter-day Saints are further blessed. Their scriptures and prophets abundantly confirm the truth of what Christ was doing for those disciples. Ancient
prophets, such as Alma, testified that Christ would come. Nephi testified that
thoughts of Christ's coming preoccupied his thoughts. He wrote, talked, preached,
and prophesied about Christ so his children would "know to what source they
[might] look for a remission of their sins." (2 Ne. 25:26.) Elder McConkie declared
that "prophetic utterances about Christ and his atonement have been the most
prominent part of the preachments of all the prophets." (*Promised Messiah*, p. 234.)
His voluminous work, *Promised Messiah*, is an extended affirmation of this truth.

Modern and ancient prophets reject Korihor's assumption and affirm their
own conviction that the "testimony of Jesus is the spirit of prophecy." (Rev. 19:10.)
Therefore, we might protest any efforts being made to redefine prophetic power
by human standards. Scriptures that originate in the mind of God are not subject
to interpretations that originate in the mind of men. (2 Pet. 1:20–21; D&C 50:17–
20; 1 Cor. 1:18–21; 2:1–15.)

Because Alma knew by personal experience that Christ would come and atone
for his sins, he wondered what evidence Korihor had for concluding that He would
not. Without waiting for an answer, he said to Korihor: "Ye have none, save it be
your word only." (Alma 30:40) But divine truths are never based on the mere
word of man. They always come from God and are witnessed to by his Spirit. (D&C
50:13–23.)

No one is bound to accept scholarly assumptions or conclusions that contradict
the testimony of Jesus and the prophets. Assumptions that are based on the words
alone of the scholar who proposes them provide an inadequate base upon which
to establish truths upon which to base one's life. Those truths are always founded
upon his rock. (Matt. 7:24–7.)

On the practical side, one cannot see how Isaiah could have promised people
with scarlet-hued sins that their sins could be whitened if he had not known how
God, through Christ, would absolve them of their guilt. We see from Isaiah 53 that
Isaiah knew that Christ would come and be "wounded for our transgression" so
that he and we all might be healed "with his stripes." (Cf. Isa. 1:18; 53:6–7, 10.)
Therefore, he could promise his people that they would be healed.

5. See references in note 3. For one example among many, Eusebius (A.D.
260–340), early church historian, asserts matter-of-factly that the prophets knew
of Christ. "What He [Christ] did and what He suffered accorded with the prophecies,
which foretold that a man who was also god would live in the world as a worker
of miracles. . . . They foretold also the miracles of His birth, the new teaching, and
the marvels of His works, and furthermore the manner of His death, His resurrection from the dead, and also of His restoration to heaven by the power of God.
His final kingdom was shown by the Holy Spirit to Daniel the prophet, who thus
inspired described the vision of God in human terms [Dan. 7:9–10, 13–14.]." (Eu-

sebius, *The History of the Church from Christ to Constantine,*, trans. G.A. Williamson [New York: Penguin Books], 1965, pp. 39–40.)

6. A. Cressy Morrison, *Man Does Not Stand Alone* (New York: Fleming H. Revell Co., 1944), p. 13.

7. "The great Jehovah contemplated the whole of the events connected with the earth, pertaining to the plan of salvation, before it rolled into existence. . . ; the past, the present, and the future were and are, with Him, one eternal 'now.' He knew of the fall of Adam, etc., etc." (Joseph Smith, *Teachings of the Prophet Joseph Smith,* sel. Joseph Fielding Smith [Salt Lake City: Deseret News Press, 1951], p. 220; see also pp. 12–13.)

8. James E. Talmage, *Jesus the Christ* (Salt Lake City: Deseret Book Co., 1977), p. 669.

9. The *Lord* referred to here is understood to be the Father even though *Jehovah* appears in the Hebrew.

10. When Jesus first explained to his disciples what being the Messiah meant — having to go to "Jerusalem, and suffer many things . . . and be killed, and be raised again the third day," Peter rebuked him. In turn, Jesus rebuked Peter for not savoring the "things that be of God." (Matt. 16:21–23.) Isaiah, who savored the things of God very well, knew the righteous servant would have to be cut off out of the land of the living. (Other prophets knew the same thing: see Moses 7:47; JST Gen. 15:11; Num. 21:8–9; Hel. 8:14–19; John 3:14.)

11. At times, Isaiah shifts persons to provide a more direct thrust to his message: "How art *thou* fallen from heaven, O Lucifer!" (Isa. 14:12; italics added.)

12. "No subject connected with the Old Testament has been more discussed than the question of the identity of the Suffering Servant in Deutero-Isaiah. Nor can it be said that we are any nearer to a consensus of opinion to-day than we have ever been since the era of critical scholarship opened. . . . My purpose is but to emphasize how great is the variety of contemporary view, and to warn against the acceptance of mine or anyone else's view with an easy satisfaction." (H. H. Rowley, "The Servant of the Lord in the Light of Three Decades of Criticism," in *The Servant of the Lord and Other Essays on the Old Testament* (London: Lutterworth Press, [n.d.]), p.3. For a fuller discussion of the various identifications that have been posed, see Christopher R. North, *The Suffering Servant in Deutero-Isaiah,* 2d ed. (London: Oxford University Press, 1956).

13. Frederick Alfred Aston, *The Challenge of the Ages: New Light on Isaiah 53,* 19th ed., rev. (Scarsdale: Research Press, 1968).

14. Among the "fairly typical" comments by Jewish writers of the Servant being the Messiah, C. R. North cites this one from the *Pesiqta:* "The Holy One brought forth the soul of the Messiah, and said to him, 'Art thou willing to be created and to redeem my sons after 6,000 years?' He said, 'I am.' God replied, 'If so, thou must take upon thyself chastisements in order to wipe away their iniquity,' as it is written, 'Surely our weaknesses he hath carried.' The Messiah answered, 'I will take them upon me gladly.' The most famous passage is one from the Talmud: 'The Messiah — what is his name? . . . The rabbis say, The leprous one; those of the house of Rabbi (Judah han-Nasi) say, The sick one, as it is said,

Surely he hath borne our sicknesses &c.' " (North, *Suffering Servant*, p. 14.)

Franz Delitzsch has said: " 'Christian Scholars,' says Abravanel, 'interpret this prophecy as referring to that man who was crucified in Jerusalem about the end of the second temple, and who, according to their view, was the Son of God, who became man in the womb of the Virgin. But Jonathan ben Uziel explains it as relating to the Messiah who has yet too come; and this is the opinion of the ancients in many of their Midrashim.' So [Delitzsch concluded] that even the synagogue could not help acknowledging that the passage of the Messiah through death to glory is predicted here. And what interest could we have in understanding by the 'servant of Jehovah' in this section, the nation of Israel generally, as many Rabbis, both circumcised and uncircumcised have done; whereas he is that One Israelite in whom Jehovah has effected the redemption of both Israel and the heathen, even through the medium of Israel itself? Or what interest could we have in persuading ourselves that Jeremiah, or some unknown martyr-prophet, is intended, as Grotius, Bunsem and Ewald suppose; whereas it is rather the great unknown and misinterpreted One, whom Jewish and Judaizing exegesis still continues to misinterpret in its exposition of the figures before us, just as His contemporaries misinterpreted Him when He actually appeared before them." (Keil and Delitzsch, *Biblical Commentary*, 2:303.)

"R. Yose the Galilaean said, Come forth and learn the righteousness of the King Messiah and the reward of the just from the first man who received but one commandment, a prohibition, and transgressed it: consider how many deaths were inflicted upon himself, upon his own generations, and upon those that followed them, till the end of all generations. Which attribute is the greater, the attribute of goodness or the attribute of vengeance? He answered, The attribute of goodness is the greater, and the attribute of vengeance is the less; how much more, then, will the King Messiah, who endures affliction and pains for the transgressors (as it is written, 'he was wounded,' etc.) justify all generations! and this is what is meant when it is said, 'And the Lord made the iniquity of us all meet upon him.'

"The argument is this: If Adam's guilt entailed such consequences upon all his descendants, and the attribute of vengeance or justice is still not so potent as that of mercy, how much more will the sufferings of the Messiah redound to the advantage of all mankind! Compare the similar reasoning of St. Paul, Rom. 5:15–19, and Delitzsch's note in his interesting edition of this epistle in Hebrew (Leipzig, 1870)." As quoted in S. R. Driver and A. D. Neubauer, *The Fifty-third Chapter of Isaiah According to the Jewish Interpreters*, 2 vols. (Oxford and London: James Parker and Co, 1877), 2:10–11.

15. North, *Suffering Servant*, pp. 39–57.

16. As quoted in North, *Suffering Servant*, p. 23.

17. "One must not assume that the modern analysis, although it may be factually correct, was the view shared by Jesus or his contemporaries. The Qumran sectarians, who were responsible for the Dead Sea Scrolls . . . thought that the ancient prophets, like Habakkuk, had foretold the existence of the Qumran group and written about its history and destiny line by line. The Pharisees and their

successors, the rabbis, thought that, since every important event was intended by God, it must be found in the Scriptures. Thus, Matthew's insistence on fulfillment in Jesus is typical in its presupposition of prophetic foresight." As quoted in Raymond E. Brown, S.S., *The Birth of the Messiah* (Garden City, N.Y.: Image Books, 1979), p. 146, n. 39.

18. McConkie, *Promised Messiah,* p. 233.

19. Emil G. Kraeling, *The Old Testament Since the Reformation* (New York: Harper and Brothers, 1955), p. 17.

20. Keil and Delitzsch, *Biblical Commentary,* 2:303.

CHAPTER ELEVEN

The House of Israel: From Everlasting to Everlasting

Robert L. Millet

Brigham Young University

About three years ago I was startled by a question from a bright young woman in a rather large introductory Book of Mormon class. We were about two-thirds of the way through the second half of the Book of Mormon. She said, essentially, "Brother Millet, you continue to use a phrase that I don't understand. Maybe others in the class have the same problem. You keep referring to 'the house of Israel.' What do you mean?" For a full ten seconds I stood in wonder. It had never occurred to me that at this point in the two-semester course I needed to define and describe something so fundamental. I briefly explained during the period and asked her to see me after class. I learned that she was an 'A' student, had been raised in the Church, had completed four years of seminary, and had an excellent knowledge of the gospel.

Just last year in a large class on the Book of Mormon for returned missionaries, a young man raised his hand during our discussion of the Savior's teachings in 3 Nephi concerning the destiny of Israel. He asked: "Brother Millet, I don't mean to be disrespectful or irreverent in any way, but I need to know: What difference does it make if I am of the house of Israel? Why does it matter that my patriarchal blessing specifies that I am of the tribe of Ephraim?" During this same class period, I asked the class: "How many of you are adopted into the house of Israel?" Of the eighty members of the class, perhaps sixty raised their hands, evidencing their own misunderstandings concerning patriarchal declarations of lineage.

These instances and others illustrate what I sense to be a particular problem among many Latter-day Saints as this century draws to a close and as we draw nearer to the time when the Holy One of Israel will return to reign over his covenant people. I sense frequently among young and old a lack of covenant consciousness, not necessarily in regard to the covenants and ordinances required for salvation, but rather in a lack of feeling appropriate kinship and identity with ancient Israel and with the fathers — Abraham, Isaac, and Jacob — and of understanding and carrying out the responsibilities we have inherited from them.

In our democratic and egalitarian society, in a time when equality and brotherhood are all important, I fear that we are losing a feel for what it means to be a covenant people, what it means to be a chosen people. Too many even among the Latter-day Saints cry out that such sentiments are parochial and primitive, that they lead to exclusivism and racism. Others contend that to emphasize Israel's chosen status is to denigrate and degrade others not designated as Israel.

Careful and prayerful study of scripture — particularly the Old Testament and the Book of Mormon — will not only bring people to understand in their minds the origins and destiny of the descendants of Jacob, but will also cause them to know in their hearts what it means to come to earth through a chosen lineage and what God would have them do to be a light to the world, particularly to so many who sit in spiritual darkness. I feel that the words of the Lord to ancient Israel should be received by modern Israel with sobriety and humility, but they must be received and believed if we are to realize our potential to become a holy people and a royal priesthood. Jehovah spoke millennia ago of "Israel, whom I have chosen" (Isa. 44:1) and assured the Israelites that "you only have I known of all the families of the earth" (Amos 3:2; see also Isa. 45:4). This paper will deal with the house of Israel — its place and mission in the earth, how and why God has chosen them, and what things lie ahead for the people that God delights to call his "peculiar treasure." The subject is vast and obviously worthy of volumes, but I will attempt to touch only briefly upon what I perceive to be crucial elements in understanding Israel's past, present, and future.

Israel in Premortality

Zenos' allegory of the olive tree draws to a close as the millennial day witnesses the gathering of Israel by the chosen servants in great numbers and as the Gentiles join with Israel to constitute one royal family. "And thus they labored, with all diligence, according to the commandments of the Lord of the vineyard, even until the bad had been cast away out of the vineyard, and the Lord had preserved unto himself that the trees had become again the natural fruit; and they became like unto one body; and the fruits were equal; and *the Lord of the vineyard had preserved unto himself the natural fruit, which was most precious unto him from the beginning."* (Jacob 5:74; italics added.) I believe this passage refers to Jehovah's love and tender regard for Israel, which stretches beyond her mortal origins and sojournings and reaches back to the premortal day wherein certain souls qualified for a select status.

Following our birth as spirits, being endowed with agency, each of the spirit sons and daughters of God grew and developed and progressed according to their desires for truth and righteousness. "Being subject to law," Elder Bruce R. McConkie wrote, "and having their agency, all the spirits of men, while yet in the Eternal Presence, developed aptitudes, talents, capacities, and abilities of every sort, kind, and degree. During the long expanse of life which then was, an infinite variety of talents and abilities came into being. As the ages rolled, no two spirits remained alike. . . . Abraham and Moses and all of the prophets sought and obtained the talent for spirituality. Mary and Eve were two of the greatest spirit daughters of the Father. The whole house of Israel, known and segregated out from their fellows, was inclined toward spiritual things."[1]

Perhaps the greatest foreordination, based on premortal faithfulness, is foreordination to lineage and family: certain individuals come to earth through a designated channel, through a lineage that entitles them to remarkable blessings but also a lineage which carries with it burdens and responsibilities. As a people, therefore, we enjoy what my colleague Brent Top calls "a type of collective foreordination—a selection of spirits to form an entire favored group or lineage." Yet, he adds, "although it is a collective foreordination it is nonetheless based on individual premortal faithfulness and spiritual capacity."[2]

In the words of Elder Melvin J. Ballard, Israel is "a group of souls tested, tried, and proven before they were born into the world. . . . Through this lineage were to come the true and tried souls that had demonstrated their righteousness in the spirit world before they came here."[3] "Remember the days of old," Moses counseled his people, "consider the years of many generations: ask thy father, and he will shew thee: thy elders, and they will tell thee. When the most High divided to the nations their inheritance, when he separated the sons of Adam, he set the bounds of the people *according to the number of the children of Israel.* For the Lord's portion is his people; Jacob is the lot of his inheritance." (Deut. 32:7–9; italics added.) In speaking to the Athenians, the apostle Paul declared: "God that made the world and all things therein . . . hath made of one blood all nations of men for to dwell on all the face of the earth, and *hath determined the times before appointed, and the bounds of their habitation.*" (Acts 17:24, 26; italics added.) President Harold B. Lee explained that "those born to the lineage of Jacob, who was later to be called Israel, and his posterity, who were known as the children of Israel, were born into the most illustrious lineage of any of those who came upon the earth as mortal beings. All these rewards were seemingly promised, or foreordained, before the world was. Surely these matters must have been determined by the kind of lives we had lived in that premortal spirit world. Some may question these assumptions, but at the same time they will accept without any question the belief that each one of us will be judged when we leave this earth according to his or her deeds during our lives here in mortality. Isn't it just as reasonable to believe that what we have received here in this earth [life] was given to each of us according to the merits of our conduct before we came here?"[4]

It thus appears that the declaration of lineage by patriarchs is as much a statement about who and what we were as it is about who we are now and what we may become. There are those, of course, who believe otherwise, those who propose that premortality has little or nothing to do with mortality, that there is no tie between faithfulness there and lineage and station here; to believe in any other way, they contend, is racist, sexist, and exclusivistic. Despite the cleverness of the posture and the egalitarian-sounding nature of such a perspective, it is my firm belief that such views are doctrinally defenseless and even potentially hazardous. If there is no relationship between the first estate and the second, why, as President Lee might ask, should I believe that there is any relationship between what I do here and what I will receive hereafter? Our task as parents and teachers and students of the gospel is not simply to win friends and influence people through avoiding, watering down, or in some cases even denying what are "hard sayings" or difficult doctrines. Truth is not established by consensus or by popularity.

Who are we, then? President Lee answered: "You are all the sons and daughters of God. Your spirits were created and lived as organized intelligences before the world was. You have been blessed to have a physical body because of your obedience to certain commandments in

that premortal state. You are now born into a family to which you have
come, into the nations through which you have come, as a reward for
the kind of lives you lived before you came here and at a time in the
world's history, as the Apostle Paul taught the men of Athens and as
the Lord revealed to Moses, determined by the faithfulness of each of
those who lived before this world was created."[5]

And yet coming to earth through a peculiar lineage involves much
more than boasting of a blessing: it entails bearing a burden. "Once
we know who we are," Elder Russell M. Nelson said, "and the royal
lineage of which we are a part, our actions and directions in life will
be more appropriate to our inheritance."[6] Years ago a wise man wrote
of the burdens of chosenness and of why God had selected a particular
people as his own: "A man will rise and demand, 'By what right does
God choose one race or people above another?' I like that form of the
question. It is much better than asking by what right God degrades
one people beneath another, although that is implied. 'God's grading
is always upward. If He raises up a nation, it is that other nations may
be raised up through its ministry. If He exalts a great man, an apostle
of liberty or science or faith, it is that He might raise a degraded people
to a better condition. The divine selection is not [alone] a prize, a
compliment paid to the man or the race — it is a burden imposed. To
appoint a Chosen people is not a pandering to the racial vanity of a
'superior people,' it is a yoke bound upon the necks of those who are
chosen for a special service. . . .

" . . . [In short,] the Lord hath made [Israel] great for what He is
going to make [Israel] do."[7]

Israel in Mortality: The Scattering and the Gathering

Those of Israel who follow the Light of Christ in this life will be
led to the higher light of the Holy Ghost and will come to know the
Lord and come unto him. In time they come to know of their noble
heritage and of the royal blood which flows through their veins. They
come to earth with a predisposition to receive the truth, with an inner
attraction to the message of the gospel. "My sheep hear my voice,"
the Master said, "and I know them, and they follow me." (John 10:27.)
Those chosen to come to the earth through the favored lineage "are
especially endowed at birth with spiritual talents. It is easier for them
to believe the gospel than it is for the generality of mankind. Every
living soul comes into this world with sufficient talent to believe and

be saved, but the Lord's sheep, as a reward for their devotion when they dwelt in his presence, enjoy greater spiritual endowments than their fellows."[8] "The blood of Israel has flowed in the veins of the children of men," Wilford Woodruff declared, "mixed among the Gentile nations, and when they have heard the sound of the Gospel of Christ it has been like vivid lightning to them; it has opened their understandings, enlarged their minds, and enabled them to see the things of God. They have been born of the Spirit, and then they could behold the kingdom of God."[9]

And yet chosenness implies a succession of choices. Those who became Israel before the world was, those who were *called* in that premortal existence, must exercise wisdom and prudence and discernment in this life, before they become truly *chosen* to enjoy the privilege of ruling and reigning in the house of Israel forever. It was of such that Alma spoke when he declared that many were foreordained to receive transcendent privileges but who do not enjoy "as great privilege as their brethren" because in mortality they choose to "reject the Spirit of God on account of the hardness of their hearts and blindness of their minds."(Alma 13:4). The scriptures thus teach that "there are many called, but few are chosen." (D&C 121:34.) "This suggests," President Lee explained, "that even though we have our free agency here, there are many who were foreordained before the world was, to a greater state than they have prepared themselves for here. Even though they might have been among the noble and great, from among whom the Father declared he would make his chosen leaders, they may fail of that calling here in mortality."[10]

And so the vivid and harsh reality is that lineage and ancestry alone do not qualify one for a divine family inheritance. To use Paul's language, "they are not all Israel, which are of Israel: neither, because they are the seed of Abraham, are they all children." (Rom. 9:6–7.) In fact, as Nephi reminded us, only those who receive the gospel and commit themselves by obedience and continued faithfulness to the Mediator of that covenant are really covenant people. "As many of the Gentiles as will repent are the covenant people of the Lord," he said; "and as many of the Jews as will not repent shall be cast off; for the Lord covenanteth with none save it be with them that repent and believe in his Son, who is the Holy One of Israel." (2 Ne. 30:2.)

Both the Old Testament and the Book of Mormon — and it is particularly in the latter volume that we see the pattern clearly — set forth in consistent detail the reasons why over the generations Israel has been scattered and how it is they are to be gathered. Speaking on behalf of Jehovah, Moses warned ancient Israel that if they should reject their God they would be scattered among the nations, dispersed among the Gentiles: "If thou wilt not hearken unto the voice of the Lord thy God," he said, "to observe to do all his commandments and his statutes which I command thee this day . . . [you will be] removed into all the kingdoms of the earth. . . . And ye shall be plucked from off the land whither thou goest to possess it. And the Lord shall scatter thee among all people, from the one end of the earth even unto the other; and there thou shalt serve other gods, which neither thou nor thy fathers have known." (Deut. 28:15, 25, 63–64.) The Lord spoke in a similar vein through Jeremiah more than half a millennium later: "Because your fathers have forsaken me, saith the Lord, and have walked after other gods, and have served them, and have worshiped them, and have forsaken me, and have not kept my law; and ye have done worse than your fathers; . . . therefore I will cast you out of this land into a land that ye know not, . . . where I will not shew you favor." (Jer. 16:11–13.) The people of God became scattered — alienated from Jehovah and the ways of righteousness, lost as to their identity as covenant representatives, and displaced from the lands set aside for their inheritance — because they forsook the God of Abraham, Isaac, and Jacob and partook of the worship and ways of unholy men.

Though Israel is generally scattered because of her apostasy, we should also point out that the Lord scatters certain branches of his chosen people to the nethermost parts of the earth in order to accomplish his purposes — to spread the blood and influence of Abraham throughout the globe. Through this means all the families of the earth will be blessed eventually, either through being of the blood of Abraham themselves or through being ministered unto by the blood of Abraham — with the right to the gospel, the priesthood, and eternal life. (See Abr. 2:8–11.)

On the other hand, the *gathering* of Israel is accomplished through repentance and turning to the Lord. Individuals were gathered in ancient days when they aligned themselves with the people of God, with those who practiced the religion of Jehovah and received the ordinances of salvation. They were gathered when they gained a sense of tribal identity, when they came to know who they were and whose they were. They were gathered when they congregated with the former-day Saints, when they settled on those lands that were designated as promised lands – lands set apart as sacred sites for people of promise. The hope of the chosen people from Adam to Isaac, and the longing of the house of Israel from Joseph to Malachi, was to be reunited with their God and to enjoy fellowship with those of the household of faith. "But now thus saith the Lord that created thee, O Jacob," Isaiah recorded, "and he that formed thee, O Israel, Fear not: for I have redeemed thee, I have called thee by thy name; thou art mine."

"When thou passest through the waters, I will be with thee; and through the rivers, they shall not overflow thee: when thou walkest through the fire, thou shalt not be burned; neither shall the flame kindle upon thee.

"For I am the Lord thy God, the Holy One of Israel, thy Saviour. . . .

"Since thou wast precious in my sight, thou hast been honourable, and I have loved thee: therefore will I give men for thee, and people for thy life.

"Fear not: for I am with thee: I will bring thy seed from the east, and gather thee from the west;

"I will say to the north, Give up; and to the south, Keep not back: bring my sons from far, and my daughters from the ends of the earth." (Isa. 43:1–6.)

"Ye shall be gathered one by one, O ye children of Israel" (Isa. 27:12), Isaiah declared. The call to the dispersed of Israel has been and ever will be the same: "Turn, O backsliding children, saith the Lord," through Jeremiah; "for I am married unto you: and I will take you one of a city, and two of a family, and I will bring you to Zion." (Jer. 3:14.) That is to say, gathering is accomplished through individual conversion, through faith and repentance and baptism and confirmation, through the receipt of and obedience to the ordinances of the holy temple.

Indeed, the Old Testament and the Book of Mormon prophets longed for the day when the scattered remnants of Israel – those lost to their identity and lost to their relationship with the true Messiah and his church and kingdom – would be a part of a work that would cause all former gatherings to pale into insignificance. "Therefore, behold," Jeremiah recorded, "the days come, saith the Lord, that it shall no more be said, The Lord liveth, that brought up the children of Israel out of the land of Egypt; but, The Lord liveth, that brought up the children of Israel from the land of the north, and from all the lands whither he had driven them." And how is such a phenomenal

gathering to be accomplished? Jehovah answers: "Behold, I will send
for many fishers, saith the Lord, and they shall fish them; and after
will I send for many hunters, and they shall hunt them from every
mountain, and from every hill, and out of the holes of the rocks." (Jer.
16:14–16.) That is, through the great missionary work of the Church,
the elders and sisters—the Lord's legal administrators in the great
proselyting program—seek and teach and baptize and thereby gather
the strangers home.

And so people are gathered into the fold of God through learning
the doctrine of Christ and subscribing to the principles and ordinances
of his gospel. They learn through scripture and through patriarchal and
prophetic pronouncement of their kinship with, or in some instances
today, of their adoption into the house of Israel. The crowning tie to
Israel, however, comes only by the worthy reception of the blessings
of the temple, through being endowed and sealed into the holy order
of God. (See D&C 131:1–4.) "What was the [ultimate] object," Joseph
Smith asked, "of gathering the Jews, or the people of God, in any age
of the world?" He then answered: "The main object was to build unto
the Lord a house whereby He could reveal unto His people the ordinances of His house and the glories of His kingdom, and teach the
people the way of salvation; for there are certain ordinances and principles that, when they are taught and practiced, must be done in a place
or house built for that purpose."[11] "Missionary work," Elder Russell
M. Nelson observed, "is only the beginning" to the blessings of Abraham, Isaac, and Jacob. "The fulfillment, the consummation, of those
blessings comes as those who have entered the waters of baptism
perfect their lives to the point that they may enter the holy temple.
Receiving an endowment there seals members of the Church to the
Abrahamic Covenant."[12]

Joseph Smith, a Modern Abraham

In September 1823 the angel Moroni appeared to the Prophet Joseph Smith. "This messenger proclaimed himself," Joseph wrote to
John Wentworth, "to be an angel of God, sent to bring the joyful tidings
that the covenant which God made with ancient Israel was at hand to
be fulfilled, that the preparatory work for the second coming of the
Messiah was speedily to commence; that the time was at hand for the
Gospel in all its fulness to be preached in power, unto all nations that
a people might be prepared for the Millennial reign. I was informed

that I was chosen to be an instrument in the hands of God to bring about some of His purposes in this glorious dispensation."[13] Joseph of old prophesied of his latter-day namesake that he would be a "choice seer," one who would be raised up by God to bring the people of the last days to the knowledge of the covenants which God had made with the ancient fathers. (See 2 Ne. 3:7; 1 Ne. 13:26.) The name *Joseph* is a blessed and significant name. Whether the name is taken from the Hebrew word *Yasaf*, which means "to add," or from the word *Asaph*, meaning "to gather," one senses that the latter-day seer was destined to perform a monumental labor in regard to the fulfillment of the Abrahamic covenant in the final dispensation.

Joseph Smith was a descendant of Abraham. By lineage he had a right to the priesthood, the gospel, and eternal life. (See Abr. 2:8–11.) In a revelation received on 6 December 1832, the Savior said: "Thus saith the Lord unto you, with whom the priesthood hath continued through the lineage of your fathers—for ye are lawful heirs, according to the flesh, and have been hid from the world with Christ in God— therefore your life and the priesthood have remained, and must needs remain through you and your lineage until the restoration of all things spoken by the mouths of all the holy prophets since the world began." (D&C 86:8–10.) "It was decreed in the counsels of eternity," President Brigham Young stated, "long before the foundations of the earth were laid, that he [Joseph Smith] should be the man, in the last dispensation of this world, to bring forth the word of God to the people, and receive the fulness of the keys and power of the Priesthood of the Son of God. The Lord had his eye upon him, and upon his father, and upon his father's father, and upon their progenitors clear back to Abraham, and from Abraham to the flood, from the flood to Enoch, and from Enoch to Adam. He has watched that family and that blood as it has circulated from its fountain to the birth of that man."[14]

President Young declared on another occasion: "You have heard Joseph say that the people did not know him; he had his eyes on the relation to blood-relations. Some have supposed that he meant spirit, but it was the blood-relation. This is it that he referred to. His descent from Joseph that was sold into Egypt was direct, and the blood was pure in him. That is why the Lord chose him and we are pure when this blood-strain from Ephraim comes down pure. The decrees of the Almighty will be exalted—that blood which was in him was pure and he had the sole right and lawful power, as he was the legal heir to the blood that has been on the earth and has come down through a pure lineage. The union of various ancestors kept that blood pure. There is a great deal the people do not understand, and many of the Latter-day Saints have to learn all about it."[15]

What is true in regard to the Prophet's lineage—his right to the priesthood and the gospel, and his duty in regard to the salvation of the world—is equally true for other members of the Lord's Church. The Lord spoke of his Latter-day Saints as "a remnant of Jacob, and those who are heirs according to the covenant." (D&C 52:2.) "Awake, awake; put on thy strength, O Zion," Isaiah recorded; "put on thy beautiful garments, O Jerusalem, the holy city." (Isa. 52:1.) A modern revelation provides our finest commentary on this passage and explains that Jehovah "had reference to those whom God should call in the last days, who should hold the power of priesthood to bring again Zion, and the redemption of Israel; and to put on her strength is to put on the authority of the priesthood, which she, Zion, has a right to by lineage; also to return to that power which she had lost." (D&C 113:8.) The Lord also encouraged Israel through Isaiah to shake herself from the dust and loose herself from the bands about her neck. (See Isa. 52:2.) That is, "the scattered remnants are exhorted to return to the Lord from whence they have fallen; which if they do, the promise of the Lord is that he will speak to them, or give them revelation." In so doing, Israel rids herself of "the curses of God upon her," her "scattered condition among the Gentiles." (D&C 113:10.)

Joseph Smith became a "father of the faithful" to those of this dispensation, the means by which the chosen lineage could be identified, gathered, organized as family units, and sealed forevermore into the house of Israel to their God. The Patriarch in the days of the early Church, Joseph Smith, Sr., blessed his son as follows: "A marvelous work and a wonder has the Lord wrought by thy hand, even that which shall prepare the way for the remnants of his people to come in among the Gentiles, with their fulness, as the tribes of Israel are restored. I bless thee with the blessings of thy Fathers Abraham, Isaac and Jacob; and even the blessings of thy father Joseph, the son of Jacob. Behold, he looked after his posterity in the last days, when they should be scattered and driven by the Gentiles."[16]

On 3 April 1836 Moses, Elias, and Elijah appeared in the Kirtland Temple and restored priesthood keys of inestimable worth, keys that formalized much of the labor that had been under way since the organization of the Church. (See D&C 110.) Moses restored the keys of the gathering of Israel, including the right of presidency and directing powers needed to gather the ten lost tribes. Elias committed unto Joseph Smith and Oliver Cowdery the dispensation of the gospel of Abraham, making it possible that through those first elders all generations after them would be blessed. That is, Elias restored the keys necessary to organize eternal family units in the patriarchal order through the new and everlasting covenant of marriage. Elijah restored the keys necessary to bind and seal those family units for eternity as well as the power to legitimize all priesthood ordinances and give them efficacy, virtue, and force in and after the resurrection.[17] Thus through the coming of Elijah and his prophetic colleagues in Kirtland, the promises made to the fathers — the promises of the gospel, the priesthood, and the possibility of eternal life granted to Abraham, Isaac, and Jacob — are planted in our hearts, the hearts of the children. (See D&C 2.) More specifically, because of what took place through Joseph Smith in Kirtland in 1836, the desire of our hearts to have all the blessings enjoyed by the ancients can be realized. And because of the spirit of Elijah, which moves upon the faithful, there comes also a desire to make those same blessings available for our more immediate fathers through family history and vicarious temple ordinances.

Through Joseph Smith the blessings of Abraham, Isaac, and Jacob are available to all who will join the Church and prove worthy of the blessings of the temple. Jehovah's plea through Isaiah that the people of the covenant become a light to the nations, that they might be his "salvation unto the end of the earth" (Isa. 49:6), is thus realized through the restoration of the gospel. Thereby, as the Prophet himself declared, "the election of the promised seed still continues, and in the last day, they shall have the priesthood restored unto them, and they shall be 'saviors on Mount Zion.' "[18] Because Joseph Smith was the head of this dispensation and its modern Abraham, Brigham Young could appropriately say of his predecessor: "Joseph is a father to Ephraim and to all Israel in these last days."[19] In a revelation given to President John Taylor on 22 June 1882, the Lord spoke of the Prophet Joseph: "Behold, I raised up my servant Joseph Smith to introduce my Gospel, and to build up my Church and establish my Kingdom on the earth. . . . He was called and ordained to this office before the world was. He was called by me, and empowered by me, and sustained by me to introduce and establish my Church and Kingdom upon the earth; and to be a

Prophet, Seer, and Revelator to my Church and Kingdom; and to be a King and Ruler over Israel."[20]

The Lord has repeatedly affirmed the special status of the Latter-day Saint Prophet-leader: "As I said unto Abraham concerning the kindreds of the earth, even so I say unto my servant Joseph: In thee and in thy seed shall the kindred of the earth be blessed." (D&C 124:58.) Further: "Abraham received promises concerning his seed, and of the fruit of his loins—from whose loins ye are, namely, my servant Joseph—which were to continue so long as they were in the world; and as touching Abraham and his seed, out of the world they should continue; both in the world and out of the world should they continue as innumerable as the stars; or, if ye were to count the sand upon the seashore ye could not number them. This promise is yours also, because ye are of Abraham." (D&C 132:30–31.)

The Millennial Gathering of Israel

Both the Old Testament and the Book of Mormon attest that a significant part of the drama we know as the gathering of Israel will be millennial, that is, that it will be brought to pass after the second coming of Jesus Christ. Between now and then we shall see marvelous things on the earth in regard to the people of Israel coming unto their Lord and King and thereafter unto the lands of their inheritance. We have witnessed already the phenomenal gathering of many thousands of the seed of Lehi (of the tribe of Joseph) into the Church, and this is but the beginning. We have stood in awe as descendants of Jacob around the globe have been found, identified, taught, and converted to the faith of their fathers, and yet we have seen but the tip of the iceberg. Our missionaries shall soon enter into lands wherein pockets of Israelites will be baptized and confirmed and where patriarchs shall declare lineage through such tribes as Issachar, Zebulun, Gad, Asher, and Naphtali.

A major conversion of the Jews will take place near the time of the coming of the Lord in glory. "And it shall come to pass in that day," Jehovah said through Zechariah, "that I will seek to destroy all the nations that come against Jerusalem. And I will pour upon the house of David, and upon the inhabitants of Jerusalem, the spirit of grace and of supplications: and they shall look upon me whom they have pierced, and they shall mourn for him, as one mourneth for his only son, and shall be in bitterness for him, as one that is in bitterness for his firstborn. . . . And one shall say unto him, What are these wounds in thine hands? Then he shall answer, Those with which I was wounded in the house of my friends." (Zech. 12:9–10; 13:6.) A modern revelation provides a more detailed description of this poignant moment in our Lord's dealings with his own. Having set his foot on the Mount of Olives and the mountain having cleaved in twain, the Lord prophesies, "Then shall the Jews look upon me and say: What are these wounds in thine hands and in thy feet? Then shall they know that I am the Lord; for I will say unto them: These wounds are the wounds with which I was wounded in the house of my friends. I am he who was lifted up. I am Jesus that was crucified. I am the Son of God. And then shall they weep because of their iniquities; then shall they lament because they persecuted their king." (D&C 45:48–53.) Before this time Jews from around the globe will already have investigated the message of the Restoration, entered into the covenant gospel, and come home to the God of Abraham, Isaac, and Jacob. They will not only have come to acknowledge Jesus as an honorable prophet-teacher but will confess him as Lord and God, as Messiah. Their garments will have been "washed in the blood of the Lamb." (Ether 13:11.) But at the time the Master appears at Olivet, the conversion of a nation will begin. "That is to say, the Jews 'shall begin to believe in Christ' (2 Ne. 30:7) before he comes the second time. Some of them will accept the gospel and forsake the traditions of their fathers; a few will find in Jesus the fulfillment of their ancient Messianic hopes; but their nation as a whole, their people as the distinct body that they now are in all nations, the Jews as a unit shall not, at that time, accept the word of truth. But a beginning will be made; a foundation will be laid; and then Christ will come and usher in the millennial year of his redeemed."[21]

In 721 B.C. the Assyrians under Shalmanezer took the ten northern tribes captive. According to tradition, these Israelites escaped as they were being taken northward and scattered themselves throughout different parts of the earth. They were never again heard of and came thereafter to be known as the "lost tribes." Nephi explained to his brothers early in the Book of Mormon story that "the house of Israel, sooner or later, will be scattered upon all the face of the earth, and also among all nations. And behold, there are many [note that he is here making reference to the ten northern tribes] who are already lost from the knowledge of those who are at Jerusalem. Yea, the more part of all the tribes have been led away; and they are scattered to and fro upon the isles of the sea; and whither they are none of us knoweth, save that we know that they have been led away." (1 Ne. 22:3–4.) Nephi's use of the word *lost* is most interesting. The tribes are lost "from the knowledge of those who are at Jerusalem."

Let me here refer to a statement by President George Q. Cannon made in 1890. After having quoted at length from 2 Nephi 30 regarding the final gathering of Israel from among the nations, President Cannon said: "This prediction plainly foreshadows that which is now taking place, and which has been taking place for some years. 'As many of the Gentiles as will repent,' the prophet says, 'are the covenant people of the Lord.' By virtue of this promise which God has made, we are His covenant people. Though of Gentile descent, and numbered among the Gentile nations, by and through our obedience to the Gospel of the Son of God we become incorporated, so to speak, among His covenant people and are numbered with them. We say frequently that we are descendants of the house of Israel. This is undoubtedly true. . . . Our ancestors were of the house of Israel but they mingled with the Gentiles and became lost, that is, they became lost so far as being recognized as of the house of Israel, and the blood of our forefathers was mingled with the blood of the Gentile nations. We have been gathered out from those nations by the preaching of the gospel of the Son of God. The Lord has made precious promises unto us, that every blessing, and every gift, and every power necessary for salvation and for exaltation to His Kingdom shall be given unto us in common with those who are more particularly known as the covenant people of the Lord."[22]

Mormon teaches that in the last days all of the twelve tribes will come to Christ through accepting the Book of Mormon and the restored gospel. (See Mormon 3:17–22.) Will such persons gather into the true Church from the north? Yes. And they shall also come, as the scriptures attest, from the south and the east and the west. (See Isa. 43:5–6; 3 Ne. 20:13.) In fact, it just may be that the idea of gathering from "the lands of the north" may simply be a reference to a return from all parts of the earth. For example, Jehovah, speaking through Zechariah, called forth to his chosen but scattered people: "Come! Come! Flee from the land of the north, declares the Lord, for I have scattered you to the four winds of heaven." (New International Version, Zech. 2:6.)

As we have indicated, the work of the Father—the work of gathering Israel into the fold—though begun in the early nineteenth century, will continue into and through the Millennium. That is to say, the missionary effort begun in our time will accelerate at a pace that we cannot now comprehend. This is why the Book of Mormon speaks of the work of the Father "commencing" during the Millennium. In the millennial day "shall the power of heaven come down among them; and I also will be in the midst," the resurrected Lord stated. "And then shall the work of the Father commence at that day, even when this gospel shall be preached among the remnant of this people. Verily I say unto you, at that day shall the work of the Father commence among all the dispersed of my people, yea, even the tribes which have been lost, which the Father hath led away out of Jerusalem." (3 Ne. 21:26; see also 2 Ne. 30:7-15.)

We tend to speak of there being no death during the thousand years. Let us be more precise. The Saints shall live to the age of a tree, the age of one hundred (Isa. 65:20; D&C 43:32; 63:51; 101:30-31) before they are changed in the twinkling of an eye, from mortality to resurrected immortality. On the other hand, and presumably in speaking of terrestrial persons, Joseph Smith said: "There will be wicked men on the earth during the thousand years. The heathen nations who will not come up to worship will be visited with the judgments of God, and must eventually be destroyed from the earth."[23] "There will be need for the preaching of the gospel, after the millennium is brought in," President Joseph Fielding Smith explained, "until all men are either converted or pass away. In the course of the thousand years all men will either come into the Church, or kingdom of God, or they will die and pass away."[24] Or, as Elder McConkie has described this process: "There will be many churches on earth when the Millennium begins. False worship will continue among those whose desires are good, 'who are honorable men of the earth,' but who have been 'blinded by the craftiness of men.' (D&C 76:75.) Plagues will rest upon them until they repent and believe the gospel or are destroyed, as the Prophet said. It follows that missionary work will continue into the Millennium until all who remain are converted. Then 'the earth shall be full of the knowledge of the Lord, as the waters cover the sea.' (Isa. 11:9.) Then every living soul on earth will belong to The Church of Jesus Christ of Latter-day Saints."[25]

In that glorious era of peace and righteousness, the dispersed of Israel shall receive the message of the Restoration, read and believe the Book of Mormon, traverse the "highway of righteousness" (Isa. 35:8) into the true Church, and take their place beside their kinsmen in the household of faith. The revelation declares that "their enemies shall become a prey unto them." (D&C 133:28.) That is, the enemies of Israel—the wicked and carnal elements of a fallen world—will have been destroyed by the glory and power of the Second Coming. "For the time speedily cometh," Nephi prophesied, "that the Lord God shall cause a great division among the people, and the wicked will he destroy; and he will spare his people, yea, even if it so be that he must destroy the wicked by fire." (2 Ne. 30:10; see also 1 Ne. 22:17.) There will have been "an entire separation of the righteous and the wicked"; the enemies of the chosen people will be no more, because the Lord will have sent forth his angels "to pluck out the wicked and cast them into unquenchable fire." (D&C 63:54.) Truly, "such of the gathering of Israel as has come to pass so far is but the gleam of a star that soon will be hidden by the splendor of the sun in full blaze; truly, the magnitude and grandeur and glory of the gathering is yet to be."[26]

One of the most graphic prophetic statements about Israel in the Millennium is contained in the writings of Zenos, one of the prophets of the brass plates. In speaking of what appears to be the millennial day, Zenos taught:

" And there began to be the natural fruit again in the vineyard; and the natural branches began to grow and thrive exceedingly; and the wild branches began to be plucked off and to be cast away; and they did keep the root and the top thereof equal, according to the strength thereof.

"And thus they labored, with all diligence, according to the commandments of the Lord of the vineyard, even until the bad had been cast away out of the vineyard, and the Lord had preserved unto himself that the trees had become again the natural fruit; and they became like unto one body; and the fruits were equal; and the Lord of the vineyard had preserved unto himself the natural fruit, which was most precious unto him from the beginning." (Jacob 5:73–74.)

In that glorious day, the promise of God to his chosen seed will be well on the way to fulfillment. Paul's words, spoken in the meridian of time, will then have particular application and fulfillment. "As many of you as have been baptized into Christ," he observed, "have put on Christ. There is neither Jew nor Greek, there is neither bond nor free, there is neither male nor female: for ye are all one in Christ Jesus. And if ye be Christ's then are ye Abraham's seed, and heirs according to the promise." (Gal. 3:27–29.) All those who come unto Christ, who is the Holy One of Israel, shall, under Christ, rule and reign in the house of Israel forever. In the millennial day the Lord Jehovah will reign personally upon the earth. (Articles of Faith 1:10.) More specifically, "Christ and the resurrected Saints will reign over the earth during the thousand years. They will not probably dwell upon the earth, but will visit it when they please, or when it is necessary to govern it."[27] In that day he shall preside as King of Kings and Lord of Lords: Israel's Good Shepherd shall be with them and minister to them in everlasting splendor.

The blossoming and ultimate fulfillment of the everlasting covenant restored through Joseph Smith shall be millennial. The principles and ordinances of the gospel, the "articles of adoption"[28] by which men and women are received into the royal family and given a rightful place in the house of Israel, shall continue during the thousand years. "During the Millennium," a modern Apostle has written, "children will be named and blessed by the elders of the kingdom. When those of the rising generation arrive at the years of accountability, they will be baptized in water and of the Spirit by legal administrators appointed so to act. Priesthood will be conferred upon young and old, and they will be ordained to offices therein as the needs of the ministry and their own salvation require. At the appropriate time each person will receive his patriarchal blessing, we suppose from the natural patriarch who presides in his family, as it was in Adamic days and as it was when Jacob blessed his sons. The saints will receive their endowments in the temples of the Lord, and they will receive the blessings of celestial marriage at their holy altars. And all the faithful will have their callings and elections made sure and will be sealed up unto that eternal life which will come to them when they reach the age of a tree."[29]

"Behold," Jeremiah wrote, "the days come, saith the Lord, that I will make a new covenant with the house of Israel, and with the house of Judah:

"Not according to the covenant that I made with their fathers in the day that I took them by the hand to bring them out of the land of Egypt; which my covenant they brake, although I was an husband unto them, saith the Lord:

"But this shall be the covenant that I will make with the house of Israel; After those days, saith the Lord, I will put my law in their inward parts, and write it in their hearts; and will be their God, and they shall be my people.

"And they shall teach no more every man his neighbour, and every man his brother, saying, Know the Lord: for they shall all know me, from the least of them unto the greatest of them, saith the Lord: for I will forgive their iniquity, and I will remember their sin no more." (Jer. 31:31–34.)

"How is this to be done?" Joseph Smith asked. "It is to be done by this sealing power, and the other Comforter spoken of, which will be manifest by revelation."[30]

Conclusion

"When the Lord shall come," a modern revelation explains, "he shall reveal all things—things which have passed, and hidden things which no man knew, things of the earth, by which it was made, and the purpose and the end thereof—things most precious, things that are above, and things that are beneath, things that are in the earth, and upon the earth, and in heaven." (D&C 101:32–34.) When the Lion of the tribe of Judah finally unseals the scrolls which contain "the revealed will, mysteries, and the works of God," even "the hidden things of his economy concerning this earth during the seven thousand years of its continuance, or its temporal existence" (D&C 77:6; see also Rev. 5:1), surely we shall one and all come to know of his peculiar dealings with Israel, of the strange but masterful manner in which he has moved upon and through his covenant people in mysterious ways his wonders to perform.

In 1882 Elder Erastus Snow delivered one of the most penetrating discourses on the role and mission of Israel that I know of. In speaking of those who come to the earth as descendants of Abraham, he said: "The Lord has sent those noble spirits into the world to perform a special work, and appointed their times; and they have always fulfilled the mission given them, and their future glory and exaltation is secured unto them; and that is what I understand by the doctrine of election spoken of by the Apostle Paul and other sacred writers." Such persons, Elder Snow continued, "were called and chosen and elected of God to perform a certain work at a certain time in the world's history and in due time he fitted them for that work. . . .

"Their blood has permeated European society, and it coursed in the veins of the early colonists of America. And when the books shall be opened and the lineage of all men is known, it will be found that they have been first and foremost in everything noble among men in the various nations in breaking off the shackles of kingcraft and priest-craft and oppression of every kind, and the foremost among men in upholding and maintaining the principles of liberty and freedom upon this continent and establishing a representative government, and thus preparing the way for the coming forth of the fullness of the everlasting Gospel. And it is the foremost of those spirits whom the Lord has prepared to receive the Gospel when it was presented to them, and who did not wait for the Elders to hunt them from the hills and corners of the earth, but they were hunting for the Elders, impelled by a spirit which then they could not understand; and for this reason were they among the first Elders of the Church; they and the fathers having been watched over from the days that God promised those blessings upon Isaac and Jacob and Joseph and Ephraim. And these are they that will be found in the front ranks of all that is noble and good in their day and time, and who will be found among those whose efforts are directed in establishing upon the earth those heaven-born principles which tend directly to blessing and salvation, to ameliorating the condition of their fellow-men, and elevating them in the scale of their being; and among those also who receive the fullness of the Everlasting Gospel, and the keys of Priesthood in the last days, through whom God determined to gather up again unto himself a peculiar people, a holy nation, a pure seed that shall stand upon Mount Zion as saviors."[31]

And so, we say in summary, as Mormon said to the latter-day descendants of Lehi: "Know ye that ye are of the house of Israel." (Mormon 7:2.) Or as Jesus explained to the Nephites: "Ye are the children of the prophets; and ye are of the house of Israel; and ye are of the covenant which the Father made with your fathers, saying unto Abraham: And in thy seed shall all the kindreds of the earth be blessed." (3 Ne. 20:25.) Our patriarchal blessings specify literal blood descent and — because of our connection to father Abraham and through the call and ministry of a modern Abraham and the keys and powers delivered to him — ours is the right to the gospel, the priesthood, and the glories of eternal life. We need not misunderstand this matter and should not confuse ancestry with adoption.[32] Nor should those who are not directly descended from Israel who join the Church feel in any way less than chosen. Chosenness is a status based upon the choice to follow the Lord and associate with his people, and entrance into the true Church qualifies one for the blessings of Ephraim, as though he or she had been born a child of Abraham. Our duty is to walk with fidelity and humility and be worthy of the name and lineage that is ours. By so doing we shall help to bring to pass the foreordained purposes of God for us and our families. It can then be said of us as it was of Abraham: "I know him, that he will command his children and his household after him, and they shall keep the way of the Lord, to do justice and judgment." (Gen. 18:19.) "I am reminded," President Harold B. Lee said in his last address to Brigham Young University students, "of the old court jester who was supposed to entertain his king with interesting stories and antics. He looked at the king who was lolling on his throne, a drunken, filthy rascal; [he] doffed his cap and bells, and said with a mock gesture of obeisance, 'O king, be loyal to the royal within you.' "[33] Such is our opportunity and our great challenge, our glory or our condemnation.

NOTES

1. Bruce R. McConkie, *The Mortal Messiah*, 4 vols. (Salt Lake City: Deseret Book Co., 1979–81), 1:23; italics added.

2. Brent L. Top, *The Life Before* (Salt Lake City: Bookcraft, 1988), p. 144.

3. "The Three Degrees of Glory," in *Melvin J. Ballard: Crusader for Righteousness* (Salt Lake City: Bookcraft, 1966), pp. 218–19.

4. Harold B. Lee, in Conference Report, Oct. 1973, pp. 7–8.

5. Ibid., p. 7.

6. Russell M. Nelson, "Thanks for the Covenant " (devotional address at Brigham Young University), Provo, Utah, 22 Nov. 1988, p. 8. Unpublished typescript in author's possession.

7. W. J. Cameron, "Is There a Chosen People?" in James H. Anderson, *God's Covenant Race* (Salt Lake City: Deseret News Press, 1938), pp. 300–302.

8. Bruce R. McConkie, *A New Witness for the Articles of Faith* (Salt Lake City: Deseret Book Co., 1985), p. 34.

9. Wilford Woodruff, in *Journal of Discourses*, 26 vols. (Liverpool: F. D. Richards, 1851–86), 15:11.

10. Lee, in Conference Report, Oct. 1973, p. 7.

11. Joseph Smith, *Teachings of the Prophet Joseph Smith*, sel. Joseph Fielding Smith (Salt Lake City: Deseret Book Co., 1976), pp. 307–8.

12. Nelson, "Thanks for the Covenant," p. 7.

13. Joseph Smith, *History of The Church of Jesus Christ of Latter-day Saints*, ed. B. H. Roberts, 7 vols., 2d ed. rev. (Salt Lake City: Deseret Book Co., 1957), 4:536–37.

14. Brigham Young, in *Journal of Discourses*, 7:289–90.

15. Brigham Young, in *Utah Genealogical and Historical Magazine* (July 1920), 11:107.

16. In Joseph F. McConkie, *His Name Shall Be Joseph* (Salt Lake City: Hawkes Publishing, 1980), p. 103.

17. Smith, *Teachings*, p. 172.

18. Ibid., p. 189.

19. Brigham Young, *Journal History*, 9 Apr. 1837.

20. John Taylor, in *Unpublished Revelations of the Prophets and Presidents of The Church of Jesus Christ of Latter-day Saints*, ed. Fred E. Collier (Salt Lake City: Collier's Publishing Co., 1979), 1:133.

21. Bruce R. McConkie, *The Millennial Messiah* (Salt Lake City: Deseret Book Co., 1982), pp. 228–29.

22. Address delivered by George Q. Cannon at the Tabernacle in Salt Lake City on 12 Jan. 1890, in *Collected Discourses* (B. H. S. Publishing, 1988), 2:2–3; italics added.

23. Smith, *Teachings*, pp. 268–69; see also Zech. 14.

24. Joseph Fielding Smith, *Doctrines of Salvation*, 3 vols., comp. Bruce R. McConkie (Salt Lake City: Bookcraft, 1954–56), 1:86.

25. McConkie, *Millennial Messiah*, p. 652.

26. Ibid., p. 196.

27. Smith, *Teachings*, p. 268.

28. See Smith, *Teachings*, p. 328; *Orson Pratt's Works* (Salt Lake City: Parker Pratt Robison, 1965), pp. 46–48.

29. McConkie, *Millennial Messiah*, pp. 673–74.

30. Smith, *Teachings*, p. 149.

31. Erastus Snow, in *Journal of Discourses*, 23:185–87.

32. For an excellent treatment of the literal nature of our descent from Israel, as taught specifically in the Doctrine and Covenants, see Monte S. Nyman, "The Second Gathering of the Literal Seed," in *Doctrines for Exaltation: The 1989 Sperry Symposium on the Doctrine and Covenants* (Salt Lake City: Deseret Book Co., 1989), pp. 186–200.

33. Harold B. Lee, "Be Loyal to the Royal within You," *1973 Speeches of the Year* (Provo, Utah: Brigham Young University Press, 1974), p. 100.

Chapter Twelve

The Twelve Prophets Testify of Christ

Monte S. Nyman

Brigham Young University

The message of the prophets since the beginning of the world has been centered on Jesus Christ. Jacob, the younger brother of Nephi, wrote with the intent to show his latter-day brethren that his people knew of Christ and had a hope of his glory many hundred years before his coming. He further testified that "all the holy prophets which were before us" also had that hope. (Jacob 4:4.) Jacob later informed the anti-Christ Sherem "that none of the prophets have written, nor prophesied, save they have spoken concerning this Christ." (Jacob 7:11.) The Savior, after his resurrection, confirmed the teachings of Jacob. As two of his disciples walked on the road to Emmaus, Jesus joined them as they were discussing the recent events of his death and crucifixion. After listening for some time, he chastised them, saying, "O fools, and slow of heart to believe all that the prophets have spoken." (Luke 24:25.) To show that Christ's suffering had been foretold by the prophets, he began "at Moses and all the prophets" and "expounded unto them in all the scriptures the things concerning himself." (Luke 24:27.) Later that evening he appeared to his disciples and told them "that all things must be fulfilled, which were written in the law of Moses, and in the prophets, and in the psalms, concerning me."[1] (Luke 24:44.) Therefore, it is to be expected that the last twelve prophets of the Old Testament[2] centered their message on Jesus Christ.

Because Jesus Christ was the administrator God of the Old Testament by divine investiture of authority,[3] he was involved in every event considered by these prophets. Although a few of these messages will be recognized, they will not be the emphasis of this paper. Furthermore, various doctrines that are frequently mentioned by these prophets, such as the gathering of Israel or the giving of revelation, are likewise revealed to them from Jesus Christ, but these topics will not be emphasized, either. The hand of the Lord is indeed in all things (D&C 59:21), and he holds "the destinies of all the armies of the nations of the earth" (D&C 117:6), but this paper will emphasize the messianic prophecies of the last twelve prophets of the Old Testament.

Messianic prophecies are those that foretell of Christ coming to the earth to fulfill his mission. These prophecies, as recorded in the Old Testament, are sometimes related to his coming to dwell on earth in the flesh in the meridian of time and sometimes to his coming in glory at the end of the world or the destruction of the wicked or telestial people. Many of these prophecies are of a dual nature, as they were fulfilled in one sense in the meridian of time but also serve as a prototype of his second coming. There are many messianic prophecies in the twelve prophets. They will be considered in the order in which they appear in the text.

Hosea

Hosea is generally known for the strange marriages that he records. His first recorded marriage symbolizes the Lord's scattering and gathering of Israel. (Hosea 1–2.) Chapter 3 is considered by many as a second marriage that Hosea was commanded to enter. In my opinion, it is not a second marriage but the lesson given to Hosea about the first marriage. He is to love Israel and teach her as long as she will listen. The messianic prophecy comes in the message of hope after the prophecy of doom of Israel's scattering. After some time, Israel shall "return, and seek the Lord their God, and David their king." (Hosea 3:5.) This prophecy will be fulfilled in the latter days. The "Lord their God" and "David their king" have reference to the same person, Jesus the Christ. A spiritual and a political restoration to Israel will bring about the full kingdom of God with Christ as the king. The reference to Jesus as David is one of many among the Old Testament prophets.

Another prophecy that has messianic overtones is Hosea 6. It begins with Israel saying, "Come, and let us return unto the Lord." (Hosea 6:1.) The rest of the verse implies that Israel's statement is made after a lengthy period of their being smitten or punished (the apostasy). The next verse gives a time frame for their return. "After two days will he revive us: in the third day he will raise us up, and we shall live in his sight." (Hosea 6:2.)

While some look upon this verse as a prophecy of Christ's resurrection, and I recognize that all things have their likeness and bear record of him (Moses 6:63), the context suggests the verse is speaking of the nation of Israel. A day with the Lord is a thousand years with man. (Ps. 90:4; 2 Peter 3:8; Abr. 5:13; Facsimile 2, fig. 1.) Therefore, in the Lord's time, "after two days" equals two thousand years. "In the third day," spoken of in Hosea 6:2, could be any part of the next one thousand years. Israel was taken away in 721 B.C. It was some 2,551 years from the time of Israel's destruction and scattering until the Restoration in 1830, a period of two and a half days, or in the third day of the Lord's time. Furthermore, two thousand years from 721 B.C. would be A.D.1279, about the end of the thirteenth century after Christ. This date is approximately the ending of the Dark Ages and the beginning of the Age of Enlightenment. The enlightenment is possibly the Lord's beginning to revive Israel, but he would not raise her up for part of another day, after the Renaissance and the Reformation. The restoration of the gospel would begin the gathering of Israel, and they "shall live in his sight." (Hosea 6:2.) Other Old Testament prophets have prophesied of these sequential events. (Isa. 28:23–29.)

In 1843 the Prophet Joseph Smith used Hosea 6:2 as an evidence that the second coming of Christ would not be before the year 1890: "After two days, etc., − 2,520 years."[4] Unfortunately, his discussion that explained the total years as 2,520 years was summarized merely as an etc. Subtracting 2,520 years from 1890 brings one to the year 630 B.C. Although this year does not seem to fit into Hosea's lifetime, it is evidence that Joseph Smith considered the prophecy to be fulfilled in the latter days and not to be a prophecy of Christ's resurrection. It is helpful and enlightening to study his entire explanation.

Hosea 6:3 states, "Then shall we know, if we follow on to know the Lord," and describes the time period when Israel comes to know the Lord. This verse fits the time period after the restoration of the Church and the Church's growing in knowledge of the Lord.

A third messianic prophecy in Hosea is in chapter 11. The Lord declares that when Israel was a child (as a nation) he loved him and called him out of Egypt. (V. 1.) The house of Israel was in bondage in Egypt until the Lord raised up Moses and called him to lead them back to their land of promise. This of course is in similitude of Jesus' being in Egypt as a child until the death of Herod. (Matt. 2:12–15.) The Lord used this prophecy to teach Ephraim that they would not return to Egypt but were to go into bondage in Assyria because of their iniquities.

(Hosea 1:5.) At the time of Hosea, Ephraim was seeking an alliance with Egypt.

One more prophecy in Hosea has messianic symbolism. Out of context it sounds like a prophecy of the resurrection in connection with the Second Coming. Through Hosea, the Lord declares: "I will ransom them from the power of the grave; I will redeem them from death: O death, I will be thy plagues; O grave, I will be thy destruction: repentance shall be hid from mine eyes." (Hosea 13:14.)

In context, the Lord is using the resurrection as a teaching symbol. He promises to redeem Ephraim from the death (scattering) that is coming upon her. She will be destroyed, or die, as a nation but will be resurrected, or gathered again. As in the resurrection, the power of the Lord will do it.

Joel

Most members of The Church of Jesus Christ of Latter-day Saints are familiar with Joel 2:28–32 because the angel Moroni quoted it to Joseph Smith on the morning of 22 September 1823 as not yet fulfilled but soon to be. (JS–H 1:41.)

"And it shall come to pass afterward, that I will pour out my spirit upon all flesh; and your sons and your daughters shall prophesy, your old men shall dream dreams, your young men shall see visions:

"And also upon the servants and upon the handmaids in those days will I pour out my spirit.

"And I will shew wonders in the heavens and in the earth, blood, and fire, and pillars of smoke.

"The sun shall be turned into darkness, and the moon into blood, before the great and terrible day of the Lord come.

"And it shall come to pass, that whosoever shall call on the name of the Lord shall be delivered: for in mount Zion and in Jerusalem shall be deliverance, as the Lord hath said, and in the remnant whom the Lord shall call." (Joel 2:28–32.)

The second chapter sets the stage for Moroni's quotation. It begins with a warning to "blow ye the trumpet in Zion, and sound an alarm in my holy mountain: let all the inhabitants of the land tremble: for the day of the Lord cometh, for it is nigh at hand." (Joel 2:1.)

Drawing upon the teachings of the modern-day prophet, Joseph Smith, we know that Zion refers to the Americas.[5] The second phrase, "sound an alarm in my holy mountain," is Hebrew parallelism, a repetition of the same concept. The coming of the Lord being nigh at hand that should cause the inhabitants to tremble in the last days supports Moroni's telling Joseph Smith that the last verses of Joel 2 would soon be fulfilled. (JS–H 1:41.)

The succeeding verses of Joel 2 describe the day of the Lord that is to come. The Prophet Joseph Smith cited verse 2 in urging the Saints to prepare for the Second Coming: "It seems to be deeply impressed upon our minds that the Saints ought to lay hold of every door that shall seem to be opened unto them, to obtain foothold on the earth, and be making all the preparation that is within their power for the terrible storms that are now gathering in the heavens, 'a day of clouds, with darkness and gloominess, and of thick darkness,' as spoken of by the Prophet, which cannot be now of a long time lingering."[6]

The day of darkness and gloominess is accompanied by a great and strong people unequaled in previous generations. (Joel 2:2–7.) These people are probably destroying angels who will eliminate the wicked or telestial people. A fire is prophesied to precede them. The fire may be the glory that attends these angels. Just as God is a consuming fire (Heb. 2:12–29), the angels appearing in glory will also consume the corruptible things of man and beast, as will the Lord's second coming. (See also D&C 101:23–24.) Further support for there being angelic people is given in Joel 2:8–9 where it is stated that they cannot be wounded by mortal weapons. This army of the Lord will cause the earth and heaven to quake and tremble. The sun and moon will be dark, and the stars will not shine. The Lord's voice will precede the army, his great and terrible day will be ushered in, and many inhabitants of the earth will be unable to abide it. (Joel 2:10–11.) Joel 2:10–11, along with verse 31, are quoted or paraphrased in four sections of the Doctrine and Covenants that talk about the Second Coming. (D&C 29:14; 34:8–9; 43:18; 84:118.)

The people of Zion are invited to turn to the Lord and repent. By doing so, they can escape this terrible evil and receive a blessing that will result in the people's offering a sacrifice or oblation in thanksgiving to the Lord. (JST, Joel 2:12–14.) The trumpet blown in Zion will bring about the gathering of the people in preparation for the coming of the bridegroom. (Joel 2:15–17.) The bridegroom is, of course, Jesus Christ, and the bride is those gathered, or the Church. (See also Rev. 19:7–9.)

The wonders in the heavens and the earth foretold in Joel 2:30–

31 were to happen before the second coming of the Lord. The terminology used by Joel is common to other scriptures. (See Matt. 24:39; Isa. 13:10; D&C 29:14.) The specifics of the fulfillment of this prophecy will be better understood at the time they come to pass, as Nephi said concerning the prophecies of Isaiah. (2 Ne. 25:7.) Joel concludes his soon-to-be fulfilled prophecy with the declaration that those who call upon the Lord in these perilous times will be delivered from the terrible destruction. Deliverance will be initiated and fulfilled through the gathering of a remnant of Israel. (See Isa. 6:13; 10:20–22; 49:1–6; D&C 133:30–32; Abr. 2:11.) Joseph Smith, the Lord's servant, was to bring about the fulfillment of these prophecies. The angel Moroni announced that God had a work for Joseph Smith to do. (JS–H 1:33.) Later, after quoting Joel 2:28–32, Joseph Smith commented:

"It is very difficult for us to communicate to the churches all that God has revealed to us, in consequence of tradition; for we are differently situated from any other people that ever existed upon this earth; consequently those former revelations cannot be suited to our conditions; they were given to other people, who were before us; but in the last days, God was to call a remnant, in which was to be deliverance, as well as in Jerusalem and Zion. Now if God should give no more revelations, where will we find Zion and this remnant? The time is near when desolation is to cover the earth, and then God will have a place of deliverance in his remnant, and in Zion.

"Take away the Book of Mormon and the revelations, and where is our religion? We have none; for without Zion, and a place of deliverance, we must fall; because the time is near when the sun will be darkened, and the moon turn to blood, and the stars fall from heaven, and the earth reel to and fro. Then, if this is the case, and if we are not sanctified and gathered to the places God has appointed, with all our former professions and our great love for the Bible, we must fall; we cannot stand; we cannot be saved; for God will gather out his Saints from the Gentiles, and then comes desolation and destruction, and none can escape except the pure in heart who are gathered."[7]

The work begun by Joseph Smith has progressed since then and is rapidly spreading throughout the world.

Having spoken of the two gathering places in general, Joel returns in chapter 3 to enlarge upon the prophecies concerning Judah and Jerusalem. As announced, all nations of the Gentiles will be gathered against Judah in the valley of Jehoshaphat where the Lord will plead for his people (Judah) as well as for others of Israel who have been scattered among the Gentile nations. (Joel 3:1–2.) The valley of Je-hoshaphat is located outside of Jerusalem and will be the place of the last battle before the long-awaited Messiah comes to rescue his people. The Lord's pleading for his people was also foretold by Isaiah and is used in conjunction with judgment. (Isa. 3:13–14.) Both prophets speak of the injustices that have come upon the Lord's people. (Joel 3:3; Isa. 3:15.) Joel speaks of Tyre and Sidon (modern Lebanon) and the coasts of Palestine having mistreated the Lord's people and his promise to make recompense upon their heads. (Joel 3:4–8.) Again, the symbolic representation of Tyre and Sidon will be fully understood at some later day, but vengeance is the Lord's and he will repay. (Mormon 3:15.)

The Lord challenges the Gentiles and the heathens (those who worship other gods) to come to the valley of decision where he will sit to judge the nations. (Joel 3:9–14.) At that time he will show who his people are by his coming to defend them in this great battle. While many multitudes will be gathered, they will be no match for the God of the whole earth. Elder Bruce R. McConkie describes the multitudes gathered in the valley of decision as "the hosts of men who must decide whether they will be gathered with the Lord's harvest into his kingdom or be left for the day when the tares and the grain that are not harvested shall be burned."[8]

The battle in the valley of decision will be fought just prior to the Lord's coming in glory to the whole world and at the time of the sun, moon, and stars prophecies being fulfilled. The Lord also shall roar out of Zion and utter his voice from Jerusalem; and the heavens and the earth shall shake. (Joel 3:14–16.) This shaking is also confirmed in modern revelation, which adds that the shaking is for the Saints' good. (D&C 21:6; 35:24.) It will be when the Lord will have established his people in his two gathering places, Zion and Jerusalem, and he will be their strength. The roaring out of Zion is the proclaiming of his gospel from the center place of the Church in the Americas, his holy mountain. (Joel 3:16–17; see also Isa. 2:3; 4:2–3.) At that time Jerusalem will also become a holy city as prophesied by Ether, the Jaredite prophet. (Ether 13:5, 11.) The land of Judah will prosper, and all her rivers will flow with water. Some of this water will come as a fountain from under the temple built in Jerusalem. (Joel 3:18.)

The Prophet Joseph Smith commented about these events: "Judah must return, Jerusalem must be rebuilt, and the temple, and water come out from under the temple, and the waters of the Dead Sea be healed. It will take some time to rebuild the walls of the city and the temple, &c.; and all this must be done before the Son of Man will make his appearance. There will be wars and rumors of wars, signs in the heavens above and on the earth beneath, the sun turned into darkness and the moon to blood, earthquakes in divers places, the seas heaving beyond their bounds; then will appear one grand sign of the Son of Man in heaven. But what will the world do? They will say it is a planet, a comet, etc. But the Son of man will come as the sign of the coming of the Son of Man, which will be as the light of the morning cometh out of the east."[9]

The messianic prophecies of Joel center on the gathering of all the house of Israel in Zion and Jerusalem in the last days prior to the Second Coming.

Amos

The book of Amos is one of the best examples of the Lord as the administrator God holding "the destinies of all the armies of the nations of the earth." (D&C 117:6.) His prophecies begin with a scathing pronouncement of the Lord's judgments upon the seven nations surrounding Israel and upon Israel herself. (Amos 1–2.) His prophecies are also rich in showing the Lord's calling of a prophet (Amos 7:10–17) and how he reveals his will to the prophets. (Amos 3:7.) The prophecies of Amos also show the Lord's role in the scattering of Israel and their being gathered in the last days. (JST, Amos 7:1–6; 9:8–9.) There is, however, only one messianic prophecy in this fascinating book.

The last prophecy recorded in Amos concerns the eventual result of the gathering out of the house of Israel from among the nations. In the day of the gathering, the Lord will "raise up the tabernacle of David that is fallen . . . and . . . build it as in the days of old." (Amos 9:11.) This passage refers to the establishment of the full kingdom of God among all of the original twelve tribes of Jacob. The twelve tribes will be reunited with one king ruling over them all. That king will be Christ, "THE LORD OUR RIGHTEOUSNESS." (Jer. 23:5–6.) He will be the descendant of David, who was promised that his seed would reign forever, or eternally. (2 Sam. 7:16.) He is the "KING OF KINGS, AND LORD OF LORDS." (Rev. 19:16.)

Obadiah

Although it is indirect, there is one messianic prophecy in the book of Obadiah. One of the well-known phrases among Latter-day Saints is taken from the last verse of Obadiah—"saviors upon mount Zion." The term was used by the Prophet Joseph Smith, which accounts for its use among members of the Church. Although most Church members could not justify its use in the context of Obadiah, it is a valid interpretation. First of all, let us examine Joseph Smith's statements.

In May 1841 Joseph spoke about election in the flesh of the seed of Abraham: "The election of the promised seed still continues, and in the last day, they shall have the Priesthood restored unto them, and they shall be the 'saviors on Mount Zion,' the ministers of our God; if it were not for the remnant which was left, then might men now be as Sodom and Gomorrah."[10]

In October 1841 Joseph Smith "presented baptism for the dead as the only way that men can appear as saviors on Mount Zion."[11] In April 1842, as he preached on baptism for the dead, he declared: "We are commanded to be baptized for our dead, thus fulfilling the words of Obadiah, when speaking of the glory of the latter-day: 'And saviors shall come upon Mount Zion to judge the remnant of Esau, and the kingdom shall be the Lord's.' "[12]

In January 1844 the Prophet discoursed on the sealing power of the priesthood. He again referred to the Saints' being saviors on mount Zion and asked: "But how are they to become saviors on Mount Zion? By building their temples, erecting their baptismal fonts, and going forth and receiving all the ordinances, baptisms, confirmations, washings, anointings, ordinations and sealing powers upon their heads, in behalf of all their progenitors who are dead, and redeem them that they may come forth in the first resurrection and be exalted to thrones of glory with them."[13]

In the context of Obadiah, work for the dead ancestors of Edom will also be done in the temples established through the restoration of the gospel to the house of Joseph in America. Those millions of people of the lineage of Edom or other surrounding nations who have not had the opportunity to hear the gospel in this life will hear in the spirit world and will then be saved through the ordinances performed in the temples built in the latter days. Obadiah's prophecy is not limited to Edom. President John Taylor said that men who administer in the temples of God "become saviors of their own nations; they administer and operate in their interests and in the interests of their fathers and their friends and associates."[14] This interpretation of Obadiah and of Joseph Smith has been repeated throughout the history of the Church.

Part of the mission of Jesus in the meridian of time was to open the spirit world to the preaching of the gospel and the vicarious work for the dead. Isaiah foretold it (Isa. 42:7; 61:1), as well as Zechariah and Malachi, as will be shown later. It was also verified by Jesus (John 5:28–29), by Peter (1 Peter 3:18–20; 4:5–6), and by Paul. (1 Cor. 15:29.) The work begun in the meridian of time was reinstituted in the latter-day restoration as a part of the preparation for the second coming of the Messiah. (D&C 128.)

Jonah

On two different occasions, Jesus referred to the teachings of the prophet Jonah as a sign of his being killed and buried in the heart of the earth for three days and three nights. (Matt. 12:38–41; 16:1–4.) The account of Jonah was thus a type and shadow of Jesus' death and resurrection. It also bears record of Jesus Christ as he (the Lord) taught Adam that "all things are created and made to bear record of [him]." (Moses 6:63.)

Micah

Micah begins his record with a witness against the people of Samaria and Jerusalem. (Micah 1:1–2.) "For, behold, the Lord cometh forth out of his place, and will come down, and tread upon the high places of the earth. And the mountains shall be molten under him, and the valleys shall be cleft, as wax before the fire, and as the waters that are poured down a steep place." (Micah 1:3–4.)

The first prophecy of Micah is undoubtedly a dual prophecy. The two separate time periods for the prophecy are the conquest of Samaria by Assyria, 722 B.C., and the second coming of Christ. The Assyrian conquest left "Samaria as an heap of the field, and as plantings of a vineyard." (Micah 1:6.) The iniquities of Samaria were "incurable" and had spread over into Jerusalem. (Micah 1:5, 9.) On this occasion, however, the mountains were not "molten under [the Lord], and the valleys [were not] cleft, as wax before the fire, and as the waters that are poured down a steep place." (Micah 1:4.) Although the description of the Lord's coming down and treading upon the earth (Micah 1:3) may symbolize the Samarian conquest and not a literal treading down, it will be literally fulfilled in the second coming of Christ. (See Isa. 40:3–5; JST, Luke 3:4–11.)

A second messianic prophecy of Micah relates to the latter-day political kingdom of God. After the mountain of the house of the Lord (the temple) has been built in the top of the mountains in the last day (Micah 4:1–2; Independence, Missouri — see D&C 57, headnote and v. 3), the Lord will gather in from all nations those Israelites who had previously been "driven out" of their promised lands and assemble them in "Mount Zion" where he will personally "reign over them." (Micah 4:6–7.) The "strong nation" (Micah 4:7) over which the Lord will reign and which will be made strong by him is the restored nation of Israel. Christ, "whose right it is to reign" will be there, in Zion, as king. (D&C 58:22.) His kingdom will first have "dominion" in Zion and then "shall come to the daughter of Jerusalem." (Micah 4:8.) That is the same political kingdom that was delivered by the woman (the Church) in the meridian of time to rule all nations with a rod of iron (the word of God), but because of the great red dragon (the devil), was caught up unto God. The woman (the Church) was driven into the wilderness for a long time (the Apostasy), but will now be delivered from the hands of her enemies and established. (See Rev. 12:1–6; Micah 4:9–10.) Isaiah likewise predicts the birth of this man child, the political kingdom of God. (Isa. 66:5–10.) Although the kingdom is born, it is born in Babylon, or among the wickedness of the world (D&C 133:14), and will thus be opposed by the world. The world, however, knows "not the thoughts of the Lord." (Micah 4:12; see also Isa. 55:8.) The Lord will gather his people, the house of Israel, out of the world as a thresher in the ancient world gathered the grain "sheaves into the floor" and brought forth the seed of grain from the straw and chaff. (Micah 4:13.) This same concept was taught to the Nephites by the Savior. He quoted the prophecy of Micah in the context of the gathering of Israel from the Gentiles to establish the New Jerusalem in the Americas in fulfillment of the covenant to his people. (3 Ne. 20:12–22.) The two witnesses of this gathering and establishing of the political kingdom, Micah and Isaiah, are thus interpreted and confirmed by the Book of Mormon. Another witness is given by the Lord in the Appendix to the Doctrine and Covenants (section 133) and also adds another dimension. In explaining why he restored the fulness of the gospel, the Lord used the terminology of Micah 4:13, "And by the weak things of the earth the Lord shall thrash the nations by the power of his Spirit." (D&C 133:59.) The power of the Lord's Spirit will be the major factor in this latter-day movement.

One of the Christian world's favorite scriptures from Micah is the third messianic prophecy of Christ, his being born in Bethlehem. Most people who are familiar with this prophecy, however, fail to put the prophecy in its context and fail to analyze the entire prophecy. The context of the prophecy is the last days and the subject is again the gathering of the remnant of Israel.

The first verse of the prophecy speaks of the gathering of troops, "O daughter of troops." The daughter of troops seems to be the gathering of Israel to Zion and her stakes similar to the Gentiles who have gathered against Zion. The mother nations (Babylon) gathering against Zion have set the pattern for the daughter (Israel), who has been scattered among them, to gather as a refuge from the threatened gentile storm. (See Isa. 4:5–6; D&C 115:6.) The nations of Babylon will lay siege to Zion and will smite the judge of Israel (Christ) with a rod upon the cheek. (Micah 5:1.) The rod here seems to symbolize a verbal barrage against the people of Zion who are gathering under the direction of the Lord, or judge of Israel.

Apparently to explain why these events will happen in the last days, the Lord, through Micah, refers to the humble beginning of the "ruler in Israel" in the little town of Bethlehem. He then quickly confirms that that was not the beginning of his rulership, because he had been administering the affairs of the house of Israel "from of old, from everlasting." (Micah 5:2.) The interpretations of this prophecy being of Christ's birth are given by two New Testament apostles. (Matt. 2:6; John 7:42.) As an explanation of this being a last-days prophecy, however, Micah explains that the Lord would give Judah up "until the time that she which travaileth hath brought forth." (Micah 5:3.) This refers to the travailing of Zion to establish the political kingdom as prophesied earlier. (Micah 4:10.) Not until this kingdom is established will the tribe of Judah, "the remnant of his [Christ's] brethren," return unto the children of Israel. (Micah 5:3.) In other words, the conversions of Judah will not happen until after the building of the New Jerusalem in Missouri. (3 Ne. 21:23–29.)

Micah adds some depth to the messianic prophecies that are not covered by others of the twelve prophets.

Nahum

There are no messianic prophecies in the book of Nahum as defined in this work; however, there are general prophecies of Christ. There is a probable dual prophecy of the destruction of Ninevah in about 712 B.C. as a type of the destruction of the last days, as the headnote to this book suggests in the LDS edition of the Bible. This conclusion is drawn from the descriptions of chariots with flaming torches that rage in the streets and jostle one against another. The chariot combat of ancient times is supposedly used to describe the tanks and other armored vehicles with modern lighting systems. (Nahum 2:3–4.) Thus, again we see evidence of the Lord holding "the destiny of all the armies of the nations of the earth." (D&C 117:6.)

Habukkuk

At sometime in everyone's life the question arises about whether or not God is aware of and concerned with his or her life. As a person is given more responsibility for the lives of other people, that question enlarges to how involved God is or will be in the lives of those over whom the person has jurisdiction. The book of Habakkuk answers these questions with a declaration that "the Lord is in his holy temple" (he is on the job and in full control); therefore the inhabitants of the earth and his servants should "keep silence before [God]" (they should listen to and obey his voice rather than question his involvement). (Hab. 2:20.)

Habukkuk's opening statement, "O Lord, how long shall I cry, and thou wilt not heart" (Hab. 1:2) shows he is perplexed. He has repeatedly warned the people of their wickedness, yet to his knowledge the Lord has done nothing about it. (Hab. 1:2–4.) Jeremiah had similar feelings. (Jer. 20:7–13.) The Prophet Joseph Smith also cried out against the suffering of the Saints in Missouri. (D&C 121:6.)

The Lord's answer to Habukkuk pertained to the latter days: "Behold ye among the heathen, and regard, and wonder marvelously: for I will work a work in your days, which ye will not believe, though it be told you." (Hab. 1:5.) Although the Prophet Joseph Smith made no changes in this passage as he translated the Bible, "your days" was not referring to, or at least limited to, Habukkuk's day. The work that the Lord referred to was to be fulfilled in the latter days among the heathen, or Gentile nations, as shown in the Book of Mormon. The Lord is obviously quoting or paraphrasing Habakkuk, or another prophet who taught the same principle, when he says to the Nephites: "For in that day, for my sake shall the Father work a work, which shall be a great and a marvelous work among them; and there shall be among them those who will not believe it, although a man shall declare it unto them." (3 Ne. 21:9.) The context of the Savior's quotation to the Nephites shows the marvelous work of the Father to be the bringing forth of the Book of Mormon through his servant Joseph Smith. (3 Ne. 21:1–11.) The Lord allows evil to exist because of the agency of man and as a witness against the wicked. (Alma 60:12–13.) He will eventually intervene. After he leads the righteous people out, he will destroy the nations of the wicked. (1 Ne. 17:37–38.) In the future, however, he will give other generations an opportunity to accept the gospel. That is Habukkuk's message from the Lord.

After some other questions by Habukkuk and answers by the Lord, Habukkuk prays to the Lord. (Hab. 3.) He acknowledges the Lord's involvement in his dealings with the people of Israel in the past and his power over the earth and the elements of the earth. (Hab. 3:3–12.) He further acknowledges that the Lord's actions have always been for the salvation of his children. (Hab. 3:13–15.) All people will someday learn or be forced to acknowledge that God is in his temple and is in command, controlling the final outcome of the earth and its inhabitants. That is Habukkuk's testimony of Christ.

Zephaniah

Zephaniah knew well the messianic prophecies of the second coming of Christ; however, he used them differently from the way most other prophets used them. Zephaniah 1:2–3 speaks of the consumption of all things — man and beast, fowls and fishes. This wording had led some to suggest that it is a description of the Second Coming, but as the chapter headnote in the LDS edition of the Bible suggests, "the destruction of Judah is a type of the Second Coming." The wording of verse 4, "I will also stretch out mine hand upon Judah, and upon all the inhabitants of Jerusalem," suggests another possibility. Zephaniah is using the already-known prophecy of destruction at the second coming of Christ as an attention-getter so he can deliver his message of destruction to Judah.

Zephaniah uses the Second Coming as an example of a similar destruction upon Judah as he speaks of the day of the Lord being at hand. (Zeph. 1:7.) In this verse, the bidding of the guests to the sacrifice the Lord has prepared is similar to the parable of the great supper (Luke 14:15–24) or the parable of the marriage of the king's son (Matt. 22:1–4), both referring to the Second Coming. Assuming this verse has reference to the Second Coming, the following verses (8–10), introduced with phrases like "in the same day," bring the present audience of Zephaniah back to their own day. Verse 8 speaks of those clothed with strange apparel. (Zeph. 1:8.) This is like the Matthew parable. Perhaps there were similar parables at one time in the Old Testament before the plain and precious parts were removed (1 Ne. 13:24–29), and Zephaniah is referring to things the people had already been taught.

Once more Zephaniah uses latter-day prophecies to illustrate the coming destruction of their goods and houses. As Isaiah had prophesied that in the Millennium people would build houses and inhabit them and plant vineyards and eat the fruit of them (Isa. 65:22), Zephaniah specifies that just the opposite was to occur with the people of Judah. (Zeph. 1:13.) The great day of the Lord was near for the people of Judah. It would be a day of wrath, trouble, distress, and darkness for them, just as the Second Coming would be for the people in the last days. (Zeph. 1:14–16.) These conditions would come because the people had sinned against the Lord, and their silver and gold would not be able to deliver them. (Zeph. 1:17–18.) Thus Zephaniah is using the messianic prophecies of the destruction of the wicked at the Lord's second coming to warn his present generation of the coming destruction of the nation because of their collective wickedness. His use of those prophecies verifies that all of the prophets knew of Christ and had a hope of his glory. (Jacob 4:5.)

Haggai

Haggai was one of the two prophets raised up to inspire the men of Judah to rebuild the temple of the Lord. (Ezra 5:1–2; 6:14.) As the work on the temple commenced, the Lord through Haggai asked the people to remember the glory of the first temple and compare it with how they were presently building. Apparently, their efforts were not producing a very impressive building, because the Lord answered his own question by saying the comparison was as nothing. (Hag. 2:1–3.) He encouraged them to be strong and beautify the building and promised that he will be with them if they will respond. (Hag. 2:4–5.) The Lord then gave them a reason for the house to be beautified. In a little while (in the Lord's time), he is going to shake the heavens and the earth, and the sea, and the dry land and all the nations and the desire of all nations shall come (the Messiah). When he comes, the temple will be filled with glory. (Hag. 2:6–7.) That is the only specific messianic prophecy in the book of Haggai. The shaking of the heaven and earth is probably a dual prophecy that refers to the catastrophic signs that occurred at the time of Christ's birth (3 Ne. 1:15–21; Luke 2:8–15; Matt. 2:1–2) and also what will take place at his second coming. While the gospel testaments do not record the temple's being filled with glory at his birth, it probably was, and there were spiritual manifestations given to faithful people. (Luke 2:25–38.) All the prophets had foretold this glorious birth, and all nations would be blessed by his advent into mortality — thus "the desire of all nations" would come. Since the gospel will "be preached in all the world, for a witness unto all nations" before the destruction of the wicked (JS–M 1:31), it is logical that the Lord will again be the desire of all nations in the latter days. The beautiful Latter-day Saint hymn "Come, O Thou King of Kings" was written by Parley P. Pratt from this inspired verse.

Zechariah

Zechariah has more messianic prophecies than any of the other eleven prophets. In Zechariah 3, an angel seems to speak by divine investiture of authority for the Father, declaring that his servant the BRANCH will be brought forth. (V. 8). The capitalization of the name for the servant designates that it is a messianic prophecy. The prophet Jeremiah identifies the servant as the BRANCH. (Jer. 23:5–6; 33:15.) The context of the chapter suggests his coming forth at the time of his birth, although verses 9 and 10 suggest his second coming. Perhaps it is another dual prophecy.

In chapter 6, Zechariah is instructed to take silver and gold and make crowns, and one was for the head of Joshua the high priest. (Zech. 6:11.) This crowning was apparently symbolic of Christ being the king of kings, the BRANCH. (Zech. 6:12–13.) The text seems to represent both Joshua as the present-day high priest who shall be the presiding authority in the temple and Jesus Christ who shall sit upon the throne of David forever. (See also 2 Sam. 7:16.) The message to Zechariah is that the temple will be built and Joshua will serve, which symbolizes Christ reigning through eternity.

There are three prophecies in chapter 9 about the ministry of Christ. Jesus' riding of a colt into the city at the beginning of the last week of his ministry was foretold by Zechariah. Jerusalem was to shout because "thy King cometh unto thee: he is just, and having salvation; lowly, and riding upon an ass, and upon a colt the foal of an ass" (Zech. 9:9). As he rode down from Bethphage on the Mount of Olives, the people laid their garments in his path or cut palm branches and laid them before him, proclaiming that he was the Son of David, king of Israel. Both Matthew and John quote Zechariah as being fulfilled with this incident. (Matt. 21:1–9; John 12:12–15.) The Christian world today celebrates Palm Sunday to commemorate this event.

The second prophecy of chapter 9 foretells that the chariot of Ephraim and the horse from Jerusalem will be cut off. He was to speak peace to the heathen, and his dominion was to cover to the ends of the earth. (Zech. 9:10.) This prophecy was another way of foretelling that the gospel would be taken from the Jews to the Gentiles. Jesus proclaimed this concept during his ministry (Matt. 19:30; 21:43), and it was fulfilled when Peter received the revelation to take the gospel to the Gentiles (Acts 10). Through the gospel going to both Jew (Israel) and Gentile, Christ's dominion would go to the ends of the earth in fulfillment of the covenant made to Abraham to bless all nations of the earth. (Abr. 2:11; 1 Ne. 22:9; 3 Ne. 20:25.)

The third prophecy of Christ's ministry was his opening of the spirit world to the preaching of the gospel and the performing of ordinances for those spirits in prison. Through the blood of Christ's covenant, he visited the spirit world and organized the forces of righteous, departed spirits to preach the gospel in the spirit prison and perform the ordinances to bring "thy prisoners out of the pit wherein is no water." (Zech. 9:11; see also D&C 138:18–30.) There being no water is reminiscent of the parable taught by Jesus during his ministry of Lazarus and the rich man. The rich man desired that Lazarus dip his finger in water and cool the rich man's tongue, but that was not possible because of the gulf between them. (Luke 16:19–31.) The water is probably representative of there being no source of the living water of Christ and his gospel in the spirit prison. Christ had not yet bridged the gulf that enabled the gospel to be taught. The rest of the verses in the chapter are addressed to the "prisoners of hope" (Zech. 9:12) and seems to be an invitation for those in the spirit prison to accept the gospel: "The Lord their God shall save them in that day" when the gospel is preached and they shall be exalted (Zech. 9:16).

In chapter 11, Zechariah foretells of Judah betraying the Christ for thirty pieces of silver and casting the money into the potter's field. (Zech. 11:12–13.) Credit for this prophecy is given to Jeremiah in the New Testament. (Matt. 27:1–10.) Perhaps Jeremiah made a similar prophecy that was lost from his prophecies, but, regardless, it was fulfilled by Judas.

The last three chapters of Zechariah (12 through 14) refer to the coming of the Lord in the latter days or his second coming. The chronology given is not consistent with itself nor with latter-day scripture, but the teachings of these chapters are confirmed by modern revelation.

The burden, or message of doom, to Israel opens the last section of Zechariah. The Lord promises to make Jerusalem a cup of trembling unto all the people round about when they lay siege against Judah and Jerusalem. All of the people of the earth will be gathered against Jerusalem. The governors, or leaders, of Judah are to devour the people round about and the Lord will defend Jerusalem. (Zech. 12:1–8.) This is another description of the battle of Armageddon (Rev. 16:16) or the valley of decision. (Joel 3.) At the conclusion of the battle, the Lord will appear to his people, the embattled Jews, and they will recognize him as their Messiah, but they "will look upon me whom they have pierced." (Zech. 12:10.) There is a dual fulfillment of this prophecy. It was quoted by John in his Gospel as being fulfilled while Christ was on the cross (John 19:37); however, the same author spoke of his coming in the clouds of heaven "and every eye shall see him, and they also which pierced him" (Rev. 1:7). The context of Zechariah supports the latter fulfillment. The text continues with a declaration that there would be great mourning in Jerusalem in that day. (Zech. 12:11–14.)

The following chapter speaks of a day of restoration among Judah. It speaks of a fountain being "opened to the house of David and to the inhabitants of Jerusalem for sin and for uncleanness." (Zech. 13:1.) The fountain refers to the ordinance of baptism for the remission of individual sins and is supported by the prophet Isaiah's declarations of Judah's opening the gate of baptism as well as a political invitation to the nation that keepeth the truth. (Isa. 26:2.) Thus the gospel will be preached in the homeland of the Jews to the Jews.

Zechariah continues with the prophecy of the idols and false prophets being cut off in the land. (Zech. 13:2–5.) The text returns to an extension of Zechariah 12:10. As they look upon him whom they have pierced, one shall say to the Savior, "What are these wounds in thine hands?" Then he shall answer, "Those with which I was wounded in the house of my friends." (Zech. 13:6.) The Doctrine and Covenants records these same words as given by Jesus on the Mount of Olives to his disciples prior to his crucifixion, regarding the events of the last days. The Doctrine and Covenants further equates these words with the mourning mentioned in Zechariah 12. (D&C 45:51–53.) Zechariah 13 concludes with a prophecy that two-thirds of the Jewish people will be killed in the battle of Armageddon, but the third that survive will be refined and made the people of the Lord. (Zech. 13:7–9.)

The final chapter of Zechariah speaks of the coming of the "day of the Lord." It is the day when all nations shall gather against Jerusalem to battle and the Lord will fight against those nations. (Zech. 14:1–3.) When the Lord appears, his feet shall stand upon the Mount of Olives, and it shall cleave in the midst towards the east and the west with the mount being moved half to the north and half to the south. (Zech. 14:4.) The Lord also referred to this catastrophic event in the appendix of the Doctrine and Covenants. (D&C 133:18–20; see also D&C 45:48.) He compares the fleeing of the people at this time to the earthquake in the days of Uzziah. (Zech. 14:5.) There is no record of an earthquake in Uzziah's day but there must have been one. The earthquake in the days of Uzziah is a pattern or a type of the earthquake that was to come in the last days. (Moses 6:63.)

The earthquake was to accompany the coming of the Lord and all the Saints with him. (Zech. 14:5.) The Savior's instructions to his disciples on the Mount of Olives qualifies the Saints coming with him as the Saints from the four quarters of the earth who have slept or died, being resurrected at his coming. (D&C 45:43–46.) This event was to happen before the arm of the Lord fell upon the surrounding nations. (D&C 45:47.)

Another sign apparently to be repeated is the day and a night and a day of no darkness given to the Nephites at the birth of Christ happening again at the Second Coming. (3 Ne. 1:15–19.) In Zechariah's words, the light shall not be clear nor light but at evening time it shall be light. (14:6–7.) The wording of this prophecy is a bit nebulous, but it seems similar to the Nephite sign.

Zechariah next speaks of living water coming out from Jerusalem, half toward the former sea (Dead Sea) and half toward the hinder sea (Mediterranean). This water was to run in the winter as well as the summer. (Zech. 14:8.) The living water suggests that it is symbolic of Christ. (See also John 4:10–15; 7:37.) The Prophet Joseph Smith, however, spoke of the actual water that would come out from under the temple that was to be built in Jerusalem.[15] (See also Joel 3:18.)

After these events, the Lord will be king over all the earth and Jerusalem shall be inhabited safely. (Zech. 14:9–11.) The Doctrine and Covenants repeatedly speaks of Jesus' reign as the king. (D&C 38:21; 41:4; 45:59; 58:22; 65:5–6.) Other Old Testament prophets also prophesied of his role as king. (Jer. 23:5; Ezek. 34:23–24; 37:24–27.)

Zechariah then speaks of the plague that will come upon those who fight against Jerusalem. The flesh, the eyes, and the tongue shall fall away. (Zech. 14:12.) This plague sounds like the plagues mentioned in Doctrine and Covenants 29:18–20 that will come before the great day of the Lord. Zechariah speaks further of those who will not come up to Jerusalem to worship. (Zech. 14:16–19.) Although the feast of the tabernacles is mentioned, a festival under the law of Moses, it probably symbolizes the higher law that will be followed in the Millennium.

The text concludes with an announcement that even the bells of the horses shall have engraved upon them "Holiness to the Lord" as well as pots and other items. There will be no more Canaanites or Gentiles in the house of the Lord. (Zech. 14:20–21.) The Prophet Joseph reaffirmed this as a latter-day practice.[16] It is another way of describing Jerusalem as a holy city unto the Lord occupied by a holy or sanctified people. (See Ether 13:5, 11.)

The prophet Zechariah saw the meridian of time and the mission of the Lord Jesus Christ. His prophecies extended to the final winding-up scenes in Jerusalem and the coming of the great day of the Lord. Zechariah has left us a challenging text to study, and the Lord has confirmed his prophecies in the Doctrine and Covenants.

Malachi

The prophecies of Malachi are and should be of great interest to the Latter-day Saints. They speak of things that must happen before the second coming of Christ and how one must prepare for that great event. Christ agreed to come to earth and shed his blood, making an atonement for all mankind. (3 Ne. 27:13–14; see also Heb. 13:20.) Through his atoning blood, he was able to provide a plan to bring all mankind to immortality and eternal life. (3 Ne. 27:15–21; Moses 1:39.) To qualify for the blessings of the Atonement, mankind must comply with the new and everlasting covenant. This covenant was to be restored upon the earth in preparation for the great and dreadful day of the Lord—great for those who are prepared and dreadful for those who are not prepared.

The Lord promised to send his messenger to prepare the way before his coming. (Mal. 3:1.) A surface reading and cross-referencing to the New Testament suggest this promise to be fulfilled through the mission of John the Baptist. (Matt. 11:10; Mark 1:2; Luke 7:27.) Because we are dealing with dual prophecy, the ultimate fulfillment will be in the latter days. That is obvious because the Savior quoted this passage to the Nephites after his resurrection in the context of future fulfillment, the angel Moroni quoted it among the prophecies soon to be fulfilled, and the Savior revealed it to Joseph Smith in the past tense in March 1831: "And even so I have sent mine everlasting covenant into the world, to be a light to the world, and to be a standard for my people, and for the Gentiles to seek to it, and to be a messenger before my face to prepare the way before me." (D&C 45:9.)

The messenger to prepare the way before the second coming of the Lord is, therefore, the restoration of the everlasting covenant, or the fulness of the gospel. The rest of Malachi 3:1 further confirms the latter-day fulfillment.

Malachi prophesied that the Lord would come suddenly to his temple. (Mal. 3:1.) Following the restoration of the new and everlasting covenant, the Lord reaffirmed his future sudden appearance in his temple. (D&C 36:4; 133:2.) He could not make this appearance until a temple of the Lord had been built. The first temple to the Lord was the Kirtland Temple, completed and dedicated on April 3, 1836. On this occasion, Christ came to the Kirtland Temple suddenly. Following the prayer of Joseph Smith and Oliver Cowdery, the veil was taken from their minds and eyes and they saw him. (D&C 110:1.) His appearance fulfilled in part the promise made through Malachi. The message of the everlasting covenant had been fulfilled and the messenger of the everlasting covenant had suddenly come to his temple in preparation for his Second Coming or the great day of the Lord for those who have accepted and followed the gospel plan of salvation.

That Malachi's prophecy is about the second coming of Christ and not his first coming or his mortal ministry is further attested to by the declaration, "But who may abide the day of his coming, and who shall stand when he appeareth? For he is like a refiner's fire and like fuller's soap." (Mal. 3:2.) There is no evidence that people could not abide his first coming. His second coming, however, will constitute a cleansing of the earth—thus the analogy of a refiner's fire where the impurities are cleansed from ores to make metals or the fuller's soap of ancient days that was also a purifier often used to whiten cloth. Later Malachi speaks of all the proud and all that do wickedly burning as stubble. (Mal. 4:1.) As quoted earlier, in latter-day revelation, the Lord has declared that "every corruptible thing, both of man, or of the beasts of the field, or of the fowls of the heavens, or of the fish of the sea, that dwells upon all the face of the earth, shall be consumed." (D&C 101:24.) That is the dreadful part of his coming.

As Malachi continues his prophecy, the Lord holds out hope to those who fear his name. Following the burning of the proud and the wicked, the Son of Righteousness will arise with healing in his wings. (Mal. 4:2; 3 Ne. 25:2.) The Book of Mormon text changes the word "sun" to "Son," which clarifies it as a reference to the Son of God. (See also 2 Ne. 25:13; 26:9.) Those who are left after the judgment of the Second Coming will be able to raise up their children as calves are raised in a stall. (Mal. 4:2; see also 1 Ne. 22:24.) The calf is protected from the elements and his environment is controlled. The children in the Millennium will similarly "grow up without sin unto salvation." (D&C 45:58.) The telestial element will be removed and Satan will be bound. (Rev. 20:1–3; 1 Ne. 22:26; D&C 101:28.) Thus the environment will be more controlled. The wicked who do not survive his coming, the telestial people, will be as ashes under the feet of those who do survive the burning. (Mal. 4:3.) The wicked will come to their end just as Malachi ends the prophecies of the Old Testament.

Conclusion

All of the last twelve prophets of the Old Testament testified of Jesus Christ. Their prophecies were many and varied. They confirm Jesus as the administrator God of this world in the past, the present, and the future and show his involvement in all things. There are many specific messianic prophecies of his advent in the flesh upon the earth and of his coming in glory in the latter days. Many of the prophecies are confirmed, clarified, or enlarged upon in modern-day scripture: the Book of Mormon, the Doctrine and Covenants, the Pearl of Great Price, the Joseph Smith Translation of the Bible, and by the prophet of the Restoration, Joseph Smith. The prophecies of these twelve Old Testament prophets are another witness that all the prophets testified of Jesus Christ. We are commanded to search them. (3 Ne. 23:5.) If we do search them, we will see that they truly testify of him (see John 5:39), and we will be the beneficiaries of that search.

NOTES

1. The psalms referred to by Jesus were probably the third section of the Jewish canon, the Writings, or the Hagiographa. Such a meaning would confirm that all of the Old Testament testified of him.

2. The writings of these twelve prophets were considered one book in the Hebrew canon and called the "Twelve Prophets."

3. James R. Clark, comp., *Messages of the First Presidency*, 6 vols. (Salt Lake City: Bookcraft, 1971), 5:31–33.

4. Joseph Smith, *Teachings of the Prophet Joseph Smith*, sel. Joseph Fielding Smith (Salt Lake City: Deseret Book Co., 1976), p. 286.

5. Ibid., p. 362.

6. Ibid., p. 141.

7. Ibid., pp. 70–71; see also p. 17.

8. Bruce R. McConkie, *The Mortal Messiah*, 4 vols. (Salt Lake City: Deseret Book Co., 1979), 1:503.

9. Ibid., pp. 286–87.

10. Ibid., p. 189.

11. Ibid., p. 191.

12. Ibid., p. 223.

13. Ibid., p. 330.

14. John Taylor, in *Journal of Discourses*, 26 vols. (Liverpool: F. D. Richards, 1851–86), 21:97.

15. Smith, *Teachings*, pp. 286–87.

16. Joseph Smith, *History of The Church of Jesus Christ of Latter-day Saints*, ed. B. H. Roberts, 7 vols., 2d ed. rev. (Salt Lake City: Deseret Book Co., 1957), 2:257–58.

CHAPTER THIRTEEN

The Marriage of Hosea and Gomer: A Symbolic Testament of Messianic Love and Mercy

Brent L. Top

Brigham Young University

Jehovah, the God of the Old Testament, dealt with his people Israel in ways which might seem strange, austere, or even cruel to us today. A superficial study of the Bible may leave some with the impression that the God of the Old Testament was a God of vengeance and retribution, a God to be feared; whereas the New Testament God was a God of love and compassion, a God to be worshiped and adored. A more in-depth and thoughtful examination of the Old Testament, however, reveals Jehovah as a long-suffering, tenderhearted, loving, and merciful Shepherd who is continually imploring his lambs to return to his flock and watchful care. Perhaps no place in the Old Testament is this image clearer than in the intriguing and important account of the marriage of the prophet Hosea to the harlot Gomer. (See Hosea 1–3.) The story is intriguing because of the unusual circumstances surrounding the marriage, but it is important because it demonstrates so poignantly and painfully God's perfect love and his unfailing offer of mercy. "By no other of the Old Testament witnesses," wrote one scholar, "is the tender intimacy and the triumphant power of the love of God so deeply comprehended and so fully expressed as by Hosea."[1]

Hosea's Marriage to Gomer: Actual or Allegorical?

In Hosea 1 we read of the Lord's divine injunction to the prophet to "Go, take unto thee a wife of whoredoms." (Hosea 1:2). Would God actually ask his chosen prophet to marry a promiscuous woman? Would not such a marriage compromise Hosea's prophetic position and pronouncements? These and other similar questions reflect the problematic nature of this command that has caused scripture scholars through the centuries to call into question the actuality of this marriage. The views of Bible commentators seem to fall into two camps — those who believe there was indeed a marriage between Hosea and a woman of questionable morality and those who believe the marriage account is merely an allegory used in Hosea's teachings. Moreover, within these basic schools of thought there are many variations of these theories.

The Literal View

Many of the ancient interpreters and those of the rabbinical period held a more strict and literal interpretation of this episode.[2] Today, however, only a few seem to hold to a strict literalist view.[3] Some scholars feel that whereas there was indeed an actual marriage between Hosea and Gomer, which served as a symbolic basis for his prophetic message, they contend that she had neither prostituted herself nor committed immoral acts but merely had those inclinations as indicated by her later unfaithfulness. This common interpretation suggests that Gomer was faithful and virtuous at the time of her marriage to Hosea but later became "an adulteress." (Hosea 3:1.)[4] This view in some respects best fits the symbolism of the text. Another modified-literal view is that Gomer had been immoral in some unspecified way previous to her marriage, had repented and reformed, yet later rejected her marriage to Hosea and became unfaithful and immoral again.[5] Still others indicate that the text gives evidence that Gomer was a Baal worshiper, not a common harlot. Guilty of spiritual harlotry and driven by her own fanatic devotion, she had perhaps participated in the sexual fertility rites of Baalism.[6]

The Allegory View

In more modern commentaries the trend has been away from the literal view of the marriage (and all of the before-mentioned modifications) to the allegory theory. One interesting variation of this view is that the marriage and family imagery of Hosea 1 through 3 was given to Hosea through a dream or a vision.[7] It seems that most of the writers and scholars who adopt the allegory view of the marriage do so because of the perceived problem created by the commandment of God to Hosea to marry a "wife of whoredoms." The eminent Bible commentators Keil and Delitzsch reject the literal nature of the marriage for two main reasons. First, such a marriage would undermine the prophetic example and teaching of Hosea, and second, God would not command a prophet to sin or do anything at odds with the laws of God. "That by such a command and the prophet's obedience on his first entering upon his office, all the beneficial effects of that office would inevitably be frustrated. For if it were a well known fact, that the woman whom the prophet married had hitherto been leading a profligate life, and if the prophet declared freely and openly that he had taken her as his wife for that very reason, and with this intention, according to the command of God; the marriage, the shame of which the prophet had taken upon himself in obedience to the command of God . . . would be a practical and constant sermon to the nation. . . .

"The instruction given to a prophet to set forth a sin in a symbolical form, for the purpose of impressing upon the hearts of the people its abominable character, and the punishment it deserved, is not at variance with the holiness of God; whereas the command to commit a sin would be. God, as the Holy One, cannot abolish the laws of morality, or command anything actually immoral, without contradicting himself, or denying His own nature."[8]

Dr. Sidney B. Sperry, respected Latter-day Saint scholar in whose honor this symposium is held, embraced the allegorical view of Hosea's marriage. His views reflect those of Keil and Delitzsch: "I cannot believe the marriage to be a literal one, for, as those who have taken it as an allegory or parable have always pointed out, to do so would be imputing to God a command inconsistent with His holy character. Furthermore, for Hosea to marry a woman with a questionable past would make it impossible for him to preach to his people and expose their sexual immoralities. They could point the finger of scorn at him and say, 'You are as guilty as we are; don't preach to us.' "[9]

The Latter-day Saint View

Dr. Sperry's views have generally been accepted and incorporated into Latter-day Saint curriculum through the years and have even been characterized as "the Latter-day Saint view," "authoritative to the Latter-day Saint," and "the Latter-day Saint rejection of this [literalist] thesis."[10] Nevertheless, Brother Sperry would also acknowledge that his opinions on this matter do not necessarily represent "the Latter-day Saint view" any more than does the view of any other Latter-day Saint scholar or religious educator. Even among thoughtful and faithful Latter-day Saint scholars there are diverse views on this problem of interpretation. What, then, is the LDS view of the nature of the marriage recorded in the book of Hosea? Perhaps the most appropriate answer to that question is, "There is no official LDS view," or perhaps, "What the scriptures say is the LDS view."

Elder Bruce R. McConkie gave several important keys to understanding the Bible. One of those keys was to distinguish between literal and figurative passages. He commented: "This is difficult to do, it requires considerable experience and discernment. . . . In general we are safer in taking things literally, although the scriptures abound in figurative matters."[11] With specific reference to the marriage of Hosea and Gomer, it would be wise to consider the three following arguments before categorically rejecting the literal nature of the episode.

1. Although some have maintained that God's command to Hosea to marry a harlot was "inconsistent with His holy character," it could also be argued that such a command was indeed consistent with His character and practices as evidenced by other scriptural precedents. Abraham was commanded of God to sacrifice his own beloved son, even though as a child Abraham had been rescued by an angel of God when his own father sought to kill him as a religious sacrifice. (See Gen. 22:1–18; Abr. 1:5–18.) To Joshua came the command to utterly destroy Israel's heathen enemies, killing "both man and woman, young and old, and ox, and sheep, and ass." (Joshua 6:21.) They were to take no spoils from the conquest and were punished severely if anyone or anything was spared. (See Joshua 7.) Isaiah was commanded to walk "naked and barefoot" as a prophetic testimony that the Assyrians would "lead away the Egyptians prisoners . . . naked and barefoot, with their buttocks uncovered, to the shame of Egypt." (Isa. 20:2–4.) The Lord commanded Jeremiah not to marry or have a family as a sign of the impending destruction that was to fall upon the families of Jerusalem. (See Jer. 16.) Ezekiel, who had never before defiled himself in such a manner, was commanded to break the dietary laws of the Mosaic code as a symbolic testimony against his people. (See Ezek. 4:9–17.) Nephi recoiled from the command he received to slay Laban. (See 1 Ne. 4:10–19.) In each of these cases the commandments issued from Jehovah to His holy prophets appear repugnant or in some way contrary to gospel principles. Numerous other examples in the Old Testament attest that God used dramatic, sometimes even harsh means to warn, teach, and discipline Israel. Although these means may be troubling to some or even appear "inconsistent to His holy character," God's mercy

and love are also consistently manifested. As we struggle to understand why God issues difficult commands or does certain things, we should remember, as the Prophet Joseph taught, "Whatever God requires is right, no matter what it is, although we may not see the reason thereof till long after the events transpire."[12]

2. Some have claimed that symbolic instruction was adequately understood by the ancients; therefore, there was no need for literal, personal examples such as Hosea's marriage. The hardness of the hearts and the spiritual stubbornness of these ancient Israelites as seen in the scriptures, however, would seem to indicate otherwise. Literal, rather than merely figurative, examples in such a case would have far greater effect. Of this important argument one scholar has written: "By means of these dramatic demonstrations, engaging the eyes as well as the ears of the people, the message of God was driven home. That which the prophet had proclaimed in words was expressed and embodied in actions. It would be a mistake, however, to regard these symbolic acts as little more than 'visual aids' to a deeper understanding of the truth. 'Like the spoken word, they are instrumental acts, helping to bring about that which they signify. They are part of the divine activity, that part which the prophets initiate.' . . . Yet they are far more than pictures of the truth. They convey the unseen realities they symbolize, even although they symbolize far more than they convey."[13]

Abraham, through his own actual and agonizing experience, could better understand the significance of the "great and last sacrifice" of God's Only Begotten Son than if he had merely been told about it. Likewise, Hosea's teaching and experiential testimony of Jehovah's steadfast love for wayward Israel would have greater poignancy and power and stand as an indisputable witness if his marriage to a "harlot" was indeed real.

3. The Old Testament account itself does not state specifically that the marriage was actual, but there is virtually no textual evidence to indicate otherwise. Rejecting the literal nature of this or any other scriptural episode that we find disturbing, illogical, or at odds with our own finite view of God and his dealings with man opens a Pandora's box of issues surrounding the historicity of the scriptures. What do we take in the scriptures to be literal and what is merely figurative? Did Moses really part the Red Sea? Was Jonah really swallowed by a fish? Was there really such a person as Job? Were Christ's miracles real? Did Jesus literally suffer for our sins?

Classifying things we have difficulty understanding or accepting them as simply figurative can have rippling implications beyond a few sensational stories from the Old Testament. An allegorical or figurative approach to problematic passages can actually undermine the fundamentals of our religious beliefs. Some theologians and scholars in the world today call into question the literal nature of such important doctrines as priesthood authority and the resurrection of Christ and all mankind. Even within the Church there are some who advance the notion that foundational events and doctrines of the Restoration such as the coming forth of the Book of Mormon and accounts of the First Vision and other heavenly ministrations are simply figurative. Although there are translation and textual problems with the Bible, as evidenced by the eighth article of faith, we are on safer ground doctrinally if we allow the scriptures and the prophets to speak for themselves. "Now taking it for granted," declared the Prophet Joseph Smith, "that the scriptures say what they mean, and mean what they say, we have sufficient grounds to go on and prove from the Bible that the gospel has always been the same."[14] Numerous Bible commentaries and helps may provide perceptive assistance in discerning the figurative from the literal, but perhaps the most important aids to understanding difficult passages in the Bible are passages from the other standard works that relate to or comment on those incidents, and authorized declarations and interpretative commentary of the Lord's modern prophets, seers, and revelators. In the absence of such clarifications, it is defensible to accept the passages as accurate accounts of real events.

The debate and controversy surrounding the marriage of Hosea and Gomer will continue, perhaps not to be resolved in this life. While the nature of Hosea's relationship to Gomer may be in question, we are nonetheless able to see a profound and unmistakable message to Israel—one with another, deeply personal meaning to us today. The historicity of the marriage may indeed be a peripheral issue, but Jehovah's love and mercy are at the very heart of the scriptural account of Hosea's marriage to Gomer.

Jehovah's "Steadfast Love" for Israel

There is perhaps as much consensus among the scholars concerning the meaning of Hosea's message as there is controversy concerning the nature of the marriage. Hosea 2 alludes to the adulterous abandonment of Hosea by his wife, Gomer. In that chapter her return to a life of immorality graphically represents the idolatry and wickedness of Israel. Just as Gomer had been unfaithful to her marriage covenant with Hosea, so had Israel been unfaithful to her covenants with Jehovah. The graphic imagery of physical adultery is used many times in the scriptures to characterize Israel's spiritual idolatry and unfaithfulness. "When a man and a woman enter into the sacred covenant of marriage, they make certain promises to each other, either explicitly or implicitly, which form the very foundation of their union. Chief among these covenant promises are honesty, unfailing love, and strict faithfulness. Often in the scriptures the covenant which God made with Israel is referred to as a marriage covenant. The same conditions which are at the core of the bond of marriage are also at the core of the bond between Jehovah and Israel — honesty, love, and fidelity. The covenant of marriage and God's covenant with his chosen people are, in fact, very similar. Hosea's message concerning Jehovah and his people is expressed in that kind of language. Yet even more graphically, the violation of that covenant of honesty, love, and fidelity is expressed as adultery — the violation of the sanctity of marriage. The dissolution of that covenant is described as divorce."[15]

Hosea was the first Israelite prophet to testify of Jehovah's covenant with Israel by comparing it to marriage, but others who followed amplified the imagery. "For thy Maker is thine husband; the Lord of Hosts is his name," declared Isaiah as he spoke of Israel as Jehovah's "wife of youth." (See Isa. 54:5–6.) To Israel and Judah, the Lord declared through Jeremiah, "I am married unto you." (Jer. 3:14.) Both Jeremiah and Ezekiel built upon the metaphor of adultery as they testified of Israel's and Judah's wickedness. Jeremiah wrote: "The Lord said also unto me in the days of Josiah the king, Hast thou seen that which backsliding Israel hath done? she is gone up upon every high mountain and under every green tree, and there hath played the harlot. And I said after she had done all these things, Turn thou unto me. But she returned not. And her treacherous sister Judah saw it. And I saw, when for all the causes whereby backsliding Israel committed adultery I had put her away, and given her a bill of divorce; yet her treacherous sister Judah feared not, but went and played the harlot also." (Jer. 3:6–8.)

Ezekiel used similar symbolism in his testimony against Jerusalem: "I [Jehovah] sware unto thee [Judah], and entered into a covenant with thee, saith the Lord God, and thou becamest mine. Then washed

I thee with water; yea, I thoroughly washed away thy blood from thee, and I anointed thee with oil. . . . And thy renown went forth among the heathen for thy beauty: for it was perfect through my comeliness, which I had put upon thee, saith the Lord God. But thou didst trust in thine own beauty, and playedst the harlot because of thy renown, and pouredst out thy fornications on every one that passed by." (Ezek. 16:8–9, 14–15.)

Not only does Gomer's infidelity represent the collective wickedness of Israel and Judah but her consequent suffering also symbolized the destruction and bondage that awaited them. Hosea spoke gloomily of the humiliation, heartache, and hardships that would befall Gomer. (See Hosea 2:2–13.) Her humiliation was but a foreshadowing of Israel's own fate. Hosea seems to signify in his own reaction to Gomer's infidelity that Jehovah's judgments against wayward Israel are not intended merely for punishment but also for rehabilitation. "And just as a great crisis in an individual's life sometimes makes possible a new beginning, so Hosea believed that the historical catastrophe about to befall the nation was intended by God as an opportunity for Israel to recover her health. . . . God's 'wrath' or judgment is redemptive. God's purpose is not to destroy, but to heal."[16] God's redemptive designs are reflected in Hosea's reference to a "door of hope." (Hosea 2:15.) This hopeful theme in Hosea's teachings bespeaks an "optimism of grace" and a "promise of restoration and renewal" by virtue of "the constancy of [Jehovah's] love for his people."[17]

Just as Gomer represented Israel both in committing wickedness and in suffering its painful consequences, Hosea represents Jehovah in extending love and mercy and in His untiring efforts to reestablish His covenant with Israel. In contrast to Gomer's fickleness and infidelity, Hosea demonstrated long-suffering love. In the Hebrew, this type of love is called *chesed* — "loyal love" or "steadfast love." "*Chesed* presupposes the existence of a bond or covenant between two or more parties. It is the love which operates within the covenant, and maintains it by discharging all the accepted obligations. The word is often used in conjunction with or as a parallel to the word 'faithfulness.' (e.g. Ps. 36:5.) *Chesed* is loyal love, steadfast love, bonded love, covenant love. Because the Lord has betrothed Israel to himself in loyal love, in spite of her infidelity he cannot and will not let her go. . . . His love is strong and mighty, patient and persistent, warm and compassionate. [In the story of Hosea and Gomer] we see into the heart of God; and here in the heart of God there is tension, passion, a tumult of feelings, a conflict of emotions. Punish Israel he will, for he is holy; cease to love her he will not, for he is God and not man. His nature is love, inexhaustible and invincible."[18]

Because of Gomer's blatant and willful violation of her covenants, there was a deserved divorce with its accompanying pain, punishment, and deprivation of covenantal blessings. This divorce, which symbolizes the suffering and punishment inflicted upon Israel during her captivity, did not minimize or negate Hosea's steadfast love for his former wife. Combining this love with mercy, Hosea later reclaims Gomer as his wife: "Then said the Lord unto me, Go yet, love a woman beloved of her friend, yet an adulteress, according to the love of the Lord toward the children of Israel, who look to other gods, and love flagons of wine. So I bought her to me for fifteen pieces of silver, and for an homer of barley, and an half homer of barley: and I said unto her, Thou shalt abide for me many days; thou shalt not play the harlot, and thou shalt not be for another man: so will I also be for thee." (Hosea 3:1–3.)

The reclaiming of scattered Israel and the renewal of Jehovah's covenant with her, as symbolized by Gomer's reunion with her husband, were later prophesied by Isaiah, Jeremiah, Ezekiel, and others of the prophets. (See Isa. 62; Jer. 3; Ezek. 16; 36.) These teachings, as well as Hosea's, are as timeless as they are timely. There were indeed timely warnings and prophecies to the ancient kingdoms of Israel and Judah. The message of the marriage of Hosea and Gomer is not, however, merely an ancient prophecy about some ancient peoples with ancient applications and fulfillments. It is also timeless in that it beckons covenant Israel of all generations to abandon her unfaithfulness and return to Jehovah. The symbolism of the bride and the bridegroom, so clearly set forth in Hosea, is not unique to the Old Testament but is also found in the New Testament and in modern scriptures. John the Baptist alluded to Christ as the Bridegroom. (See John 3:27–30.) John the Revelator referred many times to the Church as the bride who would be made ready through righteousness and repentance to receive the bridegroom at his glorious Second Coming. (See Rev. 19:7–9; 21:9.) The Savior himself spoke of this in symbolic form as he taught the parable of the ten virgins. (See Matt. 25:1–13.) To the modern Church, The Savior then reemphasized this redemptive relationship: "Wherefore, be faithful, praying always, having your lamps trimmed and burning, and oil with you, that you may be ready at the coming of the

Bridegroom—For behold, verily, verily, I say unto you, that I come quickly." (D&C 33:17.) Just as Hosea symbolically testified of Jehovah's "steadfast love" for ancient Israel, modern scriptures also testify of the Messiah's ongoing redemption of covenant Israel. "Yea, let the cry go forth among all people: Awake and arise and go forth to meet the Bridegroom; behold and lo, the Bridegroom cometh; go ye out to meet him. Prepare yourselves for the great day of the Lord." (D&C 133:10.) "That [the] church may come forth out of the wilderness of darkness, and shine forth fair as the moon, clear as the sun, and terrible as an army with banners; and be adorned as a bride." (D&C 109:73–74.) As evidenced in these passages, the symbolism of Hosea's marriage and the subsequent teachings of the prophets are not merely instructional but also invitational. The Book of Mormon prophet Jacob summarizes it best in his prophetic declaration: "And how merciful is our God unto us, for he remembereth the house of Israel, both roots and branches; and he stretches forth his hands unto them all the day long; and they are a stiffnecked and a gainsaying people; but as many as will not harden their hearts shall be saved in the kingdom of God. "Wherefore, my beloved brethren, I beseech of you in words of soberness that ye would repent, and come with full purpose of heart, and cleave unto God as he cleaveth unto you. And while his arm of mercy is extended towards you in the light of the day, harden not your hearts." (Jacob 6:4–5.)

The Bride and the Bridegroom: A Personal Application

Volumes of commentaries and hundreds of articles in scholarly journals have been written about the message of Hosea. Almost all of these works, however, focus on the meaning of Hosea's ministry to his own people and its collective application to the gathering and redemption of the house of Israel. Such an application is doctrinally significant and must not be overlooked, but there is a further application of this story that can do more than just instruct in doctrine. It also testifies of the perfect love of Christ and the possibility of personal redemption, which he extends to every person individually through his atoning blood. By likening the scriptures to ourselves, as Nephi admonished (see 1 Ne. 19:23), we can see in this beautifully symbolic marriage account a personal message of hope amidst despair, a message of love for the sinner amidst feelings of self-rejection. Three main messages with direct and personal application to our own individual lives stem from the example of Hosea's relationship with his wife—

the divine love of the Savior, the availability of personal forgiveness and redemption, and our responsibility to love and forgive others.

The Divine Love of the Savior

One debilitating by-product of sin is the notion that by virtue of our own disobedience and unfaithfulness we are unlovable and unforgivable. This mistaken impression, spawned by self-doubts such as "How can the Lord still love me after what I have done?" and "How can I ever be forgiven?" can become a major roadblock to repentance. Of this common challenge, Elder Jeffrey R. Holland, former president of Brigham Young University said: "There are multitudes of men and women—in and out of the Church—who are struggling vainly against obstacles in their path. Many are fighting the battle of life—and losing. Indeed, there are those among us who consider themselves the vilest of sinners. . . .

"How many broken hearts remain broken because those people feel they are beyond the pale of God's restorative power? How many bruised and battered spirits are certain that they have sunk to a depth at which the light of redeeming hope and grace will never again shine?"[19]

How can we overcome these sometimes overwhelming, ill-inspired feelings that seem to chain us down, especially when we feel unworthy to approach the only Being who can deliver us? We will find relief only as we "lay hold upon the word of God, which is quick and powerful, which shall divide asunder all the cunning and the snares and the wiles of the devil, and lead the man of Christ in a strait and narrow course across that everlasting gulf of misery." (Hel. 3:29.) It is in the scriptures that hope for the hopeless and love for the unlovable can be found. The scriptural account of Hosea's love for Gomer offers a motivating message to all whose hearts are or have been heavy with burdens of unworthiness and spiritual rejection.

Gomer, the "wife of whoredoms," not only symbolizes wayward Israel who went "whoring" after other gods (see Deut. 31:16–17; Hosea 9:1) but also represents each of us individually. Just as she was unfaithful to Hosea and to the covenants she had made with him, each of us to some degree has also been remiss. We all have in some manner broken covenants and been unfaithful in our spiritual duties. Hosea, on the other hand, stands as a graphic reminder of the steadfast love that the Savior has for each of us. We cannot help but marvel at the continued compassion and love Hosea demonstrated for his wicked wife. Of course he abhorred her adultery. He could not and did not minimize the severity of her sins or ignore her infidelity, but he loved her still and yearned for her return. Jehovah, God of the Old Testament, Savior, and Bridegroom, declared to Jeremiah: "I have loved thee with everlasting love: therefore with loving kindness have I drawn thee." (Jer. 31:3.) His love for us is perfect and divine. While others may reject or withhold love because of our sins and unworthy ways, Jehovah stands ever ready to encircle us about "in the arms of his love." (2 Ne. 1:15.) Despite our moments of spiritual infidelity, we are loved with His *chesed* or "steadfast love" described by the Apostle Paul as "the love of Christ, which passeth knowledge." (Eph. 3:19.) Almost as if echoing from eternity we can hear Hosea testifying from painful personal experience that no matter who we are, no matter how low and unworthy we may feel, we are not rejected or alone—Jehovah, even Jesus Christ loves us still. "Certainly the Lord loves the sinner," wrote President Spencer W. Kimball, "and especially the one who is trying to repent, even though the sin is abhorrent to him (D&C 1:31.). . . .

"The image of a loving, forgiving God comes through clearly to those who read and understand the scriptures."[20]

Hosea's anguish over his wife's infidelity, as painful as it must have been, is a microcosm of the infinitely more significant suffering of another loving Bridegroom. "He suffereth the pains of all men," testified Jacob, "yea, the pains of every living creature, both men, women, and children, who belong to the family of Adam." (2 Ne. 9:21.) In both cases, they were willing to suffer because of the sins of the wicked by virtue of their perfect and unconditional love for their bride. Of the Savior's perfect and divine love, Nephi testified: "And the world, because of their iniquity, shall judge him to be a thing of naught; wherefore they scourge him, and he suffereth it; and they smite him, and he suffereth it. Yea, they spit upon him, and he suffereth it, because of his loving kindness and his long-suffering towards the children of men." (1 Ne. 19:9.) "He doeth not anything save it be for the benefit of the world; for he loveth the world, even that he layeth down his own life that he may draw all men unto him." (2 Ne. 26:24.)

Hosea's tender love for Gomer, as a symbol of Jehovah's "steadfast love," beckons us individually, as it also was intended to beckon collectively to ancient Israel, to come unto Christ and know him in the truest sense. That is the inspirational and invitational purpose of the symbolism. As Elder David B. Haight so powerfully testified: "If we could feel or were sensitive even in the slightest to the matchless love of our Savior and his willingness to suffer for our individual sins, we would cease procrastination and 'clean the slate' and repent of all our transgressions."[21] When we, or those around us, feel unloved, rejected or forgotten by the Lord, the story of Hosea and Gomer can convey a personal message of hope and love. It is no wonder that Hosea is often referred to as "Prophet of Love" — a special witness of this "steadfast love," even "the pure love of Christ." Through the marriage of Hosea and Gomer and the rich symbolism that attends the scriptural account, we catch a spiritual glimpse of Jehovah's "steadfast love," of which Isaiah also testified. "But Zion said, The Lord hath forsaken me, and my Lord hath forgotten me. Can a woman forget her sucking child, that she should not have compassion on the son of her womb? yea, they may forget, yet will I not forget thee. Behold, I have graven thee upon the palms of my hands; thy walls are continually before me." (Isa. 49:14–16.)

The Availability of
Personal Forgiveness and Redemption

There are among us those who feel that they have sinned to such an extent that they cannot have any claim upon the mercy of God. "While wallowing in deep despair, true repentance is impossible," wrote Elder Neal A. Maxwell. "The feeling of futility can render one powerless to further resist the adversary; it can blur the vital difference between understanding the possibility of forgiveness for the sinner, while rejecting the sinful act."[22] To these dejected souls, Hosea's marriage account offers the most hopeful and significant message in the scriptures — the central focus of the "glad tidings" of the gospel: "And this is the gospel, the glad tidings, which the voice out of the heavens bore record unto us — That he came into the world, even Jesus, to be crucified for the world, and to bear the sins of the world, and to sanctify the world, and to cleanse it from all unrighteousness." (D&C 76:40–41.) Not only is Hosea, like Christ, willing to take his adulterous wife back but he actually purchases her back. That is one of the most important symbols in the marriage account, because it represents the atonement of Jesus Christ whereby He, as the apostle Paul testified, "bought us with a price." (1 Cor. 6:20.)

Although Hosea's love for Gomer was continual and unconditional, his forgiveness of her wickedness and his reacceptance of her as his wife was conditioned upon a probationary period of repentance and rehabilitation. (See Hosea 3:3.) Just as Israel had to abandon her worship of false gods and return to faithful worship of and obedience to Jehovah to be reclaimed as God's chosen people, so must we meet certain conditions to receive redemption from personal sins. Just as Hosea reached out to reclaim his bride, the Savior also "sendeth an invitation unto all men, for the arms of mercy are extended towards them, and he saith: Repent, and I will receive you. Yea, he saith: Come unto me and ye shall partake of the fruit of the tree of life; yea, ye shall eat and drink of the bread and the waters of life freely." (Alma 5:33–34.) The Savior as our spiritual husband stands willing to forgive us of our unfaithfulness and infidelity. His love for us may be *unconditional*, but his forgiveness and acceptance of us into his presence is *conditional* upon faith in him, true repentance, and faithful observance of his laws and commandments. Isaiah's words reflect the meaning of Hosea's experience and teachings: "Let the wicked forsake his way, and the unrighteous man his thoughts: and let him return unto the Lord, and he will have mercy upon him; and to our God, for he will abundantly pardon." (Isa. 55:7.) Hosea's symbolic message of messianic mercy — described by a modern prophet as "the miracle of forgiveness" — is a message of individual hope, a personal promise of redemption of lost lambs as well as the collective promise of the gathering of the flock of Israel. The words of President Spencer W. Kimball serve as another witness with those of Hosea: "God will wipe away from their eyes the tears of anguish, and remorse, and consternation, and fear, and guilt. Dry eyes will replace the wet ones, and smiles of satisfaction will replace the worried, anxious look.

"What relief! What comfort! What joy! Those laden with transgressions and sorrows and sin may be forgiven and cleansed and purified if they will return to their Lord, learn of him, and keep his commandments. And all of us needing to repent of day-to-day follies and weaknesses can likewise share in this miracle."[23]

Our Responsibility to Love and Forgive Others

The example of Hosea's love and forgiveness of Gomer is not only a powerful symbol of Christ's perfect love for all mankind and his mercy and forgiveness of those who repent but also a reminder of how we should treat our fellowmen. Many who have come to experience Jehovah's perfect love and the miracle of his forgiveness may still face another major obstacle — forgiveness and loving acceptance by others. Hosea's exemplary dealings with his unfaithful wife teach us that we too must be willing to continue loving and showing concern for those who, much like Gomer, have gone astray, broken covenants, and wounded the hearts of those who love them. As a symbol of Christ's love for the sinner, the story of Hosea also illustrates this Christlike love that we too must possess: "A new commandment I give unto you," declared the Savior to his disciples, "That ye love one another; as I have loved you, that ye also love one another. By this shall all men know that ye are my disciples, if ye have love one to another." (John 13:34–35.) In contrast to Jehovah's *conditional* redemption of Israel and Christ's *conditional* forgiveness of our sins, our forgiveness of others must be *unconditional*. The Lord declared: "My disciples, in days of old, sought occasion against one another and forgave not one another in their hearts; and for this evil they were afflicted and sorely chastened. Wherefore, I say unto you, that ye ought to forgive one another; for he that forgiveth not his brother his trespasses standeth condemned before the Lord; for there remaineth in him the greater sin. I, the Lord, will forgive whom I will forgive, but of you it is required to forgive all men." (D&C 64:8–10.)

As Hosea lovingly and mercifully reclaimed his beloved bride, we also have a sacred obligation to reach out to those around us who not only desire to return to the Lord and partake of his "steadfast love" and mercy but who also need to feel of our love, forgiveness, and acceptance. Our voices should be raised with a loving invitation to return to the Messiah. Our arms of mercy should be extended to "succor the weak, lift up the hands which hang down, and strengthen the feeble knees." (D&C 81:5.) The words of Elder Vaughn J. Featherstone epitomize the love and mercy, reflected in Hosea's life and teachings, that must also become a part of our lives. "And we invite all those who are not here to come home. We gaze steadily down the road, anxious for your return. We will run with open arms, and hearts filled with compassion. . . . Come home and we will rejoice together."[24]

The marriage of Hosea and Gomer may be one of the most overlooked and underused passages in the Bible. Perhaps that is because the nature of the marriage seems so repugnant to some. That repugnance, however, is the very point that drives home the lesson so

powerfully because it represents us. Our own sins make us feel repugnant and filthy before God in that "we would fain be glad if we could
command the rocks and the mountains to fall upon us to hide us from
his presence." (Alma 12:14.) Yet, Christ loves us with a "steadfast
love" and not only wants us back but has in very deed purchased us
with his own blood. The scriptural account of Hosea and Gomer, like
the law of Moses and many Old Testament types and symbols, serves
as a "schoolmaster" (Gal. 3:24) who is "pointing our souls to [Christ]."
(Jacob 4:5.) Stephen F. Winward, a Christian Bible scholar, perceptively
summarizes the marriage of Hosea and Gomer: "The love of God is
stronger than the sin of his people, and through suffering will, in the
end, be triumphant. This good news Hosea proclaimed with his lips
and embodied in his life. In thus bearing witness to the divine love in
its tender intimacy and triumphant power, Hosea was foreteller and
forerunner. He points forward to Jesus Christ, the Mediator of the New
Covenant, whose loyal love, through the sufferings of the cross, was
triumphant."[25]

NOTES

1. Artur Weiser, quoted in *The Interpreter's Bible*, 12 vols., ed. Nolan B.
Harmon (New York: Abingdon Press, 1956), 6:690.

2. Sidney B. Sperry, *The Voice of Israel's Prophets* (Salt Lake City: Deseret
Book Co., 1961), p. 280; see also *Encyclopedia Judaica*, ed. Cecil Roth [Jerusalem:
Keter Publishing House, n.d.], 8:1011.

3. Henry Cowles, *The Minor Prophets* (New York: D. Appleton & Co., 1867),
pp. 3–4; see also the commentary by Henry B. Keating, *The Cambridge Bible
Commentary; The Books of Amos, Hosea and Micah*, ed. P. R. Ackroyd, A. R. C.
Leaney, J. W. Packer (London: Cambridge University Press, 1971), pp. 74–77.

4. See several references to this theory in *The Interpreter's Bible*, 6:560–61;
this view is also advanced in *The New Bible Commentary*, ed. F. Davidson, A. M.
Stibbs, E. F. Kevan (Grand Rapids, Mich.: Eerdmans Publishing Co., 1956), p. 683.

5. Victor L. Ludlow, *Unlocking the Old Testament* (Salt Lake City: Deseret
Book Co., 1981), p. 198.

6. Sidney B. Sperry, *The Voice of Israel's Prophets* (Salt Lake City: Deseret
Book, 1961), p. 280. For a more thorough discussion of all of these theories the
reader should see George Adam Smith's *The Book of the Twelve Prophets*, 2 vols.
(New York: Doubleday, 1929), 1:246–53. A thorough bibliography of Hosea and
the various interpretations of the marriage can be found in *The Anchor Bible: Hosea,
a New Translation with Introduction and Commentary*, Francis I. Andersen and
David Noel Freedman (New York: Doubleday, 1980), pp. 81–111.

7. *Old Testament Student Manual 1 Kings—Malachi* (Salt Lake City: The Church of Jesus Christ of Latter-day Saints, 1981–82), p. 104; there are also references to this possible explanation in *Encyclopedia Judaica*, 8:1011–13 and Abraham J. Heschel, *The Prophets* (New York: Harper Torchbooks, 1969), 1:53–55.

8. C. F. Keil and F. Delitzsch, *Biblical Commentary on the Old Testament*, trans. James Martin (Grand Rapids, Mich.: William B. Eerdmans Publishing Co., 1877; reprint 1967), pp. 30, 35 n. 1.

9. Sperry, *Voice of Israel's Prophets*, p. 281.

10. *Old Testament Student Manual 1 Kings—Malachi*, p. 104.

11. Bruce R. McConkie, "The Bible, a Sealed Book," *Supplement to a Symposium on the New Testament*, 1984, Brigham Young University, Provo, Utah (Salt Lake City: The Church of Jesus Christ of Latter-day Saints, 1984), p. 4.

12. Joseph Smith, Jr., *The Personal Writings of Joseph Smith*, comp. Dean C. Jessee (Salt Lake City: Deseret Book Co., 1984), p. 508.

13. Stephen F. Winward, *A Guide to the Prophets* (Atlanta, Ga.: John Knox Press, 1977), pp. 157–58.

14. Joseph Smith, Jr., *Times and Seasons*, 1 Sept. 1842, p. 904.

15. Kent P. Jackson, "The Marriage of Hosea and Jehovah's Covenant with Israel," *Isaiah and the Prophets*, ed. Monte S. Nyman (Provo: Religious Studies Center, Brigham Young University, 1984), p. 60.

16. Bernhard W. Anderson, *Understanding the Old Testament* (Englewood Cliffs, N.J.: Prentice-Hall, 1975), pp. 290–91.

17. See ibid., p. 284.

18. Winward, *Guide to the Prophets*, pp. 59–60.

19. Jeffrey R. Holland, *However Long and Hard the Road* (Salt Lake City: Deseret Book Co., 1985), p. 77.

20. Spencer W. Kimball, *The Miracle of Forgiveness* (Salt Lake City: Bookcraft, 1969), p. 344.

21. David B. Haight, *Ensign*, May 1988, p. 23.

22. Neal A. Maxwell, "Hope for the Hopeless," *Instructor*, Aug. 1966, p. 318.

23. Kimball, *Miracle of Forgiveness*, p. 368.

24. Vaughn J. Featherstone, *Ensign*, Nov. 1982, p. 73.

25. Winward, *Guide to the Prophets*, p. 60.

CHAPTER FOURTEEN

The Two Davids

Rodney Turner

Brigham Young University

Two Davids appear in the Old Testament. Although separated by three millennia, they are bound to one another by blood and by promise. The first ruled Israel in the eleventh century before Christ; the second will rule Israel in the coming age. Of the first much is known; of the second, much remains to be revealed.

The Historical Setting

The house of Israel arose in Syria and Canaan. It spent centuries of servitude in Egypt where it became a nation and from whence it was delivered by Moses, the man of God. After the translation of Moses, Joshua led the Israelites in a partially successful conquest of Canaan.

For about a century after Joshua's death, the Israelites looked to their individual tribal heroes, called judges, for leadership. It was a time of spiritual and political disarray. Idolatry was rife; the people were at least semiapostate. The anonymous author of Judges summed up conditions when he wrote: "In those days there was no king in Israel: every man did that which was right in his own eyes." (Judg. 21:25; see also 17:6.)

Then came Samuel, Israel's dominant prophet-leader in that age. In his later years Israel demanded a king: "Behold, thou art old, and thy sons walk not in thy ways: now make us a king to judge us like all the nations." (1 Sam. 8:5.) Offended, Samuel went to the Lord, who instructed him to "hearken unto the voice of the people," adding, "for they have not rejected thee, but they have rejected me, that I should not reign over them." (1 Sam. 8:7.)

The Lord further instructed Samuel to warn the people of the burdens and evils a king could bring upon them, but they were adamant: "Nay; but we will have a king over us; that we also may be like all the nations; and that our king may judge us, and go out before us, and fight our battles." (1 Sam. 8:19–20.)

King Saul

So a king they got. Unlike alien rulers, however, he was to be the "anointed of the Lord" — a messiah — one obedient to Jehovah's will as that will was made known by the prophets. Although 1 Samuel describes the institution of a monarchy in negative terms, it was designed to serve Israel's eternal best interests. Israel was meant to have a king. As we shall see, the divine patriarchal order mandated it.[1]

The Lord, seeking "a man after his own heart" (1 Sam. 13:14), selected Saul from the tribe of Benjamin. He was anointed by Samuel, but within two years Saul fell out of favor for, among other things, presuming to offer sacrifice on his own recognizance. For this, he and his posterity were rejected as the ruling house in Israel.[2] It was foreordained that Judah, not Benjamin, should be the kingly tribe.

The First David

To replace Saul, Samuel was inspired to anoint David, a shepherd boy and the youngest of Jesse's eight sons. His life was one of triumph and tragedy. It is recounted by the anonymous authors of Samuel, Kings, and Chronicles. Of the three, Chronicles, seeking to depict him as the ideal ruler, provides the least critical and least historical version of David's life.[3]

In any case, he came to epitomize the golden age of the Jews, an age Jesus' generation longed to see restored by another king, another messiah, another who would be the Lord's anointed.[4] But when he came, he was crucified. As the Spirit of the Lord descended upon David, it departed from Saul, and a certain madness seized the king. David's skill on the lyre and as a sweet singer of songs brought him to Saul's court where he became his armorbearer and dispeller of evil spirits.

Then followed David's surprising defeat of Goliath the Philistine champion, his deep friendship with Saul's son, Jonathan, his brief appointment as commander of Israel's armies, and Saul's obsessive jealousy. The king looked upon David with narrow eyes after the people cried: "Saul hath slain his thousands, and David his ten thousands." (1 Sam. 18:7.)

Driven by a consuming fear of being overthrown, Saul murdered eighty-five priests who had befriended David, together with every man, woman, child, and beast in the city of Nob.[5] Saul became obsessed with capturing his supposed rival.

On one occasion David crept into Saul's camp while he slept.[6] An officer, Abishai, asked permission to slay the king but David refused: "Destroy him not: for who can stretch forth his hand against the Lord's anointed, and be guiltless?" (1 Sam. 26:9; see also 24:6.)

The Lord's anointed was in the Lord's hands. God, old age, or battle would end Saul's life; David would not. In spite of all, David revered his king as God's chosen servant. Loyalty to God and his anointed one was perhaps David's major virtue.

Saul's spear and jar of water lay by his head. David took them and, from a distance, protested his innocence to the then awake Saul, who responded: "I have sinned: return, my son David: for I will no more do thee harm, because my soul was precious in thine eyes this day: behold, I have played the fool, and have erred exceedingly." (1 Sam. 26:21; see also 24:17.)

David did not trust Saul's words; he fled with six hundred men to the Philistine city of Gath and for sixteen months served Achish, its king. During that time he led a series of bloody raids to the south against various Canaanitish peoples. Learning that David had joined the Philistines, Saul made no further efforts to capture him.

In a battle with the Philistines at Mount Gilboa, Saul and three sons, including Jonathan, perished. Severely wounded, Saul deliberately fell upon his own sword; however, a young Amalekite told David that at the king's request, he had slain him. Assuming the Amalekite was telling the truth, David had him killed because he had "slain the Lord's anointed." (2 Sam. 1:16.)

King David

Samuel the prophet and Saul the king were dead. At the age of thirty, David was anointed king of Judah at Hebron (possibly by the prophet Nathan). He ruled there seven and a half years and in Jerusalem, as king of all Israel, for thirty-three years. His reign marked the beginning of the unbroken Davidic dynasty of twenty-one kings of Judah, which lasted almost five hundred years, ending only with the fall of Jerusalem in 587 B.C.[7]

David had at least nineteen sons, plus daughters, by a number of wives, not including Saul's daughter Michal, who bore him no children.[8] This number does not include his concubines and their children.

Six wives are mentioned by name during David's reign in Hebron. He married additional wives and concubines during his reign in Jerusalem. The total number is not given, but since the Lord denounced his "many wives and concubines" as being "abominable before me," it was excessive. (Jacob 2:24.)

After the death of Saul's son Ishbosheth, David was anointed king of all Israel. He soon conquered the Jebusite city of Jerusalem, "the stronghold of Zion," the last bastion of Canaanite power in the land, and declared it the city of David.[9]

The ark of the covenant was removed from Kiriath-jearim where it had been kept for more than twenty years. David, literally dancing for joy, brought it to Zion. Jerusalem became the spiritual as well as the political capital of the kingdom of Israel.

David and Bathsheba

As the Psalms attest, David gloried in the Lord, who had abundantly blessed him. Then tragedy struck. David remained in Jerusalem while his armies fought the Ammonites east of the Jordan. It was springtime. Arising from an afternoon rest, he walked upon the flat roof of his cedar palace. As he did so he saw a beautiful woman performing a ritual bath for uncleanness.[10] Upon inquiry, he learned that her name was Bathsheba, the wife of Uriah, one of his Hittite officers.

The ruler of others failed to rule himself. Driven by desire, David commanded that she be brought to him. No five stones protected him against his own moral Goliath, nor was there a great army present to cheer him on to victory. He was alone with the dark side of his nature, and he was defeated by it. He humbled Bathsheba.

Thereafter she sent word that she was with child. To hide his own responsibility for her condition, David ordered Uriah's return to Jerusalem and then urged him to go to his wife. But Uriah, under a soldier's vow of continence[11] and sensitive to the plight of his comrades in the field, refused to do so.

The king plied him with wine, but Uriah stubbornly remained with the king's servants. In desperation, David wrote an order to his commander, Joab, to put Uriah in the fiercest battle and abandon him. The order was hand carried by Uriah himself. Joab obeyed, and Uriah was killed. His loyalty to his king and his comrades cost him his life.

But that same order cost David far more. In one unguarded moment he set in motion a series of events that undid virtually all that he had achieved since his anointing by Samuel the prophet.

How do we account for David's behavior? We can only suggest some possibilities. For one thing, he was a man of war, one who had ordered the death of a number of men through the years; perhaps he had become somewhat hardened to killing. Then, too, apparently he did not know Uriah well because he did not know Bathsheba's identity. As for taking a woman of his choosing, he was accustomed to that, being a king with numerous wives and concubines.

But, ironically, perhaps his fatal flaw was his earlier unquestioning loyalty toward the Lord's anointed. He well may have transferred that very loyalty to himself. Like Saul, he, too, had become untouchable and beyond judgment. Was he not the king? Did he not have rights and privileges denied lesser men? He saw the woman. He wanted her. He took her.

Another irony, as Saul had sought the life of loyal David, so David took the life of loyal Uriah. Both kings were motivated by the desire to protect their thrones and the honor of the Lord's anointed.

Had David stopped at adultery, the Lord could have forgiven him; but murder doomed him. And it was all for naught. Nathan the prophet came to David and told him the classic parable of the one ewe lamb belonging to a poor man that a rich man having "exceeding many flocks and herds" callously took from him. Incensed by the injustice, David swore an oath: "As the Lord liveth, the man that has done this thing shall surely die: and he shall restore the lamb fourfold, because he did this thing, and because he had no pity." Nathan answered: "Thou art the man." (2 Sam. 12:6–7.)

The death of Uriah was the deliberate shedding of innocent blood. It violated the standards of even that violent age. Being so, it robbed David of the everlasting kingdom that might have been his.

In seeking to hide his sordid sin, he committed a far more grievous crime and lost those wives who had been sealed to him by Nathan and other prophets. "I gave them," said the Lord, "unto another." (D&C 132:39.) Perhaps that man was Uriah.

Nathan reminded David that God had saved him from Saul, given him all that Saul possessed, made him king over Israel, and would have given him even more had he asked. But David had "despised the commandment of the Lord" and killed Uriah. Nathan then prophesied:

"Thus saith the Lord, Behold, I will raise up evil against thee out of thine own house, and I will take thy wives before thine eyes, and give them unto thy neighbour, and he shall lie with thy wives in the sight of this sun. For thou didst it secretly: but I will do this thing before all Israel, and before the sun." (2 Sam. 12:11–12.)

David acknowledged his guilt. Psalm 51 is said to be his cry for forgiveness: "Have mercy upon me, O God, according to thy loving kindness: according unto the multitude of thy tender mercies blot out my transgressions. Wash me thoroughly from mine iniquity, and cleanse me from my sin. For I acknowledge my transgressions: and my sin is ever before me." (Ps. 51:1–3.)

Nevertheless, the merciless murder of Uriah placed David beyond the mercy of Christ. More, it placed him beyond the security of the sealing powers of the priesthood. According to the Prophet Joseph Smith, there is "a reserve [restriction] made in the seals and power of the Priesthood" rendering the sealing power void for those who commit the unpardonable sin against the Holy Ghost, or the lesser but unforgiveable sin of shedding innocent blood.[12]

The Prophet cited David as an example of such a man: "A murderer, for instance, one that sheds innocent blood, cannot have forgiveness [via the Atonement]. David sought repentance at the hand of God carefully with tears, for the murder of Uriah; but he could only get it through hell: he got the promise that his soul should not be left in hell."[13]

There he has been for three thousand years. What has been his anguish of soul as he has contemplated all that he might have had and all that he might have become! David is surely the most poignant figure in all scripture because he had the potential for genuine greatness. Still, forever is a long time; who can say what the future will bring him?

Although he forfeited the crown of exaltation,[14] eventually he will be saved in a kingdom of glory. But like those repentant Jews who crucified Jesus, he must remain in the spirit world until the next general resurrection.[15] "Even David," said Joseph Smith, "must wait for those times of refreshing [or redemption] before he can come forth and his sins be blotted out."[16]

Although it is often assumed that David will inherit a telestial glory, the "times of refreshing," as the Prophet made clear, occur in connection with Christ's second coming when only celestial and terrestrial souls are resurrected.[17] It seems, therefore, that in the infinite mercy of God, David will obtain a terrestrial salvation.

Tamar and Absalom

David married Bathsheba, but their son died at birth. Then another tragedy, painfully similar to the first, engulfed David and three of his children. His firstborn son, Amnon, became lovesick over his half-sister Tamar and was advised to feign illness to have her wait upon him in his room. When Amnon forced himself on Tamar, she pleaded with him to ask their father David for her in marriage. But Amnon was interested in gratification, not matrimony. The author of Samuel tells us that when he had spent his passion, "then Amnon hated her exceedingly; so that the hatred wherewith he hated her was greater than the love wherewith he had loved her." He told her to get out. She cried: "There is no cause: this evil in sending me away is greater than the other that thou didst unto me." Ignoring her pleas, Amnon called his servant: "Put now this woman out from me, and bolt the door after her." Tamar put ashes of mourning on her head, tore her virgin's apparel of many colors, and "remained desolate in her brother Absalom's house." (2 Sam. 13:15–20.)

The affair angered David, yet he did nothing. But Absalom, her full brother, was enraged, and two years later, to avenge Tamar's honor and at the same time remove a rival for the throne, successfully plotted Amnon's death. Absalom fled from Jerusalem and was only reconciled to his grieving father five years later.

A flawlessly handsome man and David's heir apparent, Absalom was impatient for power. He flattered the people and "stole the hearts of the men of Israel." (2 Sam. 15:6.) After four years he raised a rebellion that prompted David to leave Jerusalem through the Kidron Valley and over the Mount of Olives to Jericho and beyond.

Absalom entered Jerusalem in triumph, and in a symbolic act of claiming the throne "went in unto his father's concubines in the sight of all Israel." (2 Sam. 16:22.) Nathan's prophecy was fullfilled.

Civil war ensued in which David's well-trained armies vanquished Absalom's inept forces. Absalom, fleeing on his mule, caught his head in the limbs of an oak tree. As he hung "between the heaven and the earth" (2 Sam. 18:9.) he was slain by Joab, David's commander.

Overcome by his son's death, David cried out: "O my son Absalom, my son, my son Absalom! would God I had died for thee, O Absalom, my son, my son." (2 Sam. 18:33.)

David's final years saw wars, insurrections, famines, and further affronts to the Lord—but he endured. As David lay dying, his son Adonijah conspired to seize the throne. But David, heeding Nathan and Bathsheba, named Solomon, who was not first in line of succession, his heir. Despite his weaknesses, David lived and died loyal to Israel's God: "The Lord [Jehovah] is *my* shepherd." In doing so, he became a larger-than-life symbol of Israel at its finest.

Solomon

In accordance with David's dying instructions, Solomon was anointed king by Nathan the prophet and Zadok the priest at the Gihon spring in the Kidron Valley east of Jerusalem. The spring still flows today.[18] In his later years Solomon betrayed Jehovah by marrying literally hundreds of foreign wives and erecting altars on "the mount of offense" to their alien gods.[19] Thus Solomon "the wise" introduced the practice of officially sanctioned idolatry, which plagued Israel until the fall of Jerusalem and the Babylonian captivity of the Jews.

His death, about 925 B.C., brought about the prophesied division of his kingdom into the southern kingdom of Judah and the northern kingdom of Israel, or Ephraim (the ten tribes). Israel's division and scattering has continued to the present time.

But it must end. Peace must come to Israel before peace can come to the world. Isaiah prophesied that the Lord would set up an ensign and gather the "outcasts of Israel" and the "dispersed of Judah." That ensign is Mount Zion—not the "mount Zion" of old Jerusalem, but the "Mount Zion" centered in the New Jerusalem of the Saints.[20] Sometime after it is established in glory, Isaiah's words will be fulfilled: "The envy also of Ephraim shall depart, and the adversaries of Judah shall be cut off: Ephraim shall not envy Judah, and Judah shall not vex Ephraim." (Isa. 11:13.)

The ingathering of scattered Israel, which began with Ephraim in 1830, will continue until all twelve tribes stand united before the Holy One of Israel. This union is symbolized by the two sticks that became one in the hand of Ezekiel.[21] Said Jehovah: "And I will make them one nation in the land upon the mountains of Israel; and one king shall be king to them all: and they shall be no more two nations, neither shall they be divided into two kingdoms anymore at all." (Ezek. 37:22.)

"Branch"

The prophecy of Ezekiel brings us to the second David, but before considering those passages that explicitly mention him, we will consider a figure that has been identified with him: the "Branch."

"Branch" is a rather common figure of speech in the Old Testament. In the Book of Mormon, it almost always refers to Israel as represented by the olive tree. (Jacob 5:3.)[22] For example, in writing that God would "raise up a righteous branch unto the house of Israel," Nephi explained that this branch was "not the Messiah, but a branch which was to be broken off." (2 Ne. 3:5.) The most extensive use of the figure is found in the complex allegory of Zenos (Jacob 5), which deals with the various branches of Israel down through time.

Just as "branch" may apply to more than one group, so may it apply to more than one person. The first mention in the Old Testament of a "Branch" personality is found in Isaiah: "And there shall come forth a rod out of the stem of Jesse, and a Branch shall grow out of his roots." (Isa. 11:1.)[23]

A partial explanation of this enigmatic prophecy is provided by the Lord in Doctrine and Covenants 113 where he declares himself to be the "Stem of Jesse."[24] Like the trunk (stem) of a great tree, Jehovah is the life-source of Israel with its many branches. A "rod" (shoot) will grow out of the "Stem," meaning a man will come forth from Christ. This "rod" is "a servant in the hands of Christ, who is partly a descendant of Jesse as well as of Ephraim." That is, this "servant" will have a dual lineage, being a descendant of both Judah and Joseph. Most commentators assume that Isaiah is employing synonymous parallelism[25] in this passage and equate the "rod" with the "Branch." If the two clauses are wholly synonymous, then both "stem" and "roots" represent Christ, whereas the "rod" and the "Branch" represent his unidentified servant. If, however, Isaiah does not intend synonymous parallelism (as he sometimes does not), then at least *three* individuals are symbolized in verse one: the "rod," the "Stem of Jesse," and the "Branch."

A fourth individual is described in verse 10 as "the root of Jesse." The Lord explained that this "root of Jesse" will be a "descendant of Jesse, as well as of Joseph, unto whom rightly belongs the priesthood, and the keys of the kingdom, for an ensign, and for the gathering of my people in the last days." Like the "rod," he, too, will descend from both Judah and Joseph.

The actual identities of the "rod," the "Branch," and the "root of
Jesse" in Isaiah are conjectural. Some believe that both "rod" and
"Branch" symbolize the second David. Others believe that the "rod"
is David, and the "Branch" another latter-day figure.

Regardless, the "root of Jesse" is almost surely the Prophet Joseph
Smith. He holds the keys of this kingdom in both time and eternity
and is the president of the last and greatest of all dispensations, the
dispensation of the fulness of times.[26] He is the living ensign to which
the present generation must gather. We cannot, in reality, come to
Christ if we do not accept his servant, Joseph Smith.

The Lord's works are first spiritual and then temporal, or physical.[27]
All of the spiritual keys, powers, doctrines, and ordinances revealed
through the Prophet Joseph Smith must be honored and implemented
before Zion, the second ensign, can be literally established in fulness
and glory.[28] That day is not far off.

"Branch" Passages

Jeremiah and Zechariah contain several passages that identify a
"Branch" with a latter-day ruler.

"Behold, the days come, saith the Lord, that I will raise unto David
a righteous Branch, and a King shall reign and prosper, and shall execute
judgment and justice in the earth. In his days Judah shall be saved, and
Israel shall dwell safely: and this is his name whereby he shall be called,
The Lord our righteousness." (Jer. 23:5–6.) A companion passage in
Jeremiah reads: "In those days, and at that time, will I cause the Branch
of righteousness to grow up unto David; and he [the "Branch"] shall
execute judgment and righteousness in the land. In those days shall
Judah be saved, and Jerusalem shall dwell safely: and this is the name
wherewith she shall be called, The Lord our righteousness." (Jer.
33:15.)[29]

Some commentators have identified Jeremiah's "Branch" with the
Messiah. Aware of their position, my mentor, Dr. Sperry, for whom
this symposium is named, commented as follows: "The fact that the
'Branch' is to be a descendent of David and the further fact that he is
called 'Lord' by the words in italics seems to decide the identification
in favor of the Messiah. But we call attention to the fact that in Jeremiah
33:16 it is not the 'Branch' but Jerusalem that is called *The Lord our
righteousness.* Furthermore, the original Hebrew may be translated *The*

Lord is our righteousness, which changes the sense considerably, especially in the first quoted passage in Jeremiah."[30]

In one of a series of eight visions Zechariah beheld an unclean high priest named Joshua who, becoming sanctified, was promised rule over the Lord's house and told, "I will bring forth my servant the "Branch." (Zech. 3:1–8.) In a subsequent vision Zechariah crowned Joshua and told him: "Behold the man whose name is The Branch; and he shall grow up out of his place, and he shall build the temple of the Lord: Even he shall build the temple of the Lord; and he shall bear the glory, and shall sit and rule upon his throne; and he shall be a priest upon his throne: and the counsel of peace shall be between them both." (Zech. 6:12–13.)

This prophecy is usually associated with the building of the second temple by Zerubbabel (the presumed "Branch") in the sixth century before Christ; however, as with Peter's use of Joel 2 (Acts 2:14–21; JS–H 1:41), it is a dual prophecy and has been only partially fulfilled.

I believe its real fulfillment is yet future when the "Branch" builds the great temple in the New Jerusalem assisted by those who come from "far off" — not from ancient Babylon but from the "Babylon" of these last days.[31]

We cannot be certain that the "Branch" of Isaiah 11, of Jeremiah 23 and 33, and of Zechariah 3 and 6 are one and the same individual. Christ, "the stem of Jesse" has many branches. As for "Joshua" and the "Branch," are they two different men, or does the unclean Joshua become the sanctified "Branch"? Time will tell. In any event, a king designated the "Branch" will yet reign in Israel.

The Second David

The king who will yet reign in Israel is the second David. A descendant of David, he will be the first king since Solomon to rule over all twelve tribes. He is mentioned by name in Hosea, Jeremiah, and Ezekiel.[32] Hosea, a prophet to the northern kingdom of Israel in the eighth century before Christ, wrote: "And afterward shall the children of Israel return, and seek the Lord their God, and David their king; and shall fear the Lord and his goodness in the latter days." (Hosea 3:5.)

Over two hundred years later Jeremiah prophesied: "But they [Israel] shall serve the Lord their God, and David their king, whom I will raise up unto them." (Jer. 30:9.) And in the days of the Babylonian captivity, Ezekiel expanded Jeremiah's prophecy: "And I will set one shepherd over them, and he shall feed them, even my servant David; he shall feed them, and he shall be their shepherd. And I the Lord will be their God, and my servant David a prince among them; I the Lord have spoken it." (Ezek. 34:23–24.) Later Ezekiel added: "I will be their God. And David my servant shall be king over them; and they all shall have one shepherd: they shall also walk in my judgments, and observe my statutes, and do them. . . . and my servant David shall be their prince forever." (Ezek. 37:23–25.)

Note that these passages speak only of this king's reign over Israel; they are silent about his relationship to the gentile and heathen nations.

Zion and Jerusalem

The Shepherd of Israel is going to gather all of his scattered sheep. His labors begin with Ephraim and Zion and end with Judah and Jerusalem. Where, therefore, does King David fit into the prophetic scheme of things? How does he relate to the Latter-day Saints? The answer given by Joseph Smith and his associates is that Christ's church will beget Christ's millennial kingdom; however, the church of Christ is not the kingdom of God. They will be two related but separate institutions.[33] Consequently, the fulfillment of the prophecies concerning the Jews and the second David will follow and be a direct result of the fulfillment of the prophecies pertaining to the establishment of Zion and the New Jerusalem in America. The Lord will redeem Zion many years before he redeems Jerusalem.[34]

Indeed, "the kingdom of Zion" (D&C 105:32) will provide the pattern and the power for the government of God as it will be organized in Jerusalem. President Charles W. Penrose declared that after the Messiah appears to the Jews, "the government of God *as established in Zion* will be set up among them."[35]

Heber C. Kimball said that he, himself, together with many early leaders of the Church who were then deceased, would be in Jackson County "in the flesh." He then added: "And the day will be when I will see those men in the general assembly of the Church of the First-Born, in the great council of God in Jerusalem. . . . I heard Joseph [Smith] say twice that brother Brigham and I should be in that council in Jerusalem, when there should be a uniting of the *two divisions of God's government.*"[36]

In fulfillment of Isaiah's words, "Out of Zion shall go forth the law, and the word of the Lord from Jerusalem" (Isa. 2:3; see also D&C 133:21), there will be two world capitals, Zion in the west and Jerusalem in the east. But Zion will retain its preeminence as the spiritual and political center of the Church and the kingdom of God.

This worldwide order will have one head, Jesus Christ, and two arms to serve the body politic: a spiritual arm consisting of the Church of the Firstborn in all of its priestly and ecclesiastical ramifications and powers, and a political arm, the kingdom of God, to govern the nations.[37] In their totality the Church and kingdom constitute "the holy order." Extensive in organization and diverse in administration, it will be a perfect theocracy.

I believe that the prophets wrote of those who would be called at various times to critical positions in both arms of the Lord's latter-day and millennial order. Their identities are hidden behind such figures as rod, Branch, root of Jesse, ensign, and one mighty and strong. Understanding the prophetic code is a challenging business; no one should dogmatize their opinions on these matters. Only the word of the Lord can provide us with certitude.

Modern revelation indicates that the second David will come on the scene sometime after Zion's redemption, the return of the lost tribes, and the selection of the 144 thousand. He will appear in connection with the climactic events associated with Armageddon and the deliverance of a remnant of Judah in Jerusalem as described in Revelation 11 and 16 and Doctrine and Covenants 45. He is essentially a millennial figure.

Joseph Smith's Teachings

Neither the Prophet Joseph Smith nor any of the earlier leaders of the Church ever established the actual identity of this David. After the Prophet's martyrdom, however, it was rumored in Nauvoo that he believed that one of his posterity—possibly David Hyrum Smith, a son born in November 1844—would be that David. While such a notion is ludicrous to us—gifted as we are with one hundred and forty-five years of hindsight—it must have seemed plausible at the time.

In late 1844 Oliver B. Huntington was living in the Prophet's home, the Mansion House. In his diary he wrote of David Hyrum Smith: "At the time of his birth, it was intimated by old Mrs. Durphee and others that Joseph the Prophet said that he (David Hyrum, which name Joseph gave him before his death)[38] was to be the David the Bible speaks of to rule over Israel forever, which David spoken of most people took to be old king David."[39]

While there is no solid evidence that the Prophet had such aspirations for his son,[40] the very rumor suggests that he had not publicly identified the second David with anyone else. Had he done so, Huntington and others would probably have countered the rumor with the Prophet's actual teachings.

Joseph Smith's only known relevent statement is that "the throne and kingdom of David is to be taken from him and given to another by the name of David in the last days, raised up out of his lineage."[41] If he understood — and this is still unclear — that this David would be one of his own posterity, Joseph Smith had to be, in part, of the lineage of Judah. He was, if he is Isaiah's "root of Jesse."

Denouncing what he called "The Davidic Myth," however, Elder Bruce R. McConkie wrote: "This wresting of the written word assumes that someone of prophetic stature will arise in the Church in the last days, to preside as a Second David, and to prepare the way before the Second Coming of the Son of Man. That there may be one or many brethren called David who preside over the Church in this dispensation is of no moment. The scriptures that speak of King David reigning in the last days are Messianic; they have reference to the Millennial reign of the Lord Jesus Christ."[42]

His most extensive discussion of this subject is found in *The Millennial Messiah*, published in 1982. In it he identifies Christ as "the Branch," the "Second David," the "Eternal David, the Son of David, the one of whom David of old was a type and a shadow."[43]

A New Exegesis

This view is reflected in the LDS edition of the Bible published in 1979. The headnotes to Jeremiah 30 and Ezekiel 34 and 37 identify Christ as the prophesied David. The headnotes to Jeremiah 23 and 33 and Zechariah 3 and 6 state that the Messiah, or Christ, is the "Branch."[44] Thus the Messiah, the "Branch," and the second David are identified as being one and the same person: Jesus Christ.[45] This position is primarily based on those indisputable scriptures, both ancient and modern, which declare the Lord Jesus Christ to be Israel's supreme king and lawgiver.[46] For example, in Luke, Mary is told by the angel Gabriel that God would give Jesus "the throne of his father

David: and he shall reign over the house of Jacob for ever; and of his kingdom there shall be no end." (Luke 1:32–33; see also Acts 2:30.)

As we shall see, however, Christ is not the only king in Israel; he is "King of kings." Then too, the relevant passages in Hosea, Jeremiah, and Ezekiel distinguish between the Lord God and that "servant" whom he will raise up in the last days as a Davidic king. Is Jehovah a servant to himself? Joseph Smith's brief reference to this king does not suggest divinity. But, as with so many theological questions, we need not close and bolt the door on this matter. It is not imperative that we have the final answer now; in good time we will see "eye to eye" on the second David.

The Everlasting Kingdom of David

A number of prophets, including Joseph Smith, have testified to the enduring nature of the house of David.[47] Although ancient David has lost his own kingdom, nevertheless the Lord said through Nathan: "Thy kingdom shall be established for ever before thee: thy throne shall be established for ever." (2 Sam. 7:16.) And Jeremiah added: "David shall never want a man to sit upon the throne of the house of Israel." (Jer. 33:17; see also vss. 19–26.)

The Psalmist wrote: "Once have I sworn by my holiness that I will not lie unto David. His seed shall endure for ever, and his throne as the sun before me. It shall be established for ever as the moon, and as a faithful witness in heaven." (Ps. 89:35–37; see also 132:11–18.)

King of Kings

Why is the house of David so highly favored of the Lord? The answer lies not in David the man but in his lineage and in the kingdom he symbolizes. In blessing his son Judah, Jacob said: "The sceptre [kingly authority] shall not depart from Judah, nor a lawgiver from between his feet, until Shiloh [the Messiah] come;[48] and unto him shall the gathering of the people be." (Gen. 49:10.)

Judah was designated the kingly tribe in Israel and, as we have seen, the house of David its ruling dynasty. The promised Messiah-King must be of that house; a non-Davidic Messiah was, and is, prophetically inconceivable. Therefore it was ordained that the Son of Man, being both "the root and offspring of David" (Rev. 22:16; see also 5:5;

Matt. 22:41–46), should be born into that house as *the* Son of David
and the only legitimate heir to the immortal throne of Israel.

So kingship belongs to Jesus the Messiah both by lineage and by
divine decree. He alone possesses "the key of the house of David"
(Isa. 22:22; see also Rev. 3:7), the key to the governance of Israel. The
house of David reigns forever because the Son of David reigns forever.
He will be the God-King of this celestialized earth.[49]

He is preeminently "the Lord's anointed." Although, as we have
seen, this title was bestowed upon Israel's ancient kings, it did not
originate with them nor with the ancient patriarchs and prophets. It
originated with the Son of Man. Paul wrote: "But unto the Son he [the
Father] saith, Thy throne, O God, is for ever and ever: a sceptre of
righteousness is the sceptre of thy kingdom. Thou hast loved righteousness, and hated iniquity; therefore God, even thy God, hath
anointed thee with the oil of gladness above thy fellows." (Heb. 1:8–
9.) That anointing was performed in the first estate in a general assembly of the Father's spirit family.[50] The Messiah is the prototype of
all upon whom the designation "the Lord's anointed" is sealed. He is
the begetter of kings. For he shares his throne with all who prove
worthy of joint-heirship under him in the Father's kingdom.[51]

Clearly, his throne is not literally one throne, his kingdom not
literally one kingdom. Rather, it consists of the myriad "thrones, kingdoms, principalities, and powers" (D&C 132:19) that compose the house
of Israel in the celestial world.

Anointed "with the oil of gladness above his fellows" (Heb. 1:9),
the Messiah stands at the apex of royal Israel as the King of her kings
and the Lord of her lords.[52] He is the David of Davids, the Melchizedek
of Melchizedeks[53] — the righteous King of righteous kings during and
following the millennial age. Hence Isaiah's words: "Of the increase of
his government and peace there shall be no end, upon the throne of
David, and upon his kingdom, to order it. . . . even for ever." (Isa. 9:7.)

Priest of Priests

The Savior is not only King of kings, but Priest of priests.[54] To be
a celestial king is to be a celestial priest. No man can be a king forever
who is not a priest forever. No woman can be a queen forever who is
not a priestess forever. And only those who receive a fulness of priesthood will be celestial priests and priestesses and, therefore, celestial

kings and queens. That is the patriarchal order now under attack by a few misguided members of the Church.

Receiving only a portion of priesthood, David could not be exalted. "Although David was a king," said the Prophet, "he never did obtain the spirit and power of Elijah and the fullness of the Priesthood."[55]

Divine kingship and priesthood constitute exaltation. The Son of Man was anointed a King and a Priest from eternity.[56] Those men and women who are adopted into his family, becoming his sons and his daughters, inherit like powers. As Jesus' priesthood was not based on a Levitical lineage but on oath and covenant (Heb. 7:14– 21), so may all receive a fulness of priesthood by oath and covenant without regard to any earthly lineage.[57]

When a man becomes a king and a priest and a woman a queen and a priestess, they are linked into the eternal order of celestial Israel. He is a king over his posterity and a priest to his God. She is a queen to her children and a priestess to her divine husband. Thus each is linked to their endless posterity and each to their Lord in a "whole and complete and perfect union" (D&C 128:18) from eternity to eternity.

This royal union of the Father's sons and daughters is achievable only through a fulness of the Melchizedek Priesthood. For it is only by entering this holy order that the kingly authority, as represented by Judah, and the priestly authority, as represented by Ephraim, can be received. Joseph Smith, with selected brethren and sisters, initiated this order in Nauvoo in 1843.[58]

Ephraim

In a latter-day context Jehovah said, "I am a father to Israel, and Ephraim is my firstborn." (Jer. 31:9; see also v. 20.) Now Ephraim is coming into his own as the the elder son of Jacob, the heir of the spiritual birthright. The redemption of Israel is primarily, but not exclusively, Ephraim's responsibility.

The foundation of the Restoration was laid through the Ephraimite Joseph Smith, who also initiated the temple order — the straight and narrow way to exaltation. Even as ancient Joseph's brothers came to him for the wheat of temporal and physical survival, so must his brethren come to Ephraim, Joseph's son of the right-hand blessing (Gen. 48:10–20), for the wheat of salvation and exaltation. And they will do so. The lost tribes will come to Zion, "and there shall they fall down and be crowned with glory, even in Zion, by the hands of the servants of the Lord, even the children of Ephraim. . . . Behold, this is the blessing of the everlasting God upon the tribes of Israel, and the richer blessing upon the head of Ephraim and his fellows." (D&C 133:32–35.)

Only after the other tribes are gathered, redeemed, and sealed will Judah be blessed in like manner. It is then that Israel will once more have a king named David.

Conclusion

David of old personifies those who, aspiring to the Father's richest blessings, enter into the most solemn of covenants in the house of the Lord. Those who prove faithful in these covenants—as David did not prove faithful to his—will be numbered among the kings and priests, queens and priestesses composing celestial Israel. The second David personifies them.

We must never forget, however, that all aspirants for exaltation ultimately rely upon the merits of the Holy One of Israel. Enoch testified: "Thou hast made me, and given unto me a right to thy throne, *and not of myself*, but through thy own grace." (Moses 7:59; italics added.)

Jesus himself said: "I am the vine, ye are the branches: He that abideth in me, and I in him, the same bringeth forth much fruit: for without me ye can do nothing." (John 15:5.) A "branch" is just that, a branch; it is not the life-giving vine itself. Thus it is altogether fitting that the anthem of Israel and her millennial king should be, "The Lord is our righteousness."

As we approach the last decade of the twentieth century, the tide of prophecy flows ever faster. We are poised on the very brink of unprecedented events pertaining to the Church, America, and the world. It will be some years before the second David makes his grand entrance on the prophetic stage. But when he does so, he will reign over a united Israel as a gracious ruler, a glorious king—one whom the first David will look upon with gratitude and joy.

NOTES

1. Abraham was told, "Kings shall come out of thee." (Gen. 17:6.) Moses predicted that Israel would desire a king and counseled that he should be chosen by the Lord. (Deut. 17:14– 15.)

2. 1 Sam. 13:8–4; 15.

3. For example, compare the account of David's adultery and his subsequent murder of Uriah in 2 Sam. 11 with 1 Chron. 20:1–3.

4. See Luke 3:15; John 6:15; 10:24; Acts 1:6.

5. 1 Sam. 22:17–22.

6. There appear to be two versions of this narrative in 1 Samuel, the first in chapter 24 and the second in chapter 26. I have quoted the latter as probably the more correct account.

7. The succession of Davidic kings was broken once when Athaliah, the mother of Ahaziah, murdered all but one of his sons and ruled Judah for eleven years. See 2 Kgs. 11:1–16.

8. Six sons by six wives were born to David in Hebron and at least thirteen sons by an unspecified number of wives were born in Jerusalem. See 2 Sam. 5:13–16; 14:3–7; 1 Chron. 3:1–9.

9. 2 Sam. 5:6–7. The original city of David covered about fifteen acres.

10. See Lev. 15:19–24.

11. 1 Sam. 21:4–5.

12. Joseph Smith, *Teachings of the Prophet Joseph Smith,* sel. Joseph Fielding Smith (Salt Lake City: Deseret Book, 1969), p. 339; see Andrew F. Ehat and Lyndon W. Cook, *The Words of Joseph Smith* (Salt Lake City: Bookcraft, 1980), pp. 334–35

13. Smith, *Teachings of the Prophet Joseph Smith,* p. 339.

14. See Ehat and Cook, *Words of Joseph Smith,* p. 335.

15. See Acts 3:12–21.

16. Smith, *Teachings of the Prophet Joseph Smith,* p. 188.

17. See Acts 3:19–21; D&C 88:95–100; Bruce R. McConkie, *Mormon Doctrine,* 2d ed. (Salt Lake City: Bookcraft, 1966), pp. 640, 795–96.

18. The Gihon spring was the main source of water for ancient Jerusalem. It is also known as Mary's Spring and the Virgin's Fountain.

19. See 1 Kgs. 11:1–10.

20. Although Jerusalem is sometimes described as "mount Zion" (see 2 Kgs. 19:31; Ps. 48:11), the truly glorious Mount Zion will be centered in the New Jerusalem of the Latter-day Saints. From thence the spirit of Zion will spread forth until Jerusalem and eventually the whole earth become Zion. See Smith, *Teachings of the Prophet Joseph,* pp. 17, 362; *Journal of Discourses,* 26 vols. (London: Latter-day Saints' Book Depot, 1854–86), 9:138; D&C 58:13, 64; 76:66; 84:2–5; 133:18, 56.

21. Ezek. 37:15–17.

22. See 1 Ne. 15:12; 19:24; Jacob 2:25.

23. "Branch" is not capitalized in 2 Nephi 21:1.

24. D&C 113:1–2. Note that "Stem" is capitalized in the Doctrine and Covenants but not in Isaiah. See Rom. 15:12.

25. Synonymous parallelism occurs when the same thought is restated or

amplified in the second clause or sentence. For examples, see Isaiah 1:10; 9:6; Psalm 24:1.

26. See D&C 27:12–13; 90:1–3; 112:30–32; 128:18–21.

27. See D&C 29:31–32.

28. See D&C 64:41–43; 105:3–5.

29. The complete capitalization in the King James Version of "The Lord our righteousness" in Jeremiah 23:6 and of "Branch" in Zechariah 3:8 and 6:12 is both unique and arbitrary on the part of the translators who applied these passages to Christ. See Revelation 19:16.

30. Sidney B. Sperry, *The Voice of Israel's Prophets* (Salt Lake City: Deseret Book Co., 1961), p. 414. Modern translations in English (including Jewish) read, "The Lord is our righteousness."

31. See D&C 133:2–7.

32. Whether David will be his actual name or is only symbolic of the restored Davidic order is a moot question. My opinion is that both usages were intended by the prophets.

33. See *Journal of Discourses*, 2:317; 15:44–45.

34. See D&C 45:66–71; 64:41–43; 133:26–35.

35. N. B. Lundwall, comp., *Inspired Prophetic Warnings*, 6th ed., p. 73; see also *Millennial Star*, 10 Sept. 1859, pp. 581–84.

36. *Journal of Discourses*, 9:27; italics added.

37. The so-called Council of Fifty was organized by the Prophet Joseph Smith in March 1844 as the precursor of the political arm (kingdom) of Christ's millennial "holy order."

38. When leaving for Carthage, the Prophet told Emma, "If the child is a boy, name him David Hyrum."

39. As quoted in Hyrum L. Andrus, *Doctrinal Commentary on the Pearl of Great Price* (Salt Lake City: Deseret Book Co., 1967), p. 464, n. 109.

40. Brigham Young believed that if he made himself worthy to do so, it was David Hyrum Smith's right to preside over the Church. (See *Journal of Discourses*, 8:69; 15:136; see also 25:367.) Any statements about Joseph Smith's posterity having honored positions in the Church must be qualified by the Lord's warning to the Prophet in 1833: "Your family must needs repent and forsake some things, and give more earnest heed unto your sayings, or be removed out of their place." (D&C 93:48.) Still, in 1841 the Lord assured the Prophet that he and his posterity would bless the nations, even as had Abraham. See D&C 124:56–59.

41. Smith, *Teachings*, p. 339; see also Ehat and Cook, *Words of Joseph Smith*, pp. 331, 334–35.

42. Bruce R. McConkie, *A New Witness for the Articles of Faith* (Salt Lake City: Deseret Book Co., 1985), p. 518.

43. Bruce R. McConkie, *The Millennial Messiah* (Salt Lake City: Deseret Book Co., 1982), pp. 172, 602–11.

44. See Jeremiah 23: "King Messiah (the Branch) shall reign in righteousness"; Jeremiah 33: "Christ the Branch of righteousness is promised"; Zechariah 3: "The Branch shall come" and Zechariah 6: "Christ, the Branch, who shall come."

45. The "Branch" and "David" are not found together in any given passage.

46. See Psalm 89:18; 149:2; Isaiah 33:22; 43:15; 44:6; Zephaniah 3:15; Matthew 27:42; John 1:49; 12:13; 1 Timothy 6:15; Revelation 17:14; 19:16; D&C 38:22; 41:4; 58:22.

47. See 1 Samuel 7:12–16, 25–29; Isaiah 9:7; Jeremiah 33:17–26; Psalm 89:3–4; Ehat and Cook, *Words of Joseph Smith*, p. 335.

48. "Until Shiloh comes" does not mean that kingship will depart from Judah when he *does* come—that would negate Jeremiah 33:17 and related passages—but that it will *remain with* Judah and be perfected in Christ. "Until" is used in a similar fashion in D&C 13:1.

49. See D&C 130:9.

50. See Smith, *Teachings,* p. 265.

51. Rom. 8:14–17; D&C 84:37–38.

52. Rev. 19:16.

53. The Hebrew "Melchizedek" may be translated "King of righteousness" (Heb. 7:2) or "our king is righteous."

54. See Hebrews 2:17; 4:14–15; 6:28; 7:7–8:1; 9:11.

55. Smith, *Teachings,* p. 339.

56. See JST Revelation 12:6–9.

57. See D&C 84:33–40; JST Genesis 14:28; Hebrews 7:1–3.

58. For key references on the fulness of priesthood, see Ehat and Cook, *Words of Joseph Smith,* pp. 303–7.

CHAPTER FIFTEEN

Redeeming the Dead As Taught in the Old Testament

Bruce A. Van Orden

Brigham Young University

"Redeeming the Dead" has long been one of the top priorities in The Church of Jesus Christ of Latter-day Saints. But only recently has this labor received its present lofty stature in the eyes of most members of the Church. In the April 1981 annual general conference President Spencer W. Kimball outlined for the first time the "threefold" mission of the Church: "To proclaim the gospel of the Lord Jesus Christ to every nation, kindred, tongue, and people;

"To perfect the Saints by preparing them to receive the ordinances of the gospel and by instruction and discipline to gain exaltation;

"To redeem the dead by performing vicarious ordinances of the gospel for those who have lived on the earth.

"All three are part of one work—to assist our Father in Heaven and His Son, Jesus Christ, in Their grand and glorious mission 'to bring to pass the immortality and eternal life of man.' " (Moses 1:39.)[1]

More recently President Ezra Taft Benson identified the "grand mission of the Church" as inviting all "to come unto Christ." "This grand mission of the Church is accomplished," he added, "by proclaiming the gospel, perfecting the Saints, and redeeming the dead."[2] In harmony with that statement, the threefold mission of the Church has been expressed in a regional representatives seminar in such terms as "Come unto Christ through Proclaiming the Gospel," "Come unto Christ through Perfecting the Saints," and "Come unto Christ through Redeeming the Dead."[3]

The sacred labor of bringing individuals to the Lord Jesus Christ through redeeming the dead is no less important than proclaiming the gospel or perfecting the Saints. They are approximately equal in importance. President Ezra Taft Benson explained how and why redeeming the dead fits into the overall scheme: "Through the resurrection of our Lord and by revelations given to the Prophet Joseph Smith and other modern prophets, we know that life does not end at death when our bodies are buried in the earth. But our spirits, which give life to our bodies, continue to live in the spirit world, where we may associate again with family and friends. In the world of spirits the gospel is preached to millions of people who never had an opportunity to hear it while on the earth. The preaching of the gospel there is a more intense activity than it is here, and the ministers of the Lord number in the tens of thousands."[4] Elder Boyd K. Packer stated, "In simple terms, [the work of redeeming the dead] is a testament of our certainty of the resurrection."[5] Hence, it is appropriate that as we talk variously of testifying of Christ in the Old Testament, we discuss redeeming the dead.

But is redeeming the dead taught in the Old Testament? The answer is "Yes, but without latter-day revelation, redeeming the dead would be an obscure doctrine in the Old Testament." Elder Bruce R. McConkie explained: "Salvation for the dead is Bible doctrine. This is perfectly clear to all of us now that we have received latter-day revelation. We now know [the meaning of several biblical passages which he briefly cited: John 5:25; Luke 23:43; 1 Pet. 3:18–20; 4:6; 1 Cor. 15:29; Isa. 42:7; 49:9; 61:1; Zech. 9:11; Obad. 1:21; Mal. 4:5–6.].

"But in the beginning days of our era, we need not suppose that Joseph Smith understood these passages any more than the sectarian world does today. For that matter we have every reason to believe that he did not so much as know of their existence until the Lord began the schooling process that was to make him, before his death, one of the greatest prophets and most exalted seers ever to grace the face of this lowly planet. In spite of the biblical passages, only some of which we have noted, it is clear that neither young Joseph nor any of the professors of religion who held sway in his day had even the slightest glimmering of knowledge about this merciful and equitable doctrine until He whose doctrine it is began the modern-day revelatory processes."[6]

So, with the aid of modern revelation and latter-day, inspired commentary, we shall seek out those passages in the Old Testament that either testify to us or inform us about the sacred doctrine of redeeming the dead.

Before the dead can be redeemed, naturally genealogies must be kept. "So all Israel were reckoned by genealogies," we learn from the

Chronicles. (1 Chr. 9:1.) All of us have encountered numerous genealogies when we have read the Old Testament. We even read in Ezra and Nehemiah how genealogies were used to forbid some men access to the priesthood because they had married unfaithfully among the heathen: "These sought their register among those that were reckoned by genealogy, but it was not found: therefore were they, as polluted, put from the priesthood." (Neh. 7:64; see also Ezra 6:22.) The importance of keeping an accurate genealogy in our day is underscored in a letter from Joseph Smith in Doctrine and Covenants 85:11–12: "And they who are of the High Priesthood, whose names are not found written in the book of the law, or that are found to have apostatized, or to have been cut off from the church, as well as the lesser priesthood, or the members, in that day shall not find an inheritance among the saints of the Most High; therefore, it shall be done unto them as unto the children of the priest, as will be found recorded in the second chapter and sixty-first and second verses of Ezra."

Keeping sacred genealogies was always a prerequesite among the chosen seed of God. "And a book of remembrance was kept," we read in the Book of Moses about Adam and his posterity. "A genealogy was kept of the children of God. And this was the book of the generations of Adam." (Moses 6:5, 8.) We learn further that Adam's book of remembrance was written "according to the pattern given by the finger of God." (Moses 6:46.) Adam's book of remembrance was undoubtedly used to teach God's "chosen seed" how to function according to the patriarchal order of the priesthood. (See Moses 6:6; D&C 107:40–57.)

We in latter-day Zion likewise have been enjoined to keep a book of remembrance collectively as a church, as families, and as individuals. "And all they who are not found written in the book of remembrance shall find none inheritance in that day," warned the Lord through Joseph Smith. "Their portion shall be appointed them among unbelievers, where are wailing and gnashing of teeth." (D&C 85:9.)

In an epistle to the Saints in 1842, the Prophet Joseph Smith further explained the importance of sacred records that would go into the collective book of remembrance. He cited Revelation 20:12 about the books being opened: "The books spoken of must be the books which contained the record of their works, and refer to the records which are kept on the earth. And the book which was the book of life is the record which is kept in heaven." (D&C 128:7.) In that same epistle Joseph Smith alluded to Malachi's warning and prophecy: "But who may abide the day of his [Christ's second] coming? and who shall stand when he appeareth? . . . He shall purify the sons of Levi, and purge them as gold and silver, that they may offer unto the Lord an offering in righteousness." (Mal. 3:2–3.) Using Malachi, the Prophet Joseph Smith admonished, "Behold, the great day of the Lord is at hand; and who can abide the day of his coming, and who can stand when he appeareth? . . . Let us, therefore, as a church and a people, and as Latter-day Saints, offer unto the Lord an offering in righteousness [even as the purified sons of Levi will do]; and let us present in his holy temple, when it is finished, a book containing the records of our dead, which shall be worthy of all acceptation." (D&C 128:24.)

President Spencer W. Kimball commented on these records "worthy of all acceptation" that we would offer to the Lord in the temple: "We have asked the members of the Church to further the work of turning the hearts of the children to the fathers by getting their own sacred family records in order. These records, including especially the 'book containing the records of our dead' (D&C 128:24) are a portion of the 'offering in righteousness' referred to by Malachi (3:3) which we are to present in His holy temple and without which we shall not abide the day of his coming.[7]

"I feel the same sense of urgency about temple work for the dead as I do about the missionary work for the living," President Kimball said in 1978 in general conference. "They are basically one and the same. I have told my brethren of the General Authorities that this work for the dead is constantly on my mind." President Kimball then explained a twofold program of gathering records that would go into our individual books of remembrance and into the Church's collective book of remembrance: "First, all members should write a personal history and participate in a family organization. Also, we want to emphasize again and place squarely upon the shoulders of these individuals and their families the obligation to complete the four-generation program. Families may extend their pedigree beyond the four generations if desired.

"Secondly, we are introducing a Church-wide program of extracting names from genealogical records. Church members may now render second-mile service through participating in this regard in extracting these names in this program supervised by the priesthood leaders at the local level. . . .

"I urge all the people of this church to give serious attention to their family histories, to encourage their parents and grandparents to write their journals, and let no family go into eternity without having left their memoirs for their children, their grandchildren, and their posterity. This is a duty and a responsibility, and I urge every person to start the children out writing a personal history and journal."[8]

That which is recorded in righteousness here on earth, according to Joseph Smith, will also be recorded in heaven. (D&C 128:8.) He added that this has been the case "in all ages of the world, whenever the Lord has given a dispensation of the priesthood to any man by actual revelation." (D&C 128:9.) That, naturally, would include the dispensations recorded in the Old Testament. "Hence, whatsoever those men did in authority, in the name of the Lord," Joseph Smith concluded, "and did it truly and faithfully, and kept a proper and faithful record of the same, it became a law on earth and in heaven, and could not be annulled, according to the decrees of the great Jehovah." (D&C 128:9.)

Isaiah taught us that it is a principle of righteous people to look to their roots, that they remember their heritage and be grateful for it. "Hearken to me, ye that follow after righteousness," he said. "Look unto the rock whence ye are hewn, and to the hole of the pit whence ye are digged. Look unto Abraham your father, and unto Sarah that bare you." (Isa. 51:1–2.) We who are members of the house of Israel have not only the glorious opportunity but also the duty to seek out our kindred dead, who are also of the house of Israel, because they likewise call Abraham their father and Sarah their mother. Through Isaiah, the Lord gave a promise to those who look to their roots: "For the Lord shall comfort Zion: he will comfort all her waste places; and he will make her wilderness like Eden, and her desert like the garden of the Lord; joy and gladness shall be found therein, thanksgiving, and the voice of melody." (Isa. 51:3.)

In a *Church News* editorial on 22 April 1989, we read of a possible interpretation to this promise: "If one definition of Zion is the honest in heart, surely it is not too big a stretch to apply the promise in Isaiah spiritually and intellectually as well as physically. There are among us too many waste places — minds rendered useless by idleness or the emptiness of modern media, hearts set on material things and pleasure.

"When hearts turn to their fathers, when minds turn from idleness and trivia to the exciting search for roots, waste places do indeed turn into gardens of the Lord. Joy and gladness, thanksgiving do dwell therein, and, yes, even the melody of the ages."[9]

In connection with the lofty idea of looking to our roots, we refer to another Old Testament prophet, Malachi, who prophesied: "Behold, I will send you Elijah the prophet before the coming of the great and dreadful day of the Lord: and he shall turn the heart of the fathers to the children, and the heart of the children to their fathers, lest I come and smite the earth with a curse." (Mal. 4:5–6.)

"Now, the word *turn* here," explained the Prophet Joseph Smith, "should be translated *bind*, or seal. But what is the object of this important mission? or how is it to be fulfilled? The keys are to be delivered, the spirit of Elijah is to come, the Gospel to be established, the Saints of God gathered, Zion built up, and the Saints to come up as saviors on Mount Zion."[10]

We read in 1 Kings 17:1 that the Old Testament prophet Elijah possessed the sealing power of the priesthood, which he exercised by sealing the heavens from rain. "Elijah was the last Prophet [in the Old Testament] that held the [sealing] keys of the Priesthood," explained Joseph Smith. That is why he specifically was chosen to restore those keys in the last days.[11]

This "spirit of Elijah," also alluded to by Joseph Smith, is indeed a potent force. "When a member of the Church comes under its influence," wrote Elder Boyd K. Packer, "it is a powerful, compelling force which motivates him with a desire to be attending to genealogical and temple work. It leaves him anxious over the well-being of his forebears. When that spirit comes, somehow we desire to know more about those forebears—we desire to *know* them."[12]

Once we catch the spirit of Elijah, we are motivated to stick to our task, to seek out our kindred dead, identify which of their ordinances need yet to be performed in the temples, and compile and write their personal or family histories. No one of us can rest assured that he or she has fulfilled the duty pertaining to an individual book of remembrance until the following three things are included in it:

1. A pedigree chart or charts that list everybody on the family tree where there are written or oral tradition records in existence. For most of us, that is possible on most lines back to about 1700 or 1650, or about seven or eight generations.

2. Family group sheets (or records) as far as they can be filled out accurately for each husband and wife listed on the pedigree. That means

we identify each of the children of our ancestors, that is, our "collateral relatives." We should see to it that each person listed on these family group records has his or her baptism, endowment, and sealing ordinances performed.

3. Personal or family histories for as many individuals or families on the family tree as we can either collect or write ourselves.

Although this task may seem daunting, Elder Boyd K. Packer reasoned: "We are commanded to preach the gospel to all the living, for example. We see no way to accomplish this task in our lifetime. Many refuse to listen, some turn away, others resent and even persecute us. Nevertheless we are not released from the assignment to try. We are to do the best we can. If we do, the honest in heart can be found and sifted out of the world.

"As for those who have died, there seems no way we can find them all. We have no way of knowing whether they will accept the work we do for them. We are sure some will reject it. There may be those who are not eligible to receive it. We can only do as we do in missionary work—set our hand to the task, be about the work, do all we can to seek out the names of our kindred dead and prepare these names for temple work. Insofar as we can, too, we gather the identifying data of all who have lived in mortality."[13]

It has been my observation, as I labor on my own book of remembrance and as I teach "Introduction to Family History/Genealogy" at BYU, that once a person gets sufficiently organized and gains confidence with the basic family history principles, he or she can then dedicate approximately twenty hours per year to this work and achieve remarkable progress. He or she will continue to be motivated by the powerful spirit of Elijah. "Something happens to us in this life when we participate in this great work of genealogical research and of going to the temple for our own ancestors," observed Elder Dallin H. Oaks. "That something which happens is something we need. We also accomplish something our ancestors need. Those spiritual blessings aren't happening to enough people."[14] Presently the General Authorities in charge of family history in the Church are doing all they can to help members do this work, to "simplify" and "demystify" the procedures so that they are "do-able" by "every member of the Church."[15]

We mentioned earlier that it is the Lord's mission "to bring to pass the immortality and eternal life of man." (Moses 1:39.) One thing the

Lord does is rescue the souls in spirit prison from their bonds. As we read in Zechariah, "By the blood of thy covenant I have sent forth thy prisoners out of the pit." (Zech. 9:11.) In Isaiah we read a related graphic description of what will happen to the prisoners: "And they shall be gathered together, as prisoners are gathered in the pit, and shall be shut up in the prison, and after many days shall they be visited." (Isa. 24:22.) The wondrous fulfillment of those messianic prophecies in the Old Testament was witnessed by Joseph F. Smith in his vision of the redemption of the dead: "I beheld that they [the dead] were filled with joy and gladness, and were rejoicing together because the day of their deliverance was at hand. They were assembled awaiting the advent of the Son of God into the spirit world, to declare their redemption from the bands of death. . . . While this vast multitude waited and conversed, rejoicing in the hour of their deliverance from the chains of death, the Son of God appeared, declaring liberty to the captives who had been faithful." (D&C 138:15–16, 18.)

On two more occasions Isaiah included messianic prophecies about the role of the Lord in freeing these prisoners: "I the Lord have called thee in righteousness, and will hold thine hand, and will keep thee, and give thee for a covenant of the people, for a light of the Gentiles; to open the blind eyes, to bring out the prisoners from the prison, and them that sit in darkness out of the prison house." (Isa. 42:6–7.) "He hath sent me to bind up the brokenhearted, to proclaim liberty to the captives, and the opening of the prison to them that are bound." (Isa. 61:1.)

We have also learned from President Spencer W. Kimball that it is our duty to help the Lord with his mission of redeeming mankind. Through Isaiah the Lord tells *us* who are members of the house of Israel: "Thus saith the Lord, In an acceptable time have I heard thee, and in a day of salvation have I helped thee: and I will preserve thee, and give thee for a covenant of the people, to establish the earth, to cause to inherit the desolate heritages; that thou mayest say to the prisoners, Go forth; to them that are in darkness, Shew yourselves. They shall feed in the ways, and their pastures shall be in all high places. They shall not hunger nor thirst; neither shall the heat nor sun smite them: for he that hath mercy on them shall lead them, even by the springs of water shall he guide them." (Isa. 49:8–10.)

As these beautiful verses tell us, we who are of the house of Israel will have the privilege, after we have passed from mortality, of showing ourselves to those bound in prison and proclaim to them the tender mercies of our Savior. President Joseph F. Smith explained it this way: "I beheld that the faithful elders of this dispensation, when they depart from mortal life, continue their labors in the preaching of the gospel of repentance and redemption, through the sacrifice of the Only Begotten Son of God, among those who are in darkness and under the bondage of sin in the great world of the spirits of the dead. The dead who repent will be redeemed, through obedience to the ordinances of the house of God, and after they have paid the penalty of their transgressions, and are washed clean, shall receive a reward according to their works, for they are heirs of salvation." (D&C 138:57–59.)

While we are still in mortality, we can become "saviors [note the lower case *s* compared with the upper case *S* for Jesus Christ] on Mount Zion" (see Obad. 1:21) for scores, maybe even hundreds and thousands, of those who have passed on (especially our own kindred dead) by performing by proxy the requisite ordinances for them in the house of the Lord. "But how are [we] to become saviors on Mount Zion?" asked the Prophet Joseph Smith while the Nauvoo Temple was being built. "By building their temples, erecting their baptismal fonts, and going forth and receiving all the ordinances, baptisms, confirmations, washings, anointings, ordinations and sealing powers upon their heads, in behalf of all their progenitors who are dead, and redeem them that they may come forth in the first resurrection and be exalted to thrones of glory with them; and herein is the chain that binds the hearts of the fathers to the children, and the children to the fathers, which fulfills the mission of Elijah. And I would to God that this temple was now done, that we might go into it, and go to work and improve our time, and make use of the seals while they are on the earth."[16]

At the dedication of the Apia Samoa Temple in 1983, President Gordon B. Hinckley petitioned the Lord: "Wilt thou open the way for thy people to seek out the records of their forebears that they may serve as saviors on Mount Zion in opening the prison doors of those whose progress has been stopped beyond the veil, that these may now become the beneficiaries of the sacred ordinances of thy holy house, and go forward on the way to eternal life and exaltation in thy presence."[17]

Yes, we can have this "welding link" (see D&C 128:18) established between us and our ancestors all the way back to Abraham, Isaac, and Jacob, and from them back to Adam and Eve. I can think of no more noble appellation than that of "savior on Mount Zion." All the Lord expects of us in this is to catch the Spirit of Elijah and labor consistently, not inordinately, on our genealogies, family histories, and visits to the temple. May we be imbued with that Spirit of Elijah and may we become literally "saviors on Mount Zion."

NOTES

1. Spencer W. Kimball, in Conference Report, Apr. 1981, p. 3.

2. Ezra Taft Benson, in Conference Report, Apr. 1988, p. 97.

3. See *Church News*, 11 Apr. 1987, pp. 5, 23.

4. *Friend*, Apr. 1981, p. 6.

5. Boyd K. Packer, in *Church News*, 4 Mar. 1989, p. 7.

6. Bruce R. McConkie, "A New Commandment: Save Thyself and Thy Kindred!" *Ensign*, Aug. 1976, p. 8.

7. Spencer W. Kimball at Genealogical Society Seminar, Brigham Young University, Aug. 1977, pp. 34–35, as quoted in Daniel H. Ludlow, *A Companion to Your Study of the Old Testament* (Salt Lake City: Deseret Book Co., 1981), p. 401.

8. Spencer W. Kimball, in Conference Report, Apr. 1978, p. 4.

9. *Church News*, 22 Apr. 1989, p. 16.

10. Joseph Smith, *History of The Church of Jesus Christ of Latter-day Saints*, ed. B. H. Roberts, 7 vols., 2d ed. rev. (Salt Lake City: Deseret Book Co., 1957), 6:184.

11. Ibid., 4:211.

12. Boyd K. Packer, *The Holy Temple* (Salt Lake City: Bookcraft, 1980), p. 210.

13. Ibid., p. 211.

14. Dallin H. Oaks, in *Church News*, 6 June 1987, p. 11.

15. James E. Faust, in *Church News*, 6 June 1987, p. 11.

16. *History of the Church*, 6:184.

17. Gordon B. Hinckley, in *Church News*, 14 Aug. 1983, p. 5.

CHAPTER SIXTEEN

The Abrahamic Covenant

S. Michael Wilcox

Brigham Young University

"And I will bless them through thy name; for as many as receive this Gospel shall be called after thy name, and shall be accounted thy seed, and shall rise up and bless thee, as their father; and I will bless them that bless thee, and curse them that curse thee; and in thee (that is, in thy Priesthood) and in thy seed (that is, thy Priesthood), for I give unto thee a promise that this right shall continue in thee, and in thy seed after thee (that is to say, the literal seed, or the seed of the body) shall all the families of the earth be blessed, even with the blessings of the Gospel, which are the blessings of salvation, even of life eternal." (Abr. 2:10–11.)

Every member of the Church is encouraged to obtain a patriarchal blessing. One of the most important aspects of every blessing is the declaring of lineage which indicates to the individual his or her place in the house of Israel. This lineage gives each person the blessings and obligations of the Abrahamic covenant. It is essential that all understand the importance of this covenant, how it relates to their lives, the mission of the Church in the latter days, and its importance to past dispensations. With an understanding of this covenant, all scripture takes on added significance. If there is a unifying theme in the Old and New Testaments that goes hand in hand with the mission of the Messiah, it is the Abrahamic promises.

An Elect People

Various aspects of God's promises to Abraham and his descendants can be found throughout scripture, chiefly in Abraham 1 and 2 and in Genesis 12, 15, 17, 26, and 28. God called Abraham's covenant children an "elect" (Isa. 45:4) and a "chosen" (Ps. 105:6) people. Almost all of the prophets spoke of the Abrahamic promises and responsibilities. Many people believed this meant they were favored above other nations because they were more loved of God; however, the words *elect* and *chosen* refer to certain responsibilities. Abraham's seed were elected to service. They were chosen to perform a service, just as we elect and choose public servants today. During the Savior's visit to the Nephites he explained: "And behold, ye are the children of the prophets; and ye are of the house of Israel; and ye are of the covenant which the Father made with your fathers, saying unto Abraham: *And in thy seed shall all the kindreds of the earth be blessed.*

"The Father having raised me up unto you first, and sent me to bless you in turning away every one of you from his iniquities; and this because ye are the children of the covenant—

"And after that ye were blessed then fulfilleth the Father the covenant which he made with Abraham, saying: *In thy seed shall all the kindreds of the earth be blessed.* (3 Nephi 20:25–27; italics added.)

Every covenant contains promises and blessings. The Lord promised Abraham that his seed would be granted the blessings of the priesthood. (Abr. 1:18.) The Savior told the Nephites, who were a part of covenant Israel, that he would "bless" them by "turning away every one of you from his iniquities." That is a wonderful promise. What turns people from their iniquities, whether it be Old Testament Israel, Book of Mormon Nephites, or Latter-day Saints? Only the principles of truth and righteousness contained in the gospel can keep a society or an individual righteous. And righteousness is the only means to happiness, peace, and rest. Lehi told his sons on his deathbed, "If there be no righteousness there be no happiness." (2 Nephi 2:13.)

To Abraham's seed went the most precious gifts of God. They were given prophets. They were given the priesthood and its accompanying ordinances, including the all-important gift of the Holy Ghost. They were given scriptures, truth, and knowledge. They were given chosen and promised lands that would be protected as long as they remained righteous. They were given the privilege of taking the Savior's name and becoming his people. Their children, born into this covenant, would share in all these blessings. If they obeyed the law of the gospel, these gifts would turn them from the iniquities of the world and eventually lead them to the Eternal Father. The promise was given that each succeeding generation would be privileged to have these gifts, if they lived worthily and fulfilled their part of the covenant. This was their birthright under the covenant.

All the Families of the Earth

It is important to remember that the people of Abraham were chosen and elected, not because God loved them more, but because they were to take on a vital responsibility. That responsibility is suggested in the most often quoted passage of the Abrahamic covenant: "In thy seed shall all the kindreds of the earth be blessed." (3 Ne. 20:27.) The following verses from the promises given to Abraham in other scriptures show the importance of this promise: "And I will bless them that bless thee, and curse him that curseth thee: and in thee shall all families of the earth be blessed." (Gen. 12:3.) "And this covenant I make, that thy children may be known among all nations." (JST Gen. 17:9.) "Seeing that Abraham shall surely become a great and mighty nation, and all the nations of the earth shall be blessed in him?" (Gen. 18:18.) "And I will make thy seed to multiply as the stars of heaven, and will give unto thy seed all these countries; and in thy seed shall all the nations of the earth be blessed; because that Abraham obeyed my voice, and kept my charge, my commandments, my statutes, and my laws." (Gen. 26:4–5.) "And I will make of thee a great nation, and I will bless thee above measure, and make thy name great among all nations, and thou shalt be a blessing unto thy seed after thee, that in their hands they shall bear this ministry and Priesthood unto all nations." (Abr. 2:9.) Later in this same chapter the Lord told Abraham the specific blessings his seed would bestow upon all the families of the earth. They were the "blessings of the Gospel, which are the blessings of salvation, even of life eternal." (Abr. 2:11.)

It is clear that Abraham's seed was elected and chosen to bless all the nations of the earth with the treasures of eternity God bestowed on them. This truth was well understood by Paul, and he used all his abilities to help in its fulfillment. In his epistle to the Romans, Paul beautifully explained covenant Israel's responsibility: "For there is no difference between the Jew and the Greek: for the same Lord over all is rich unto all that call upon him. For whosoever shall call upon the name of the Lord shall be saved. How then shall they call on him in whom they have not believed? and how shall they believe in him of whom they have not heard? and how shall they hear without a preacher? And how shall they preach, except they be sent? as it is written, How beautiful are the feet of them that preach the gospel of peace, and bring glad tidings of good things!" (Rom. 10:12–15.)

The Abrahamic Covenant is inseparably connected to the priesthood, particularly the Melchizedek Priesthood. In the oath and covenant of the priesthood, men who magnify their calling are called "the seed of Abraham." (D&C 84:34.) Upon the bearer of the Melchizedek Priesthood, the Lord has placed a sacred responsibility to fulfill the Abrahamic charge because he is literally the "seed of Abraham." This truth was plainly taught to Abraham in the Pearl of Great Price. Immediately after Abraham was saved from the idolatrous priests of Ur, the Lord gave him the commission to bless all the nations of the earth: "I will take thee, to put upon thee my name, even the Priesthood of thy father, and my power shall be over thee. . . . but through thy ministry my name shall be known in the earth forever, for I am thy God." (Abr. 1:18–19.) The seed of Abraham are elected to make known the Lord's name forever. This responsibility ties in directly with the covenant of baptism and the sacrament, wherein followers take upon themselves the name of Christ and through obedience to covenants and righteous living, make his "name known" throughout the earth. This same focus was given to Abraham later: "For I have purposed to take thee away out of Haran, and to make of thee a minister to bear my name in a strange land which I will give unto thy seed after thee for an everlasting possession, when they hearken to my voice." (Abr. 2:6.)

Just before Abraham's removal to Canaan the Lord reemphasized his responsibility to bless all the nations. At this moment the Lord spoke of specific blessings to be carried to the world, and of their direct relationship to the priesthood:

"And I will make of thee a great nation, and I will bless thee above measure, and make thy name great among all nations, and thou shalt be a blessing unto thy seed after thee, that in their hands they shall bear this ministry and Priesthood unto all nations;

"And I will bless them through thy name; for as many as receive this Gospel shall be called after thy name, and shall be accounted thy seed, and shall rise up and bless thee, as their father;

"And I will bless them that bless thee, and curse them that curse thee; and in thee (that is, in thy Priesthood) and in thy seed (that is, thy Priesthood), for I give unto thee a promise that this right shall continue in thee, and in thy seed after thee (that is to say, the literal seed, or the seed of the body) shall all the families of the earth be blessed, even with the blessings of the Gospel, which are the blessings of salvation, even of life eternal." (Abr. 2:9–11.)

It is plain in this last scripture that the priesthood bearer is under covenant to share the blessings he has received with the world. He must "bear this ministry and priesthood" to all nations, that all nations may be blessed with "the Gospel," "salvation," and "life eternal." Only in this way can all God's children be "turned from [their] iniquities" and enjoy happiness, peace, and rest. These responsibilities under the direction of the priesthood apply to all Church members and constitute the chief mission of the Lord's kingdom, for the Lord explained to Abraham that all who accept the gospel become his seed. Upon baptism the covenant is immediately extended to the new member, who must be willing to accept not only the blessings of his or her newly acquired birthright but also its responsibilities.

As if to impress upon us the need to preach the gospel, we are told that Abraham was not idle with this responsibility as he traveled to the promised land. When he left for Canaan he took with him "the souls that we had won in Haran." (Abr. 2:15.) Abraham had already made an earlier attempt to win souls for Christ, in particular those of his family. (See Abr. 1:5–7.) In Egypt he is portrayed as the teacher of Pharaoh and his court, emphasizing again his role of teacher.

It is very easy to see within this framework why the leaders of the Church have identified the mission of the Church as centering on three main objectives:

"1. To proclaim the gospel of the Lord Jesus Christ to every nation, kindred, tongue, and people;

"2. To perfect the Saints by preparing them to receive the ordinances of the gospel and by instruction and discipline to gain exaltiation;

"3. To redeem the dead by performing vicarious ordinances of the gospel for those who have lived on the earth." (Spencer W. Kimball, in Conference Report, Apr. 1981, p. 3.)

Through accomplishing these objectives, the Church, under the direction of the priesthood, fulfills the Abrahamic covenant. It is not coincidental that newly ordained nineteen-year-old Melchizedek Priesthood bearers are counseled to fill a mission. For two years the young men keep their covenant with the Lord with all their time and ability, as do sister missionaries and couples.

It is also not difficult to see how completely the Savior fulfilled the Abrahamic responsibility of blessing all the world with the gospel, salvation, and life eternal. He fulfilled all with his atonement, teachings, example, visits to the Nephites and the lost tribes, etc. He was in truth a son of Abraham—literally the seed of Abraham and as such the

ultimate fulfiller of Abrahamic responsibilities. More than that, Christ
made the covenant with Abraham; he was its author. In this we find
added insight to Paul's words that Christ was the "author and finisher"
of our faith. (Heb. 12:2.)

The Lord's Rest

We find an additional witness to these truths in the Book of Mormon. There Alma the Younger explains the role of high priests to the
people of Ammonihah. They were to "teach these things [the saving
principles of the gospel] unto the people . . . that thereby the people
might know in what manner to look forward to his Son for redemption."
Alma stressed that their "calling" was to "teach his commandments
unto the children of men, that they also might enter into his rest."
(Alma 13:1–2, 6.) The word *rest* is often seen in conjunction with the
gospel. Abraham wanted "rest" (Abraham 1:2) and sought to administer
this blessing of the priesthood to others. The Doctrine and Covenants
gives us a distinct definition of *rest* as it relates to Moses' desire to
obtain rest for the children of Israel: "And this greater priesthood
administereth the gospel and holdeth the key of the mysteries of the
kingdom, even the key of the knowledge of God. Therefore, in the
ordinances thereof, the power of godliness is manifest. . . . Now this
Moses plainly taught to the children of Israel in the wilderness, and
sought diligently to sanctify his people that they might behold the face
of God; but they hardened their hearts and could not endure his presence; therefore, the Lord in his wrath, for his anger was kindled against
them, swore that they should not enter into his rest while in the
wilderness, which rest is the fulness of his glory." (D&C 84:19–20,
23–24.)

Rest, then, is the fulness of God's glory, and all God's servants
have strived to bring their people into its enjoyment. The seed of
Abraham's responsibility, therefore, is to administer the blessings of
the gospel to the world so that all humanity can enter into the rest of
the Lord and enjoy the fulness of his glory.

The emphasis of the gospel has always been on others. To accept
the blessings of the priesthood and the gospel and not share them is
to deny the very meaning of an Abrahamic birthright. It is an act of
selfishness and blindness that not only shows a lack of gratitude but
also an ignorance of the most fundamental truths of the covenant. The
spirit of this responsibility and the charity which should betoken every

member of the Church, particularly bearers of the priesthood, is eloquently summarized by the apostle Paul in his letter to the Hebrews: "For every high priest taken from among men is ordained for men in things pertaining to God, that he may offer both gifts and sacrifices for sins: Who can have compassion on the ignorant, and on them that are out of the way." (Heb. 5:1–2.)

Of the World or above the World

If a member of the Church is to bless the world and thus fulfill the obligation inherent in the Abrahamic covenant, he or she must be aware of two attitudes that hinder the effective influencing of the world for righteousness: being of the world, or like it, and being above the world, or aloof from others not yet part of the covenant. Both attitudes caused failures in the Old and the New Testaments. They stand in opposition to the very essence of the birthright, yet they are still pervasive among us. We must guard against them.

When God established his covenant people, he placed them in the center of the ancient world. Egypt, Babylon, Assyria, Persia, Greece, Rome, and other empires all came into contact with the people of the covenant, not to mention the Philistines, Moabites, Ammonites, Edomites, and the citizens of Sidon and Tyre. It was the Lord's purpose from the beginning to make Israel a holy and a peculiar people: "Now therefore, if ye will obey my voice indeed, and keep my covenant, then ye shall be a peculiar treasure unto me above all people: for all the earth is mine: And ye shall be unto me a kingdom of priests, and an holy nation." (Ex. 19:5–6.) This injunction was later applied by Peter to the New Testament Saints. (See 1 Peter 2:9.)

God placed his people in the center of the ancient world, for there they could, if they remained righteous, holy, and peculiar, exert their beneficial influence on, and be an example to, all the nations of the earth. Some of the ancient prophets accomplished that objective. The Old Testament relates the positive influence Abraham, Joseph, and Moses exerted on Egypt; Daniel and Shadrach, Meshach, and Abednego, on Babylon and Persia; Jonah, on the Assyrians; Elisha, on Naaman; and so forth. The New Testament follows the same principle with the influence Peter, Paul, and the other disciples had on the Greeks, Romans, and Samaritans.

There is, however, a chance that a peculiar, covenant, and elect people may allow the world's cultures, laws, values, and standards to infiltrate their own. They become like the world rather than serving as an example to the world. Instead of serving Jehovah in Sinai, the Israelites desired to return to the "fleshpots" of Egypt and their former bondage. Ahab was influenced by Jezebel. Samson was more Philistine than the Philistines, and the people under Samuel wanted to have a king "like all the nations." (1 Sam. 8:5.) Throughout the history of the Old Testament, the children of the covenant embraced the standards and desires of the world. For that reason the prophets constantly reminded them of their responsibility to choose between being distinguished from the world or being part of the world. Joshua issued this challenge—"Choose you this day whom ye will serve." (Joshua 24:15.) Elijah offered the same choice on Mount Carmel—"How long halt ye between two opinions? if the Lord be God, follow him: but if Baal, then follow him." (1 Kings 18:21.)

Obviously if the Lord's elect become like the world, they can no longer fulfill their covenant. This is what Christ meant when he spoke of the salt of the earth losing its savor. "Wherewith shall it [the earth] be salted?" (Matt. 5:13.) Every episode related in the Old Testament can be seen as a success or a failure to fulfill the obligations of Abraham's promises. It is very fitting we are introduced to its features early in Genesis.

The biblical challenge of being in the world without accepting its influences remains a major stumbling block today. The temptation is ever present to be "like all the nations." Therefore a true son or daughter of Abraham will remain peculiar and holy (not aloof), and let his or her light shine for others to see. The standards and images of the world must never become the ideals of any member of the Church. Alma spoke of the proper attitude while conversing with the citizens of Ammonihah about high priests: "Now they, after being sanctified by the Holy Ghost, having their garments made white, being pure and spotless before God, could not look upon sin save it were with abhorrence; and there were many, exceedingly great many, who were made pure and entered into the rest of the Lord their God." (Alma 13:12.) The birthright children of Abraham must not enter the spacious building of the world but cling to the rod of iron and eat only from the tree of life. As Lehi did, they will invite others to partake of that fruit also.

The second dangerous attitude is more easily seen in the New Testament. When Christ came, the "elect" had done a complete turnaround in attitude. Instead of embracing the world, they shunned the world, considering themselves superior to it. They believed contact with the world rendered one unclean. Their attitude was one of self-righteousness. So strong was their attitude that Nicodemus listened and marveled as Christ explained to him that, "God so loved the world that he gave his only begotten Son, that whosoever believeth in him should not perish, but have everlasting life. For God sent not his Son into the world to condemn the world; but that the world through him might be saved." (John 3:16–17.) To Nicodemus and most of the Jews, the Messiah would come as a conquering warrior to put an end to their oppressors. The concept of a Messiah who would die to save all men — Greeks, Romans, and Samaritans included — was foreign to them. He was not coming as a condemning Messiah but as one who saved.

The attitude of complete separation from the world was evident even among the disciples and apostles of Christ. After the Resurrection and the command to take the gospel to "all the world," it still took the thrice-repeated dream of the unclean animals before Peter understood and preached the gospel to Cornelius. When apprised of Peter's actions, other early Christians were dismayed, saying, "Thou wentest in to men uncircumcised, and didst eat with them." (Acts 11:3.) After Peter's careful explanation, they concluded with wonder, "Then hath God also to the Gentiles granted repentance unto life." (Acts 11:18.) In spite of repeated efforts by Paul and other leaders, the contention concerning the Gentiles continued and finally became a major contributor to the apostasy. That is clearly seen in the epistles of the early leaders.

It does not require great insight to understand that a self-righteous attitude will also prevent a covenant son or daughter of Abraham from blessing the world with happiness, peace, and rest. Those of us in the Church today must radiate to the world a spirit of love and acceptance in order to bring others to the truths of the gospel. We must love all people, even when their actions should be condemned. A spirit of pride, superiority, condemnation, or intolerance will prevent a righteous influence as effectively as worldliness will prevent it. Though members of the covenant cannot "look upon sin save it were with abhorrence" (Alma 13:12), they must look on people as the children of deity and worthy of salvation and love.

Christ, as in all things, is the supreme example of this spirit. The troubled and guilt-ridden sought him out, knowing his attitude toward them was the opposite of that of condemning Pharisees. A chosen and elect people must not let worldliness or self-righteousness stand in the way of blessing "all the families of the earth."

There are many practical methods by which the Abrahamic covenant regarding "the families of the earth" can be fulfilled. The best place for us to start blessing the world is in our own family, ward, and neighborhood. The greatest challenges given to any ward involve non-members, part-member families, less active members, troubled youth, and others with special needs. These are found in every ward and branch of the Church. The scriptures provide excellent models of effective ways to bless all the families of the earth with the blessings of the gospel, salvation, and eternal life. If we search them, these truths will unfold and the Old Testament will truly become a book for our time.

CHAPTER SEVENTEEN

The Waters Which Make Glad the City of God: The Water Motif of Ezekiel 47:1–12

Fred E. Woods

Brigham Young University

This paper focuses on the meaning of the water motif of Ezekiel 47:1–12. I will begin by giving you my own translation of this passage.[1]

"1. And he brought me to the entrance of the temple, and behold water went out from under the threshold of the temple eastward, for the front of the temple was facing eastward. And water descended underneath on the right side of the temple, south of the altar.

"2. And he brought me out through the north gate round the outside to the outside gate which faces east and the water trickled from the right side.

"3. And the man came out to the east with the measuring line in his hand and he measured a thousand cubits more and allowed me to pass through the water up to the ankles.

"4. And he measured a thousand cubits more and allowed me to pass through the water up to the knees. And he measured a thousand cubits more and he let me pass through water up to the loins.

"5. And he measured a thousand cubits more a river which I could no longer pass through, for the water had raised, water to swim in, and a river which could no longer be passed through.

"6. And he said to me: Have you seen, Son of man?[2] And he brought me back to the bank of the river.

"7. When I came back, there were on the bank of the river many trees on each side.

"8. And he said to me: These waters go out to the eastern region and flow down into the Arabah and come to the sea, into the bitter, salty waters and the waters will become fresh.

"9. And it will be that all living creatures which swarm there where the streams reach will live. And the fish will be very numerous because these waters reach there, and they will be healed and where the river reaches, everything will live.

"10. And fishermen will stand by it; from En-gedi until En-eglaim nets will be spread out to dry. Of many kinds will its fish be, like the fish of the great sea, very numerous.

"11. But its swamps and its marshes will not be healed; they will be used for salt.[3]

"12. And by the river upon its banks grow every kind of tree for food. And their leaves do not wither, nor does their fruit cease and it will bear new fruit according to its months because their water flows out of the temple and their fruit is used for food and their leaves for healing."

The waters that flow from the temple have both literal and figurative meaning. The meaning is literal in the physical sense of the waters' renewing and fructifying effects on the land. In the figurative sense they symbolize first the restoration of Israel as a land and a people, eventually including the entire earth. At the same time, they are figurative for the voice, presence, power, and pedagogy of Jehovah, which flows down from heaven as revelation to renew and sanctify man. Ezekiel uses the imagery of trees as a symbol of mankind. Just as the waters cause the trees to grow, so hearkening to the voice of Jehovah causes mankind to grow. Thus the relationship between God and man is symbolized by the water-tree motif.

Perhaps the Garden of Eden was the genesis of this motif. Just as those Edenic waters flowed through the Garden, so shall water flow from the temple to renew the earth to its paradisiacal state. At that millennial day Jehovah's voice will also flow to all mankind who will then say, "There is a river, the streams thereof shall make glad the city of God." (Ps. 46:4.)

Historical Geography of Dead Sea Region

It is important to describe the desolate region around the Dead Sea accurately to allow full appreciation of the miraculous fructifying and healing effects of the temple waters. The Dead Sea is located in an area known as the Arabah or the sea of Arabah. (Deut. 3:17; 4:49.) In Hebrew the word *carabhah* is used to describe a remote desert region.[4] Certainly that word is an understatement when applied to the forbidding wasteland of the Arabah. The biblical geographer George Adam Smith writes: "Perhaps there is no region of our earth where

Nature and History have more cruelly conspired, where so tragic a drama has obtained so awful a theatre."[5]

This desolate area encompasses the deep depression of the Jordan Rift from the Sea of Galilee to the Gulf of Akabah. The Dead Sea lies not only at the lowest elevation of this great depression but also, in fact, at the lowest land area on the surface of the earth, dropping to 1,275 feet below sea level.[6] About the Dead Sea itself, George Adam Smith commented, "The history of the Dead Sea opens with Sodom and Gomorrah, and may be said to close with the Massacre of Masada."[7]

It is surprising to learn in Genesis 13:10 that this desolate land known as the Arabah was once a very fertile area. The verbal root of Arabah, c-r-b, can mean "to be sweet" or "pleasing."[8] Genesis 13:10 indicates that it was pleasing to the eyes of Lot: "And Lot lifted up his eyes, and beheld all the plain of Jordan, that it was well watered every where, before the Lord destroyed Sodom and Gomorrah, even as the garden of the Lord."[9] Yet the Lord sent fire and sulphur to utterly destroy Sodom and Gomorrah and its inhabitants (Gen. 19:24–25, 28.) as a punishment for their grievous sins. (Gen. 18:20; 19:13.) This desolate condition is not to remain. Ezekiel states, "And the desolate land will be tilled, whereas it lay desolate in the sight of all that passed by. And they shall say, This land that was desolate is become like the garden of Eden; and the waste and desolate and ruined cities are become fenced, and are inhabited." (Ezek. 36:34–35.)[10] Hence, in the geographic history of the Dead Sea region it begins as a well-watered garden, is then destroyed by fire and sulphur as a consequence of sin, and will be restored to its Edenic state. The extent of Ezekiel's awareness of these things is revealed in that portion of his writing under investigation here.

Ezekiel's Understanding of Dead Sea Symbolism

Ezekiel, a priest (Ezek. 1:3), would have been familiar with passages from the Pentateuch concerning the consequences of sin against Jehovah that befall lands and peoples. One such passage explained the curses that would fall upon the Israelites as a consequence for breaching their covenants with the Lord: "And the Lord will not spare him, but then the anger of the Lord and his jealousy shall smoke against that man, and all the curses that are written in this book shall lie upon him, and the Lord shall blot out his name from under heaven." (Deut. 29:20.) It is likely that Ezekiel perceived the fate of Sodom and Gomorrah as a type for rebellious Israel. Another passage that reflects the geographic cursing of Israel as a result of broken covenants is found in Deuteronomy: "And that the whole land thereof is [sulphur], and salt, and burning, that it is not sown, nor beareth, nor any grass groweth therein, like the [destruction] of Sodom, and Gomorrah." (Deut. 29:23.)

Ezekiel was familiar with the figurative usage of Sodom and Gomorrah as symbols of both wickedness and desolation. The Lord compares the wickedness of Jerusalem to that of Sodom: "As I live, saith the Lord God, [your sister Sodom] hath not done, she nor her daughters, as thou hast done, thou and thy daughters." (Ezek. 16:48.) The Lord consequently declares to Jerusalem that "I will even deal with thee as thou hast done, which hast despised the oath in breaking the covenant." (Ezek. 16:59.) Yet he promises, "I will remember my covenant with thee in the days of thy youth, and I will establish unto thee an everlasting covenant." (Ezek. 16:60.) Among these covenants was the promise that the land that lay desolate would once again become like the Garden of Eden. (Ezek. 36:34–35.)

Ezekiel's priestly background and his writings speak of his knowledge of the literal and figurative nature of this desolate region. He understood that when his people kept the Lord's commandments the land would become fertile and the people would prosper. Ezekiel's prophecy using the water motif signals the commencement of the Edenic day of restoration.

The Garden of Eden

The etymology of the Hebrew word *Eden* is uncertain. It may be related to the Sumerian word *edinu,* which denotes either "wilderness" or "flatland."[11] The Septuagint interpreted the word from the root of the Hebrew verb *cdn,* "to delight," and thus translated the "garden of Eden" as "the garden of delight." This interpretation was the basis for the traditional view of the Garden of Eden as paradise.[12]

Eden is cited as a location or a condition fourteen times in the Old Testament. It is used six times both in Genesis and in Ezekiel and once each in Joel and Isaiah.[13] Nicholas Wyatt notes that the references after the book of Genesis are given after the scattering of Israel, indicating that these prophets use Eden to suggest the notion of a return to a restored condition or an Edenic land.[14]

Ezekiel uses the word *Eden* as many times as the book of Genesis does. This usage gives preliminary support to the proposal that the water motif of Ezekiel is based upon the Garden of Eden theme. That prototype reference in Genesis 2:8–10 states:

"And the Lord God planted a garden eastward in Eden; and there he put the man whom he had formed.

"And out of the ground made the Lord God to grow every tree that is pleasant to the sight, and good for food; the tree of life also in the midst of the garden, and the tree of knowledge of good and evil.

"And a river went out of Eden to water the garden; and from thence it was parted, and became into four heads."

The source of this river may have been the underground waters known in biblical Hebrew as *tehom,* which is translated as the "deep." These waters symbolize both life-giving power and the chaotic waters of destruction that existed before the Creation. These waters are first mentioned in Genesis 1:2: "And the earth was without form, and void; and darkness was upon the face of the [*tehom*]. And the Spirit of God moved upon the face of the waters." In his Near Eastern studies of temple typology, John Lundquist states that "the temple is often associated with the waters of life which flow from a spring within the building itself. . . . The reason such springs exist in temples is that they were perceived as the primeval waters of creation."[15]

The waters that issue forth from the threshold of Ezekiel's temple appear to represent the waters of creation. Herbert May states, "Since it was not fed by tributaries, it must have been the deep [*tehom*] which was the source of the river of life which flowed from beneath the threshold of Ezekiel's temple."[16] I suggest the *tehom* is not only the source for the river in the Garden of Eden but may also be the source of the waters that flow from Ezekiel's temple.

Figurative Meaning of Water in Ezekiel's Motif

Ezekiel 47:1 provides the basis for the figurative meaning of the temple waters: "Afterward he brought me again unto the door of the house; and behold, waters issued out from under the threshold of the house eastward." The Hebrew word translated "threshold" is *miptan.* It is mentioned eight times in the Old Testament. Five of the eight instances are in the book of Ezekiel. (See Ezek. 9:3; 10:4, 18; 46:2; 47:1.) From Ezekiel 9:3 and 10:4 we learn that the glory of the Lord appeared first where the cherubim protected the ark of the covenant and then extended to the threshold of the temple. The *miptan* (threshold) is thus the place where the presence of Jehovah is first experienced by the person entering the temple. When Joseph Smith dedicated the first latter-day temple in Kirtland, he prayed to God that "all people who shall enter upon the *threshold* of the Lord's house may feel thy power." (D&C 109:13.)

The water that issues forth from Jehovah's presence thus represents the podium of his power, glory, and divine attributes, suggesting figurative implications for Ezekiel's water motif. Ezekiel 47:12 emphasizes that these waters have fructifying and special healing power because the "waters . . . issued out of the sanctuary." This water embodies Jehovah's power and his divine attributes because it flows from the podium of his power.

Several passages from the Old Testament support this concept. Among these is Jeremiah 2:13, wherein the Lord declares: "For my people have committed two evils; they have forsaken me the fountain of living waters, and hewed them out cisterns, broken cisterns, that can hold no water." A similar passage from Isaiah states, "Therefore with joy shall ye draw water out of the wells of salvation." (Isa. 12:3.) The psalmist adds in reference to the Lord, "with thee is the fountain of life." (Ps. 36:9.) These references illustrate a clear understanding and use of water by Old Testament prophets as a figurative symbol of Jehovah's power and presence.

Ezekiel also symbolically describes Jehovah's voice in terms of water. In his first vision he describes the voice of the Almighty as the sound of great waters. (Ezek. 1:24.) In his last vision he states that "his voice was like a noise of many waters." (Ezek. 43:2.) That is the same extended vision in which Ezekiel saw the waters flowing from the temple. Clearly the waters that flow from Jehovah's presence symbolize his voice and might. The psalmist writes this beautiful passage: "The voice of the Lord is upon the waters: the God of glory thundereth: the Lord is upon many waters. The voice of the Lord is powerful; the voice of the Lord is full of majesty." (Ps. 29:3–4.) As a whole these passages indicate that the waters that flow from Ezekiel's temple figuratively represent Jehovah and his various divine attributes.

Ezekiel's Use of the Edenic Garden and Trees

Ezekiel referred to Eden far more often than any other prophet. That in itself suggests that the Edenic theme influences much of his writing. In her dissertation entitled "Garden As a Symbol of Sacred

Space," Susan Carol Walter Lau helps us understand Ezekiel's use of the garden and of the trees in Eden.

Ezekiel first uses the imagery of Eden in his prophecy of doom against Tyre and its king. (See Ezek. 28.) Lau proposes that Ezekiel uses the king of Tyre as a type of Adam.[17] The king, like Adam, had been blessed to be living in a place that is likened to Eden. Ezekiel 28:13 states: "Thou hast been in Eden the garden of God." But like Adam, the king of Tyre was forced to withdraw from the garden as a consequence of sin: "Thou hast sinned: therefore I will cast thee as profane out of the mountain of God." (Ezek. 28:16; compare Gen. 3:17, 23.)

Interestingly, the sanctuary of Eden appears to be located in the holy mountain of God. Ezekiel 28:14 and 16 are the only verses in the entire Old Testament that allude to the Garden of Eden being on a holy mountain. Lau suggests that "this probably reflects some 'Zion theology' on Ezekiel's part, which seeks in some way to identify the original Garden with Mt. Zion in Jerusalem."[18] In fact, Mircea Eliade views the Garden of Eden as the prototype of later temples in Israel as well as of other Near Eastern cultures.[19] If we view the temple of Ezekiel with that concept in mind, we can see there is a correlation with water. Just as there was water flowing to the east to provide life for the Garden of Eden, so also waters flow to the east to re-create a garden of God.[20]

The Water-Tree Motif

The second series of references to Eden in the book of Ezekiel appears four times in chapter 31. (See vv. 8–9, 16, 18.) Each time the trees of Eden are the salient feature, and in every case they symbolize kings and kingdoms. Ezekiel uses a great cedar in Lebanon as a symbol for Pharaoh and the kingdoms of Assyria and Egypt. It is revealing to compare Ezekiel's characterization of Pharaoh as a great tree with Daniel's figurative use of King Nebuchadnezzar as a mighty tree. (Dan. 4:10–26.) Each of these trees was the largest in its location, and both were brought down low. (Ezek. 31:10–13; Dan. 4:10–12, 23–25.) Ezekiel uses this same motif in describing the king of Tyre. (Ezek. 28.) In all three of these cases, the rulers were brought down because they were lifted up in the pride of their hearts. (Compare Ezek. 28:17; 31:10–11 with Dan. 4:22, 27.)

Ezekiel 31:4 notes that it was water that made these trees mighty.

In specific reference to the kingdoms of Assyria and Egypt as well as to Pharaoh this verse states, "The waters made him great, the deep set him up on high with her rivers running round about his plants, and sent out her little rivers unto all the trees of the field." The trees that were lifted up did not understand the source of their greatness and so, eventually, they fell. Ezekiel's lesson is clear. The water represents the power of Jehovah. These foreign people would not acknowledge Jehovah as their creator and their sustainer of life. Therefore, once they accomplished his divine purpose, they were left to themselves and died.

Ezekiel also uses the water-tree motif to refer to Israel. In Ezekiel 15 Jerusalem and her inhabitants are referred to as a useless vine tree that will be burned. In Ezekiel 19:10 Israel is likened unto a vine that is "planted by the waters: she was fruitful and full of branches by reason of many waters." Ezekiel 19:11–12 instructs us that Israel too was lifted up in pride and is therefore cast down to the ground, where her fruit dried up. Ezekiel 19:13 states concerning Israel: "And now she is planted in the wilderness, in a dry and thirsty ground." The result is that there is "no strong rod to be a scepter to rule." (Ezek. 19:14.) Walter Zimmerli views this vine as the Davidic house, which has had its royal roots transplanted into a desolate garden through the exile.[21] They, like the foreign kings and kingdoms, also forgot that it was the water (Jehovah) that made them fruitful.

In Ezekiel 17:22–24 we read of a high tree that is made low and also of a low tree that will be exalted. As in the case of Ezekiel 31:1–9, this tree seems to represent the kingdom of Israel.

Ezekiel continues his water-tree motif as a symbol of the relationship between God and man in Ezekiel 47:1–12. There are numerous trees on both sides of the river of water: "And by the river upon its banks grow every kind of tree for food. And their leaves do not wither, nor does their fruit cease and it will bear new fruit according to its months because their water flows out of the temple and their fruit is used for food and their leaves for healing." (Ezek. 47:12.) The water spoken of here is both literal and figurative. The fruit trees, I suggest, are not only fruit trees but are a figure of righteous men who produce good works that will heal the nations. Speaking messianically, Isaiah uses this symbolism when he refers to men as potential "trees of righteousness." (Isa. 61:3.)[22]

In the book of Revelation we see the same water-tree motif used by John the Revelator. John appears to have been highly influenced by Ezekiel's writings.[23] The water motif of Ezekiel serves as a bridge between the waters of Eden and the pure river in the book of Revelation that restores again paradise.[24] The influence of Ezekiel on John culminates in Revelation 22:1–3: "And he shewed me a pure river of water of life, clear as crystal, proceeding out of the throne of God and of the Lamb. In the midst of the street of it, and on either side of the river, was there the tree of life, which bare twelve manner of fruits, and yielded her fruit every month: and the leaves of the tree were for the healing of the nations. And there shall be no more curse: but the throne of God and of the Lamb shall be in it; and his servants shall serve him."

The similarity between John and Ezekiel is clear. In both Revelation and Ezekiel waters flow from the throne of God to create a river that causes trees to flourish. From these trees comes the healing of nations. I suggest that this healing of nations is accomplished by righteous men (represented by the trees) who share the knowledge of the gospel (in the Millennium) and thus plant anew the seedlings of potentially righteous men, bearers of good works. (See Jacob 5:74.)[25] Joseph Fielding Smith stated, "The gospel will be taught far more intensely and with greater power during the millennium, until all the inhabitants of the earth shall embrace it."[26]

The water-tree relationship may indeed have its origin in the Garden of Eden. George Widengren suggests there is a "connection between water and tree, between temple basin and sacred grove, which clearly reflects the Water of Life and Tree of Life in paradise [or Garden of Eden]."[27] In Genesis 2:9 we learn that from the ground of the Garden of Eden "made the Lord God to grow every tree that is pleasant to the sight, and good for food; the tree of life also in the midst of the garden, and the tree of knowledge of good and evil."[28] It is imperative that we remember that the gardener who planted and watered these trees was, in fact, the Lord. He is the same gardener who, in a figurative sense, plants trees (men) besides Ezekiel's waters. These waters symbolize Jehovah and produce fruit (works) and leaves (power) to heal (save a nation), both physically and spiritually. The figurative message, then, is that Jehovah places man in a position to drink from his divine knowledge and thereby men can strengthen themselves and others.

The symbolic description of the relationship between God and man replete in Ezekiel's motif appears in various passages in the Old Testament. Jeremiah 17:7–8 reads, "Blessed is the man that trusteth in

the Lord, and whose hope the Lord is. For he shall be as a tree planted
by the waters, and that spreadeth out her roots by the river, and shall
not see when heat cometh, but her leaf shall be green; and shall not
be careful in the year of drought, neither shall cease from yielding
fruit." The psalmist remarks concerning the man who does not walk
in the ways of the ungodly, "And he shall be like a tree planted by the
rivers of water, that bringeth forth his fruit in his season; his leaf also
shall not wither; and whatever he doeth will prosper." (Ps. 1:3.)[29]
Psalms 92:12–13 states: "The righteous shall flourish like the palm
tree: he shall grow like a cedar in Lebanon. Those that be planted in
the house of the Lord shall flourish in the courts of our God." The
psalmist also informs us that the house of the Lord had its beams laid
in the waters of creation; so too, Ezekiel's temple. (Ps. 104:3; Ezek.
47:1.) Perhaps Ezekiel, like Isaiah, looked forward to the day when
men would turn again to the living water of Jehovah and become "trees
of righteousness" (Isa. 61:3) and when "the trees of the field [would]
clap their hands." (Isa. 55:12.)

Further Attestation of Israel's Restoration in Ezekiel

The consistent theme concerning the restoration of Israel as a land
and as a people is richly demonstrated in the book of Ezekiel. The
following selected passages serve to support this point. In relation to
this restored condition the Lord declares the following:

"And I will make them and the places round about my hill a blessing;
and I will cause the shower to come down in his season; there shall
be showers of blessing.[30] And the tree of the field shall yield her fruit,
and the earth shall yield her increase, and they shall be safe in their
land, and shall know that I am the Lord." (Ezek. 34:26–27.)

Note, too, Ezekiel 36:25, where the Lord states, "Then will I
sprinkle clean water upon you, and ye shall be clean." The Lord then
tells Israel that he will give her a new heart and spirit. (Ezek. 36:26–
27.) Israel is told her trees will be multiplied and her cities will be
rebuilt. (Ezek. 36:30, 33.) The people in her borders will say, "This
land that was desolate is become like the garden of Eden." (Ezek.
36:35.)

In Ezekiel 37, Ezekiel is shown in vision a valley of dry bones.
This vision implies a dual symbolism of the restoration of Israel and
her inhabitants in both a temporal and spiritual way. In verse 12 the
Lord says, "I will open your graves, and cause you to come up out of

your graves, and bring you into the land of Israel."[31] The last nine chapters of Ezekiel, 40–48, contain a vision focusing on the construction of a latter-day temple and the theme of restoration.[32]

Comparative Passages to Ezekiel 47:1–12

Two other Old Testament authors refer to precisely the same event that Ezekiel describes in Ezekiel 47:1–12. Joel and Zechariah verify Ezekiel's theme and at the same time shed additional light on the motif. Joel 3:18 states, "And it shall come to pass in that day, that the mountains shall drop[33] down new wine, and the hills shall flow with milk, and all the rivers of Judah shall flow with waters, and a fountain shall come forth of the house of the Lord, and shall water the valley of Shittim."[34] Contrasting Ezekiel's motif with this verse, we learn that whereas Ezekiel speaks of but one large river, Joel notes that all the river beds in Judah will be full of water. The word for fountain here is *cyan*. The word denotes a fresh underground source, which may be related to the *tehom*, or deep. The book of Joel reflects the same theme as the book of Ezekiel concerning the restoration of Israel as a people and the renewing of the land. Joel 2:3 informs us that the land will become again like the "garden of Eden," but not before a traumatic desolation takes place. This desolation is described in Joel 1:9–12, 20, where the people are cut off from the temple, the land laid waste, and the rivers dried up. Yet we find in Joel 2:21–22 that the Lord tells Israel: "Fear not, O Land; be glad and rejoice: for the Lord will do great things. Be not afraid . . . for the pastures of the wilderness do spring, for the tree beareth her fruit, the fig tree and the vine do yield their strength." Joel 2:23 states, "Rejoice in the Lord your God: for he hath given you the former rain."[35] This passage is equally convincing evidence that the land will be renewed and the people will be restored and come to a knowledge of the source of their fruitful condition.

The other passages that refer directly to Ezekiel's water motif are Zechariah 13:1 and 14:8. Zechariah 13:1 states: "In that day there shall be a fountain opened to the house of David and to the inhabitants of Jerusalem for sin and for uncleanness." The word here translated as "fountain" is *maqor*, which is a fountain or underwater spring; this word means the same thing as *yan* in Joel 3:18.

Zechariah 14:8 sheds additional light on the reference to *fountain* in Zechariah 13:1. The passage states, "And it shall be in that day, that living waters shall go out from Jerusalem; half of them toward the

former sea, and half of them toward the hinder sea: in summer and in
winter shall it be."[36] The fountain seems to be caused by a great
earthquake that takes place when the Lord stands upon the mount of
Olives. (Zech. 14:4–5.) That this water is literal can be supported by
the Prophet Joseph Smith's prophecy: "Judah must return, Jerusalem
must be rebuilt, and the temple, and water come out from under the
temple, and the waters of the Dead Sea be healed . . . before the Son
of Man will make His appearance."[37] This fountain beneath the temple
will turn into a river flowing to the east and the west. (Zech. 14:1.)
This reference illuminates Ezekiel 47:1–12. It seems that the river in
Ezekiel's vision flows not only to the Dead Sea but also to the Mediterranean Sea. The extension of the waters of this river, which go
beyond Israel's boundaries, and the additional directional flow may be
interpreted here in a figurative sense to symbolize not only the restoration of all the land of Israel but the entire earth as well.

It is important to recognize that the word for "river" used in Ezekiel
47:4–12 is *nahal*. The word *nahal* is a key word in this chapter. In
Ezekiel 47:13–14,22–23 we learn that when the waters issued forth,
the tribes of Israel as well as non-Israelite people receive an inheritance
on the earth. The word for "inheritance" is *nahalah*. Both *nahal* and
nahalah come from the Hebrew root *n-h-l*, meaning to "possess" or
to "inherit."[38] The author appears to be using a deliberate play on
words. By this means he indicates that when the river comes forth, so
will the fruitful inheritance. One scholar suggested, "The return of
paradise, apparently at present limited to Palestine, is of its very nature
a universal event embracing the whole world. So we may take it for
granted without further demonstration that Palestine is a part that
stands for the whole."[39] The tenth article of faith states, "the earth
will be renewed and receive its paradisiacal glory." Elder Bruce R.
McConkie interpreted this phrase to mean that the earth "will return
to the edenic terrestrial state which existed when the Lord God finished
the creative enterprise."[40] The earth will be transfigured to its Edenic
state. (D&C 63:21.) Speaking of that edenic day, Isaiah 35:6–7 states,
"In the wilderness shall waters break out, and streams in the desert.
And the parched ground shall become a pool, and the thirsty land springs
of water: in the habitation of dragons, where each lay, shall be grass
with reeds and rushes."

Elder McConkie then adds: "We do not doubt that this is temporal,
for the deserts of this old earth, in its fallen and barren state, shall

become the gardens and flowering fields of the new earth in the millennial day. But it is also spiritual, for the latter-day revelations says: 'And in the barren deserts there shall come forth pools of living water; and the parched ground shall no longer be a thirsty land.' In that day all Israel shall drink from streams of living water, streams that flow direct from the great Fountain Head, streams filled with the words of eternal life of which men may drink and never thirst more."[41]

In that day of transfiguration, the righteous will receive their inheritance upon the paradisiacal earth. (D&C 63:20.)

A universal renewal of the earth appears to have its origin in the waters of the Garden of Eden. In Genesis 2:10–14 we read of the river of Eden, which divided into four different rivers and flowed in four different directions. Lau explains that there have been many attempts to try to specify the literal historical and geographical designations of these four rivers with little success.[42] She prefers to consider these rivers in a symbolic way. Lau states, "If we pursue this line of thinking, the rivers might be seen as representing the four directions of geographical space."[43] With respect to these four rivers Gerhard von Rad suggests that "the number 'four' circumscribes the entire world."[44]

Additional contextual evidence from Zechariah suggests that this universal application is plausible. Zechariah 14:8–9 informs us that "in that day, [when] living waters shall go out from Jerusalem. . . . the Lord shall be king over all the earth: in that day shall there be one Lord, and his name one." This passage lends credence to the idea of a universal renewal of the earth because the Lord is said to be reigning not just over the land of Israel but over the entire globe. Modern-day revelation also informs us that when Christ appears to usher in the Millennium, "he shall stand upon the mount of Olivet. . . . And he shall utter his voice . . . and his voice shall be heard among all people. And it shall be a voice as the voice of many waters." (D&C 133:20–22.) These references shed additional light on Ezekiel's water motif in helping us to understand that the restoration can be applied to the land and people of all the earth. In its renewed condition all the earth and its inhabitants are flooded with the knowledge of the Lord. In Jeremiah 31:34 the Lord declares that in the millennial day, "They shall all know me, from the least of them unto the greatest." Isaiah 11:9 states, "The earth shall be full of the knowledge of the Lord, as the waters cover the sea." Habakkuk 2:14 states, "For the earth shall be filled with the knowledge of the glory of the Lord, as the waters cover the sea."

Joseph Smith commented on the kind of knowledge in the Millennium when he stated that the Lord would "turn to them a pure language, and the earth will be filled with sacred knowledge, as the waters cover the great deep."[45] Joseph Fielding Smith stated, "If the knowledge of the Lord covers the earth as the waters do the sea, then it must be universally received."[46]

Conclusion

The Garden of Eden served as the foundation for Ezekiel's water motif. The term "waters" has both a literal and a figurative use. The prophecies used here will find literal fulfillment as life-giving water, indeed, flows from Jehovah's temple in the last days. But there will also be a fulfillment of the symbolic aspect as Israel and then eventually all the earth and its inhabitants are renewed through the life-giving powers of their millennial King.

Specific examples of the relationship between God and man verified the proposal that the water motif of Ezekiel was both figurative and literal for the restoration of Israel. It further symbolized the renewal of the land. Thus, water represents the commencement of the millennial day when the earth will be full of the knowledge of the Lord. For the present, these living waters bear witness of their Creator, who is Jehovah, even the Lord Jesus Christ. As he told the woman of Samaria, "Whosoever drinketh of the water that I shall give him shall never thirst." (John 4:14.) At the Feast of Tabernacles the Lord also declared, "If any man thirst, let him come unto me and drink. He that believeth on me . . . out of his belly shall flow rivers of living water." (John 7:37–38.)

Jehovah promises yesterday, today, and forever that "I will pour water upon him that is thirsty, and floods upon the dry ground: I will pour my spirit upon thy seed, and my blessing upon thine offspring." (Isa. 44:3.) The invitation is clear: "Every one that thirsteth, come ye to the waters." (Isa. 55:1.)[47] As we draw water from the Source of salvation, who is Christ, we will concur with the psalmist, who declared, "There is a river, the streams whereof . . . make glad the city of God." (Ps. 46:4.)

NOTES

1. Except for Ezekiel 47:1–12, all other biblical references in this paper cite the King James Version unless otherwise indicated.

2. The Hebrew words translated "Son of man" are *ben adam*. This phrase is used to indicate one man or, collectively, all mankind. The phrase as used in Ezekiel 47:6 may indicate that the Lord is not talking only to Ezekiel but through Ezekiel to all the descendants of Father Adam. (See Even-Shoshan 1981:14.)

3. Eichrodt (1970:581) suggests that verse 11 is a gloss. He contends that this passage is used to justify the important industry of salt. May (1956:328) agrees that the scriptural passage is being used to justify exploiting the mineral salts of the Dead Sea. Zimmerli (1979: vol. 2:514) states, "The thoroughness of this transformation frightened a later writer who was aware of the possibility of the extraction of salt from the Dead Sea. So he added the observation that the swamps and pools of the sea . . . 'keep their salt water for the extraction of salt.' " Thus we have a unanimous agreement from these authors, and I also concede that verse 11 was an addition to the text.

4. William Reed, in *Interpreter's Dictionary of the Bible*, 5 vols. (Nashville: Abingdon Press, 1982), 1:828–29.

5. George Adam Smith, *Historical Geography of the Holy Land* (London: Hodder and Stoughton, 1897), p. 499.

6. Yohanan Aharoni, *The Land of the Bible: A Historical Geography*, trans. A. F. Rainey (Philadelphia: Westminster Press, 1979), p. 21.

7. Smith, *Historical Geography*, p. 499.

8. Brown, Driver, and Briggs, *A Hebrew and English Lexicon of the Old Testament* (Oxford: Clarendon Press, 1951), p. 787, for discussion concerning this root.

9. The phrase "the garden of the Lord" implies that it is like the Garden of Eden. See Genesis 2:8, which states that the Lord planted a garden in Eden.

10. Isaiah 51:3 further clarifies this understanding: "For the Lord shall comfort Zion: he will comfort all her waste places; and he will make her wilderness like Eden, and her desert like the garden of the Lord; joy and gladness shall be found therein, thanksgiving, and the voice of melody."

11. Brevard S. Childs, "Eden, Garden of," in *The Interpreter's Dictionary of the Bible*, 2:22–23.

12. Ibid., 2:22.

13. Even-Shoshan, *A New Concordance*, p. 835.

14. Nicolas Wyatt, "Interpreting the Creation and Fall Story in Genesis 2–3," *Zeitscrift fur die Alttestamentliche Wissenschaft* 93 (1981): 13.

15. John M. Lundquist, *The Temple in Antiquity*, ed. Truman G. Madsen (Salt Lake City: Bookcraft, 1984), p. 66.

16. Hebert G. May, "Some Cosmic Connotations of Mayim Rabbim, Many Waters," *The Journal of Biblical Literature* 74 (1955): 21. The Mishna (Parah III: 3) explains that the temple was built upon the *tehom*.

17. Susan C. W. Lau, "Garden As a Symbol of Sacred Space" (PhD. diss., University of Pittsburgh, 1981), pp. 200–201.

18. Ibid., p. 202.

19. Mircea Eliade, *Patterns in Comparative Religion* (New York: American Library, 1958), p. 282.

20. The association of these waters with the east may reflect messianic overtones.

21. Walter Zimmerli, *Ezekiel: A Commentary on the Book of the Prophet Ezekiel*, 2 vols. (Philadelphia: Fortress Press, 1979), 1:397–98.

22. Isaiah also used the image of the tree in a figurative sense when he spoke of the age of people in the Millennium. He prophesied that "the child shall die an hundred years old . . . for as the days of a tree are the days of my people." (Isa. 65:20,22; see also D&C 101:30, which reiterates this same idea.

23. Out of sixty-five New Testament references from Ezekiel, forty-eight are mentioned in the book of Revelation. LaSor, Hubbard, and Bush, *Old Testament Survey: The Message, Form, and Background of the Old Testament* (Grand Rapids: William B. Eerdmans Publishing Co., 1985), p. 478.

24. Lau, "Garden," p. 207.

25. Righteous men are represented by the image of a tree in the following passages: in Zechariah 3 and 4 Joshua and Zerubbabel are likened unto two olive trees; in Revelation 11:3–4 two latter-day witnesses are likened unto olive trees; in D&C 77:15 these witnesses are identified as prophets sent to the Jewish nation in the day of restoration. Elder Bruce R. McConkie stated, "No doubt they will be members of the Council of the Twelve or of the First Presidency of the Church." (*Doctrinal New Testament Commentary* [Salt Lake City: Deseret Book Co., 1973], 3:510.)

26. Joseph Fielding Smith, *Doctrines of Salvation*, comp. Bruce R. McConkie, 3 vols. (Salt Lake City: Deseret Book Co., 1976), 3:64.

27. George Widengren, "Early Hebrew Myths and Their Interpretation," in *Myth, Ritual and Kingship*, ed. S. H. Hooke (Oxford: Clarendon Press, 1953), p. 168.

28. For further understanding of the tree of knowledge and the tree of life, see Child's article, "Tree of Knowledge, Tree of Life" in *Interpreter's Dictionary of the Bible*, 4:695–97.

29. See also D&C 97:9, where this same motif is beautifully attested in modern-day revelation.

30. The Hebrew word translated "blessing" is *berakah*. The Hebrew word for a pool of water is *berekah*. Both of these nouns are derived from the same Hebrew verbal root *b-r-k*, meaning "to bless" or "to kneel." This usage implies a connection between water and blessing. See Brown, Driver, and Briggs, *Hebrew and English Lexicon*, pp. 138–40, for complete references to these words.

31. The word "grave" here may also denote exile. Some view this in connection with the resurrection from the grave. Other scholars reject this notion and consider it a later addition. (May 1956:269.) I interpret this passage as both a literal and a spiritual restoration of the land and people of Israel.

32. The restoration theme of the land of Israel and her people is frequently attested in the book of Isaiah. (See, for example, Isa. 27:3; 30:25, 28; 35:6–7; 41:18.)

33. The Hebrew verbal root meaning to drop or drip is *n-t-p*. It is often used in a figurative sense to denote prophetic discourse or divine tutelage. See, for

example, Amos 7:16 and especially Ezekiel 21:2. I suggest that Joel 3:18 implies this symbolic concept of divine instruction.

34. The milk that flows from the hills is not meant to be taken literally. It is probably a figurative reflection of Exodus 3:8, which refers to Israel as a land flowing with milk and honey. The wine dropping on the hills is probably also figurative. Both the elements of milk and wine are used as hyperbole to reflect the fertility of the land of Israel.

35. The Hebrew word for "former rain" is *moreh*, which is also the same word for "teacher." The verbal root of this noun is *y- r-h*, meaning to throw or shoot. In the 3.m.s. hiphil form *yoreh*, it means to give instruction or to give drink. (See, for example, Hosea 6:3; 10:12.) The noun *torah* is also constructed from this same root. (See Brown, Driver, and Briggs, *Hebrew and English Lexicon*, for a further discussion of the root *y-r-h*. The word "moderately" in the KJV may be a mistranslation. This word was translated from the Hebrew word *tsedaqah*, and means righteousness (Brown, Driver, and Briggs, *Hebrew and English Lexicon*, p. 842.) With the Hebrew preposition *li* attached to it, as in Joel 2:23 of the Hebrew Bible, the word could be translated "in regards to righteousness." This phrase combined with the Hebrew word *moreh* is *hamoreh litsedaqah*, which can be interpreted as the "teacher/early rain in regard to righteousness." This combination again suggests that water is used as an image of instruction or blessing.

36. The "former sea" can also be translated as the Eastern Sea and the Dead Sea (Brown, Driver, and Briggs, *Hebrew and English Lexicon*, p. 870.) The "hinder sea" can also be translated Western Sea and refers to the Mediterranean Sea. (Brown, Driver, and Briggs, *Hebrew and English Lexicon of the Old Testament*, p. 30.)

37. Joseph Smith, *Teachings of the Prophet Joseph Smith*, sel. Joseph Fielding Smith (Salt Lake City: Deseret Book Co., 1976), p. 286.

38. See Brown, Driver, and Briggs, *Hebrew and English Lexicon*, p. 635–36.

39. Walter Eichrodt, *Ezekiel: A Commentary* (London: SCM Press Ltd., 1966), p. 585.

40. Bruce R. McConkie, *Mormon Doctrine*, 2d ed. (Salt Lake City: Bookcraft, 1976), p. 494.

41. Bruce R. McConkie, *The Millennial Messiah* (Salt Lake City: Deseret Book Co., 1982), p. 328.

42. Lau, "Garden," p. 161; however, Latter-day Saints should be aware that Joseph Smith did reveal that the location of the Garden of Eden was in Jackson County, Missouri. See *Doctrines of Salvation*, 3:74; and *Journal of Discourses*, 10:235; 11:336–37.

43. Lau, "Garden," p. 161.

44. Gerhard von Rad, *Genesis: A Commentary* (Philadelphia: Westminster Press, 1972), p. 79.

45. Joseph Smith, *Teachings*, p. 93.

46. Joseph Fielding Smith, *Doctrines*, 3:65.

47. James Kugel in his book, *The Idea of Biblical Poetry*, provides some illuminating information to this passage in Isaiah. He informs us that many times, as

in Isaiah 55:1, the midrashist says that "the word water is used where it obviously means not water but something like Torah or Divine Learning. . . . We must therefore be careful to consider this other meaning of water whenever it appears in scripture; even here where actual water seems to fit the text, perhaps we ought to understand Torah." Latter-day Saints can find more credible evidence for this passage from Isaiah in the Book of Mormon. In 2 Nephi 9:50–51, Jacob interprets this verse as an invitation to "come unto the Holy One of Israel." In this way people are invited not only to come unto the Law but, more importantly, to come unto the Lawgiver, who is Christ.

Index

Noah, 38–39, 41, 147–48

Oaks, Dallin H., 267
Obadiah, messianic prophecy in, 208–9
Offerings in ancient Israel, 21–24
Old Testament: reasons to read the, 113–14;
    leaders on value of the, 114–16; neglect of
    the, 116–17; how to understand the, 118;
    testifies of Christ, 118–22; religious
    history makes up the, 122–23; using LDS
    edition of the, 123–24; cross-references in
    the, 124; chapter headings in the, 125–28;
    appendix to the, 128–31; as a witness for
    other scriptures, 131–33. *See also* Bible
Olive tree allegory, 179–80
Ordinances in ancient Israel, 21–24

Packer, Boyd K., 62, 262, 266
Patriarchal blessings, 271
Penrose, Charles W., 251
Perfection, seeking, 97–98
Performances in ancient Israel, 24–25
Premortality of the house of Israel, 180–82
Prophecies: esoteric, 2–3; messianic, 200–201
Psalms, quotability of, 26–27

Records: Old Testament, 262–64; importance
    of keeping, 264–67
Redemption, wine as symbol of, 37–39
Repentance, ancient offerings as a part of, 22–
    23
Righteous servant, 168–69

Sacrifice, as test for Abraham, 55–57
Samuel, 240–41
Saul, fall of, 241–42
"Saviors on mount Zion," 208, 269–70
Self-awareness, testing results in, 64–65
Self-confidence, testing results in, 64–65
Self-control, as taught by the law of Moses,
    21, 24
Servant, righteous, 168–69
Smith, David Hyrum, 252–53
Smith, George Adam, 282–83
Smith, Joseph: on Abrahamic testing, 58–59;
    keeps perspective, 65–66; reveals
    "hidden" Messiah, 89–90; on the Bible,
    115, 228; on Adam's physical appearance,
    144; and Isaiah, 157; as a modern

Abraham, 186–90; on the Millennium, 193;
    on Hosea, 202; on "saviors upon mount
    Zion," 208; on water, 218–19; on king
    David, 245; on the second David, 252–53;
    on records, 263–64
Smith, Joseph F., 35, 268–69
Smith, Joseph Fielding, 141, 193, 289
Snow, Erastus, 196–97
Solomon, 247
Sperry, Sidney B., 112, 134, 225, 249–50

Tamar, 246–47
Taylor, John, 65, 144–45, 208–9
Testing: mortality is time for, 53–54;
    consequential, 57–78; generational or
    collective, 58–61; individual, 61–63;
    purposes of, 63–65; keeping perspective
    during, 65–66
Top, Brent L., 180

Water: symbolism of, 37–38; Israelite
    traditions about, 42; and wine in ancient
    traditions, 44–45; and baptism, 45–46. *See
    also* Water motif; Water-tree motif
Water motif: in Garden of Eden, 285;
    represents Jehovah, 285–86; represents
    garden of God, 287; represents
    restoration, 291–93; literal and figurative
    interpretation of, 294. *see also* Water;
    Water-tree motif
Water-tree motif: symbolizes Israel, 287–88;
    symbolizes God–man relationship, 288–90.
    See also Water; Water motif
Wentworth, John, 186
Widengren, George, 289
Wine: symbolism of, 37–39; abstaining from,
    39–40; Israelite traditions about, 42–43;
    and water in ancient traditions, 44–45;
    sacramental, 45–48
Woodruff, Wilford, 183

Young, Brigham: on the Bible, 115–16, 118–
    19, 133; on the Garden of Eden, 140; on
    foreordination of Joseph Smith, 187–88

Zechariah, messianic prophecies of, 215–19
Zephaniah, messianic prophecies of, 213–14
Zion, redemption of, 251–52
Zophar, 104–5